Horizons

Mathematics

Teacher's Guide

Author: Alan L. Christopherson, M.S.

Alpha Omega Publications, Inc. • Rock Rapids, IA

Horizons Mathematics K, Teacher's Guide

804 N. 2nd Ave. E., Rock Rapids, IA 51246-1759

Printed in the United States of America

ISBN 978-0-7403-0311-1

Table of Contents

Introduction

The Goal

The goal of this curriculum is to provide the parent and teacher with a tool that will help them effectively develop math skills by raising the level of student performance. Research of the content and methods of other existing curriculums, the concepts evaluated by achievement tests, and adopted curriculum standards resulted in selection of the Scope and Sequence. This curriculum was not planned around any particular group of students. Rather, it was determined that the material in this curriculum constituted a reasonable level of performance for kindergarten students of average maturity. The curriculum is designed so that the teacher can adapt its use to student(s) of widely varying ability. In other words, the curriculum is a tool that is capable of performing well over a broad range of student ability to help students achieve a higher minimum level of proficiency

The Design

Bright, colorful lessons and varied activities are designed to bring success and enjoyment to the student. Take a moment to look at the chart entitled *Development of Concepts*. Take note of how the curriculum concepts are developed. The first presentation is usually a brief familiarization. Then the basic teaching is accomplished as part of three to five lessons. The thoroughness of a presentation depends on how new and how important the concept is to the student's academic development. The two major components of the curriculum are the student text (in two volumes) and the Teacher's Guide. These are the absolute minimum components for accomplishing the objective of teaching the concepts in the Scope and Sequence. Since this Teacher's Guide was designed as an integral part of the curriculum, its use is absolutely required. The Teacher's Guide contains activities not found in the student texts that are essential to accomplishment of the curriculum objectives. As you will see in the following sections, this guide contains a significant number of suggestions and helps for the teacher.

The Development

Students are not expected to master a concept at its introduction. Each concept will be reviewed for one week after the complete presentation. For the next two months the concept will be presented every two weeks as a part of two or three consecutive lessons. After a break in presentation of several weeks, the concept will be thoroughly reviewed as part of the lesson for three to five days. This will be followed by a period of two months where the concept will be reviewed every two weeks as part of two or three lessons. This progression continues until the student(s) have had the opportunity to thoroughly master the concept.

A Balance of the Best Methods

Since not every child learns as easily with one given method of presentation, *Horizons* incorporates a balance of the best methods. Some curriculums drill the students into boredom. Others challenge students through reasoning to the point of frustration when they cannot comprehend what is being covered. Still others major on learning by doing, abandoning all academics. The blend of the best of each of these learning styles is found in *Horizons Mathematics* without the disadvantages associated with overemphasis on any one presentation.

Analytical reasoning skills are used in making daily decisions. These thinking skills are taught in order to help students gain a complete understanding of mathematics. Students are taught to reason from the principles taught in *Horizons Mathematics* and to apply them to real-life situations. Memorization is stressed in the learning of basic math facts and computational skills. Students will progress rapidly when they can instantly recall basic math facts. A built-in repetition and review cycle makes the process simple to follow. Drill reinforces the concepts being introduced.

An Example

Some mathematics curriculums might teach time for three weeks and then not go back to it again. In this curriculum it will be introduced and practiced for about two weeks. For the next two months, time will be presented every two weeks as a part of two or three lessons to give the student(s) continual practice to develop mastery of the concept. The third month will be considered a break from presenting the concept, and time will not be taught. In the fourth month, time will first be thoroughly reviewed and again practiced every two weeks as a part of two or three lessons. By having a series of practices every two weeks, the student(s) will retain what they have learned to a greater degree. Short periods of exposure done many times are much more effective than long periods with fewer exposures. Since time has three aspects at this level (hour, half-hour, and quarter-hour), each aspect is introduced at its own interval. The hour is taught at the introduction, half-hour comes later (following the same progression), and quarter-hour a little later on. After each aspect has a break from its presentation, the three aspects are presented together for the remainder of the year. Review the Scope and Sequence to see how the concepts are developed.

General Information

Although a guide is provided for writing the numerals in the lessons, please feel free to use the same writing style that you are teaching for handwriting and using in your other subjects. Also, there is some room on the teacher lessons for you to write your own notes. The more you personalize your Teacher's Guide in this way, the more useful it will be to you.

You will notice that there are 160 student lessons in the curriculum. This allows for the inevitable interruptions to the school year like holidays, test days, inclement weather days, and those unexpected interruptions. It also allows the teacher the opportunity to spend more time teaching any concept that the student(s) may have difficulty with. Or, you might wish to spend a day doing some of the fun activities mentioned in the *Activities* section of each teacher's lesson. If you find that the student(s) need extra drill, use the worksheets as extra lessons.

Organization of Student Lessons

Student lessons are designed to be completed in twenty-five to thirty minutes a day. If extra manipulatives or worksheets are utilized, you will need to allow more time for teaching. Each lesson consists of a major concept and practice of previously taught concepts. If the student(s) find the presence of four or five different activities in one lesson a little overwhelming at the beginning, start guiding the student(s) through each activity. By the end of two weeks, they should be able to work more independently as they adjust to the format. Mastery of a new concept is not necessary the first time it is presented. Complete understanding of a new concept will come as the concept is approached from different views using different methods at different intervals. Because of the way the curriculum is designed, the student(s) should do all the problems in every lesson every day. Directions to the student(s) are given before each activity and examples or explanations are sometimes presented. If you expect to have very many students, you will find it extremely helpful to remove all pages from the individual student books and file them (all of Lesson 1 in one file, all of Lesson 2 in another file, etc.) before school starts. This will keep the lessons from being damaged or lost in the students' desks.

Organization of Teacher Lessons

Each lesson is organized into the following sections: *Overview, Materials and Supplies, Teaching Tips, Activities.* To be a master teacher you will need to prepare each lesson well in advance.

Overview

Concepts are listed at the beginning of each lesson in the order that they are presented. This same information is available in the *Daily Lesson Planner* and can be cross-referenced with the *Appearance of Concepts* chart.

Materials and Supplies

Materials and Supplies lists the things you'll need to find before you teach each lesson. Most of the items listed are things that can be easily constructed as they are needed. Sometimes you will also find instructions in the *Activities* section on how to make your own materials and supplies. When "Number Chart" is listed, it is understood to refer to the chart for 0–100.

Teaching Tips

Each tip is related to one of the activities in the lesson. The tip will identify whether a concept is being taught, reviewed or drilled. The tips are a brief lesson plan of what needs to be accomplished during the lesson. Teaching strategies for most of the tips are given in the *Activities* section. Items listed for drill are left to the teacher's or parent's discretion whether or not they will be incorporated into the daily lesson.

Activities

The *Activities* section is where the teacher or parent will concentrate most of their time. Here the teacher or parent will find step-by-step directions for teaching each lesson. All of the activities are designed to be teacher directed both in the student lesson and in the Teacher's Guide. You will need to use your own judgement concerning how much time is necessary to carry out the activities. Be sure, however, that if at all possible the student(s) do every problem of every lesson. Each activity is important to the overall scope of the lesson and must be completed. Do not omit any portion of the activities unless the student(s) have thoroughly mastered the concept being presented. Please do not put off looking at the activities in the lesson until you are actually teaching. Taking time to preview what you will be teaching is essential. Choose the manipulatives that fit your program best.

Answer Keys

The answer keys are provided on the same pages as the teacher's lesson. Answers are provided for most of the student exercises. Penmanship activities and coloring activities have been left as the student(s) see them. You should correct every paper, but you may not grade every paper. This means that each lesson should be marked for correct and incorrect answers, but it is not necessary to record a letter or percentage grade on every lesson. The lessons should then be returned to the student(s) and sent home so that they have the opportunity to learn from their mistakes.

Worksheets

There are 40 worksheets provided for duplication masters. The first time a worksheet is suggested for use, you will find it listed in the *Materials and Supplies* section. Each worksheet has a worksheet number. Look at the *Where to Use Mathematics Worksheets* chart to identify the lesson where the worksheet concept is first taught. The worksheet can be used during that lesson and with any future lesson for additional drill and practice. NOTE: Many worksheets will be used over and over as resources, so you'll need to keep a master copy.

Customize or adapt the worksheets for your particular student(s). For example, you can make one copy of the "clocks" worksheet. Add clock hands for the hour, half-hour, or quarter-hour and make copies of the revised worksheet for the student(s).

The worksheets will be handy for many purposes. You might use them for extra work for student(s) who demonstrate extra aptitude or ability or as remedial work for the student(s) who demonstrate a lack of aptitude or ability. You may also make your own worksheets and note where you would use them in the teacher's lesson.

Horizons Kindergarten Mathematics SCOPE & SEQUENCE

1, 2, 3, 4, 5, 6, 7, 8, 9,

1. COUNTING 1–100

Counting by 1's, 5's, 10's, 2's, 3's, 4's to 100

11, 12, 23, 34, 45, 56, 67, 78, 89,

2. NUMBER RECOGNITION

Recognition of all families to 100

3. NUMBER WRITING

Writing of all families to 100

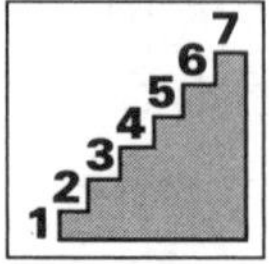

4. NUMBER VALUE

Value of all single digit numbers

5. NUMBER AFTER

Naming the number that comes after for all families to 100

6. NUMBER BEFORE

Naming the number that comes before for all families to 100

7. NUMBER BETWEEN

Naming the number that comes between for all families to 100

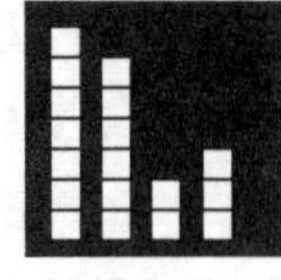

8. PLACE VALUE

(Digit Value)
Ones, tens

9. ADDITION

Adding a single digit to all families without regrouping

10. SUBTRACTION

Subtracting a single digit from all families without regrouping

11. MONEY

Recognition, value, and use of the penny, nickel, dime, quarter, half dollar, dollar bill and dollar coin

12. TIME

Naming time on the hour, half-hour quarter-hour and 5 minutes

13. CALENDAR

Naming the days of the week, the months of the year and the seasons

14. NUMBER THEORY

Recognition of ordinal numbers, even and odd numbers

15. COLORS

Recognition of black, yellow, green, red, blue, brown, orange, and purple

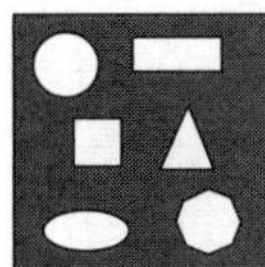

16. SHAPES

Recognition of circle, square, triangle, rectangle, diamond, star, hexagon, octagon, cone, sphere and cylinder

17. COMPARISONS

Comparisons of items and quantities that are different, pairs, twins, belong together, tall, short, long, larger number and smaller number

18. DIRECTION & POSITION

Recognition of the direction and position of right, left, up, down, top, bottom, middle, inside, outside, first, next, last, front and back

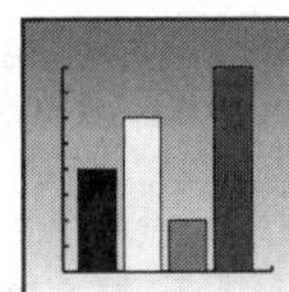

19. GRAPHS

Read and complete bar graphs and pictographs

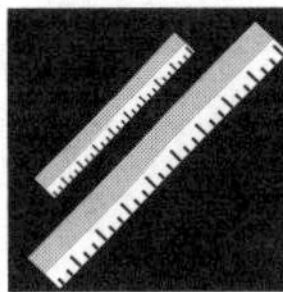

20. MEASUREMENT

Reading lengths in inches and centimeters, perimeter in inches

21. UNITS OF MEASURE

Identify and count cup, quart, gallon and liter

22. FRACTIONS

Recognize whole, 1/2, 1/3 and 1/4

23. SEQUENCE

Determine what comes next

WORKSHEET DUPLICATION MASTERS

Where To Use Mathematics Worksheets

In this Teacher's Guide you will find forty worksheets to be used as **duplication masters**. This chart shows where worksheets are used **for the first time.** The worksheet may be used during that lesson **and with any future lesson** for additional drill and practice. You will need to duplicate any worksheet used more than once.

No.	Master Worksheet Name	Lessons Where Worksheet Concepts First Appear
1	Number chart 0–100	1-160
2	Penmanship practice 1	1
3	Penmanship practice 2	4
4	Penmanship practice 3	7
5	Penmanship practice 4	9
6	Penmanship practice 5	11
7	Penmanship practice 6	13
8	Penmanship practice 7	15
9	Penmanship practice 8	17
10	Penmanship practice 9	19
11	Penmanship practice 0	21
12	Penmanship practice 1's family	23
13	Penmanship practice 10's family	28
14	Penmanship practice 20's family	31
15	Penmanship practice 30's family	40
16	Penmanship practice 40's family	46
17	Penmanship practice 50's family	58
18	Penmanship practice 60's family	70
19	Penmanship practice 70's family	80
20	Penmanship practice 80's family	90
21	Penmanship practice 90's family	100
22	Number recognition 1's family	23
23	Number recognition 10's family	28
24	Number recognition 20's family	31
25	Number recognition 30's family	40
26	Number recognition 40's family	46
27	Number recognition 50's family	58
28	Number recognition 60's family	70
29	Number recognition 70's family	80
30	Number recognition 80's family	90
31	Number recognition 90's family	100
32	Count by 2's (even numbers)	84
33	Count by 2's (odd numbers)	86
34	Count by 3's	109
35	Count by 4's	124
36	Count by 5's	55
37	Count by 10's	26
38	Ordinal numbers	18
39	Clocks (analog & digital)	19
40	Number strips	25

Appearance of Concepts
Kindergarten Math

1. COUNTING	Appears in Lesson
Counting by 1's to 10	1–5
Counting by 1's to 20	6–10
Counting by 1's to 30	11–15
Counting by 1's to 40	16–22
Counting by 1's to 50	23–36
Counting by 1's to 60	37–43
Counting by 1's to 70	44–53
Counting by 1's to 80	54–64
Counting by 1's to 90	65–74
Counting by 1's to 100	75–160
Counting by 10's to 100	26, 27, 32–35, 38, 39, 43–46, 48, 69, 77, 78, 98, 99, 103, 104, 106, 117, 129, 136, 156
Counting by 5's to 100	55–59, 62, 66, 69, 98, 99, 103, 104, 106, 127, 129, 135, 148, 157
Counting by 2's to 100	76, 84–89, 92, 96, 102–104, 113, 117, 127, 137, 158
Counting by 3's to 99	109–111, 113, 117, 127, 139, 141, 159
Counting by 4's to 100	124–127, 129, 138, 142, 160
Tally marks	10, 11, 15, 27, 39, 41, 151, 158
2. NUMBER RECOGNITION, VALUE AND WRITING	
One	1–3
Two	2–6
Three	7–8
Four	9–10
Five	11–12
Six	13–14
Seven	15–16
Eight	17–18
Nine	19–20
Zero	21–22
Ones family	21–27
Tens family	28–30
Twenties family	31, 34–38
Thirties family	40–42
Forties family	46, 47
Fifties family	57, 58
Sixties family	70
Seventies family	80, 84
Eighties family	90
Nineties family	100

5. NUMBER AFTER	
Ones family	33–37, 39–40, 48, 76, 78, 79
Tens family	48, 49, 76, 78, 79
Twenties family	56, 57, 60, 76, 78, 79
Thirties family	67–70, 76, 78, 79
Forties family	76–79
Fifties family	82, 83
Sixties family	88–90
Seventies family	93–95
Eighties family	97–99
Nineties family	108, 109, 131
6. NUMBER BEFORE	
Ones family	72–74
Tens family	81–83
Twenties family	87–90
Thirties family	110–112, 119
Forties family	117–119, 124
Fifties family	122–124
Sixties family	126
Seventies family	128
Eighties family	130
Nineties family	132
7. NUMBER BETWEEN	
Ones family	27, 28, 31
Tens family	39, 40
Twenties family	42, 43
Thirties family	45, 46
Forties family	49, 50
Fifties family	61, 62
Sixties family	74, 75
Seventies family	85, 86
Eighties family	94, 95
Nineties family	107–109
All families	153, 154, 159
8. NUMBER BEFORE & AFTER	
Ones family	134, 136, 151
Tens family	134, 136, 151
Twenties family	136, 155
Thirties family	136
9. PLACE VALUE	
Ones family	47–49, 150
Tens family	59, 60, 63–65
Twenties family	71, 72, 77, 156
Thirties family	95–97, 108, 125, 156
Forties family	115, 116, 125, 150
Fifties family	120, 121, 125, 156
Sixties family	123–125, 150
Seventies family	133
Eighties family	135
Nineties family	138, 150

10. NUMBER ORDER	
Ones family	139–141, 154, 159
Tens family	151–154, 159
11. ADDITION	
Ones family	24–32, 35–39, 41–47, 61, 62, 70, 78, 101, 126, 154
Tens family	51–58, 60, 62, 67, 154
Twenties family	62–66, 76, 88, 155
Thirties family	69–73, 82, 91, 140, 142, 155
Forties family	78–82, 92, 141, 142, 156
Fifties family	84–87, 143, 144, 156
Sixties family	91–94, 96, 130, 131, 145, 146, 148, 157
Seventies family	96–99, 111, 130, 131, 147, 148, 157
Eighties family	100–102, 108,110, 143, 144, 149, 150, 158
Nineties family	111–114, 145, 147, 152, 153, 158
Word problems	101, 102, 112, 131, 133–135, 138, 140, 142, 157
12. SUBTRACTION	
Ones family	106–109, 111, 114, 126, 136, 154
Tens family	109–113, 129, 130, 136, 154
Twenties family	113–116, 137, 155
Thirties family	116–120, 138, 140, 142, 155
Forties family	121–124, 140–142, 156
Fifties family	125, 126, 143, 144, 156
Sixties family	127, 128, 145, 146, 148, 157
Seventies family	129, 130, 147, 148, 157
Eighties family	131, 132, 149, 150, 158
Nineties family	133, 134, 144, 145, 152, 153, 158
Word problems	127, 136, 144, 159
13. MONEY	
Penny	14–16, 19, 21, 29, 32, 36, 43–46, 52, 69, 80, 84, 87, 93, 95, 100, 103–106, 115–117, 122, 135, 136, 155
Nickel	58, 59, 62, 69, 80, 84, 87, 93, 98–100, 103–106, 115–117, 122, 135, 155
Dime	26, 32–36, 38, 43–46, 52, 69, 84, 87, 93, 98–100, 103–106, 116, 117, 122, 136, 155
Quarter	51, 114–117, 122, 149, 155
Half dollar	98–100, 103–106, 117, 122, 149
One dollar bill	36, 51, 52, 54–56, 103, 104, 106, 133, 136, 149, 155
One dollar coin	103, 106, 122, 133, 149, 155
Five dollar bill	135
Ten dollar bill	27, 136, 155
14. TIME	
Hour	19, 23, 27, 43–44, 58, 59, 61, 89, 90, 100–103, 109
Half-hour	105–107, 148, 153
Quarter-hour	119–121, 125, 149, 153
Five minutes	142, 145–147, 150
Digital time hour	19, 28, 43, 44, 58, 59, 61, 100
Digital time half-hour	107
Digital time quarter-hour	122, 123, 125
Digital time 10 minutes	77, 78
Digital time 5 minutes	147, 150
Elapsed time hours	102, 103

15. CALENDAR	
Days of the week	18–20, 22, 24, 29, 33, 37, 41, 51, 54, 76, 79, 83, 110, 147
Months of the year	25, 37, 41, 51, 54, 79, 83–85, 91, 105, 128
Seasons	99, 115, 128, 132, 152
16. NUMBER THEORY	
Ordinal numbers	18–20, 22, 24, 29–33, 37, 47, 49, 50, 54, 67, 68, 84, 98, 105, 108, 141, 147, 151, 157
Even numbers	84–86, 89, 92, 102, 113, 127, 137
Odd numbers	86–88, 96, 103, 104, 127
17. COLORS	
Black	22
Yellow	8, 13, 35, 41
Green	5, 7, 8, 12, 16, 32, 36, 41
Red	12, 16, 17, 32, 35
Blue	6, 8, 12, 16, 17, 32, 36, 41
Brown	20
Orange	16
Purple	28
18. SHAPES	
Circle	6, 7, 12–14, 16, 18, 20, 22, 26, 28, 32, 39, 41,
Square	6, 7, 12, 13, 16, 18, 20, 22, 26, 28, 32, 39, 41,
Triangle	8, 13, 14, 16–18, 20, 22, 25, 26, 28, 32, 39, 41,
Rectangle	16–18, 20, 22, 26, 28, 39,
Octagon	22, 50
Diamond	28
Star	12, 14, 16, 20, 22, 25, 26,
Hexagon	20, 22, 26, 28
Sphere	73, 118–120, 135, 146, 156
Cone	73, 118, 120, 132, 135, 146, 156
Cylinder	118–120, 132, 146, 156
19. COMPARISONS	
Tall	36, 38
Short & long	37, 38,
Alike & same	5, 6
Different	4
Pairs	64, 65, 68
Twins	66, 67, 68
Belong together	75–77
More	34, 35, 52
Less	36, 53
Larger & smaller number	17, 79–82, 137, 139, 149, 150, 155
20. DIRECTION and POSITION	
Right & Left	3–5, 11, 12, 16, 75
Top	3, 7, 10, 13
Bottom	3, 13
Middle	2, 4, 5, 7, 10, 16,
Inside and outside	68, 69
First, next, and last	2, 8, 11, 12, 30, 98
Before, after	89, 90, 106
Front, back	14, 32, 58, 98, 103, 114

21. GRAPHS	
Bar graphs Pictographs	23, 40, 52, 54, 55, 64, 73, 97, 120, 137, 148, 154 31, 32, 39, 63
22. UNITS OF MEASURE	
Cup, quart, gallon, liter	92–95, 103, 104, 118, 134, 158
23. MEASUREMENT	
Inches Centimeters Perimeter in inches	50–52, 59, 65, 66, 91 139, 143, 160 60, 61, 73–75, 87, 88, 105, 116, 143, 160
24. FRACTIONS	
Whole One-half One-third One-fourth	104–107 104–107, 114, 115, 129, 146, 152 112–115, 129, 146, 152 112–115, 129, 146, 152
25. SEQUENCE	
Next in a pattern	18, 25, 41, 51

Daily Lesson Planner

Lesson 1 • Count to 10 by counting the children • Identify *top* & *bottom* • Count to 5 by counting objects • Trace and write 1	**Lesson 2** • Circle the correct number 1–3 • Identify *first*, *middle* & *last* • Count 1–10 by counting objects • Trace and write 2	**Lesson 3** • Identify *left* & *right* • Circle the correct number 1–3 • Count the steps to 10 • Identify *top* & *bottom* • Trace and write 1
Lesson 4 • Identify *same* & *different* • Identify *left*, *right* & *middle* • Circle the correct number 1–3 • Count to 10 • Trace and write 2	**Lesson 5** • Identify green color & square shapes • Identify *same* & *different* • Identify *left*, *right* & *middle* • Circle the correct number of objects 2–4 • Trace 2 • Trace and count 1–2	**Lesson 6** • Identify blue color & circle shapes • Identify circle, square & green • Identify *first*, *same* & *different* • Circle the correct number 1–3 • Trace and write 1 & 2
Lesson 7 • Teach 3 • Identify circle, square, blue, green & X • Trace and write 3 • Circle the correct number of objects 3–6 • Identify *top*, *middle* & *bottom* • Count to 10	**Lesson 8** • Identify yellow color & triangle shape • Trace 1–3 • Identify *first* & *last* • Identify green & blue • Circle the correct number of objects 3–5	**Lesson 9** • Teach 4 • Circle the correct number 4–6 • Count to 10 • Trace and write 4
Lesson 10 • Tally marks • Trace 1–4 • Identify *top*, *bottom* & *middle* • Circle the correct number 1–6	**Lesson 11** • Teach 5 • Match tally marks to the number • Identify *right*, *left*, *first* & *last* • Trace 5	**Lesson 12** • Identify red color & star shape • Read a bar graph, identify colors & square • Choose *right*, *left*, *first* & *last* • Trace 1–5

Daily Lesson Planner

Lesson 13	**Lesson 14**	**Lesson 15**
• Teach 6 • Count objects 1–15 • Determine *top, bottom,* circle, square, star, yellow & blue • Trace & write 1–6	• Recognize pennies, *front & back* • Circle correct number 1–6 • Count to 15 • Determine *same*, circle & triangle • Trace 1–6	• Teach 7 • Count pennies • Count to 15 • Match tally marks to number • Trace & write 1–7
Lesson 16 • Identify orange color & rectangle shape • Determine *left, right & middle* • Count pennies • Trace and write 5–7	**Lesson 17** • Teach 8 • Choose larger & smaller • Identify rectangle, triangle, red & blue • Trace and write 1–8	**Lesson 18** • Days of the week • Ordinals first–seventh • Complete patterns & sequence • Count to 15 • Trace and write 6–8
Lesson 19 • Teach 9 • Tell time 1:00 o'clock • Days of the week • Ordinal numbers • Count pennies • Trace & write 1–9	**Lesson 20** • Identify brown color & hexagon shape • Count to 20 • Missing number 1–9 • Ordinal numbers & days of week • Trace and write 7–9	**Lesson 21** • Teach 0 • Count to 20 • Missing number 1–9 • Count pennies • Trace and write 0–9
Lesson 22 • Identify black color & octagon shape • Ordinal numbers & days of the week • Missing number 1–9 • Connect the dots 1–9 • Trace and write 0, 7–9	**Lesson 23** • Teach 10 • Time – hour • Bar graph & colors • Trace and write 10	**Lesson 24** • Addition 0 & 1 • Days of the week & ordinal numbers • Count 0–9 • Trace and write 0–10

Daily Lesson Planner

Lesson 25 • Missing number 0–10 • Number line • Addition 0–5 • Patterns, sequence • Count to 20 • Calendar	**Lesson 26** • Count by 10s • Trace & write 10's • Dimes • Addition 0–3 • Match the shapes, line	**Lesson 27** • Number between 1's family • Vertical addition 0–4 • Use tally marks • Count by 10's • Time – hour
Lesson 28 • Identify purple color & diamond shape • Write 11–20 • Number between 1's family • Vertical addition 0–4 • Time – hour	**Lesson 29** • Ordinals first–tenth • Addition 0–7 • Count pennies • Days of the week	**Lesson 30** • Count 1–30, calendar • Ordinals first–tenth & *before* • Addition 0–8 • Missing number 0–20
Lesson 31 • Use pictograph • Ordinals first–tenth • Addition 0–9 • Number between 1's family • Trace & write 21–30	**Lesson 32** • Dimes, *front* & *back* • Count by 10's • Pictograph • Ordinals first–tenth, colors • Addition 0–9	**Lesson 33** • Number after 1–5 • Dimes • Days of week & colors • Ordinals first–tenth
Lesson 34 • More & less • Number after 1–5 • Count to 30 & trace 21–30 • Count by 10's to 40	**Lesson 35** • Addition 1's family • More & less • Number after 1–9 • Dimes • Write 1–30	**Lesson 36** • Identify tall & short • Addition 1's family • More & less • Number after 0–9 • Count to 30

Daily Lesson Planner

Lesson 37 • Identify tall & short • Addition 1's family • Ordinals, days of week, calendar • Number after 1's	**Lesson 38** • Identify long, short & tall • Write 20–29 • Count dimes • Addition 1's family	**Lesson 39** • Number between 10's • Pictograph, shapes • Number after 0–9 • Addition 1's family • Groups of 10
Lesson 40 • Count 1–40 • Number between 10's • Bar graph • Number after 0–9 • Trace & write 30–39	**Lesson 41** • Addition on number line 1's • Shapes and colors • Patterns, sequence • Calendar	**Lesson 42** • Number between 20's • Addition 1's family • Trace & write 20–39
Lesson 43 • Dimes & pennies • Number between 20's • Addition 1's family • Time – hour	**Lesson 44** • Count by 10's to 100 • Trace 10's • Dimes & pennies • Addition 1's family • Time – hour	**Lesson 45** • Number between 30's • Dimes & pennies • Addition 1's family • Count by 10's to 100
Lesson 46 • Count 1–50 • Number between 30's • Dimes & pennies • Trace and write 40–49 • Addition 1's family	**Lesson 47** • Place value 1's • Count 1–50 • Trace 41–50 • Ordinals first–tenth • Addition 1's family	**Lesson 48** • Number after 10's • Place value 1's • Ordinals first–tenth • Count & write by 10's

Daily Lesson Planner

Lesson 49 • Number between 40's • Number after 10's • Place value 1's • Ordinals first–tenth	**Lesson 50** • Ruler 1" • Number between 40's • Ordinals first–tenth • Place value 1's	**Lesson 51** • Addition 10's • Ruler 1" • Patterns, sequence • Calendar
Lesson 52 • Dollar bill • Addition 10–19 • More & less • Dimes & pennies	**Lesson 53** • Bar graph • Ruler 1" • Addition 10's • More & less	**Lesson 54** • Days of the week • Bar graph • Dollar bill • Addition 10's
Lesson 55 • Count by 5's • Dollar bill • Addition 10's • Bar graph	**Lesson 56** • Number after 20's • Count by 5's • Addition 10's • Dollar	**Lesson 57** • Count to 60 • Number after 20's • Count by 5's • Horizontal addition 10's
Lesson 58 • Nickels • Trace & write 50–59 • Time – hour • vertical addition 10's	**Lesson 59** • Place value 10's • Nickels • Ruler • Time – hour	**Lesson 60** • Find perimeter • Place value 10's • Number after 20's • Addition 10's

Daily Lesson Planner

Lesson 61	Lesson 62	Lesson 63
• Number between 50's • Find perimeter • Addition 1's • Time – hour	• Addition 20's • Number between 50's • Pennies, dimes, nickels • Addition 10's	• Place value 1's & 10's to 19 • Addition 20's • Place value 10's • Pictograph
Lesson 64 • Identify pairs • Place value 1's & 10's to 19 • Bar graph • Addition 20's	**Lesson 65** • Place value 1's & 10's to 19 • Identify pairs • Inch • Addition 20's	**Lesson 66** • Identify twins • Inch • Count by 5's • Vertical addition 20's
Lesson 67 • Number after 30's • Identify twins • Ordinals first–tenth • Addition 10's	**Lesson 68** • Identify inside & outside • Number after 30's • Identify twins & pairs • Ordinals first–tenth	**Lesson 69** • Addition 30's • Identify inside & outside • Number after 30's • Pennies, dimes, nickels
Lesson 70 • Count to 70 • Addition 30's • Addition 1's • Number after 30's	**Lesson 71** • Place value 20's • Vertical addition 30's	**Lesson 72** • Number before 1's • Place value 20's • Vertical addition 30's • Perimeter

Daily Lesson Planner

Lesson 73 • Find perimeter in inches • Number before 1's • Bar graph • Addition 30's	**Lesson 74** • Number between 60's • Find perimeter in inches • Number before 1's • Pennies, nickels	**Lesson 75** • Identify things that belong together • Number between 60's • Perimeter
Lesson 76 • Number after 40's • Identify things that belong together • Days of the week • Addition 20's	**Lesson 77** • Digital clock, minutes • Number after 40's • Identify things that belong together • Place value 20's	**Lesson 78** • Addition 40's • Number after 40's • Digital clock, minutes • Addition 1's
Lesson 79 • Determine the greater or smaller number 0–9 • Addition 40's • Days of the week • Number after 40's	**Lesson 80** • Count to 80 • Pennies, dimes, nickels • Addition 40's • Determine the greater or smaller number 0–9	**Lesson 81** • Number before 10's • Determine the greater or smaller number 0–20 • Determine the smaller number 0–20 • Addition 40's
Lesson 82 • Number after 50's • Number before 10's • Addition 30's & 40's • Smaller number 0–20	**Lesson 83** • Months of the year • Number after 50's • Number before 10's	**Lesson 84** • Count by 2's, evens • Addition 50's • Months of the year, ordinal numbers • Pennies, dimes, nickels

Daily Lesson Planner

Lesson 85 • Number between 70's • Count by 2's, evens • Months of the year • Addition 50's	**Lesson 86** • Count by 2's, odds • Addition 50's • Count by 2's • Number between 70's	**Lesson 87** • Number before 20's • Count by 2's, odds • Perimeter, inches • Pennies, dimes, nickels • Addition 50's
Lesson 88 • Number after 60's • Number before 20's • Count by 2's, odds • Perimeter, inches • Addition 20's	**Lesson 89** • Time – hour, *before, after* • Number after 60's • Number before 20's • Count by 2's, evens	**Lesson 90** • Count to 90 • Time – hour, *before, after* • Number after 60's • Number before 20's
Lesson 91 • Addition 60's • Months of the year • Addition 30's • Inches	**Lesson 92** • Identify quart, gallon, liter & cup • Addition 60's • Count by 2's, evens • Addition 40's	**Lesson 93** • Number after 70's • Identify quart, gallon, liter & cup • Pennies, dimes nickels • Addition 60's
Lesson 94 • Number between 80's • Identify quart, gallon, liter & cup • Number after 70's • Addition 60's	**Lesson 95** • Place value 30's • Number between 80's • Identify quart, gallon, liter & cup • Number after 70's	**Lesson 96** • Addition 70's • Place value 30's • Odd numbers • Addition 60's

Daily Lesson Planner

Lesson 97 • Number after 80's • Addition 70's • Bar graph • Place value 30's	**Lesson 98** • 50 cents, 1$ • Number after 80's • Addition 70's • Match first–tenths	**Lesson 99** • Seasons • 50 cents, 1$ • Number after 80's • Addition 70's
Lesson 100 • Addition 80's • Count to 100 • 50 cents, 1$ • Time – hour, *before, after*	**Lesson 101** • Word problems • Addition 80's • Time – hour • Addition 1's	**Lesson 102** • Elapsed Time • Word problems • Count by 2's, evens • Addition 80's
Lesson 103 • $1 • Elapsed Time • Count quart, gallon, cup & liter • Count by 2's, odds	**Lesson 104** • Identify whole, 1/2 & equal parts • $1 • Odd numbers • Count quart, gallon, cup & liter	**Lesson 105** • 1/2 hour • Identify whole, 1/2 & equal parts • $1 • Perimeter, inches • Months
Lesson106 • Subtract 1's • 1/2 hour • Identify whole, 1/2 & equal parts • $1	**Lesson 107** • Number between 90's • Subtract 1's • 1/2 hour • Identify whole, 1/2 & equal parts	**Lesson 108** • Number after 90's • Number between 90's • Subtract 1's • Addition 80's • Place Value 30's • Ordinals, first–tenth

Daily Lesson Planner

Lesson 109 • Subtract 10's • Count by 3's • Number after 90's • Number between 90's • Word problems	**Lesson 110** • Number before 30's • Count by 3's • Subtract 10's • Days of the week • Addition 80's	**Lesson 111** • Addition 90's • Count by 3's • Subtract 1's • Addition 70's • Subtract 10's • Number before 30's
Lesson 112 • 1/3 & 1/4 • Addition 90's • Word problems • Number before 30's • Subtract 10's	**Lesson 113** • Subtract 20's • 1/3 & 1/4 • Addition 90's • Count by 2's & 3's • Subtract 10's	**Lesson 114** • 25 cents • Subtract 20's • Identify whole, 1/2, 1/3 & 1/4 • Addition 90's • Subtract 1's
Lesson 115 • Place value 40's • 25 cents • Match seasons • Identify whole, 1/2, 1/3 & 1/4 • Subtract 20's	**Lesson 116** • Subtract 30's • Place value 40's • 25 cents • Perimeter, inches • Subtract 20's	**Lesson 117** • Number before 40's • Subtract 30's • Count by 2's, 3's & 10's • 25 cents
Lesson 118 • Sphere, cone & cylinder • Number before 40's • Subtract 30's • Count quart, gallon, liter & cup	**Lesson 119** • 1/4 hour • Identify sphere, cone & cylinder • Number before 40's • Subtract 30's	**Lesson 120** • Place value 50's • Identify sphere, cone & cylinder • Bar graph • 1/4 hour • Subtract 30's

Daily Lesson Planner

Lesson 121 • Subtract 40's • Place value 50's • 1/4 hour • Addition 1's	**Lesson 122** • Number before 50's • Subtract 40's • $1, 50 cents, 25 cents, 10 cents, 1 cent • 1/4 hour	**Lesson 123** • Place value 60's • Number before 50's • Subtract 40's • 1/4 hour
Lesson 124 • Count by 4's • Place value 60's • Number before 50's • Subtract 40's	**Lesson 125** • Subtract 50's • Count by 4's • Place value 60's • 1/4 hour	**Lesson 126** • Number before 60's • Subtract 50's • Count by 4's • Add and subtract 1's
Lesson 127 • Subtract 60's • Word problems • Count by 1's, 2's, 3's, 4's, 5's	**Lesson 128** • Number before 70's • Subtract 60's • 1/2, 1/4 hour • Months & seasons	**Lesson 129** • Subtract 70's • Count by 10's & 4's • Subtract 10's • Identify whole, 1/2, 1/3, 1/4
Lesson 130 • Number before 80's • Subtract 70's • Addition 60's & 70's • Subtract 10's	**Lesson 131** • Subtract 80's • Money, word problems • Addition 60's & 70's • Number after 90's	**Lesson 132** • Number before 90's • Subtract 80's • Identify geometric solids • Seasons

Daily Lesson Planner

Lesson 133 • Subtract 90's • Word problems, \$ • Place value 70's • Money	**Lesson 134** • Next door neighbors • Subtract 90's • Word problems • Count quart, gallon, cup & liter	**Lesson 135** • Place value 80's • Word problems (+) • Identify geometric solids • Count by 5's
Lesson 136 • Subtract all • Word problems (–) • Count by 10's • Next door neighbors	**Lesson 137** • Add & subtract 20's • Bar graph • Count by 2's • Find the largest number of 3	**Lesson 138** • Place value 90's • Count by 4's • Subtract 30's • Word problems (+)
Lesson 139 • Measure with centimeters • Put numbers in order 1's • Count by 3's • Smallest of 3 numbers	**Lesson 140** • Subtract & add 30's • Put numbers in order 1's • Money, word problems • Subtract 40's	**Lesson 141** • Subtract and add 40's • Put numbers in order 1's • Ordinals, first–tenth • Count by 3's
Lesson 142 • Time minutes • Count by 4's • Subtract and add 40's • Word problems	**Lesson 143** • Subtract and add 50's • Measure with centimeters • Addition 80's • Perimeter, inches	**Lesson 144** • Subtract 90's • Subtract and add 50's • Money, word problems, subtract • Addition 80's

Daily Lesson Planner

Lesson 145	Lesson 146	Lesson 147
• Subtract & add 60's • Time – minutes • Subtract 90's • Addition 90's	• Time minutes • Subtract & add 60's • Identify geometric solids • 1/2, 1/3, 1/4	• Subtract & add 70's • Time – minutes • Days of the week • Addition 90's
Lesson 148 • Bar graphs • Subtract & add 70's • 1/4 & 1/2 hour • Count by 5's	**Lesson 149** • Subtract & add 80's • Largest of 3 numbers • 1/4 hour • $1, 25 cents	**Lesson 150** • Place value all • Subtract & add 80's • Smallest of 3 numbers • Time – minutes
Lesson 151 • Put numbers in order 10's • Ordinals, first–tenth • Number before and after 1's • Tally marks	**Lesson 152** • Subtract & add 90's • Put numbers in order 10's • Identify whole, 1/2, 1/3 & 1/4 • Months of year, seasons	**Lesson 153** • Number between 1–100 • Subtract & add 90's • 1/4, 1/2 hour • Put numbers in order 10's
Lesson 154 • Review 1's & 10's, addition & subtraction • Number between 1–100 • Bar graph • Put numbers in order 1's & 10's	**Lesson 155** • Review 20's & 30's, addition & subtraction • Number before and after 20's • Money • Lesser number • Greater number	**Lesson 156** • Review 40's & 50's, addition & subtraction • Count by 10's • Geometric solids • Place value 10's & 1's

Daily Lesson Planner

<table>
<tr>
<td>Lesson 157
• Review 60's & 70's, addition & subtraction
• Ordinal numbers
• Count by 5's
• Word problems</td>
<td>Lesson 158
• Review 80's & 90's, addition & subtraction
• Tally marks
• Count quart, gallon, cup & liter
• Count by 2's</td>
<td>Lesson 159
• Put numbers in order 1's & 10's
• Number between 1–100
• Word problems
• Count by 3's</td>
</tr>
<tr>
<td>Lesson 160
• Ordinal numbers
• Count by 4's
• Measure with centimeter
• Measure with inches</td>
<td></td>
<td></td>
</tr>
</table>

Development of

GENERAL PATTERN:

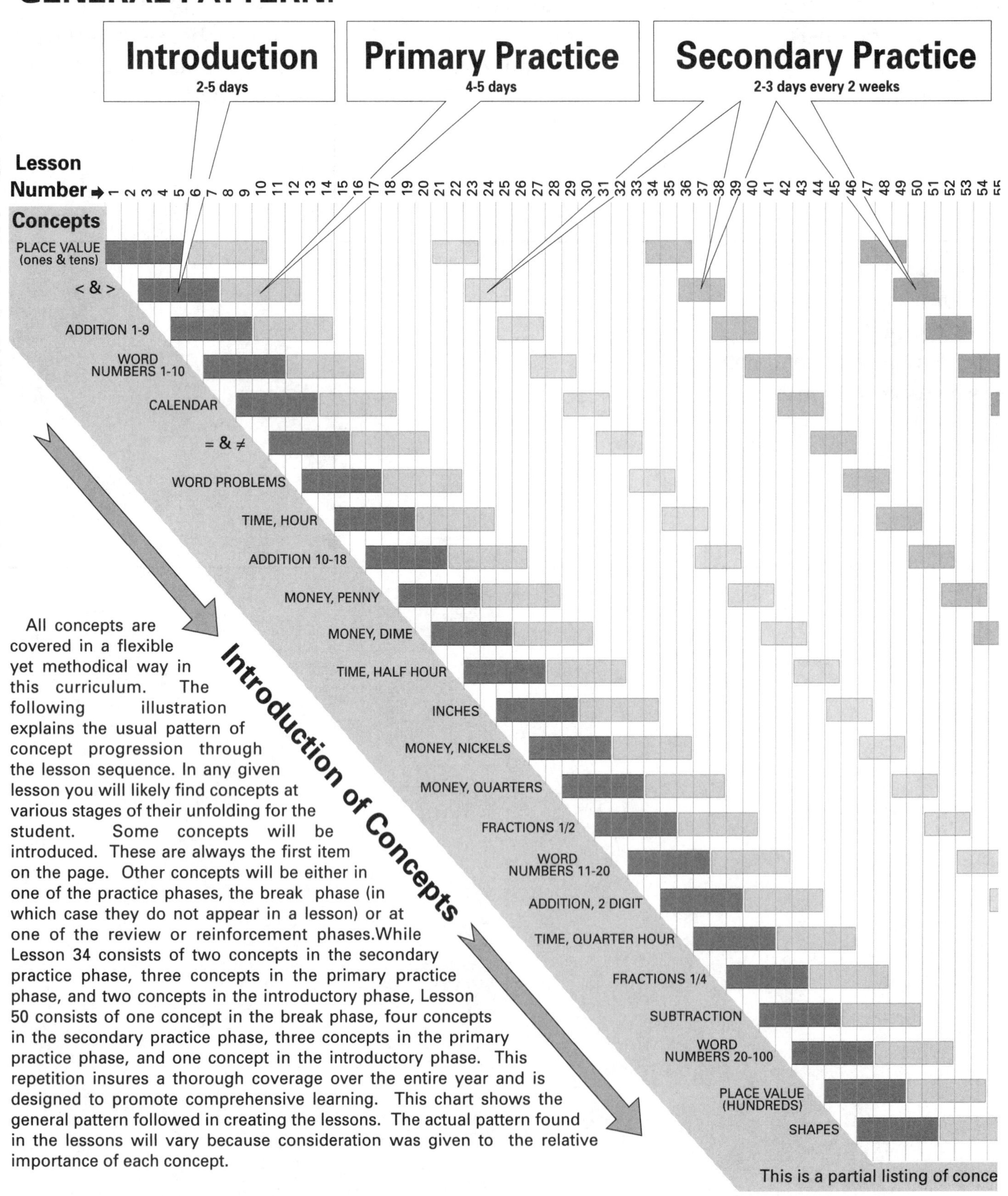

All concepts are covered in a flexible yet methodical way in this curriculum. The following illustration explains the usual pattern of concept progression through the lesson sequence. In any given lesson you will likely find concepts at various stages of their unfolding for the student. Some concepts will be introduced. These are always the first item on the page. Other concepts will be either in one of the practice phases, the break phase (in which case they do not appear in a lesson) or at one of the review or reinforcement phases.While Lesson 34 consists of two concepts in the secondary practice phase, three concepts in the primary practice phase, and two concepts in the introductory phase, Lesson 50 consists of one concept in the break phase, four concepts in the secondary practice phase, three concepts in the primary practice phase, and one concept in the introductory phase. This repetition insures a thorough coverage over the entire year and is designed to promote comprehensive learning. This chart shows the general pattern followed in creating the lessons. The actual pattern found in the lessons will vary because consideration was given to the relative importance of each concept.

Concepts Chart

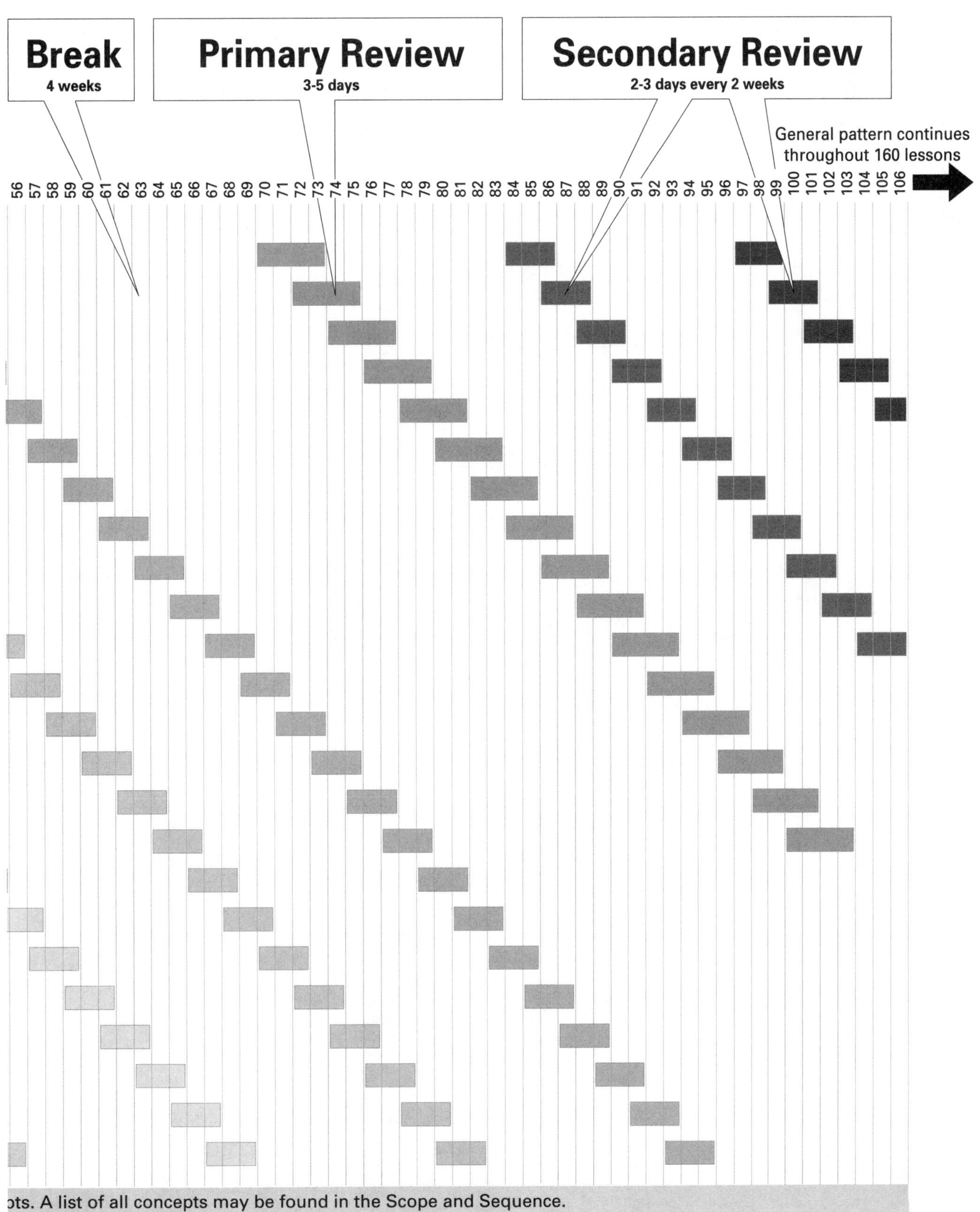

pts. A list of all concepts may be found in the Scope and Sequence.

Teacher Lessons

Lesson 1 - Counting

Overview:

- Count to 10 by counting the children
- Identify *top* & *bottom*
- Count to 5 by counting objects
- Trace and write 1

Materials and Supplies:

- Teacher's Guide & Student Workbook
- White board
- Objects for counters
- Number flash cards 1–10
- Dominos
- Worksheet 2

Teaching Tips:

During this school year it is important that you begin to count everything that you see and do with your class. Count the number of steps that are walked going from one place to another. Point out objects such as utility poles, trees, plants, birds, cats, dogs, etc., and have the class count them. Count items in the classroom. If you count 13 items, ask them how many there would be if there were 1 or 2 more or 1 or 2 less if they have started doing subtraction. Make math an important part of their everyday lives. Help them start to understand how many times numbers are used.

Introduce directions to the children by playing a game with them. Explain *right* and *left*. Ask them to hold up their *right* hands, put out their *left* legs, touch their *right* ears. Ask them to put their *right* hands on top of their heads. Ask them to put their *left* hands behind their backs. Continue this game using *right, left, up, down, high, low, top, bottom, middle, inside, outside, first, last.*

Teach counting orally to 10.

Activities:

If they are able to, have the student(s) write their name on the top of the paper. Make this the first thing they always do when they start their lesson. If they are unable to write their own names you need to write the student's names on the top of the paper before passing it out. Draw the student's attention to the name you have written. If you wish, you can have them trace over the letters. Make this an important activity and encourage the student(s) to be proud of their work.

① Point out the number 1 in the circle before the first instruction. Every new activity will have a number before the instruction. Count the children on this page out loud with the class to 10. Learning to count quickly and accurately is one of the most important objectives your student(s) can accomplish in this program. Demonstrate how you would count the children by moving from left to right and top to bottom on the page. Associate the baseball boy with (1). The jogging boy with (2). The measuring boy with (3) and etc. Show them how easy it is to get confused if they start counting randomly on the page.

② Point out the number 2 in the circle before the second instruction. Talk about *top* and *bottom*. Demonstrate the concept by pointing to a table, desk or chair. Demonstrate making a circle on the white board. Read the first instruction to the class. Check to see that they are doing the activity correctly. Read the second instruction and pick a student to show the class their work.

③ Point out the number 3 in the circle before the third instruction. Read the instruction to the class. Have them point to the number and then count the number of objects after the number. Have several student(s) do this individually for the class.

④ Point out the number 4 in the circle before the fourth instruction. Read the instruction to the class. Demonstrate writing the number (1) on the white board. Have them trace the first (1) with their pencil. Then have them trace the next two dotted 1's. Discuss the spacing between the numbers. Instruct them to write (1) five more times. Point out the objects on the bottom of the page. Ask the class for other examples of where they can find the number 1.

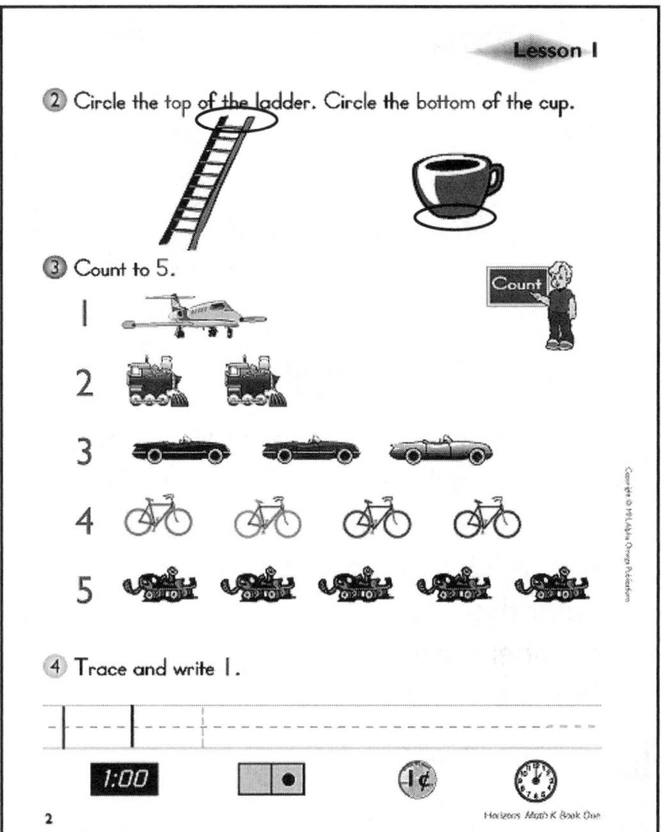

Lesson 2 - Counting

Overview:

- Circle the correct number 1–3
- Identify *first, middle* & *last*
- Count 1–10 by counting objects
- Trace and write 1

Materials and Supplies:

- Teacher's Guide & Student Workbook
- White board
- Objects for counters
- Red, yellow, green and blue crayons
- Color flash cards
- Number flash cards 1–10
- Dominos

Teaching Tips:

Place a card with the number showing (any number 1 through 10) in front of the children and ask them to pull the same number of objects from a group of 10 objects. Do this in random order until you have used all nine cards.

Introduce the red, yellow, green, and blue crayons to the children. Construct or purchase flash cards for the colors. Use them for drill and review as the colors are introduced and practiced.

Review counting orally to 10.

Activities:

If they are able to, have the student(s) write their name on the top of the paper. Make this the first thing they always do when they start their lesson. If they are unable to write their own names you need to write each student's name on the top of the paper before passing it out. Draw the student's attention to the name you have written. If you wish, you can have them trace over the letters. Make this an important activity and encourage the student(s) to be proud of their work.

Lesson 2

① Circle the correct number.

1 (2) 3 | (1) 2 3

② Circle the first one.

Circle the last one.

Circle the middle one.

③ Trace and write 1.

1:00

Horizons Math K Book One 3

① Point out the number 1 in the circle before the first instruction. Every new activity will have a number before the instruction. Read the instruction. Point out the dotted divider line. These lines and boxes are used to separate the problems. Count the elephants. Point out the numbers 1, 2 and 3. Demonstrate on the white board how the student(s) should circle the number that they choose. Point to the giraffe. Point out the numbers 1, 2 and 3. Have them circle the number that they choose.

② Point out the number 2 in the circle before the second instruction. Talk about *first, middle* and *last*. Demonstrate the concept by pointing to objects in the room or have 3 students line up at the front of the room. Demonstrate making a circle on the white board. Read the first instruction to the class. Tell them to circle the *first* butterfly. Check to see that they are doing the activity correctly. Read the second instruction and tell them to circle the *last* penguin. Read the third instruction and have them circle the monkey in the *middle*.

③ Point out the number 3 in the circle before the third instruction. Read the instruction to the class. Demonstrate writing the number (1) on the white board. Have them trace the first (1) with their pencil. Then have them trace the next two dotted 1's. Discuss the spacing between the numbers. Instruct them to write (1) five more times. Point out the objects on the bottom of the page. Ask the class for other examples of where they can find the number 1.

④ Point out the number 4 in the circle before the fourth instruction. Read the instruction to the class. Have them point to the number and then count the number of objects after the number. Have several student(s) do this individually for the class or have a different student do each row.

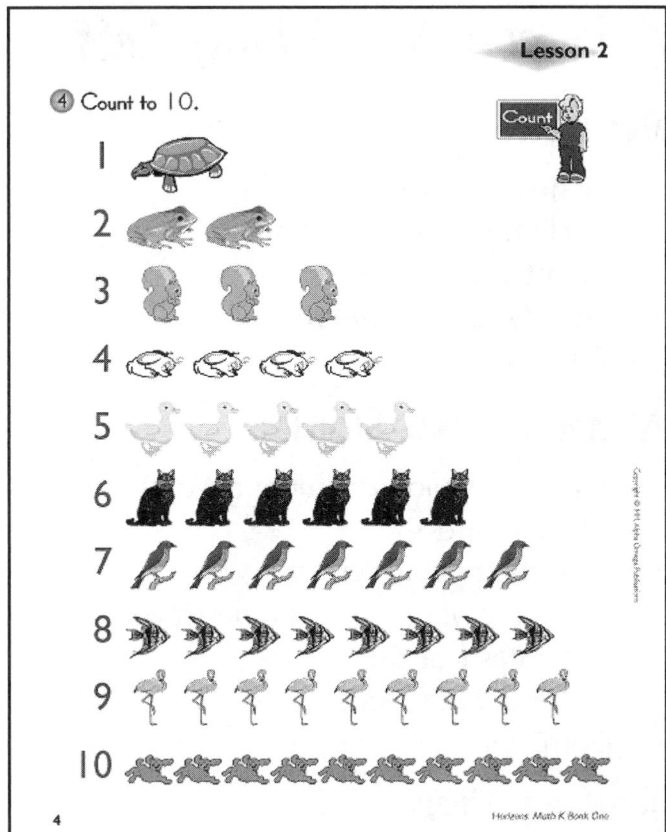

Lesson 3 - Right, Left

Overview:

- Identify *left* & *right*
- Circle the correct number 1–3
- Count the steps to 10
- Identify *top* & *bottom*
- Trace and write 1

Materials and Supplies:

- Teacher's Guide & Student Workbook
- White board
- Objects for counters
- Red, yellow, green and blue crayons
- Color flash cards
- Number flash cards 1–10
- Dominos

Teaching Tips:

Review drawing circles. Demonstrate how to make an X. Have the student(s) practice making an X.

Review directions with the children by playing a game with them. Explain *right* and *left*. Ask them to hold up their *right* hands, put out their *left* legs, touch their *right* ears. Ask them to put their *right* hands on top of their heads. Ask them to put their *left* hands behind their backs. Continue this game using *right, left, up, down, high, low, top, bottom, middle, inside, outside.*

Review counting orally to 10.

Activities:

If they are able to, have the student(s) write their name on the top of the paper. Make this the first thing they always do when they start their lesson. If they are unable to write their own names you need to write each student's name on the top of the paper before passing it out. Draw the student's attention to the name you have written. If you wish, you can have them trace over the letters. Make this an important activity and encourage the student(s) to be proud of their work.

① Point out the number 1 in the circle before the first instruction. Every new activity will have a number before the instruction. Read the instruction. Point to the boy and the girl. Ask the class which student is on the *right*. Have them circle the boy. Point to the hats. Refer to the colors. Show them other objects that are blue and yellow. Have the class put an X over the cap on the left (blue).

② Point out the number 2 in the circle before the second instruction. Read the instruction. Point out the dotted divider line. These lines and boxes are used to separate the problems. Count the pig. Point out the numbers 1, 2 and 3. Demonstrate on the white board how the student(s) should circle the number that they choose. Point to the cows. Point out the numbers 1, 2 and 3. Have them circle the number that they choose.

③ Point out the number 3 in the circle before the third instruction. Read the instruction to the class. Start on the bottom step and have the class count to 10.

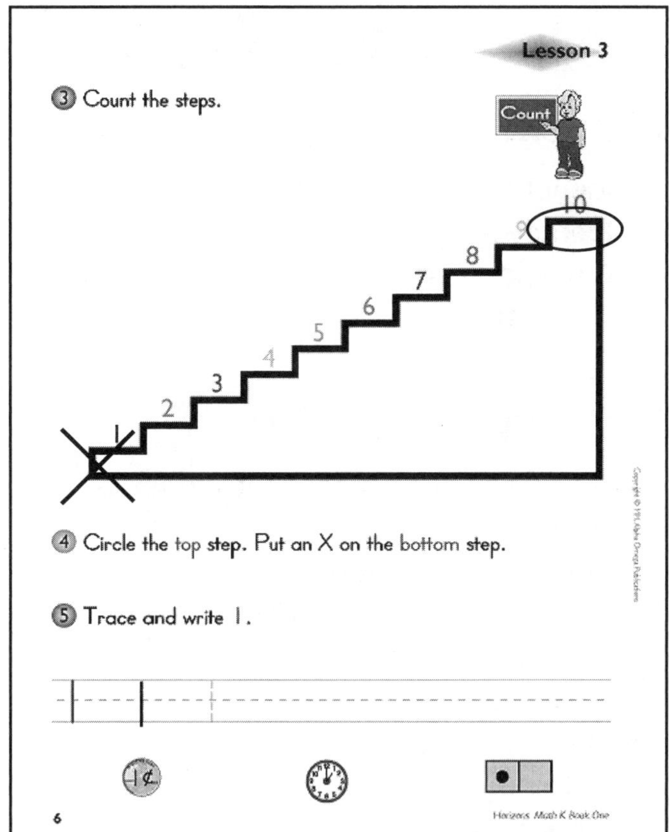

④ Point out the number 4 in the circle before the instruction. Read the instruction. Talk about *top* and *bottom*. Demonstrate the concept by pointing to a table, desk or chair. Demonstrate making a circle on the white board. Read the first instruction to the class. Check to see that they are doing the activity correctly. Read the second instruction and have the class make the X.

⑤ Point out the number 5 in the circle before the instruction. Read the instruction to the class. Demonstrate writing the number (1) on the white board. Have them trace the first (1) with their pencil. Then have them trace the next two dotted 1's. Discuss the spacing between the numbers. Instruct them to write (1) five more times. Point out the objects on the bottom of the page. Ask the class for other examples of where they can find the number 1.

Lesson 4 - Shapes

Overview:

- Identify *same* & *different*
- Identify *left, right* & *middle*
- Circle the correct number 1–3
- Count to 10
- Trace and write 2

Materials and Supplies:

- Teacher's Guide & Student Workbook
- White board
- Objects for counters
- Red, yellow, green and blue crayons
- Color flash cards
- Shape flash cards
- Number flash cards 1–10
- Dominos
- Worksheet 3

Teaching Tips:

Talk to the students about shapes. Point out different shapes in the classroom. Tell them that shapes have names and that they will learn some of these names today. Make or purchase shape flash cards. Make both flash cards that are the different shapes and rectangle cards that have the shapes drawn on them. Make a variety of sizes, positions, colors, etc.

Talk about *same* and *different*. Group objects that are the same. Look for characteristics that help identify things that are the same or different.

Review directions with the children by playing a game with them. Explain *right* and *left*. Ask them to hold up their *right* hands, put out their *left* legs, touch their *right* ears. Ask them to put their *right* hands on top of their heads. Ask them to put their *left* hands behind their backs. Continue this game using *right, left, up, down, high, low, top, bottom, middle, inside, outside.*

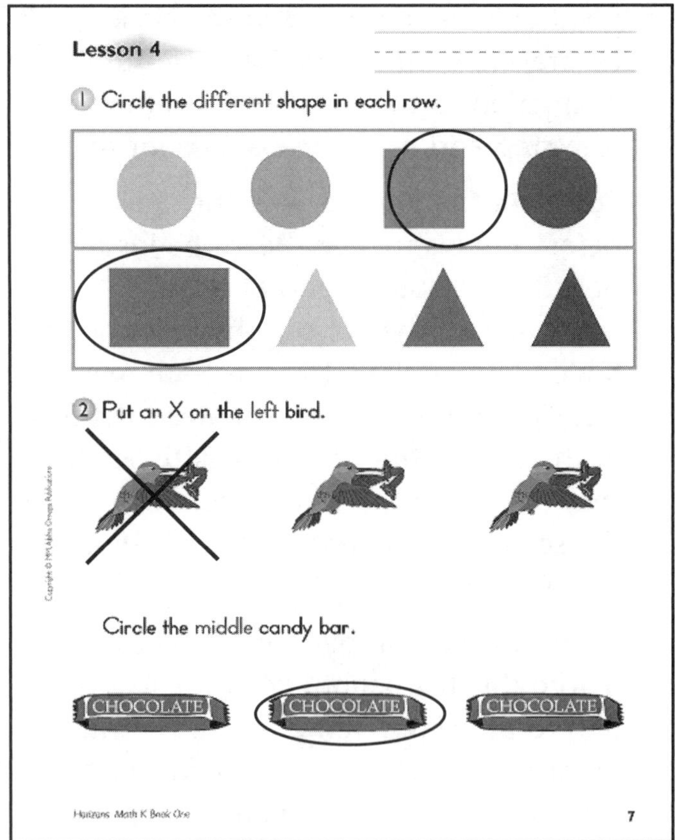

Lesson 4

① Circle the different shape in each row.

② Put an X on the left bird.

Circle the middle candy bar.

CHOCOLATE CHOCOLATE CHOCOLATE

Horizons Math K Book One 7

Review counting orally to 10.

Activities:

① Point out the number 1 in the circle before the first instruction. Read the instruction. Point out the shapes in the first row. Refer to the colors. Have the class circle their answer. Point out the shapes in the second row. Refer to the colors. Have the class circle their answer.

② Point out the number 2 in the circle before the second instruction. Read the instruction. Point to the birds. Ask the class which bird is on the left. Have them circle the bird. Read the second instruction. Point to the candy bars. Have the class circle their answer.

③ Point out the number 3 in the circle before the third instruction. Read the instruction to the class. Point out the dotted divider line. These lines and boxes are used to separate the problems. Count the hammers. Point out the numbers 1, 2 and 3. Demonstrate on the white board how the student(s) should circle the number that they choose. Point to the saws. Point out the numbers 1, 2 and 3. Have them circle the number that they choose.

④ Point out the number 4 in the circle before the instruction. Read the instruction. Start on the left of the hop-scotch figure and have the class count to 10. Do this activity outside on the sidewalk.

⑤ Point out the number 5 in the circle before the instruction. Read the instruction to the class. Demonstrate writing the number (2) on the white board. Have them trace the first (2) with their pencil. Then have them trace the next two dotted 2's. Discuss the spacing between the numbers. Instruct them to write (2) four more times. Point out the objects on the bottom of the page. Ask the class for other examples of where they can find the number 2.

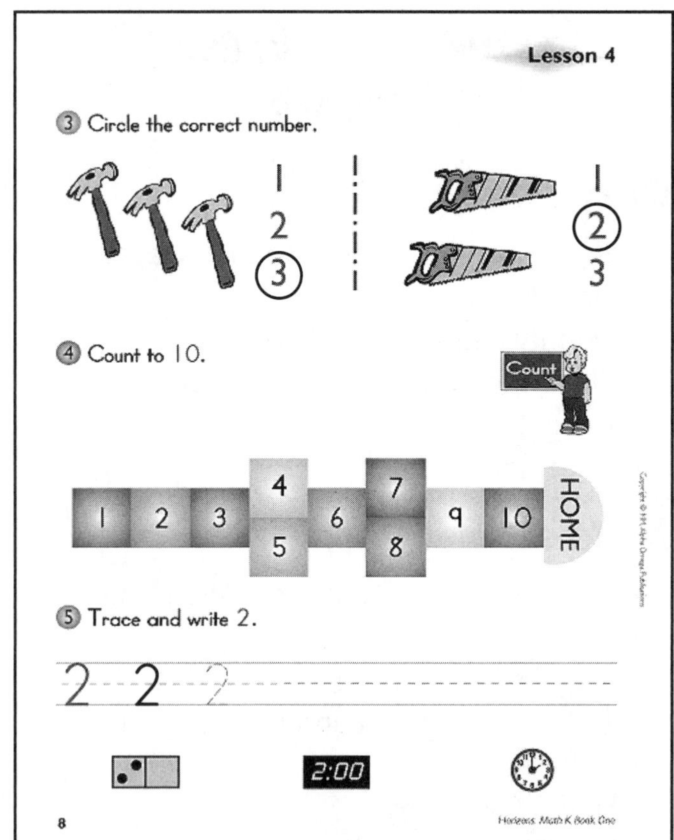

Lesson 5 - Green & Square

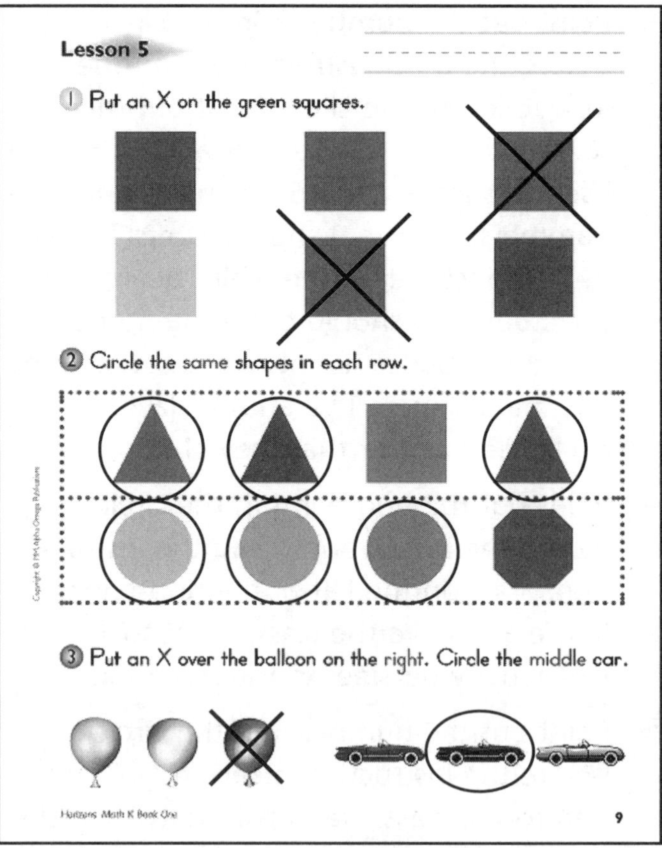

Overview:

- Identify green color & square shapes
- Identify *same* & *different*
- Identify *left, right* & *middle*
- Circle the correct number of objects 2–4
- Trace 2
- Trace and count 1–2

Materials and Supplies:

- Teacher's Guide & Student Workbook
- White board
- Objects for counters
- Red, yellow, green and blue crayons
- Color flash cards
- Shape flash cards
- Number flash cards 1–10

Teaching Tips:

Review the red, yellow, green, and blue crayons with the children.

Review *same* and *different*.

Teach squares by pointing out objects that are squares.

Review counting orally to 10.

Activities:

① Point out the number 1 in the circle before the first instruction. Read the instruction. Have the student(s) mark their answers.

② Point out the number 2 in the circle before the second instruction. Read the instruction. Point out the dotted divider lines. Refer to the colors. Have the class circle their answers.

③ Point out the number 3 in the circle before the third instruction. Read the instruction to the class. Point to the balloons and their colors. Ask the class which balloon is on the right. Have them put an X over the *right* balloon. Point to the cars. Refer to the colors. Have the class circle the *middle* car.

④ Point out the number 4 in the circle before the instruction. Read the instruction. Point out the dotted divider lines. These lines are used to separate the problems. Count the bees. Point out the numbers 2, 3 and 4. Demonstrate on the white board how the student(s) should circle the number that they choose. Do the same for the balloons.

⑤ Point out the number 5 in the circle before the instruction. Read the instruction to the class. Demonstrate writing the number (2) on the white board. Have them trace the first (2) with their pencil. Then have them trace the next two dotted 2's. Discuss the spacing between the numbers. Instruct them to write (2) four more times. Point out the objects below the lines. Ask the class for other examples of where they can find the number 2.

⑥ Point out the number 6 in the circle before the instruction. Read the instruction to the class. Demonstrate writing the numbers 1 & 2 on the white board. Have them trace the first 1 & 2 with their pencil. Then have them trace the next two dotted 1's and 2's. Discuss the spacing between the numbers. Instruct them to write the 1 & 2 two more times.

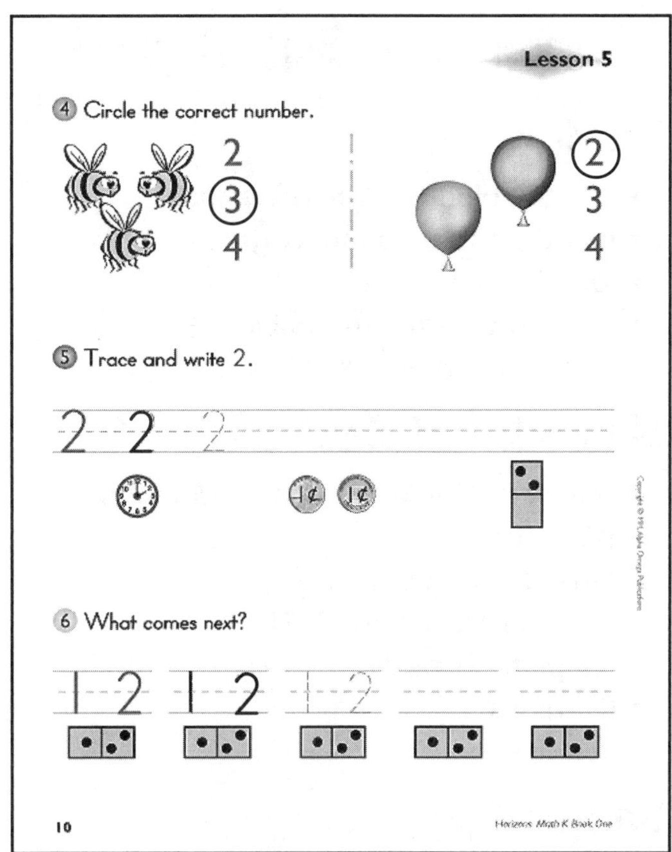
Lesson 5

④ Circle the correct number.

2 ③ 4 | ② 3 4

⑤ Trace and write 2.

⑥ What comes next?

10 Horizons Math K Book One

Lesson 6 - Blue & Circle

Overview:

- Identify blue color & circle shapes
- Identify circle, square & green
- Identify *first, same* & *different*
- Circle the correct number 1–3
- Trace and write 1 & 2

Materials and Supplies:

- Teacher's Guide & Student Workbook
- White board
- Objects for counters
- Number flash cards 1–10
- Shape flash cards
- Dominos
- Pennies

Teaching Tips:

Review the red, yellow, green, and blue crayons to the children.

Count 1–10 using flash cards and counters.

Review circles by pointing out objects that are circles.

Teach counting orally to 20.

Activities:

① Point out the number 1 in the circle before the first instruction. Read the instruction. Have the student(s) mark their answers.

② Point out the number 2 in the circle before the second instruction. Read the instruction. Refer to the colors. Have the class circle their answers.

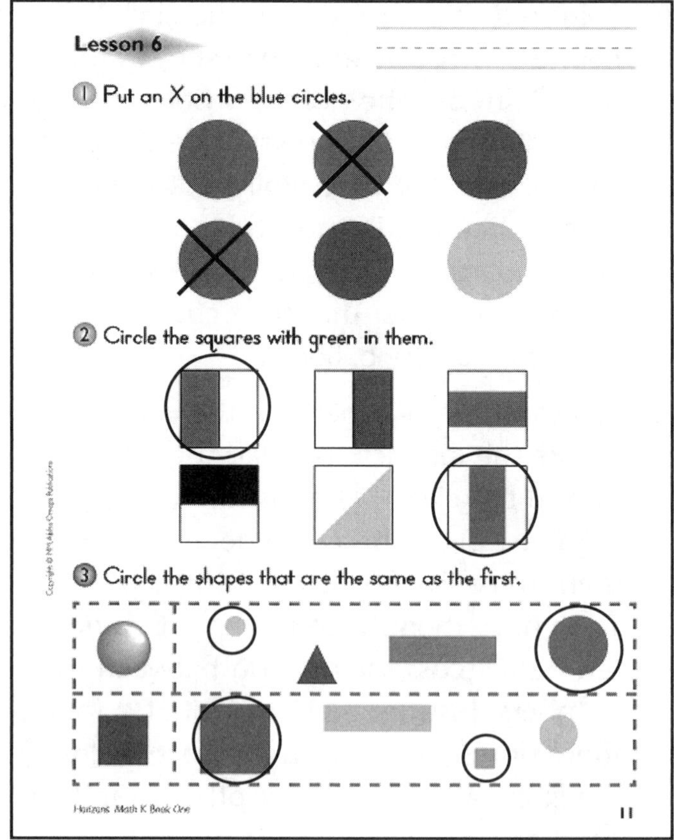

③ Point out the number 3 in the circle before the third instruction. Read the instruction to the class. Point out the dotted divider lines. These lines and boxes are used to separate the problems. Look at the first circle shape. Tell the students that not all circles are the same size. Do the same for the first square. Have the student(s) circle their answers.

④ Point out the number 4 in the circle before the instruction. Read the instruction. Point out the dotted divider lines. These lines are used to separate the problems. Count the planes. Point out the number 2. Demonstrate on the white board how the student(s) should circle the number of planes that they choose. Do the same for the other objects.

⑤ Point out the number 5 in the circle before the instruction. Read the instruction to the class. Demonstrate writing the numbers 1 & 2 on the white board. Have them trace the first (1) with their pencil. Then have them trace the next two dotted 1's. Discuss the spacing between the numbers. Have them trace the first (2) with their pencil. Then have them trace the next two dotted 2's. Instruct them to write (2) four more times. Ask the class for other examples of where they can find the numbers 1 & 2.

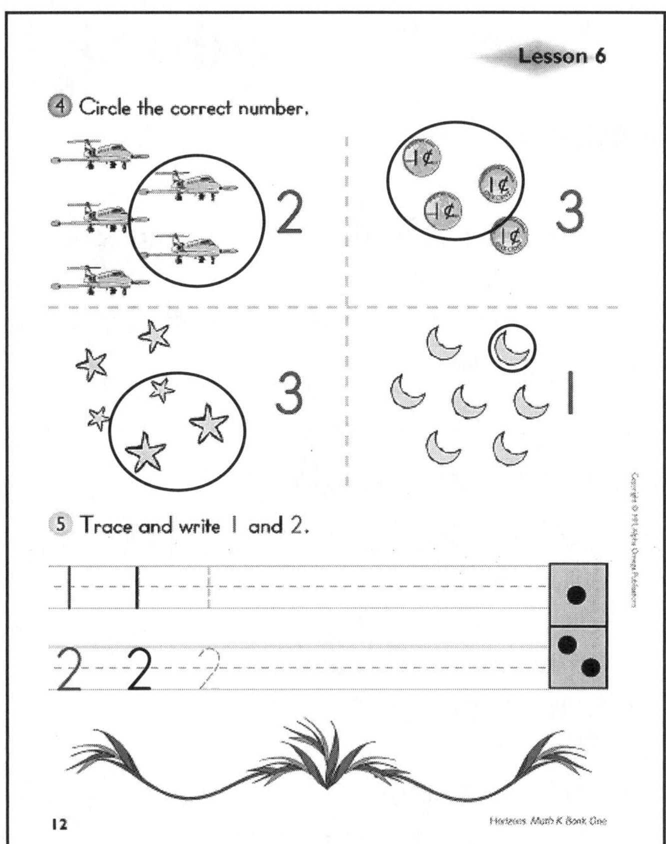

Lesson 7 - Number 3

Overview:

- Teach 3
- Identify circle, square, blue, green & X
- Trace and write 3
- Circle the correct number of objects 3–6
- Identify *top, middle* & *bottom*
- Count to 10

Materials and Supplies:

- Teacher's Guide & Student Workbook
- White board
- Objects for counters
- Number flash cards 1–10
- Shape flash cards
- Crayons
- Color flash cards
- Dominos or domino flash cards
- Pennies
- Worksheet 4

Teaching Tips:

Teach counting to three by counting objects, counters, etc.

Review the red, yellow, green and blue crayons with the student(s).

Review circles by pointing out objects that are circles.

Count 1–10 using flash cards and counters.

Review *top, bottom* and *middle.*

Review counting orally to 20.

Activities:

① Point out the number 1 in the circle before the first instruction. Read the instruction. Talk about the clock and the calculator to review uses for the number 3. Point out the dotted lines that divide parts of the activity. Have them count the objects in both rows starting on the left and moving to the right.

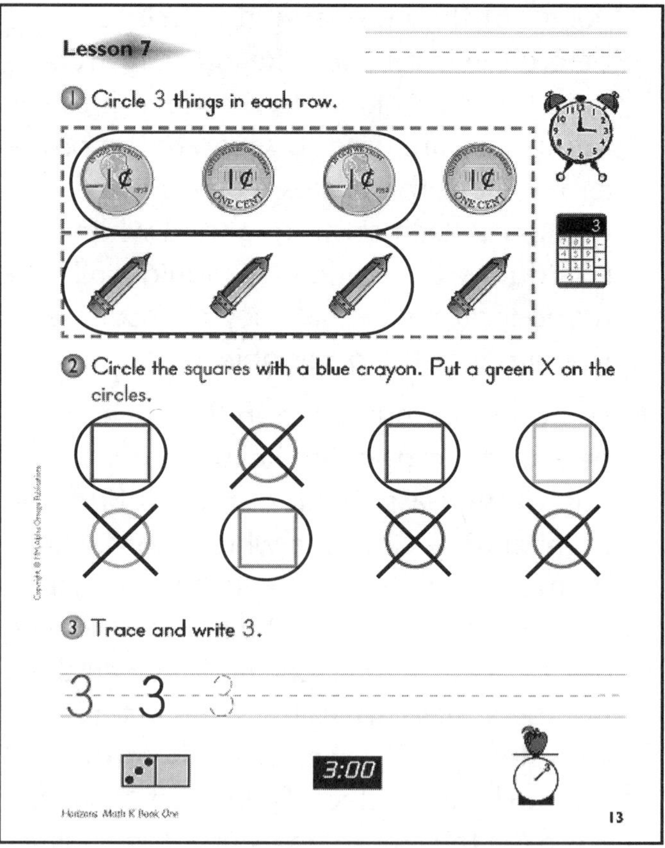

② Point out the number 2 in the circle before the second instruction. Read the first instruction. Have the student(s) circle the squares with a blue crayon. Read the second instruction. Have the student(s) put a green X on the circles.

③ Point out the number 3 in the circle before the third instruction. Read the instruction to the class. Demonstrate writing the number (3) on the white board. Have them trace the first (3) with their pencil. Then have them trace the next two dotted 3's. Discuss the spacing between the numbers. Instruct them to write (3) four more times. Point out the objects on the bottom of the page. Ask the class for other examples of where they can find the number 3.

④ Point out the number 4 in the circle before the instruction. Read the instruction. Point out the dotted divider lines. These lines are used to separate the problems. Count the bananas. Point out the numbers. Demonstrate on the white board how the student(s) should circle the number that they choose. Do the same for the other objects.

⑤ Point out the number 5 in the circle before the instruction. Read the first instruction to the class. Have them circle their choice. Read the second instruction and have them write an X over their answer.

⑥ Point out the number 6 in the circle before the instruction. Read the instruction to the class. Count the dots in each domino.

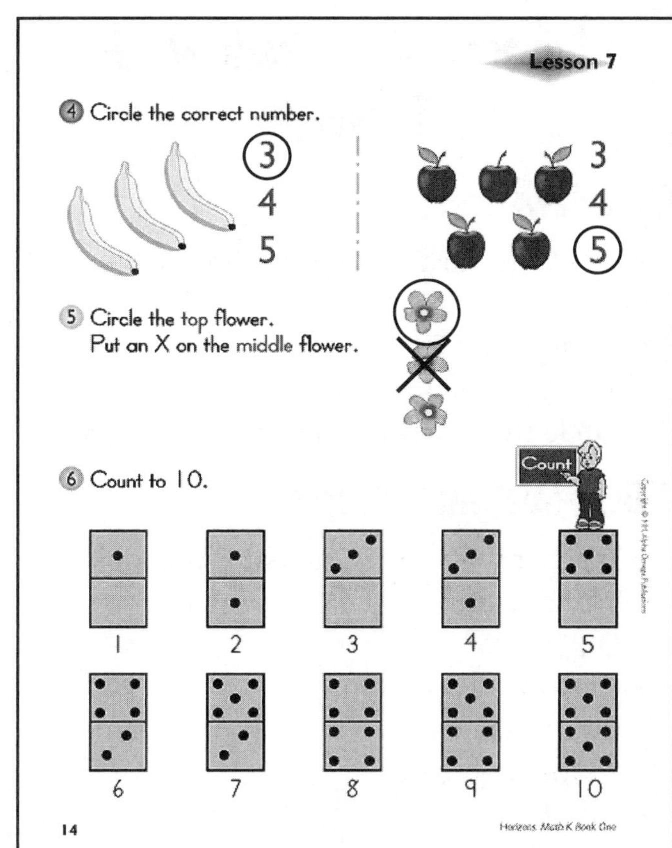

Lesson 8 - Yellow & Triangle

Overview:

- Identify yellow color & triangle shape
- Trace 1–3
- Identify *first* & *last*
- Identify green & blue
- Circle the correct number of objects 3–5

Materials and Supplies:

- Teacher's Guide & Student Workbook
- White board
- Objects for counters
- Crayons
- Color flash cards
- Shape flash cards
- Dominos
- Flash cards 1–10

Teaching Tips:

Use the number flash cards for review. Have the student(s) select certain numbers from a stack, say the the number, and then print it on the white board. Continue the review by picking out other students to do the same.

Review triangle and square.

Review colors.

Review position words.

Review counting orally to 20.

Activities:

① Point out the number 1 in the circle before the first instruction. Read the instruction. Count the number of sides that a triangle has. Show the student(s) examples of several shapes of triangles. Have the students circle their choices.

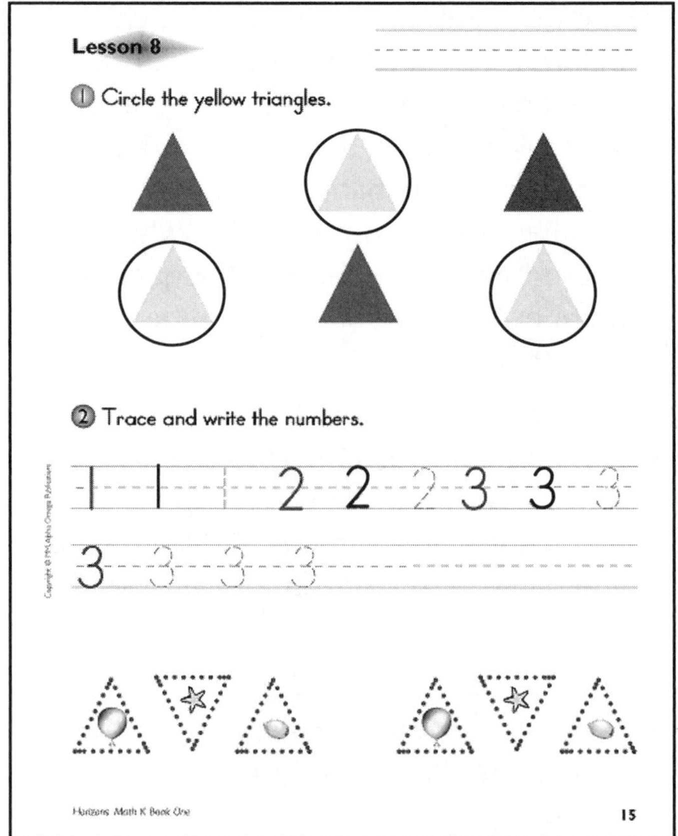

② Point out the number 2 in the circle before the second instruction. Read the instruction. Trace each red number. Write over each dotted number. Write four more 3's on the second line.

③ Point out the number 3 in the circle before the third instruction. Read the first instruction to the class. Count the number of sides in a square. Point out that the sides must be the same length. Draw a rectangle so they see how a square and a rectangle are different. Encourage them to do neat work. Read the second instruction and allow them to color their choice.

④ Point out the number 4 in the circle before the instruction. Read the instruction. Point out the dotted divider lines. These lines are used to separate the problems. Count the mice. Point out the numbers. Demonstrate on the white board how the student(s) should circle the number that they choose. Do the same for the cats.

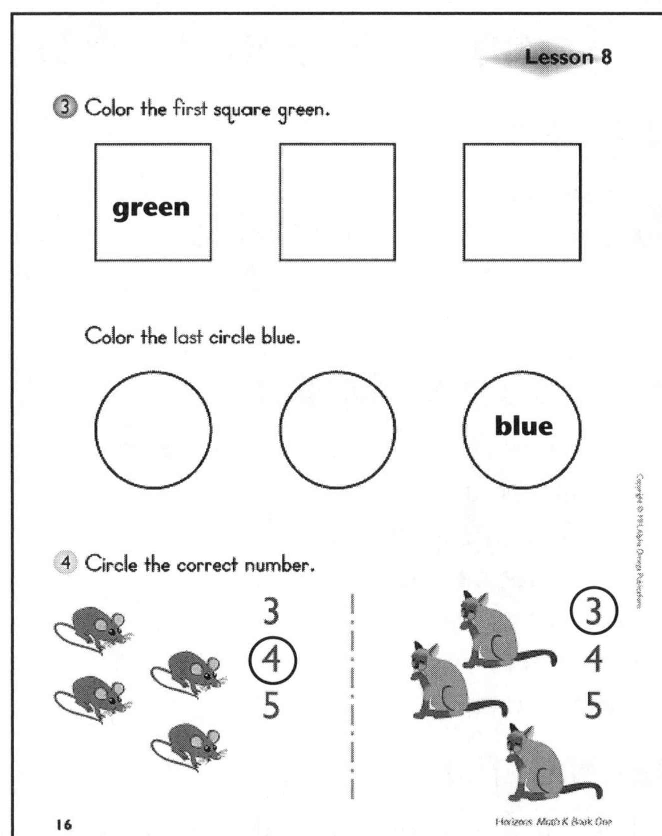

Lesson 9 - Number 4

Overview:

- Teach 4
- Circle the correct number 4–6
- Count to 10
- Trace and write 4

Materials and Supplies:

- Teacher's Guide & Student Workbook
- White board
- Objects for counters
- Number flash cards
- Dominos
- Counters
- Worksheet 5

Teaching Tips:

Teach 4 with counters or other objects. Demonstrate writing the number 4. Review counting orally to 20.

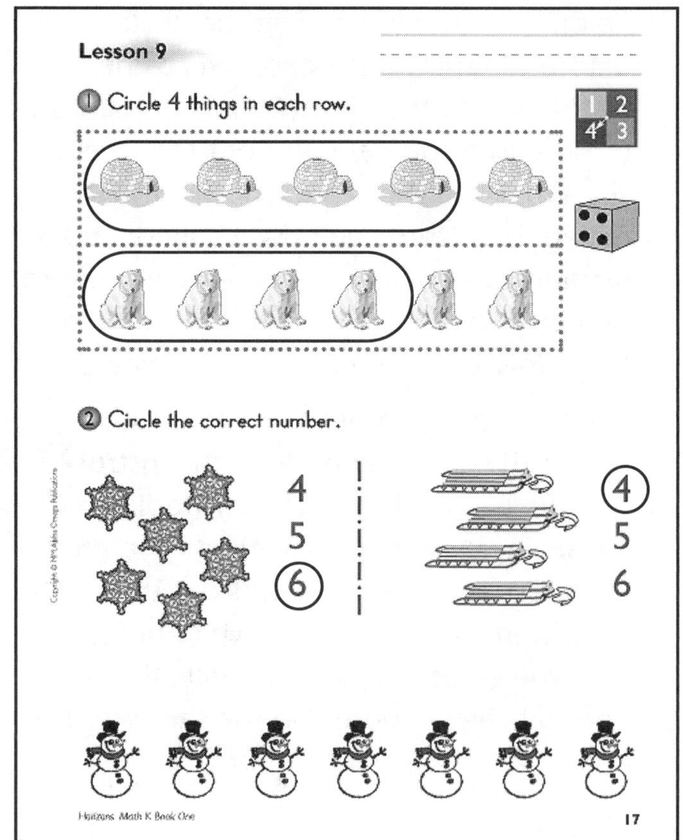

Activities:

① Point out the number 1 in the circle before the first instruction. Read the instruction. Talk about the game spinner and the die to review uses for the number 4. Point out the dotted lines that divide parts of the activity. Have them count the objects in both rows starting on the left and moving to the right. Have them circle the correct number of objects.

② Point out the number 2 in the circle before the second instruction. Read the instruction. Point out the dotted divider lines. These lines are used to separate the problems. Count the snowflakes. Point out the numbers. Demonstrate on the white board how the student(s) should circle the number that they choose. Do the same for the sleds.

③ Point out the number 3 in the circle before the third instruction. Read the instruction to the class. Do this activity as a class and then as individuals.

④ Point out the number 4 in the circle before the instruction. Demonstrate writing the number (4) on the white board. Have them trace the first (4) with their pencil. Then have them trace the next three dotted 4's. Discuss the spacing between the numbers. Instruct them to write (4) four more times. Point out the objects on the bottom of the page. Ask the class for other examples of where they can find the number 4.

NOTE: We have chosen to use a closed 4 because most of the 4's the student(s) will see are closed. The numbers and letters that the students write are in the same form as those they see in the activities.

Lesson 10 - Tally Marks

Overview:

- Tally marks
- Trace 1–4
- Identify *top, bottom* & *middle*
- Circle the correct number 1–6

Materials and Supplies:

- Teacher's Guide & Student Workbook
- White board
- Objects for counters
- Number flash cards
- Tally mark flash cards

Teaching Tips:

Review 4 with counters or other objects.

Demonstrate writing the number 4.

Teach tally marks by writing them on the white board and counting the marks with the student(s).

Review position words: *right, left, top, bottom, middle, first* & *last.*

Review counting orally to 20.

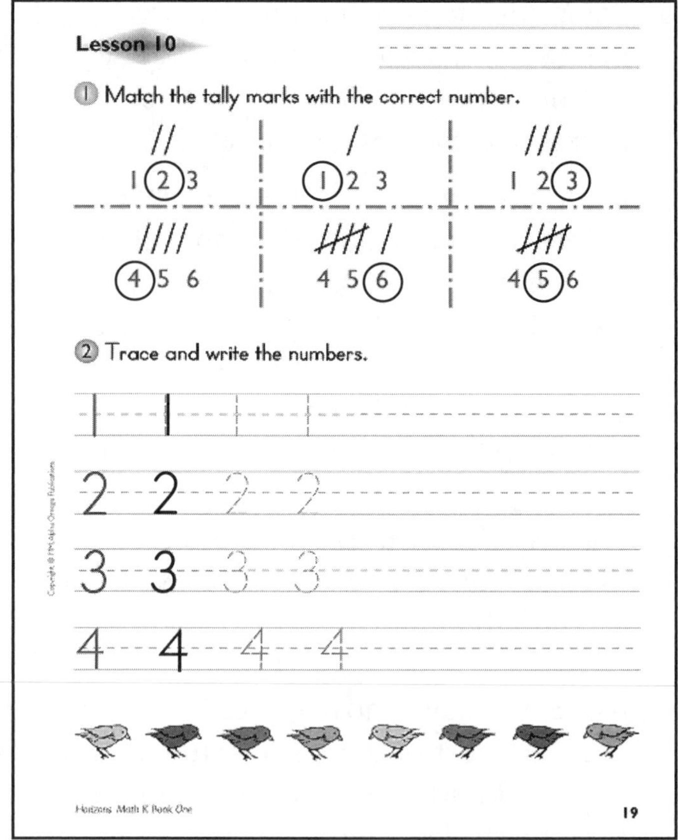

Lesson 10

① Match the tally marks with the correct number.

// 1 ②3 | / ①2 3 | /// 1 2③

//// ④5 6 | 𝍸 / 4 5⑥ | 𝍸 4⑤6

② Trace and write the numbers.

1 1 1 1

2 2 2 2

3 3 3 3

4 4 4 4

Horizons Math K Book One 19

Activities:

① Point out the number 1 in the circle before the first instruction. Read the instruction. Point out the dotted divider lines. These lines are used to separate the problems. Have the student(s) circle the number that they choose.

② Point out the number 2 in the circle before the second instruction. Read the instruction. Trace each red number. Write over each dotted number. Write four more of the same number on the line.

③ Point out the number 3 in the circle before the third instruction. Read the first instruction to the class. Have them mark their answer. Read the second instruction and have them mark their answer.

④ Point out the number 4 in the circle before the instruction. Read the instruction. Point out the dotted divider lines. These lines are used to separate the problems. Count the birds in the first group. Point out the numbers. Point out that these are not counting numbers. If they see two birds they cannot just circle the second number. They will need to know what symbol represents 2 birds, etc. Demonstrate on the white board how the student(s) should circle the number that they choose. Do the same for the other groups.

Lesson 10

③ Circle the bird on top of the fence. Put an X on the bird in the middle.

④ Circle the correct number.

(2) 4 6 | 1 (3) 5

2 4 (6) | (1) 3 5

20 Horizons Math K Book One

Lesson 11 - Number 5

Overview:

- Teach 5
- Match tally marks to the number
- Identify *right, left, first* & *last*
- Trace 5

Materials and Supplies:

- Teacher's Guide & Student Workbook
- White board
- Objects for counters
- Number flash cards
- Pennies and nickels
- Dominos
- Clock
- Worksheet 6

Teaching Tips:

Teach 5 with counters or other objects.
Teach 5 with pennies and a nickel.
Teach counting to 15 using flash cards and counters.
Demonstrate writing the number 5.
Review tally marks.
Review position words.
Teach counting orally to 30.

Activities:

① Read the instruction. Talk about the nickel, the clock and the five points on the star to review uses for the number 5. Point out the dotted lines that divide parts of the activity. Have them count the objects in both rows, starting on the left and moving to the right. Have them circle the correct number of objects.

Lesson 11

1 Circle 5 things in each row.

5¢

2 Match the tally marks to the number

///	///	////
(3) 1 2	2 (3) 4	5 6 (4)
////	///	~~////~~
(4) 6 2	1 2 (3)	3 4 (5)

Horizons Math K Book One 21

② Read the instruction. Point out the dotted divider lines. These lines are used to separate the problems. Have the student(s) circle the number that they choose for each set of tally marks.

③ Read the complete instruction in this activity to the class. Read the first part of the instruction to the class. Have them mark their answer. Read the second part of the instruction and have them mark their answer. Read the third part of the instruction and have them mark their answer. Read the fourth part of the instruction and have them mark their answer.

④ Read the instruction to the class. Demonstrate writing the number (5) on the white board. Have them trace the first (5) with their pencil. Then have them trace the next three dotted 5's. Discuss the spacing between the numbers. Instruct them to write (5) four more times. Have them trace the 5 in the second row and have them complete a row of 5's. In the third row have them trace 1–5 and then write 1–5 again. Point out the objects on the bottom of the page. Ask the class for other examples of where they can find the number 5.

Lesson 12 - Red & Star

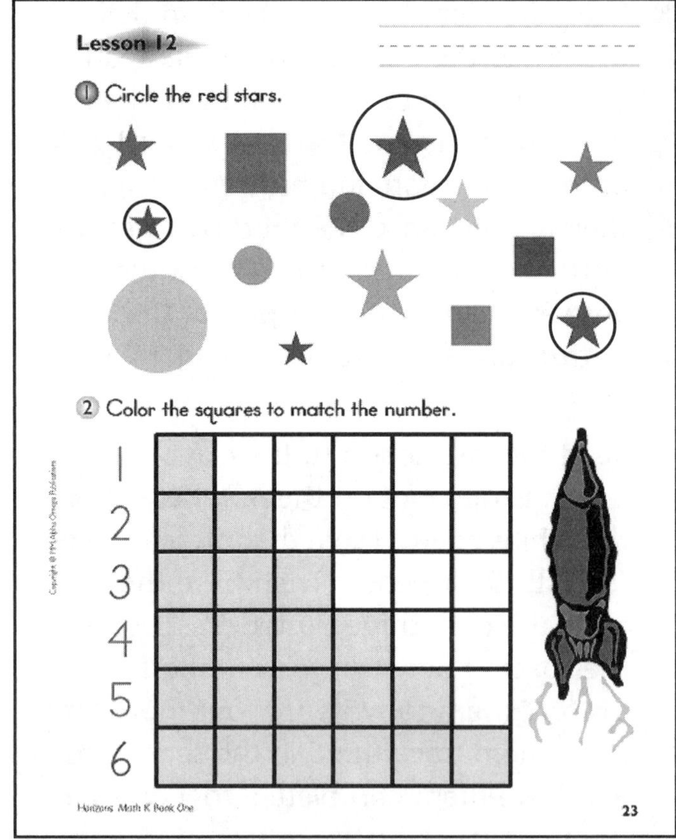

Overview:

- Identify red color & star shape
- Read a bar graph, identify colors & square
- Choose *right, left, first* & *last*
- Trace 1–5

Material and Supplies:

- Teacher's Guide & Student Workbook
- White board
- Objects for counters
- Number flash cards
- Shape flash cards
- Crayons
- Color flash cards
- Pennies & nickels

Teaching Tips:

Teach the color red.
Teach the shape of a star.
Teach a horizontal bar graph.
Review circle, triangle and square.
Use flash cards to review 1–10.
Review 5 with counters or other objects.
Review 5 with pennies and a nickel.
Review position words.
Review counting orally to 30.

Activities:

① Read the instruction. Have the student(s) circle the stars with a red crayon.

② Read the instruction. Point out that one square has been colored in the first row to represent the number 1. The number 1 is green and 1 square has been colored green. Under the 1 is a blue 2. Have the student(s) count 2 squares and color them blue. Check to see if the student(s) are doing this correctly. Point out the red 3, the green 4, the blue 5 and the red 6. Have them complete the bar graph.

③ Read the entire instruction to the class. Read the first part of the instruction to the class. Have them mark their answer. Read the second part of the instruction and have them mark their answer. Read the third part of the instruction and have them mark their answer. Read the fourth part of the instruction and have them mark their answer.

④ Read the instruction to the class. Review writing the number (5) on the white board. Have them trace 1–5 and then write 1–5 again on the first and second lines. Have them write 1–5 two times on each of the bottom lines.

Lesson 12

3 Put an X on the left star. Circle the planet on the right.

Put an X on the last rocket. Circle the first rocket.

4 Trace and write 1-5.

1 2 3 4 5

1 2 3 4 5

24 Horizons Math K Book One

Lesson 13 - Number 6

Overview:

- Teach 6
- Count objects 1–15
- Determine *top*, *bottom*, circle, square, star, yellow & blue
- Trace & write 1–6

Materials and Supplies:

- Teacher's Guide & Student Workbook
- White board
- Objects for counters
- Number flash cards
- Shape flash cards
- Crayons
- Color flash cards
- Dominos & domino flash cards
- Worksheet 7

Teaching Tips:

Teach 6.
Teach writing 6.
Review colors.
Review shapes.
Review position words.
Review counting orally to 30.

Activities:

① Read the instruction. Talk about the hexagon, the clock and the domino. Point out the dotted lines that divide parts of the activity. Have them count the objects in both rows, starting on the left and moving to the right. Have them circle the correct number of objects.

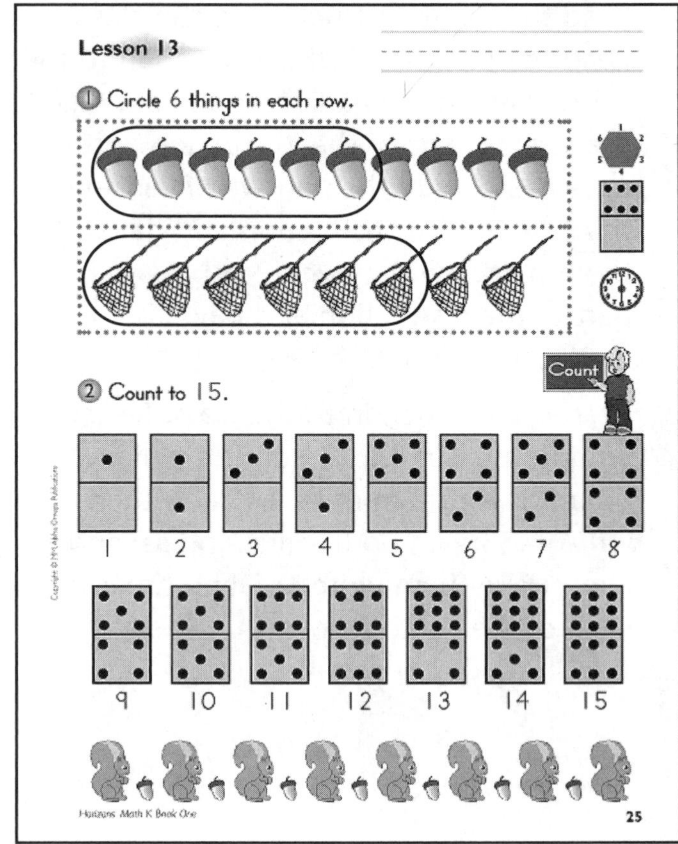
Lesson 13

① Circle 6 things in each row.

② Count to 15.

② Read the instruction. Count the dots in each domino. Help them to count left to right and top to bottom to develop patterns for counting.

③ Read the instruction to the class. Talk about the dotted lines. Review *top, bottom* and *middle*. Read the first instruction to the class. Keep them focused on the first box. Have them mark their answer. Read the second instruction and have them mark their answer also in the first box. Repeat the instructions for each box, having them work on one box at a time.

④ Read the instruction to the class. Review writing the number (6) on the white board. Have them trace the first (6) with their pencil. Then have them trace the next three dotted 6's. Discuss the spacing between the numbers. Have them write three more 6's on the line. Have them trace 1–6 on the next two lines. Have them write 1–6 on the bottom line.

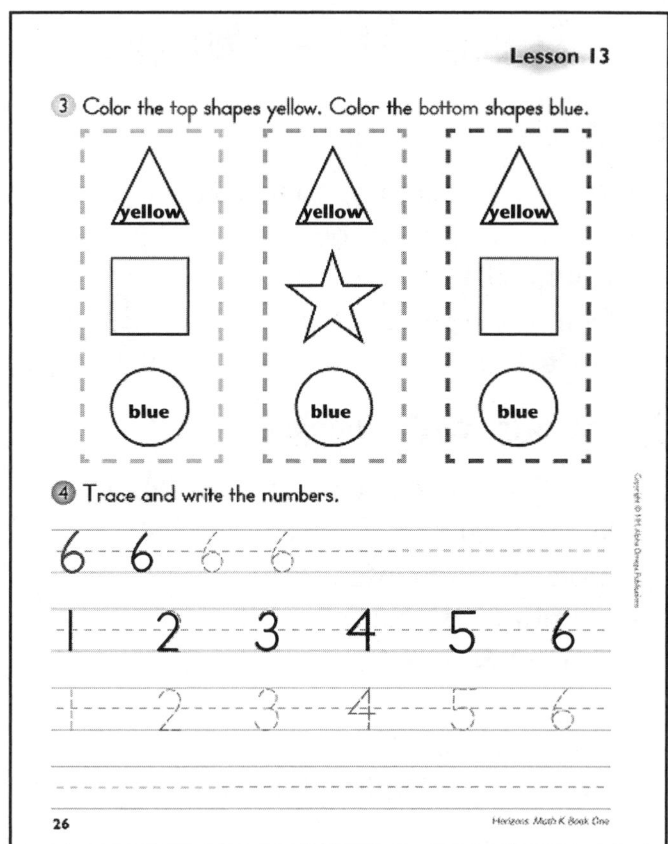
Lesson 13

③ Color the top shapes yellow. Color the bottom shapes blue.

④ Trace and write the numbers.

26 Horizons Math K Book One

Lesson 14 - Pennies

Overview:

- Recognize pennies, *front* & *back*
- Circle correct number 1–6
- Count to 15
- Determine *same,* circle & triangle
- Trace 1–6

Materials and Supplies:

- Teacher's Guide & Student Workbook
- White board
- Objects for counters
- Number flash cards
- Pennies & nickels
- Crayons
- Color flash cards
- Dominos & domino flash cards

Teaching Tips:

Teach pennies.
Teach *front* and *back.*
Teach ways of writing one cent.
Review colors.
Review shapes.
Review position words.
Review counting orally to 30.

Activities:

① Read the instruction. Point out the dotted lines that divide parts of the activity. Have them count the pennies in the first box. Have them circle the correct number for the pennies that they counted. Count the pennies in the second box and have them circle the number they choose.

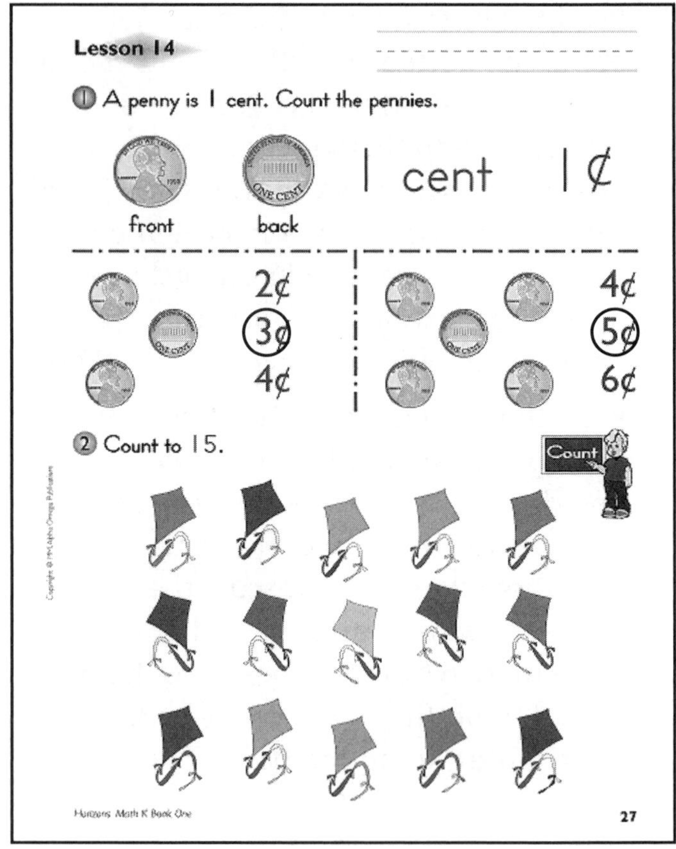

Lesson 14

① A penny is 1 cent. Count the pennies.

front back 1 cent 1¢

2¢ (3¢) 4¢

4¢ (5¢) 6¢

② Count to 15.

Count

Horizons Math K Book One 27

② Read the instruction. Count the kites. Help them to count left to right and top to bottom to develop patterns for counting.

③ Read the instruction to the class. Point out the dotted lines that divide parts of the activity. Talk about things that are in circle shapes. Have them mark their answers. Talk about things that are triangle shapes. Have them mark their answers.

④ Read the instruction to the class. Review writing the number (6) on the white board. Have them trace the first (6) with their pencil. Then have them trace the next three dotted 6's. Discuss the spacing between the numbers. Have them write three more 6's on the line. Have them trace 1–6 on the next two lines. Have them write 1–6 on the bottom two lines.

Lesson 14

③ Circle the objects that are the same shape as the first one.

④ Trace and write the numbers.

6 6 6 6

1 2 3 4 5 6

1 2 3 4 5 6

28

Horizons Math K Book One

Lesson 15 - Number 7

Overview:

- Teach 7
- Count pennies
- Count to 15
- Match tally marks to number
- Trace & write 1–7

Materials and Supplies:

- Teacher's Guide & Student Workbook
- White board
- Objects for counters
- Number flash cards
- Pennies & nickels
- Color flash cards
- Crayons
- Worksheet 8

Teaching Tips:

Teach 7.
Teach writing 7.
Review pennies.
Review *front* and *back*.
Review tally marks.
Review position words.
Review counting orally to 30.

Activities:

① Read the instruction. Talk about the clock, the digital clock and the calculator. Point out the dotted lines that divide parts of the activity. Have them count the lamps in the first box. Have them circle the 7 lamps. Count the leaves in the second box and have them circle the number they choose.

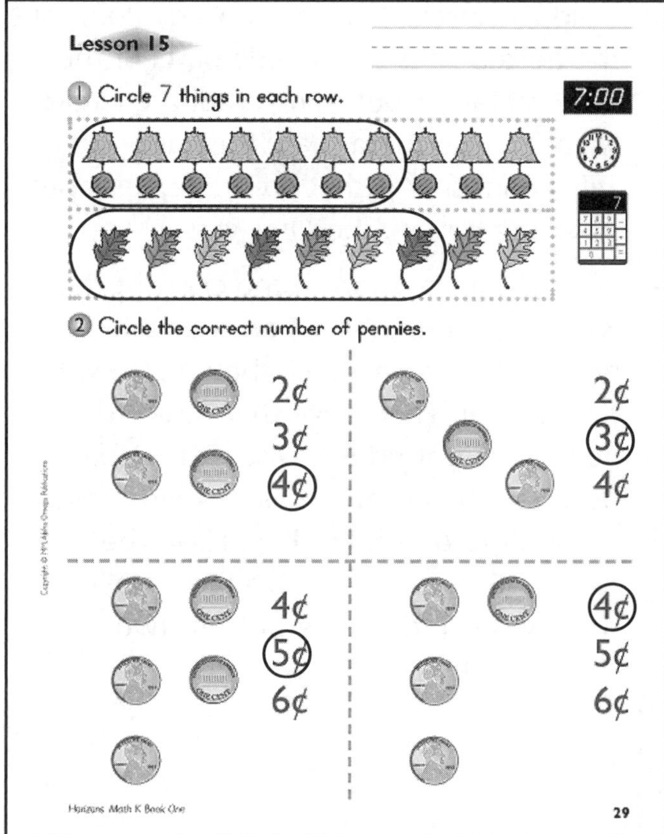

② Read the instruction. Have them count the pennies in the first box. Have them circle the correct number for the pennies that they counted. Count the pennies in the other boxes and have them circle the numbers that they choose.

③ Read the instruction to the class. Count the animals. Help them to count left to right and top to bottom to develop patterns for counting.

④ Read the instruction. Have the student(s) circle the number that they choose for each set of tally marks.

⑤ Read the instruction to the class. Review writing the number (7) on the white board. Have them trace the first (7) with their pencil. Then have them trace the next three dotted 7's. Discuss the spacing between the numbers. Have them write three more 7's on the line. Have them trace 1–7 on the next two lines. Have them write 1–7 on the bottom line.

Lesson 16 - Orange & Rectangle

Overview:

- Identify orange color & rectangle shape
- Determine *left, right* & *middle*
- Count pennies
- Trace and write 5–7

Materials and Supplies:

- Teacher's Guide & Student Workbook
- White board
- Objects for counters
- Number flash cards
- Shape flash cards
- Pennies & nickels
- Color flash cards
- Crayons

Teaching Tips:

Teach orange color.
Teach rectangles.
Review pennies.
Review position words.
Teach counting orally to 40.

Activities:

① Read the instruction. Talk about the shapes. Ask them how rectangles are similar to the other shapes. Ask them how rectangles are different. Point out that rectangles have corners like a square but that the sides are different lengths. Have them color the shapes they have chosen.

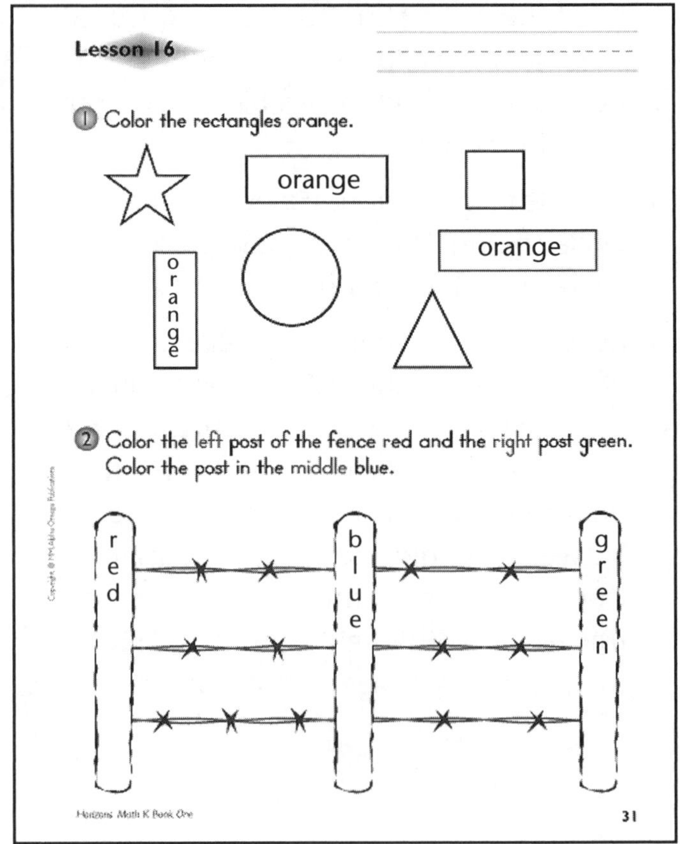

② Read the complete first instruction. Go back and read the first part of the first instruction and have the student(s) do that part of the activity. Then read the second part of the first instruction and have the students do that part of the activity. Read the final instruction and have the student(s) complete the activity.

③ Read the instruction to the class. Have them count the pennies in the first box. Have them circle the correct number for the pennies that they counted. Count the pennies in the other boxes and have them circle the numbers that they choose. Point out to the student(s) that not all of the numbers are in order.

④ Read the instruction. Review writing the numbers 5–7 on the white board. Have them trace the dotted 5–7's on the first line. Discuss the spacing between the numbers. Point out the pattern on the next three lines. Have them trace and write the remaining numbers in the pattern that is shown.

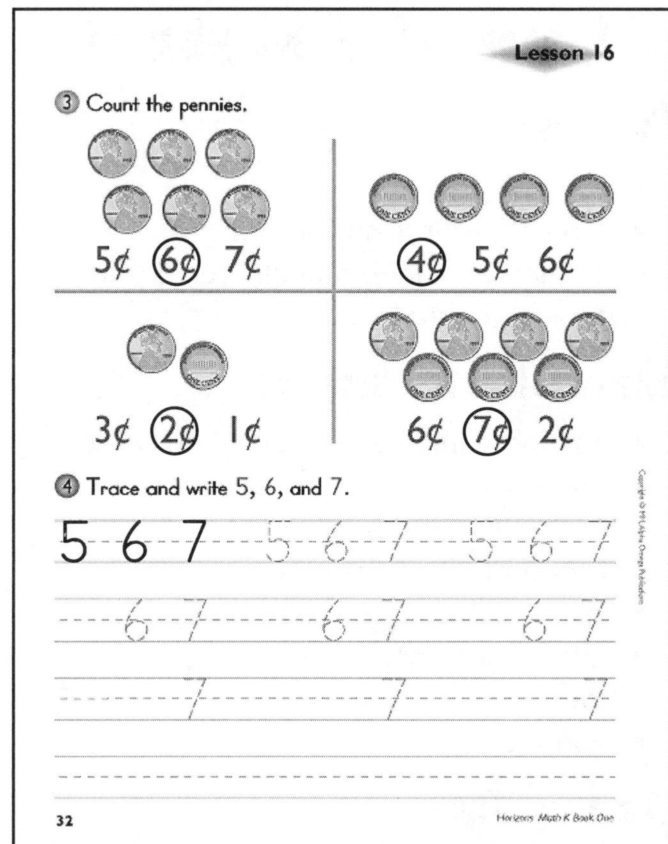

Lesson 17 - Number 8

Overview:

- Teach 8
- Choose larger & smaller
- Identify rectangle, triangle, red & blue
- Trace and write 1–8

Materials and Supplies:

- Teacher's Guide & Student Workbook
- White board
- Objects for counters
- Number flash cards
- Shape flash cards
- Color flash cards
- Crayons
- Worksheet 9

Teaching Tips:

Teach 8.
Teach writing 8.
Teach larger and smaller number.
Review position words.
Review shapes.
Review colors.
Review counting orally to 40.

Activities:

① Read the instruction. Talk about the clock and the octagon. Point out the dotted lines that divide parts of the activity. Have them count the red winged black birds in the first box. Have them circle 8 birds. Count the chickens in the second box and have them circle 8 chickens.

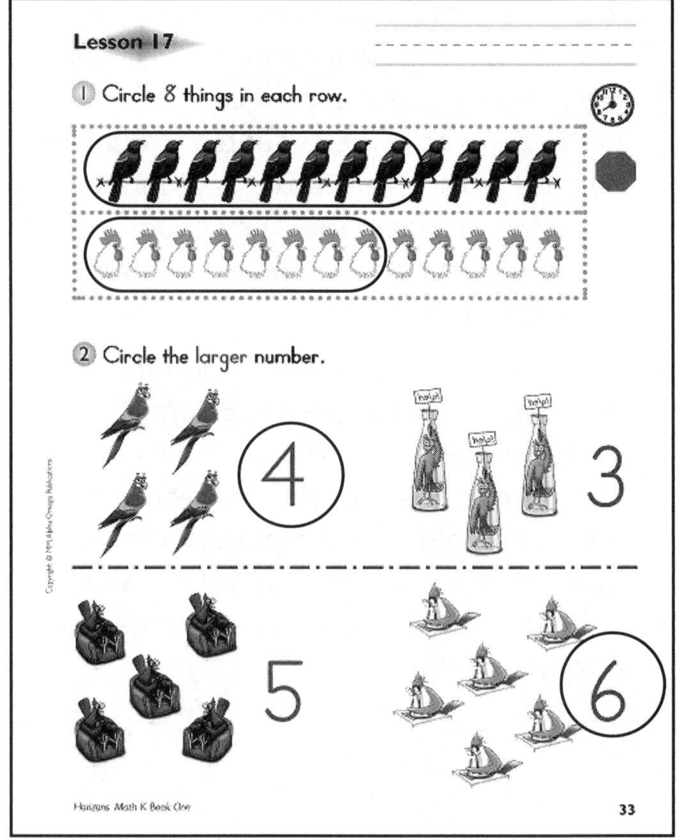

② Read the instruction. Point out the dotted line that divide parts of the activity. Present several examples on the white board to practice choosing the largest number. Have them count the birds and the bottles in the first box. Have them circle the correct number for the largest number. Count the groups in the other box and have them circle the largest number that they choose.

③ Read the instruction to the class. Have them color the house as they are instructed.

④ Read the instruction to the class. Review writing the number (8) on the white board. Have them trace the first (8) with their pencil. Then have them trace the dotted 8's. Discuss the spacing between the numbers. Have them write three more 8's on the second line. Have them trace 1–8 on the next line. Have them write 1–8 on the bottom line.

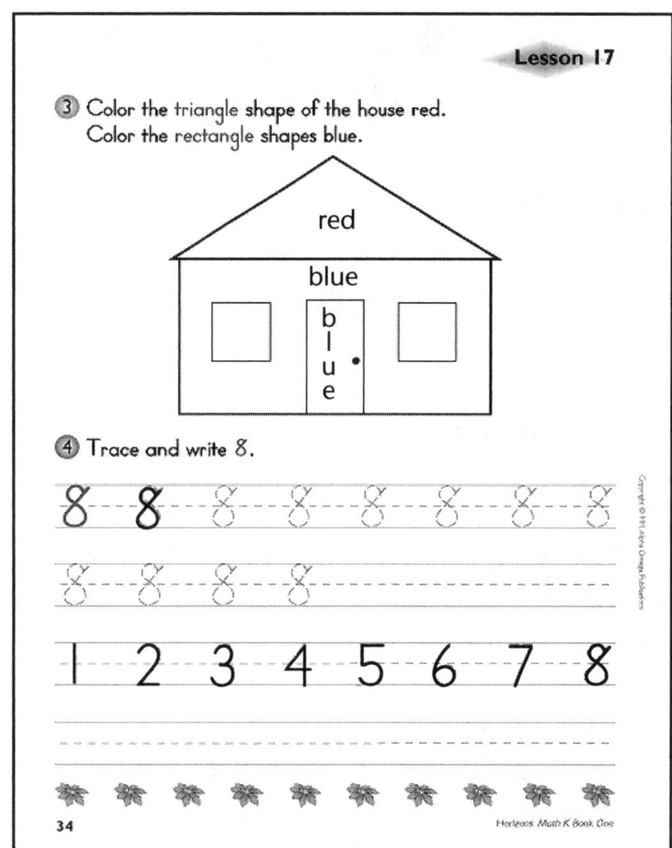

Lesson 18 - Days of the Week

Overview:

- Days of the week
- Ordinals first–seventh
- Complete patterns & sequence
- Count to 15
- Trace and write 6–8

Materials and Supplies:

- Teacher's Guide & Student Workbook
- White board
- Objects for counters
- Number flash cards
- Shape flash cards
- Calendar
- Ordinal number flash cards
- Worksheet 38

Teaching Tips:

Teach days of the week.
Teach ordinal numbers.
Teach larger and smaller number.
Teach sequence and patterns.
Review shapes.
Review counting orally to 40.

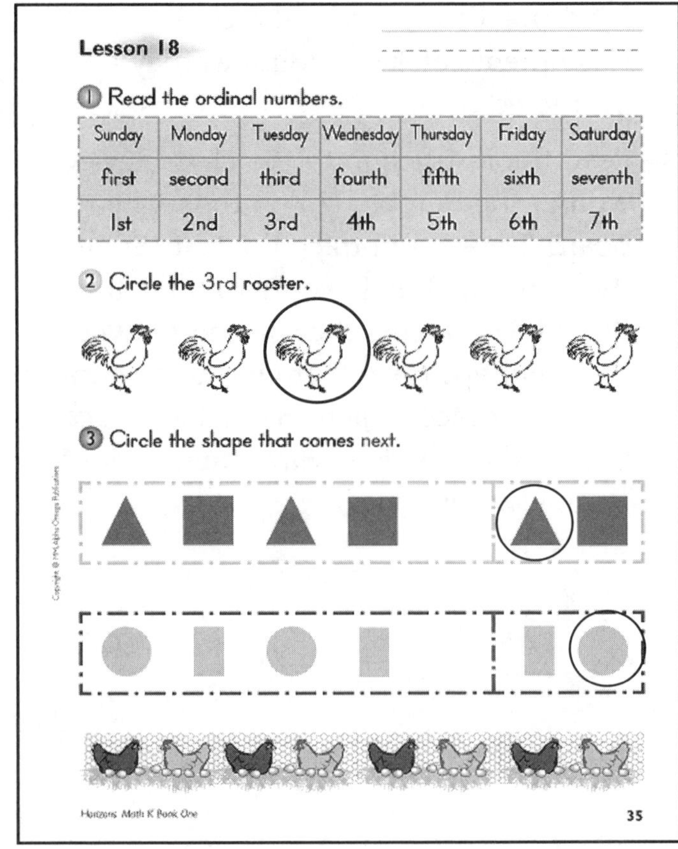

Activities:

① Read the instruction. Point out the dotted lines that divide parts of the activity. Make flash cards for the ordinal numbers. Flash a card to the class and have them say what number it is for. Read the days of the week to the class. Read the first row of ordinal numbers. Associate Sunday as the first day of the week, Monday as the second, etc. Read the second row of ordinal numbers. Tell them that this is another way to write ordinal numbers. Again associate 1st with Sunday, etc. Count the first row again counting and saying, "1, Sunday is the first day of the week; 2, Monday is the second day of the week; 3, Tuesday is the third day of the week," etc.

② Read the instruction. Have them count the chickens. Refer back to Activity ①. Count over from Sunday 1, 2, 3. Remind student(s) that Tuesday is the 3rd day of the week. Count the chickens again and have the student(s) circle their answer.

③ Read the instruction to the class. Use shape flash cards to go through a pattern of four shapes and ask what comes next in the pattern. Point out the dotted lines that divide parts of the activity. Go through the shapes in the first box and have the student(s) circle their answer. Do the same thing for the second set of shapes.

④ Read the instruction. Count the chicks and the chickens. Help them to count left to right and top to bottom to develop patterns for counting.

⑤ Read the instruction to the class. Review writing the number (8) on the white board. Have them trace the dotted 6, 7, 8 in the first row. Discuss the spacing between the numbers. Have them write a 6 on the second line. Have them trace and write 6, 7, 8 as given on the first line for the rest of the activity.

Lesson 19 - Number 9

Overview:

- Teach 9
- Tell time 1:00 o'clock
- Days of the week
- Ordinal numbers
- Count pennies
- Trace & write 1–9

Materials and Supplies:

- Teacher's Guide & Student Workbook
- White board
- Objects for counters
- Number flash cards
- Dominos
- Clock with moveable hands
- Digital clock flash cards for hours
- Days of the week flash cards
- Ordinal number flash cards
- Worksheet 10 & 39

Teaching Tips:

Teach 9.
Teach writing 9.
Teach 1 o'clock.
Review the days for the week.
Review ordinal numbers.
Review counting orally to 40.

Activities:

① Read the instruction. Talk about the clock and count the dots on the domino. Point out the dotted lines that divide parts of the activity. Have them count the moon crescents in the first box. Have them circle 9 of them. Count the suns in the second box and have them circle 9 suns.

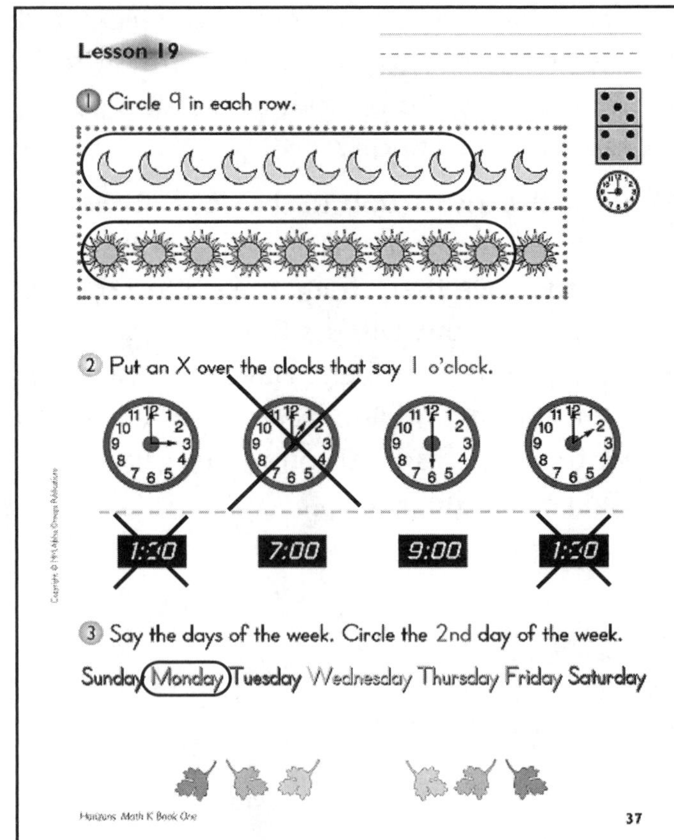

Lesson 19

1 Circle 9 in each row.

2 Put an X over the clocks that say 1 o'clock.

1:00 7:00 9:00 1:00

3 Say the days of the week. Circle the 2nd day of the week.

Sunday Monday Tuesday Wednesday Thursday Friday Saturday

Horizons Math K Book One 37

② Read the instruction. Point out the dotted line that divides the parts of the activity. Talk about the hands of a clock. The short or hour hand is the one to focus on. The long or minute hand will be taught later. Talk about digital clocks. Focus on the numbers before the dots. have the student(s) put on X over their answers.

③ Read the instruction to the class. Say the days of the week. Have them circle the 2nd day of the week.

④ Read the instruction to the class. Have them count the pennies in the first group. Have them write their number on the line next to the group of coins. Count the pennies in the other groups and have them write the numbers that they choose.

⑤ Read the instruction to the class. Review writing the number (9) on the white board. Have them trace the first (9) with their pencil. Then have them trace the dotted 9's. Discuss the spacing between the numbers. Have them write three more 9's on the second line. Have them trace 1–9 on the next line. Have them write 1–9 on the bottom line.

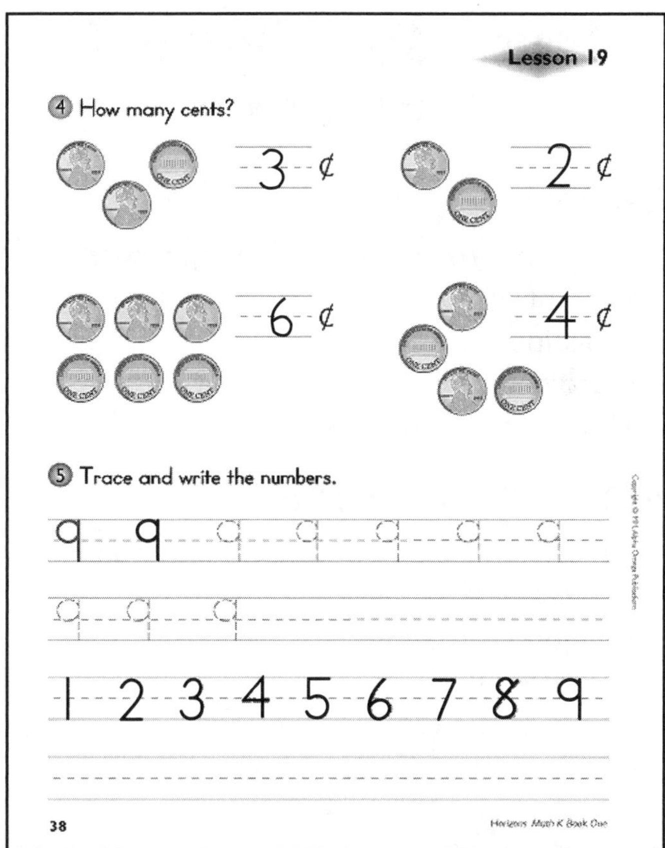

Lesson 20 - Brown & Hexagon

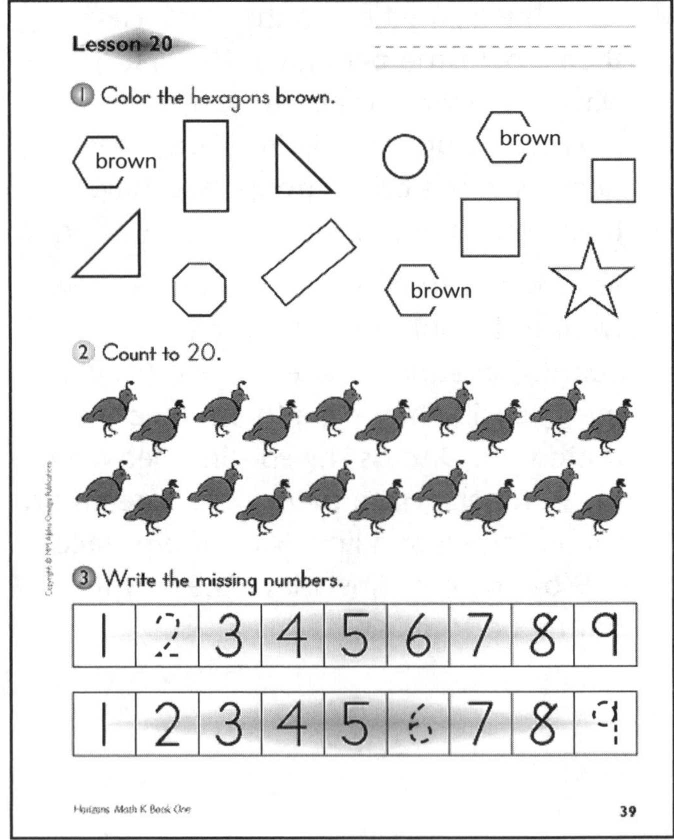
Lesson 20

1 Color the hexagons brown.

brown

brown

brown

2 Count to 20.

3 Write the missing numbers.

1	2	3	4	5	6	7	8	9
1	2	3	4	5	6	7	8	9

Horizons Math K Book One 39

Overview:

- Identify brown color & hexagon shape
- Count to 20
- Missing number 1–9
- Ordinal numbers & days of week
- Trace and write 7–9

Materials and Supplies:

- Teacher's Guide & Student Workbook
- White board
- Objects for counters
- Number flash cards
- Days of the week flash cards
- Ordinal number flash cards

Teaching Tips:

Teach hexagon.
Review shapes.
Review sequence and patterns.
Review the days for the week.
Review ordinal numbers.
Review counting orally to 40.

Activities:

① Read the instruction. Talk about the shapes. Ask them how hexagons are similar to the other shapes. Ask them how hexagons are different. Point out the six sides in a hexagon. Ask the student(s) where they might see a hexagon. Have them color the shapes they have chosen.

② Read the instruction. Count the quail. Help them to count left to right and top to bottom to develop patterns for counting.

③ Read the instruction to the class. Count to 9 together a few times. Have the student(s) write the missing numbers.

④ Read the instruction to the class. Say the days of the week. Have them circle the 5th day of the week.

⑤ Read the instruction to the class. Use shape flash cards to go through a pattern of alternating shapes and ask what comes next in the pattern. Point out the dotted lines that divide parts of the activity. Go through the items in the first box and have the student(s) circle their answer.

⑥ Read the instruction to the class. Review writing the numbers 7, 8 & 9 on the white board. Have them trace the dotted 7, 8, 9 in the first row. Discuss the spacing between the numbers. Have them write a 7 on the second line. Have them trace and write 7, 8, 9 as given on the first line for the rest of the activity.

Lesson 21 - Number 0

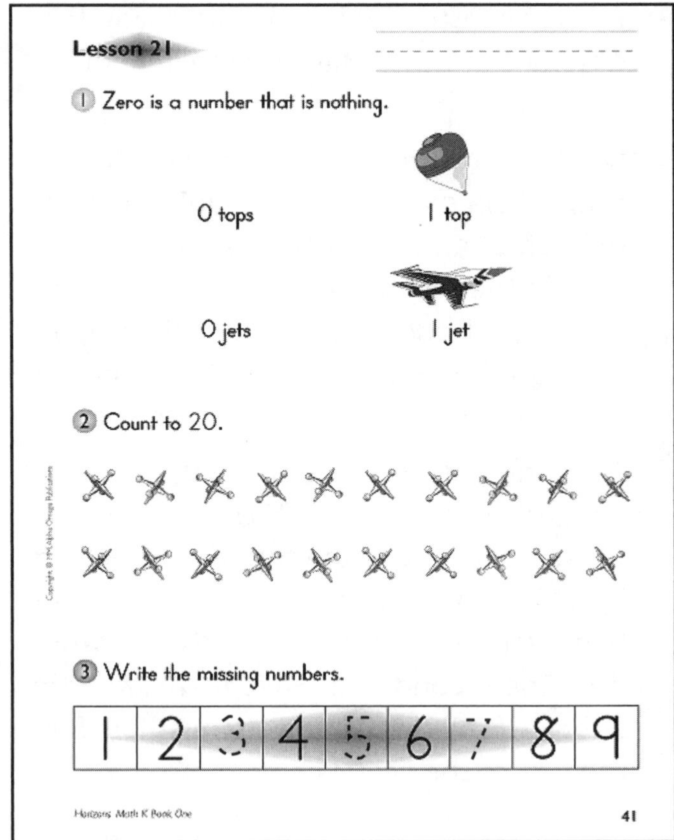

Lesson 21

① Zero is a number that is nothing.

0 tops 1 top

0 jets 1 jet

② Count to 20.

③ Write the missing numbers.

1	2	3	4	5	6	7	8	9

Horizons Math K Book One 41

Overview:

- Teach 0
- Count to 20
- Missing number 1–9
- Count pennies
- Trace and write 0–9

Materials and Supplies:

- Teacher's Guide & Student Workbook
- Objects for counters
- Number flash cards
- Pennies
- Days of the week flash cards
- Ordinal number flash cards
- Worksheet 11

Teaching Tips:

Teach 0.
Review counting pennies.
Review counting orally to 40.

Activities:

① Read the instruction. Talk about the number 0 and how it represents nothing. Demonstrate this by taking away objects in a set until there are 0 objects left. Look at the student activity. On the left there are 0 tops. On the right there is 1 top. There is 1 jet on the right but 0 jets on the left. A short discussion of place value could be had with this lesson that would show how 0 is a place holder. You can have a 0 in the ones' place but a 5 in the tens' place.

② Read the instruction. Count the jacks. Help them to count left to right and top to bottom to develop patterns for counting. Have them look at the zero in the number 20. Zero is used as a place holder. Where else have they seen the number zero?

③ Read the instruction to the class. Count to 9 together a few times. Have the student(s) write the missing numbers.

④ Read the instruction to the class. Have them count the pennies in the first group. Have them write their number on the line next to the group of coins. Count the pennies in the other groups and have them write the numbers that they choose.

⑤ Read the instruction to the class. Demonstrate writing the number (0) on the white board. Have them trace the first (0) with their pencil. Then have them trace the dotted 0's. Discuss the spacing between the numbers. Have them write four more 0's on the second line. Have them trace 0–9 on the next line. Have them write 0–9 on the bottom line. 0–9 is the ones' family, and when activities are done using numbers from the ones' family they will be the numbers 0–9.

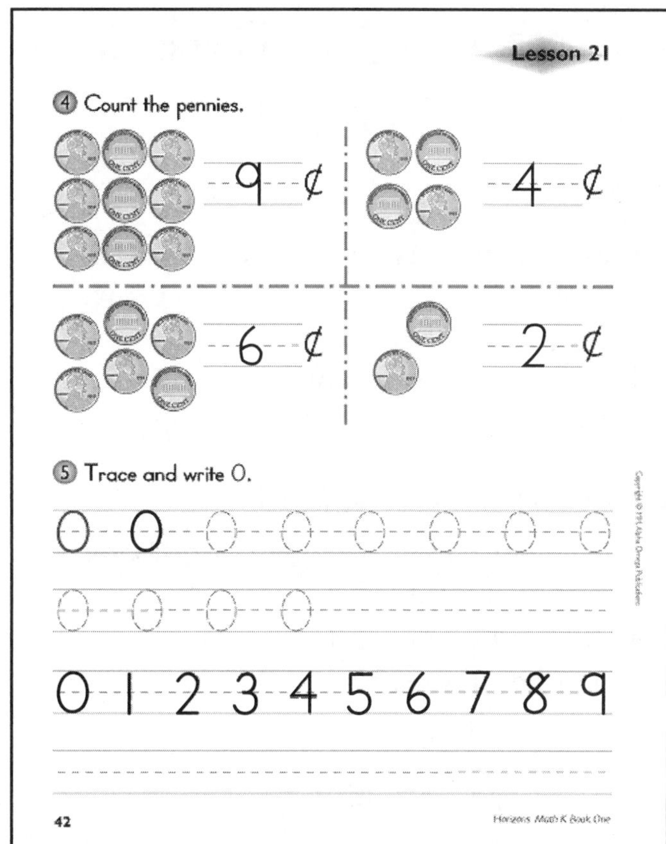
Lesson 21

④ Count the pennies.

9 ¢ 4 ¢

6 ¢ 2 ¢

⑤ Trace and write 0.

0 0 0 0 0 0 0 0

0 0 0 0

0 1 2 3 4 5 6 7 8 9

42 Horizons Math K Book One

Lesson 22 - Black & Octagon

Overview:

- Identify black color & octagon shape
- Ordinal numbers & days of the week
- Missing number 1–9
- Connect the dots 1–9
- Trace and write 0, 7–9

Materials and Supplies:

- Teacher's Guide & Student Workbook
- White board
- Objects for counters
- Number flash cards
- Shape flash cards
- Calendar
- Day of the week flash cards
- Crayons
- Color flash cards
- Ordinal number flash cards

Teaching Tips:

Teach black color.
Teach octagon shape.
Review days of the week.
Review ordinal numbers.
Review shapes.
Review counting orally to 40.

Activities:

① Read the instruction. Talk about the shapes. Ask them how octagons are similar to the other shapes. Ask them how octagons are different. How many sides does an octagon have? Where do we see the octagon shape? (stop sign) Have them color the shapes they have chosen. You can have them color the other shapes in colors other than black.

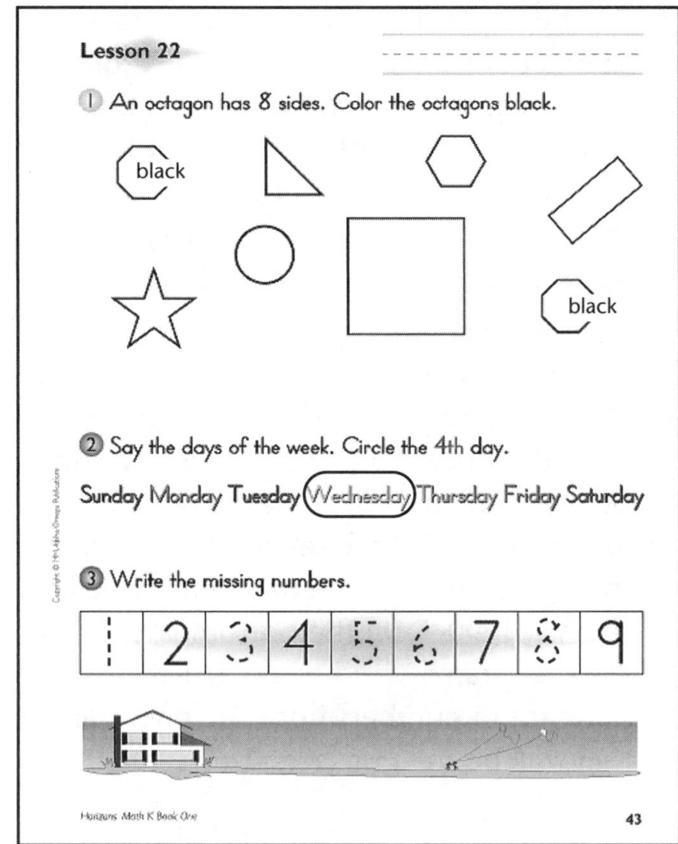
Lesson 22

① An octagon has 8 sides. Color the octagons black.

black

black

② Say the days of the week. Circle the 4th day.

Sunday Monday Tuesday (Wednesday) Thursday Friday Saturday

③ Write the missing numbers.

1	2	3	4	5	6	7	8	9

Horizons Math K Book One 43

② Read the first instruction. Say the days of the week together. Read the second instruction and let them circle their answer.

③ Read the instruction to the class. Count 1 to 9 together a few times. Have the student(s) write the missing numbers.

④ Read the instruction. Count 1 to 9 together a few times. Demonstrate how to connect the dots. Encourage them to draw straight and neat lines to connect the dots.

⑤ Read the instruction to the class. Review writing the number (0) on the white board. Have them trace the 0, 7, 8, 9 in each row. Discuss the spacing between the numbers. Have them write a complete row of each number.

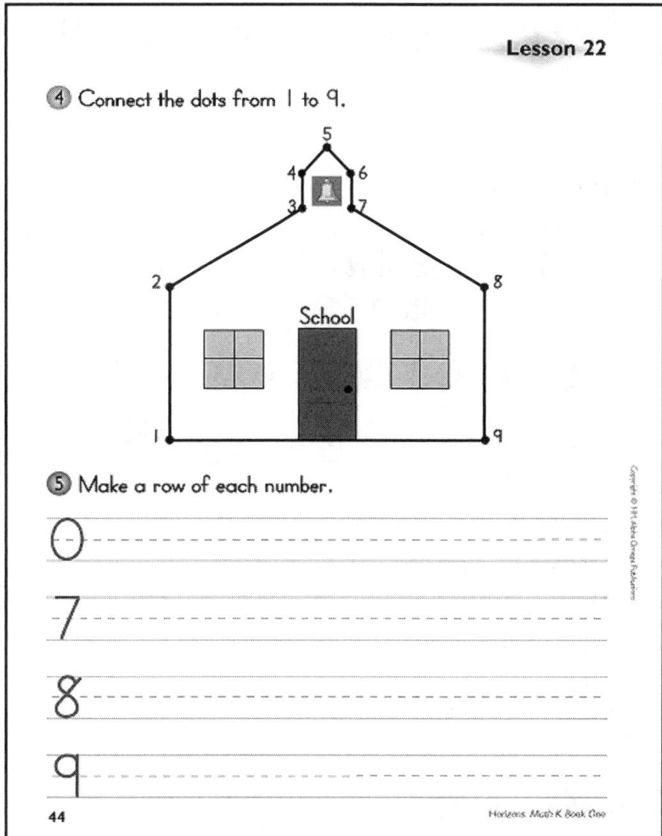

Lesson 23 - Number 10

Overview:

- Teach 10
- Time – hour
- Bar graph & colors
- Trace and write 10

Materials and Supplies:

- Teacher's Guide & Student Workbook
- White board
- Objects for counters
- Number flash cards
- Dominos
- Crayons
- Clock with moveable hands
- Worksheet 12 & 22

Teaching Tips:

Teach 10.
Teach writing 10.
Teach time – hour.
Review bar graph.
Teach counting orally to 50.

Activities:

① Read the instruction. Talk about the clocks and the dime. Point out the dotted lines that divide parts of the activity. Have them count the watches in the first box. Have them circle 10 of them. Count the watermelons in the second box and have them circle 10 watermelons.

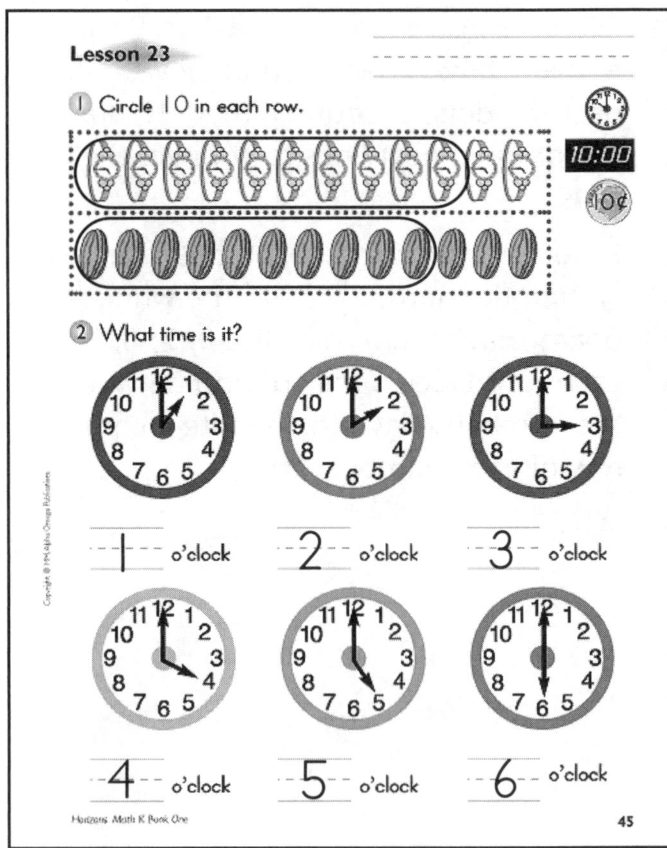

Lesson 23

① Circle 10 in each row.

10:00

10¢

② What time is it?

1 o'clock 2 o'clock 3 o'clock

4 o'clock 5 o'clock 6 o'clock

Horizons Math K Book One 45

② Read the instruction. Talk about the hands on a clock. The short or hour hand is the one to focus on. The long or minute hand will be taught later. Demonstrate by moving the hands on a clock all of the hours. Have them write the number for the hour on the blanks under each clock.

③ Read the instruction. Point out that one square is to be colored in the first row to represent the number 1. Have the student(s) count 2 squares in the second row and color them. Check to see if the student(s) are doing this correctly. Have them complete the bar graph.

⑤ Read the instruction to the class. Review writing the number (10) on the white board. Have them trace the first (10) with their pencil. Then have them trace the dotted 10's. Discuss the spacing between the numbers. Have them write three more 10's on the second line. Have them write 10's on the bottom line. Review place value and how 0 holds a place in the number 10.

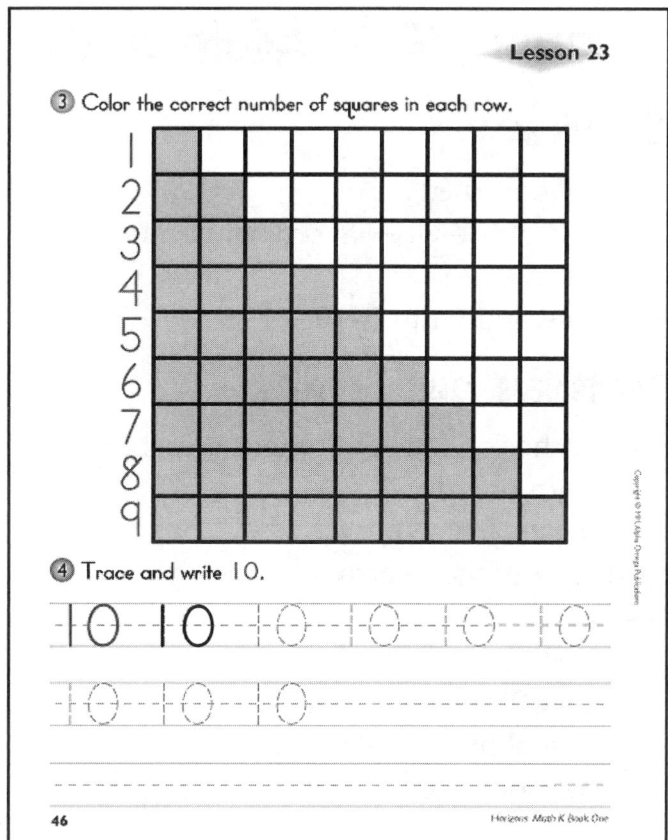
Lesson 23

③ Color the correct number of squares in each row.

1
2
3
4
5
6
7
8
9

④ Trace and write 10.

10 10 10 10 10 10

10 10 10

46 Horizons Math K Book One

Lesson 24 - Addition 1's

Overview:

- Addition 0 & 1
- Days of the week & ordinal numbers
- Count 0–9
- Trace and write 0–10

Materials and Supplies:

- Teacher's Guide & Student Workbook
- White board
- Objects for counters
- Number flash cards
- Dominos
- Calendar
- Day of the week flash cards
- Ordinal number flash cards
- Worksheet 40

Teaching Tips:

Teach addition 1's family.
Teach calendar.
Review days of the week.
Review ordinal numbers.
Review counting orally to 50.

Activities:

① Read the instruction. Talk about the dominos. The dots are to help the student(s) count the addition problems. Talk about the (+) sign and that it means addition. Talk about the (=) sign and that it means equals. Have them count the dots and trace the numbers below the dots. Say "1 plus 1 equals" and then count all of the dots on the domino and trace 2 for the answer. Do the rest of the problems in the same way.

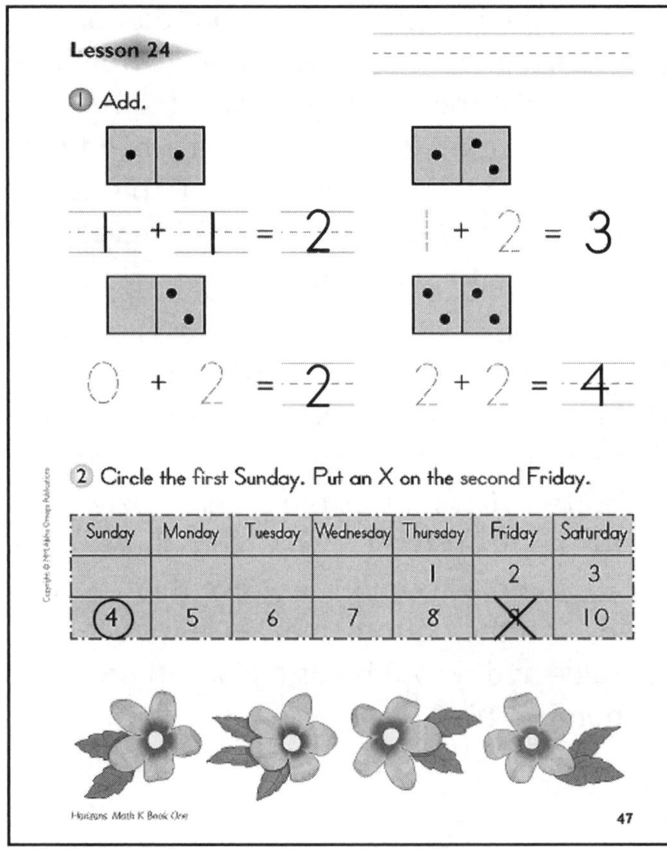

② Read the instruction. Review the days of the week. Talk about a calendar and how each month has several Sundays, Mondays, etc. Talk about weeks and that each week starts with Sunday. Have them locate Sunday and circle the first Sunday. Ask what day of the month the Sunday is on. Talk about Thursday, Friday and Saturday and how there are two days given on the calendar for those days. The first day of the month is on Thursday and the first is also the first Thursday in the month. The 8th is the second Thursday. Complete the activity.

③ Read the instruction to the class. Count 1 to 9 together a few times. Have the student(s) write the missing numbers.

④ Read the instruction to the class. Review writing the number (0) on the white board. Have them trace the 0–10 in the two rows. Discuss the spacing between the numbers. Have them write 0–5 in the 2nd row and 6–10 in the 4th row.

Lesson 24

③ Count the number in each row.

6

4

8

2

④ Trace and write the numbers.

0 1 2 3 4 5

6 7 8 9 10

48 Horizons Math K Book One

Lesson 25 - Missing Number 1's

Overview:

- Missing number 0–10
- Number line
- Addition 0–5
- Patterns, sequence
- Count to 20
- Calendar

Materials and Supplies:

- Teacher's Guide & Student Workbook
- White board
- Objects for counters
- Number flash cards
- Dominos
- Calendar
- Number line strips
- Day of the week flash cards
- Ordinal number flash cards

Teaching Tips:

Teach number line strips.
Review addition 1's family.
Review calendar.
Review days of the week.
Review counting orally to 50.

Activities:

① Read the instruction. Count 0 through 10 together a few times. Have the student(s) write the missing numbers. Talk about the number line and that each mark represents a number. Look at the numbers on a ruler and point out how the numbers on a ruler stand for inches. The numbers on a number line stand for objects that are being counted. Have the student(s) write the missing numbers under the number line.

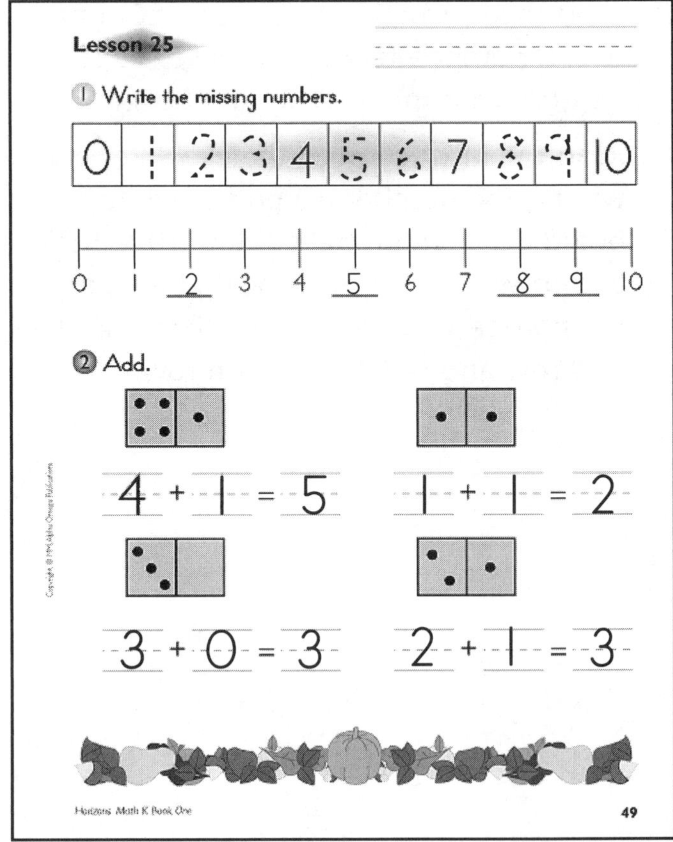

② Talk about the dominos. The dots are to help the student(s) count the addition problems. Talk about the (+) sign and that it means addition. Talk about the (=) sign and that it means equals. Have them count the dots and trace the numbers below the dots. Say "4 plus 1 equals" and then count all of the dots on the domino and write 5 for the answer. Point out that the number for the dots on the left side of the domino is written on the left side of the + sign. Do the rest of the problems in the same way.

③ Read the instruction to the class. Use shape flash cards to go through a pattern of alternating shapes and ask what comes next in the pattern. Point out the dotted lines that divide parts of the activity. Go through the items in the first box and have the student(s) circle their answer. Do the same for the second box.

④ Read the instruction. Review the days of the week. Talk about a calendar and how each month has several Sundays, Mondays, etc. Talk about weeks and that each week starts with Sunday. Use the dates to count to 20. Review ordinal numbers by asking the student(s) for the 3rd Sunday, the 2nd Saturday, etc.

Lesson 25

③ Circle what is next.

④ Count to 20.

October

Sunday	Monday	Tuesday	Wednesday	Thursday	Friday	Saturday
1	2	3	4	5	6	7
8	9	10	11	12	13	14
15	16	17	18	19	20	

50 Horizons Math K Book One

Lesson 26 - Count by 10's

Overview:

- Count by 10's
- Trace & write 10's
- Dimes
- Addition 0–3
- Match the shapes, line

Materials and Supplies:

- Teacher's Guide & Student Workbook
- White board
- Objects for counters
- Number flash cards
- Dominos
- Count by 10's flash cards
- Shape flash cards
- Dimes, pennies
- Worksheet 37

Teaching Tips:

Teach counting by 10's.
Teach dimes.
Review addition 1's family.
Review shapes.
Review counting orally to 50.

Activities:

① Read the instruction. Count 1 through 10 together a few times. Have the student(s) count to ten by counting the first row of numbers. Count 1–10 for each row and circle the 10th number. Say the numbers that have been circled: 10, 20, 30, 40 and 50. Make a set of flash cards to count by 10's, 10–100 for review in future lessons.

② Read the instruction. Have them trace the 10–50 in the first row. Discuss the spacing between the numbers. Have them write 10–50 in the 2nd row.

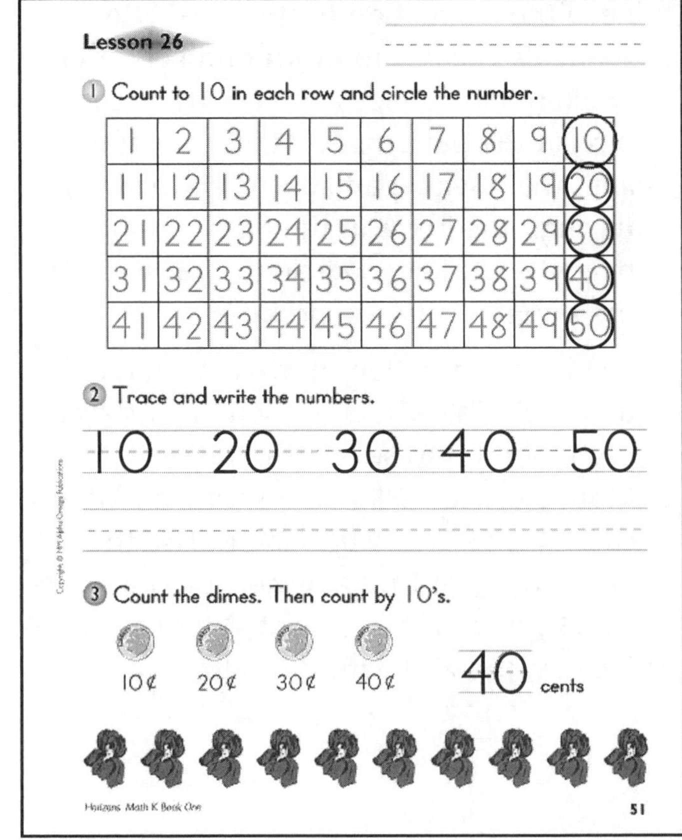

③ Read the instruction to the class. Talk about dimes and that each dime is worth 10 pennies. Demonstrate groups of 10 pennies and that 1 dime has the same value. Count orally by 10's to 50. Count the dimes by 10's and trace the 40.

④ Read the instruction. Talk about the flowers. The flowers are to help the student(s) count the addition problems like the dots did on the dominos. Talk about the (+) sign and that it means addition. Talk about the (=) sign and that it means equals or the total in an addition problem. Have them count the flowers and write the numbers below the dots. Say "3 plus 1 equals" and then count all of the flowers and write 4 for the answer. Do the rest of the problems in the same way.

⑤ Read the instruction to the class. Draw lines to match the shapes. Look for shapes that are the same. A difference in color does not matter.

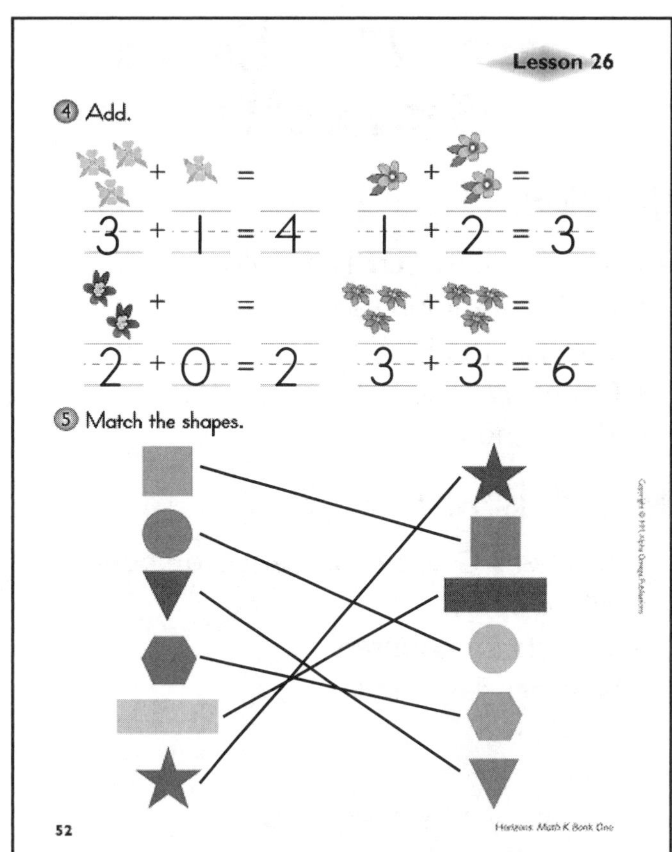

Lesson 27 - Number Between 1's

Overview:

- Number between 1's family
- Vertical addition 0–4
- Use tally marks
- Count by 10's
- Time – hour

Materials and Supplies:

- Teacher's Guide & Student Workbook
- White board
- Objects for counters
- Number flash cards
- Dominos
- Clock
- Count by 10's flash cards
- Ten dollar bills
- Number line strips
- Ordinal number flash cards

Teaching Tips:

Teach number between.
Teach vertical addition.
Review addition 1's family.
Review tally marks.
Review counting by 10's to 50.
Review time – hour.
Review counting orally to 50.

Activities:

① Read the instruction. Use number line strips to demonstrate the number between. Also point out that number between is counting by 1's. Have the student(s) write their answers.

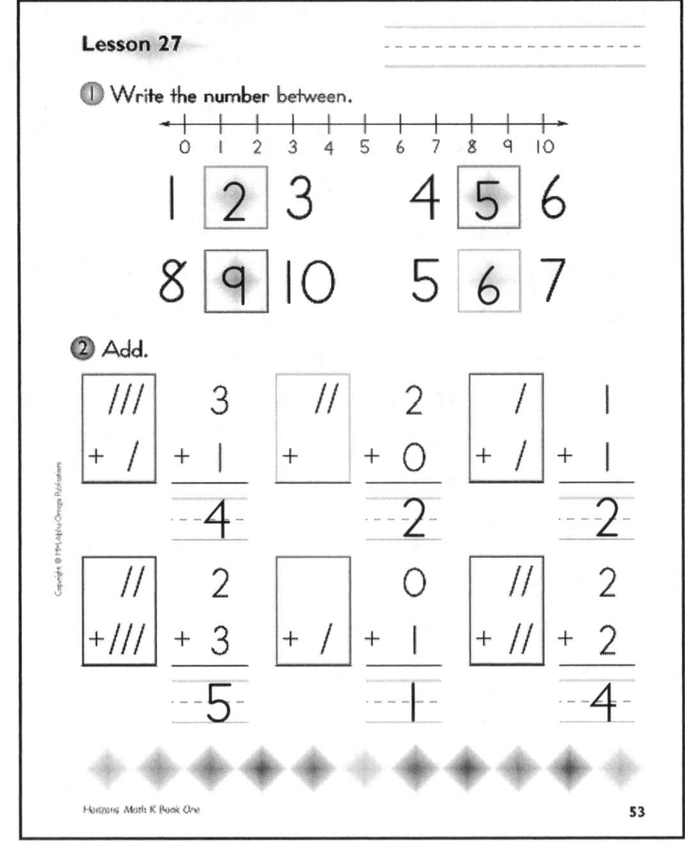

② Read the instruction. Talk about the tally marks. The marks are to help the student(s) count the addition problems. Talk about the (+) sign and that it means addition. Point out that one set of marks is on top and one set is on the bottom. This is vertical addition. Have them count the top tallys in the first problem and trace over the number 3. Count the bottom tally and trace over the 1. Say "3 plus 1 equals" and then count all of the tallys and write 4 for the answer. Point out that the line in a vertical problem is the same as the = sign in a horizontal problem. It means "equals." Do the rest of the problems in the same way.

③ Read the instruction to the class. Orally count by 10's to 50. Talk about tens and that each group of dots has 10 dots. Count by 10's to 40. Have the student(s) write 10, 20, 30, 40 in the blanks. Show that a 10 dollar bill is the same as ten $1 bills. Count the $10 bills by tens.

④ Read the instruction to the class. Talk about the hands on a clock. The short or hour hand is the one to focus on. The long or minute hand will be taught later. Demonstrate by moving the hands on a clock all of the hours. Have them write the number for the hour on the blanks under each clock.

Lesson 28 – Purple & Diamond

Overview:

- Identify purple color & diamond shape
- Write 11–20
- Number between 1's family
- Vertical addition 0–4
- Time – hour

Materials and Supplies:

- Teacher's Guide & Student Workbook
- White board
- Objects for counters
- Number flash cards
- Dominos
- Number line strips
- Color flash cards
- Crayons
- Shape flash cards
- Digital clock
- Worksheet 13 & 23

Teaching Tips:

Teach diamond shape.
Teach color purple.
Teach writing 11–20.
Teach time – hour on digital clock.
Review number between.
Review addition 1's family.
Review colors.
Review shapes.
Review counting orally to 50.

Activities:

① Read the instruction. Teach the diamond shape. Note that it has four sides like a square but it is placed so that the corners point to the top and bottom, left and right of the page. Demonstrate what the color purple looks like.

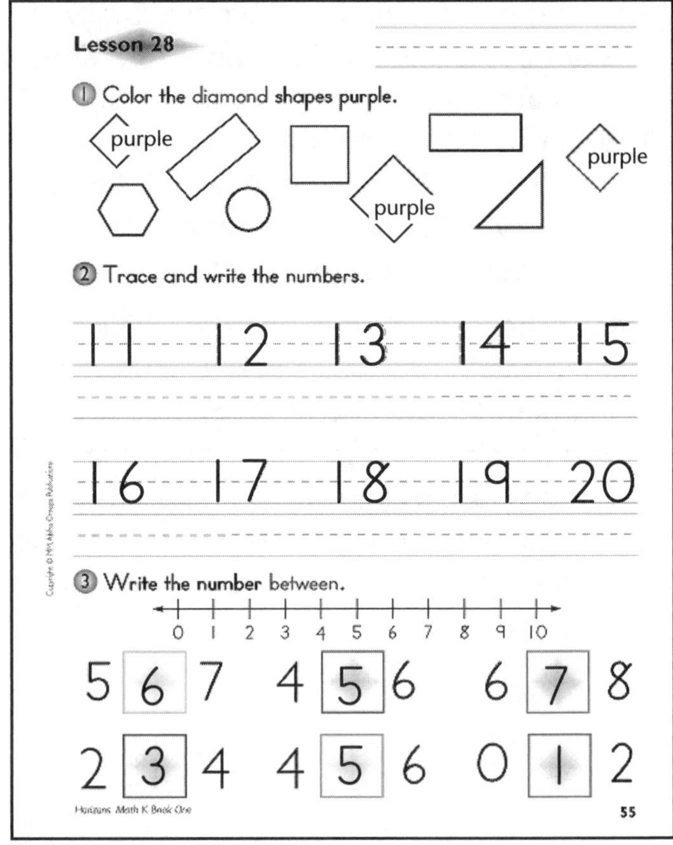

② Read the instruction. Have them trace the 11–15 in the first row. Discuss the spacing between the numbers. Have them write 11–15 in the 2nd row. Do the same for 16–20.

③ Read the instruction to the class. Use number line strips to demonstrate the number between. Also point out that number between is counting by 1's. Have the student(s) write their answers.

④ Talk about the dominos. The dots are to help the student(s) count the addition problems. Talk about the (+) sign and that it means addition. Point out that the line in a vertical problem is the same as the = sign in a horizontal problem. It means "equals." Have them count the dots and write the number on the lines to the right of the dots. Say "3 plus 2 equals" and then count all of the dots on the domino and write 5 for the answer. Point out that the number for the dots on the top of the domino is written on the top line of the addition problem and the number for the bottom dots is written on the bottom line of the problem. Do the rest of the problems in the same way.

⑤ Read the instruction to the class. Talk about where the hour number is found on a digital clock. Have the student(s) write the time on the lines below each clock.

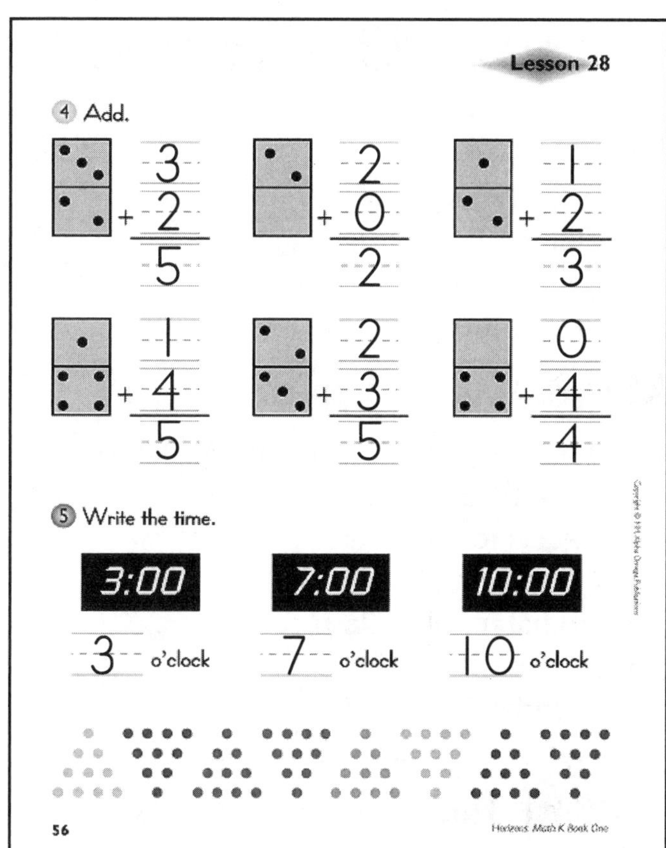

Lesson 28

④ Add.

$3 + 2 = 5$ | $2 + 0 = 2$ | $1 + 2 = 3$

$1 + 4 = 5$ | $2 + 3 = 5$ | $0 + 4 = 4$

⑤ Write the time.

3:00	7:00	10:00
3 o'clock	7 o'clock	10 o'clock

56 Horizons Math K Book One

Lesson 29 - Ordinals

Overview:

- Ordinals first–tenth
- Addition 0–7
- Count pennies
- Days of the week

Materials and Supplies:

- Teacher's Guide & Student Workbook
- White board
- Objects for counters
- Number flash cards
- Ordinal number flash cards
- Pennies
- Calendar
- Days of the week flash cards

Teaching Tips:

Teach ordinal numbers 1–10.
Review days of the week.
Review addition 1's family.
Review counting pennies.
Review counting orally to 50.

Activities:

① Read the instruction. Point out the stick figures in the activity. Count the figures 1–10. Count the figures again counting and saying, "1–first, 2–second, 3–third," etc. Read the row of 1st, 2nd, 3rd ordinal numbers in the same way. Have the student(s) circle the eighth balloon and put an X on the fifth chick.

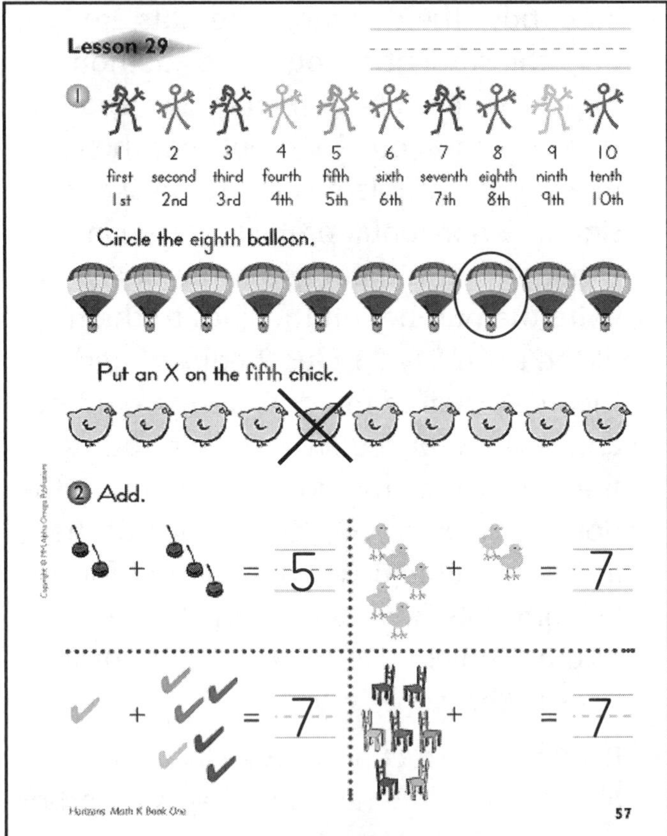

② Read the instruction. Talk about the cherries and the other figures. The figures are to help the student(s) count the addition problems. Review the (+) sign and that it means addition. Review the (=) sign and that it means equals or the total in an addition problem. Have them count the cherries and write the answer. Do the rest of the problems in the same way.

③ Read the instruction to the class. They should be able to independently count the pennies and write the answer.

④ Read the instruction. Read each list of days of the week. Have the student(s) circle the row that they feel is correct.

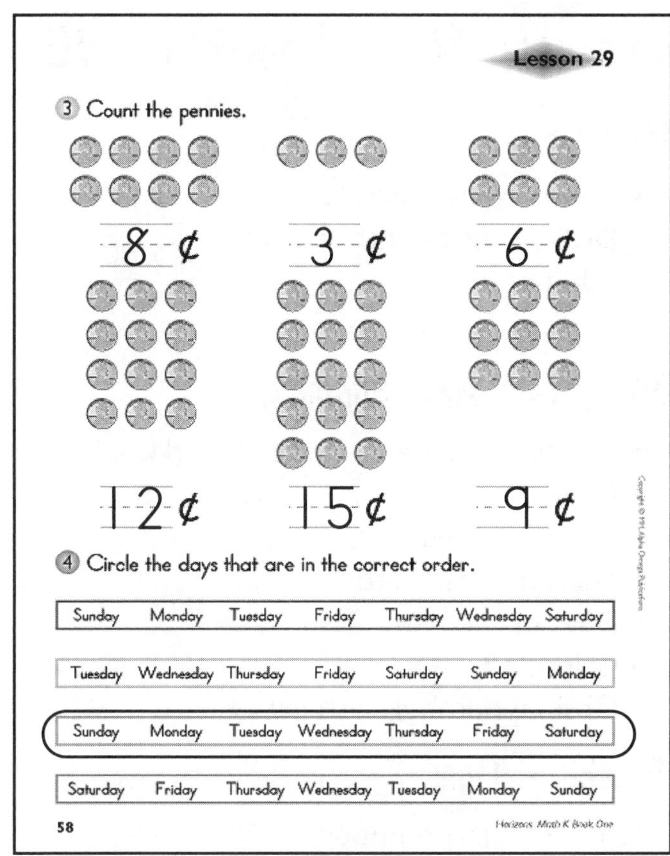

Lesson 30 - Count to 30

Overview:

- Count 1–30, calendar
- Ordinals first–tenth & *before*
- Addition 0–8
- Missing number 0–20

Materials and Supplies:

- Teacher's Guide & Student Workbook
- White board
- Objects for counters
- Number flash cards
- Days of the week flash cards
- Calendar
- Ordinal number flash cards

Teaching Tips:

Teach reading numbers to 30.
Teach the calendar.
Review the days for the week.
Review ordinal numbers.
Review oral counting to 50.

Activities:

① Read the instruction. Talk about the calendar. Note the days of the week across the top. Read the numbers 1–30. Point out that the dates in vertical rows are the same day of the week. Read the numbers under Sunday, Monday, etc.

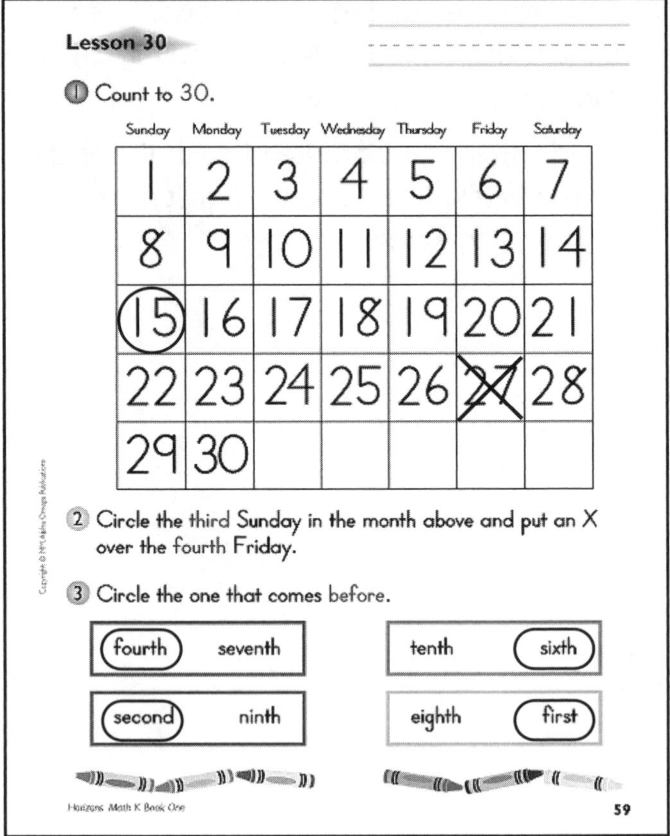

Lesson 30

1 Count to 30.

Sunday	Monday	Tuesday	Wednesday	Thursday	Friday	Saturday
1	2	3	4	5	6	7
8	9	10	11	12	13	14
15	16	17	18	19	20	21
22	23	24	25	26	27	28
29	30					

2 Circle the third Sunday in the month above and put an X over the fourth Friday.

3 Circle the one that comes before.

fourth	seventh
second	ninth

tenth	sixth
eighth	first

Horizons Math K Book One 59

② Read the instruction. Help them find the correct row. Make sure that they circle the first answer and put an X over their second answer.

③ Read the instruction to the class. Review with ordinal flash cards. They are to circle just one word in each rectangle.

④ Read the instruction to the class. Talk about the dolphins and the other figures. The figures are to help the student(s) count the addition problems. Review the the (+) sign and the line under the problem. Have them count the first dolphins and write the number in the box. Do the same for the second group. Say "3 plus 2 equals" and then count all of the dolphins and write 5 for the answer. Do the rest of the problems in the same way.

⑤ Read the instruction to the class. Orally review counting to 20. Have them fill in the missing numbers.

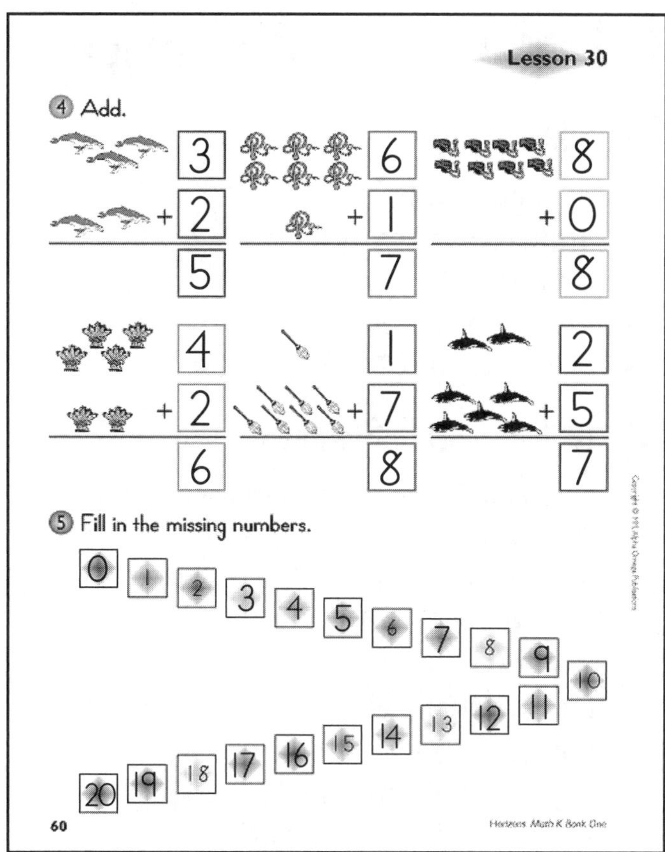

Lesson 31 - Pictograph

Overview:

- Use pictograph
- Ordinals first–tenth
- Addition 0–9
- Number between 1's family
- Trace & write 21–30

Materials and Supplies:

- Teacher's Guide & Student Workbook
- White board
- Objects for counters
- Number flash cards
- Dominos
- Number chart
- Number line strip
- Shape flash cards
- Ordinal number flash cards
- Worksheet 14 & 24

Teaching Tips:

Teach pictograph.
Review ordinal numbers.
Review addition 1's family.
Review shapes.
Review number between 1's.
Review oral counting to 50.

Activities:

① Read the instruction. Talk about the pictograph and how items are drawn in each row. Count the number of items in each row and have the student(s) write their answer on the blanks.

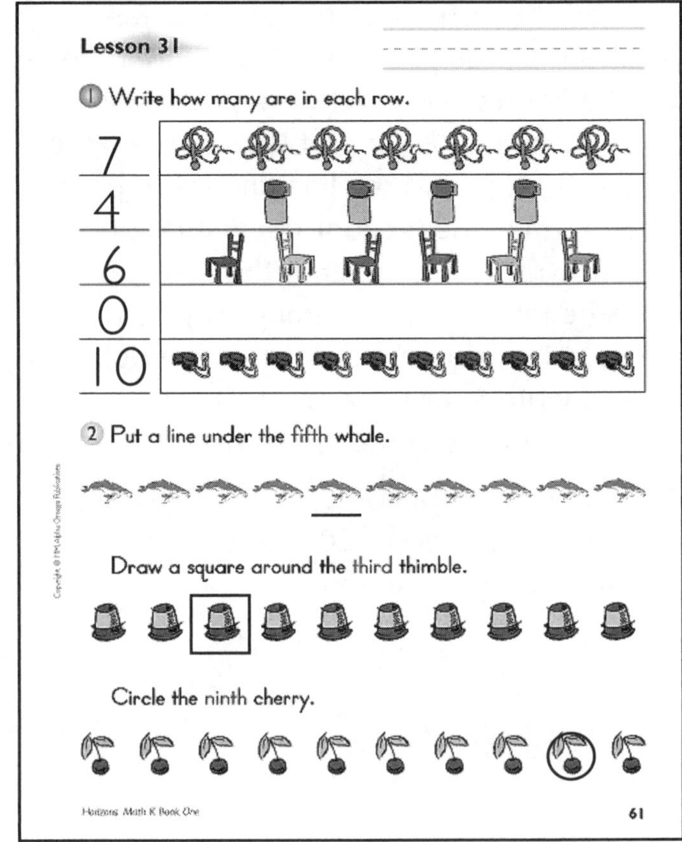
Lesson 31

① Write how many are in each row.

7
4
6
0
10

② Put a line under the fifth whale.

Draw a square around the third thimble.

Circle the ninth cherry.

Horizons Math K Book One 61

② Review with ordinal flash cards. Review shapes. Read each instruction and have them mark their answers.

③ Read the instruction to the class. Talk about the dominos. The dominos are to help the student(s) count the addition problems. Review the the (+) sign and the (=) sign. Have them count the first dots and write the number on the line. Do the same for the second group. Say "1 plus 4 equals" and then count all of the dots and write 5 for the answer. Do the rest of the problems in the same way.

④ Read the instruction to the class. Use number line strips to demonstrate the number between. Also point out that number between is counting by 1's. Have the student(s) write their answers.

⑤ Read the instruction to the class. Orally review counting to 30. Have them trace the numbers.

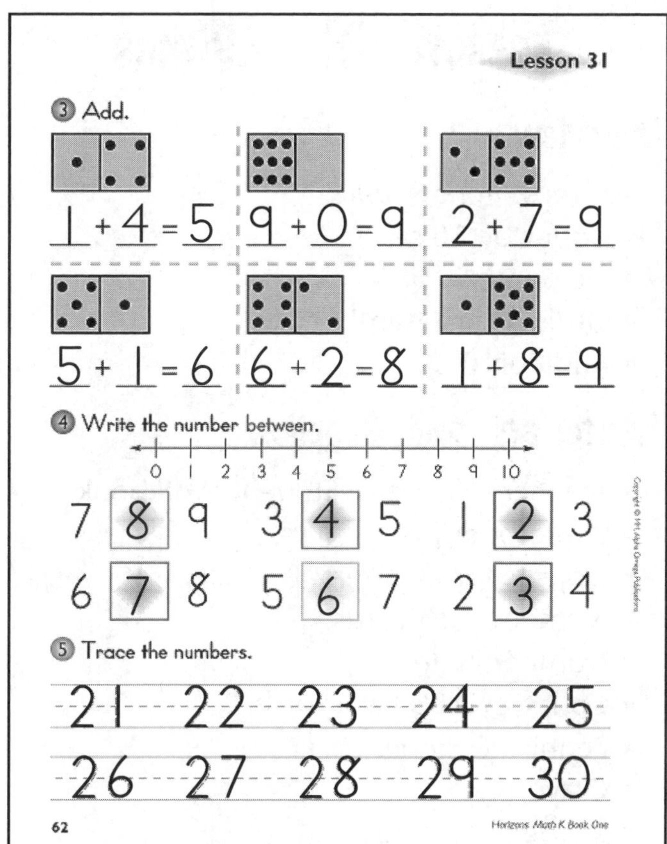

Lesson 31

③ Add.

1 + 4 = 5 | 9 + 0 = 9 | 2 + 7 = 9

5 + 1 = 6 | 6 + 2 = 8 | 1 + 8 = 9

④ Write the number between.

0 1 2 3 4 5 6 7 8 9 10

7 8 9 | 3 4 5 | 1 2 3

6 7 8 | 5 6 7 | 2 3 4

⑤ Trace the numbers.

21 22 23 24 25

26 27 28 29 30

62 Horizons Math K Book One

Lesson 32 - Dimes

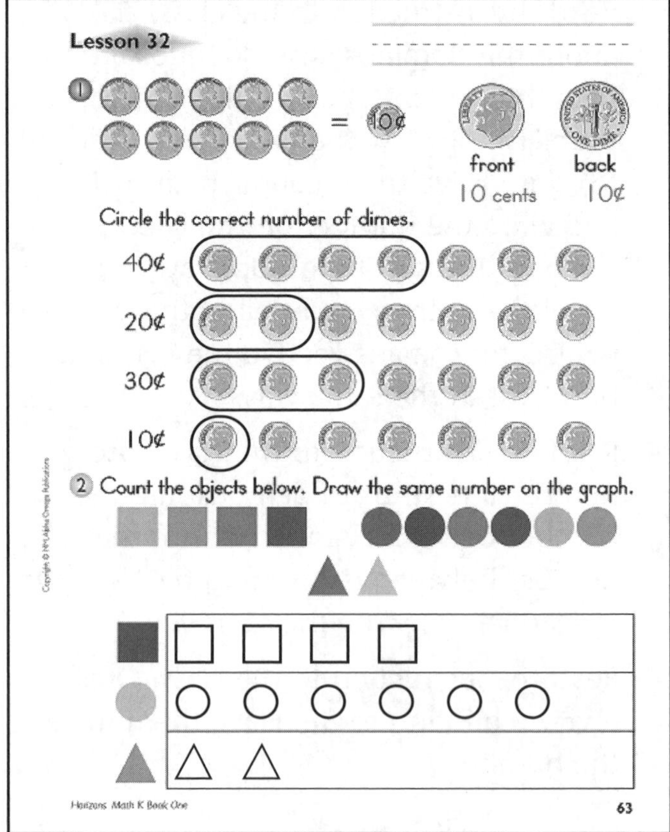

Overview:

- Dimes, *front* & *back*
- Count by 10's
- Pictograph
- Ordinals first–tenth, colors
- Addition 0–9

Materials and Supplies:

- Teacher's Guide & Student Workbook
- White board
- Objects for counters
- Number flash cards
- Number chart
- Count by 10's flash cards
- Pennies & dimes
- Crayons
- Shape flash cards
- Ordinal number flash cards

Teaching Tips:

Teach dimes.
Review front and back.
Review counting by 10's.
Review colors.
Review shapes.
Review ordinal numbers.
Review addition 1's.
Review oral counting to 50.

Activities:

① Have the student(s) count the pennies. Point out that a dime is the same as 10 pennies in value. Review *front* and *back*. Review counting by 10's. Instruct the student(s) to circle the number of dimes for the correct amount by counting by tens.

② Read the instruction. Do several sample activities of this concept on the white board. Point out that the graph represents the information given below the instruction line. Count the squares. Tell the student(s) to draw the same number of squares as they have counted in the top box of the graph. Do the same for the circles and the triangles.

③ Read the instruction to the class. Review diamond shape, colors and ordinal numbers. Have the student(s) complete the activity.

④ Read the instruction to the class. Point out the dotted lines that divide the activity. Talk about the hot dogs and the other figures. The figures are to help the student(s) count the addition problems. Review the the (+) sign and the bar which stands for the (=) sign. Have them count the first hot dogs and write the number on the first line. Do the same for the second group. Say "3 plus 2 equals" and then count all of the hot dogs and write 5 for the answer. Read the problem again "3 plus 2 equals 5." Do the rest of the problems in the same way.

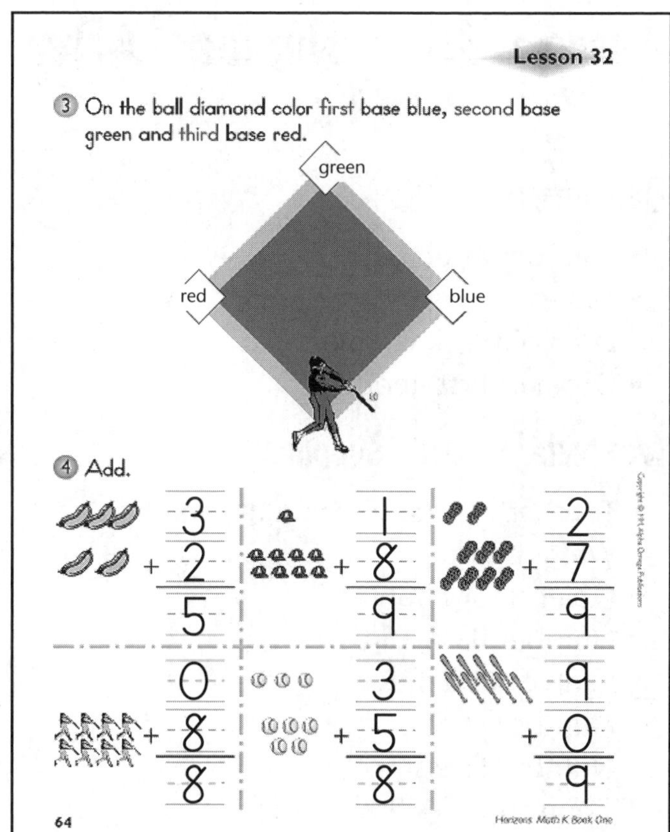

Lesson 33 - Number After 1's

Overview:

- Number after 1–5
- Dimes
- Days of week & colors
- Ordinals first–tenth

Materials and Supplies:

- Teacher's Guide & Student Workbook
- White board
- Objects for counters
- Number flash cards
- Pennies & dimes
- Number chart
- Number line strip
- Count by 10's flash cards
- Calendar
- Crayons
- Color flash cards
- Ordinal number flash cards

Teaching Tips:

Teach number after 1's.
Review dimes.
Review counting by 10's.
Review ordinal numbers.
Review days of the week.
Review colors with flash cards.
Review oral counting to 50.

Activities:

① Read the instruction. Demonstrate with a number line and/or with counters the number after.

Lesson 33

① Write the number after.

0 1 2 3 4 5 6 7 8 9 10

1 2   4 5   2 3

5 6   3 4   0 1

② Count by 10's.

20¢

40¢

30¢

10¢

Horizons Math K Book One 65

② Read the instruction. Have the student(s) count the first row of dimes. Point out that a dime is the same as 10 pennies in value. Instruct the student(s) to write the number for the amount of the dimes they have counted. Let the student(s) complete the activity.

③ Read the instruction. Review the days of the week. Read each instruction again and have the student(s) complete the activity.

④ Read the instruction. Count orally 1–20 with the student(s). Read each instruction again and have the student(s) complete the activity.

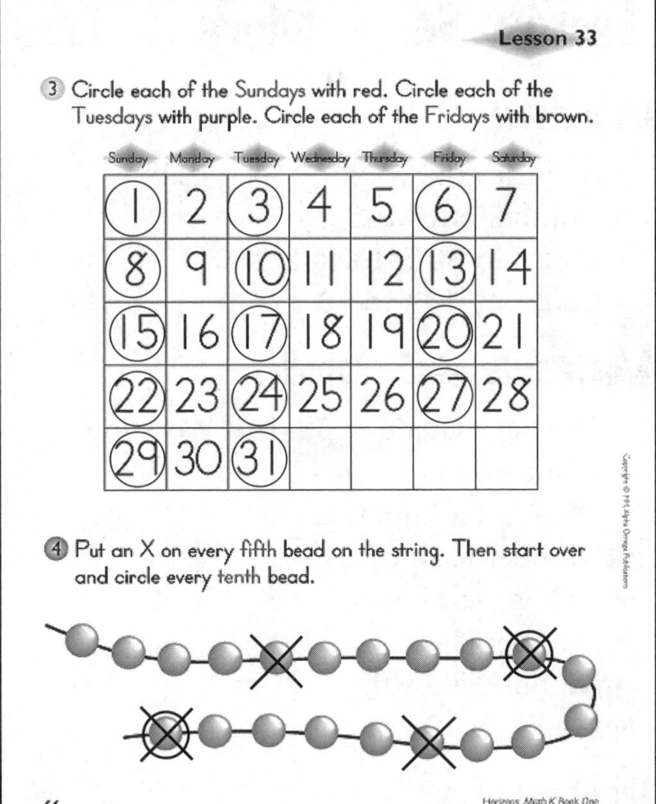

Lesson 33

③ Circle each of the Sundays with red. Circle each of the Tuesdays with purple. Circle each of the Fridays with brown.

Sunday	Monday	Tuesday	Wednesday	Thursday	Friday	Saturday
1	2	3	4	5	6	7
8	9	10	11	12	13	14
15	16	17	18	19	20	21
22	23	24	25	26	27	28
29	30	31				

④ Put an X on every fifth bead on the string. Then start over and circle every tenth bead.

66 Horizons Math K Book One

Lesson 34 - More & Less

Overview:

- More & less
- Number after 1–5
- Count to 30 & trace 21–30
- Count by 10's to 40

Materials and Supplies:

- Teacher's Guide & Student Workbook
- White board
- Objects for counters
- Number flash cards
- Pennies & dimes
- Number chart
- Number line strip
- Count by 10's flash cards

Teaching Tips:

Teach more and less.
Review number after 1's.
Review dimes.
Review counting by 10's.
Review oral counting to 50.

Activities:

① Read the instruction. Demonstrate this concept on the white board several times. Have samples of several items. Have the student(s) tell you which group is more. Point out the dotted lines that separate the groups. Look at the first group. Count the wheels. Count the whales. Have the students(s) circle the group that is more. Allow the student(s) to complete the activity.

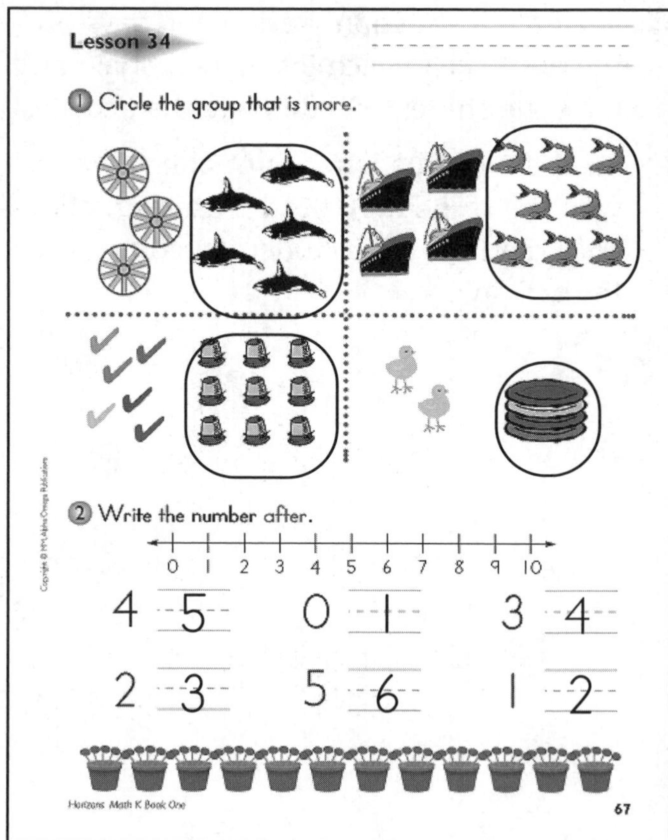

② Read the instruction. Demonstrate with a number line and/or with counters the number after and have the student(s) complete the activity.

③ Read the first instruction. Count orally 1–30 with the student(s). Read the numbers 1–30 in the activity. Read the second instruction and have the student(s) complete the activity.

④ Read the instruction. Have the student(s) count by 10's to find and write the answers for the activity.

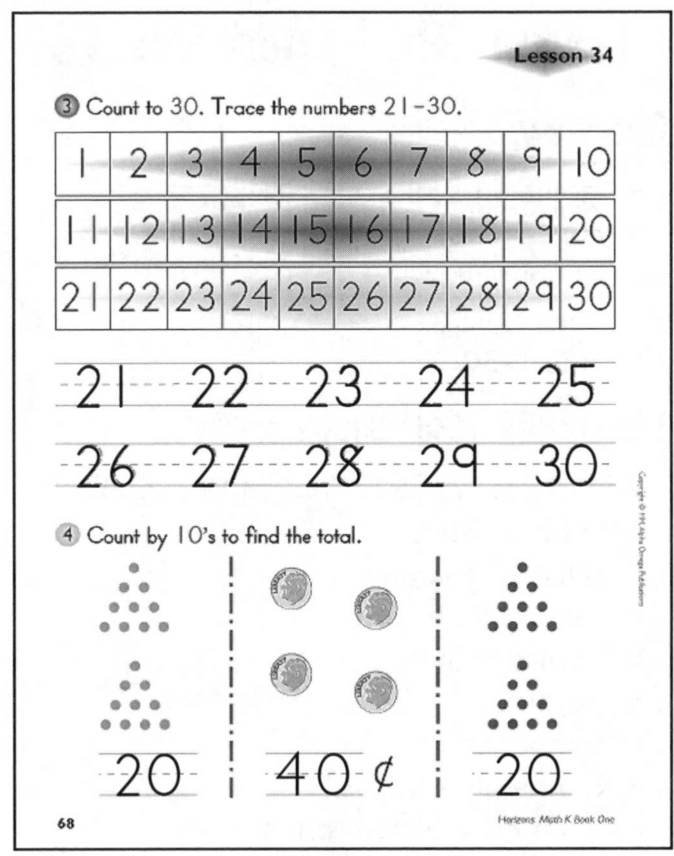

Lesson 35 - Addition 1's

Overview:

- Addition 1's family
- More & less
- Number after 1–9
- Dimes
- Write 1–30

Materials and Supplies:

- Teacher's Guide & Student Workbook
- White board
- Objects for counters
- Number flash cards
- Pennies & dimes
- Crayons
- Number chart
- Number line strip
- Count by 10's flash cards

Teaching Tips:

Teach addition.
Review more and less.
Review dimes.
Review number after 1's.
Review counting by 10's.
Review oral counting to 50.

Activities:

① Read the instruction. Talk about the squares in each strip. The squares are to help the student(s) count the addition problems. Talk about the (+) sign and that it means addition. Talk about the (=) sign and that it means equals. Have them count the red squares and trace the numbers below the squares. Have them count the orange squares and trace the number after the + sign. Count all of the squares for the answer. Instruct the student(s) to color the number of squares for each addition problem and to answer the problems.

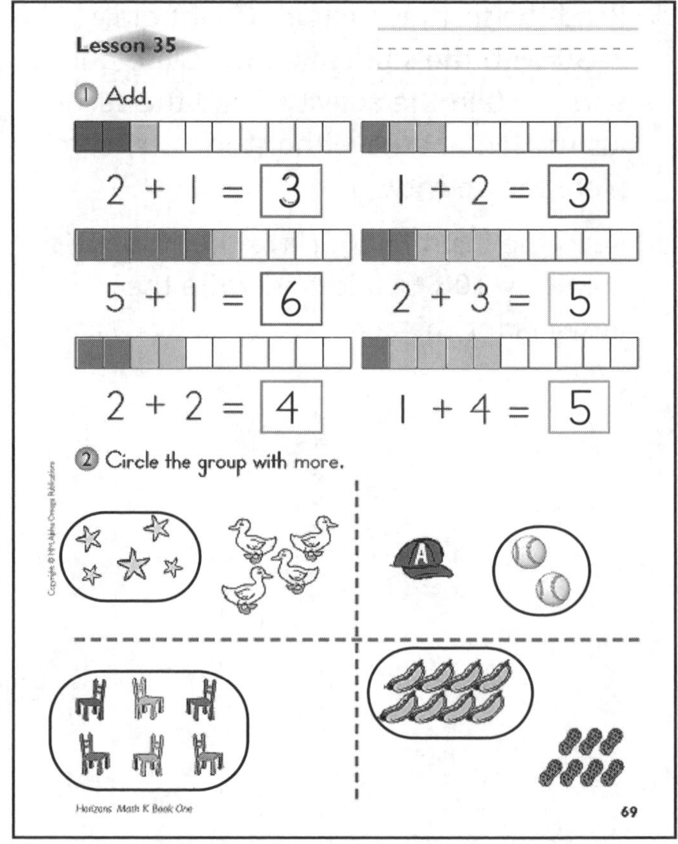

② Read the instruction. Demonstrate this concept on the white board several times. Have samples of several items. Have the student(s) tell you which group is more. Point out the dotted lines that separate the groups. Look at the first group. Count the stars. Count the ducks. Have the students(s) circle the group that is more. The student(s) are to compare the set of chairs to nothing. Allow the student(s) to complete the activity.

③ Read the instruction. Demonstrate with a number line and/or with counters the number after and have the student(s) complete the activity.

④ Read the instruction. Have the student(s) count by 10's to find the number of dimes needed for the items.

⑤ Read the instruction. Count orally 1–30 with the student(s). Have the student(s) write the numbers 1–30.

Lesson 36 - Tall & Short

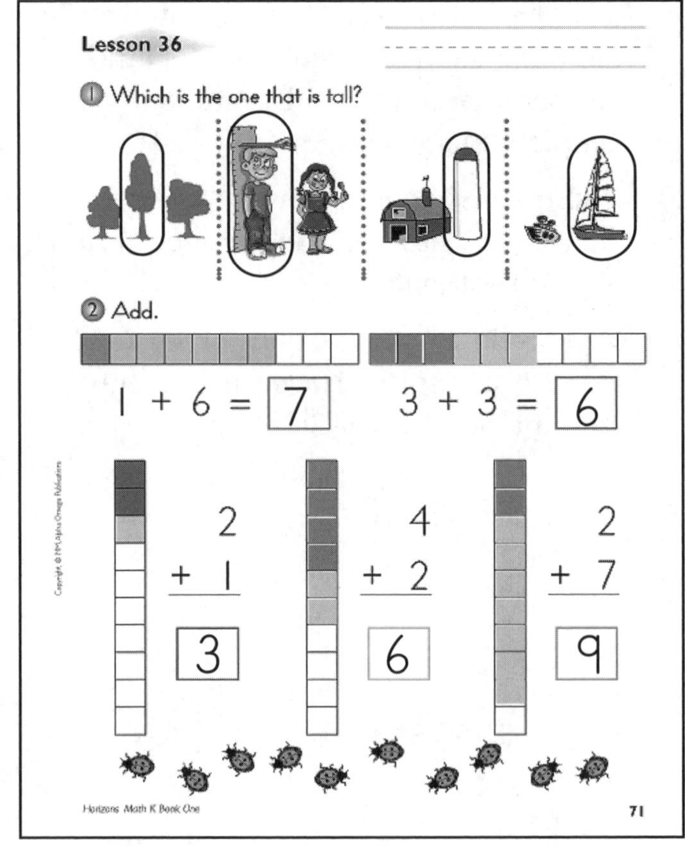

Overview:

- Identify tall & short
- Addition 1's family
- More & less
- Number after 0–9
- Count to 30

Materials and Supplies:

- Teacher's Guide & Student Workbook
- White board
- Objects for counters
- Number flash cards
- Pennies & dimes
- Number chart
- Number line strip
- Count by 10's flash cards

Teaching Tips:

Teach tall and short.
Review addition 1's.
Review more and less.
Review dimes.
Review number after 1's.
Review oral counting to 50.

Activities:

① Read the instruction. Explain and give examples of tall and short. Have the student(s) circle the one that is tall in each group.

② Read the instruction. Talk about the squares in each strip. The squares are to help the student(s) count the addition problems. Talk about the (+) sign and that it means addition. Talk about the (=) sign and that it means equals. Have them count the blue square and trace the number below the squares. Have them count the green squares and trace the number after the + sign. Count all of the squares for the answer and answer the addition problem. The vertical problems are done the same way. Instruct the student(s) to color the number of squares for each addition problem and to answer the problems.

③ Read the instruction. Demonstrate this concept on the white board several times. Have samples of several items. Have the student(s) tell you which group is less. Point out the dotted lines that separate the groups. Look at the first group. Count the first group of pennies. Count the second group of pennies. Have the students(s) circle the group that is less. Allow the student(s) to complete the activity.

④ Read the instruction. Demonstrate with a number line and/or with counters the number after and have the student(s) complete the activity.

⑤ Read the instruction. Count orally 1–30 with the student(s). Have the student(s) count the balls and write the answer.

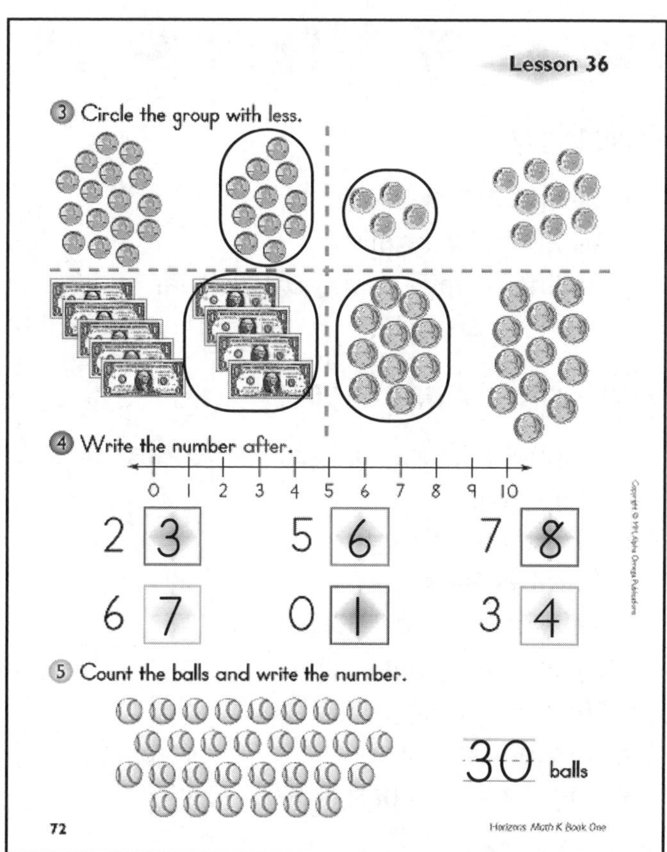

Lesson 37 - Short & Tall

Overview:

- Identify tall & short
- Addition 1's family
- Ordinals, days of week, calendar
- Number after 1's

Materials and Supplies:

- Teacher's Guide & Student Workbook
- White board
- Objects for counters
- Number flash cards
- Days of the week flash cards
- Ordinal number flash cards
- Number chart
- Number line strip
- Count by 10's flash cards

Teaching Tips:

Teach tall and short.
Review addition 1's.
Review calendar.
Review days of the week.
Review ordinal numbers.
Review number after 1's.
Teach oral counting to 60.

Activities:

① Read the instruction. Explain and give examples of tall and short. Have the student(s) circle the one that is short in each group.

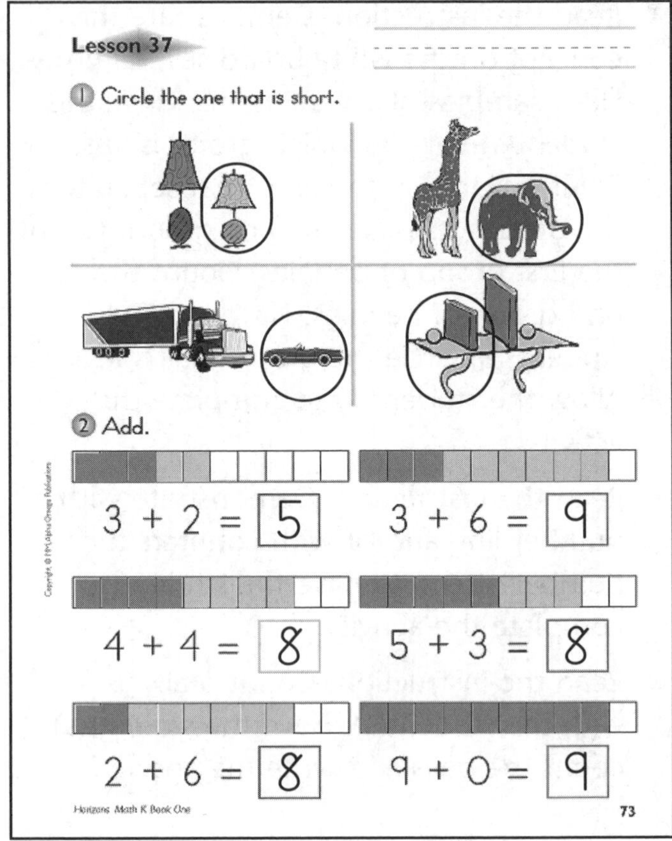

② Read the instruction. Instruct them to color the squares for the numbers in the addition problems with two different colors. The student(s) should complete the activity.

③ Read the instruction. Count orally 1–30 with the student(s) by using the numbers on the November calendar. This might be a good time to make flash cards of the months of the year.

④ Read the first instruction and have the student(s) choose their answer. Do the same for the second instruction.

⑤ Read the instruction. Demonstrate with a number line and/or with counters the number after and have the student(s) complete the activity.

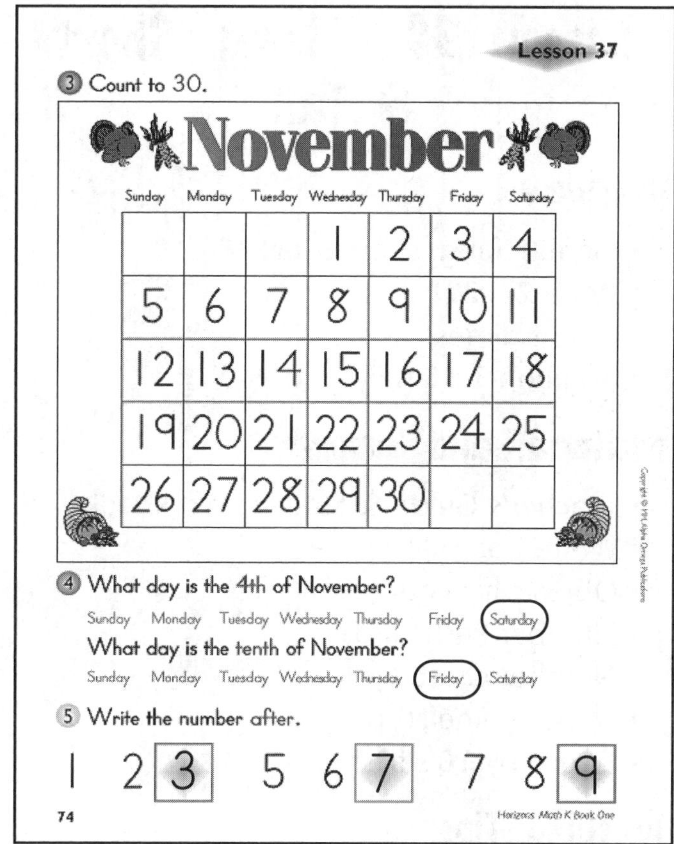

Lesson 38 - Long, Short & Tall

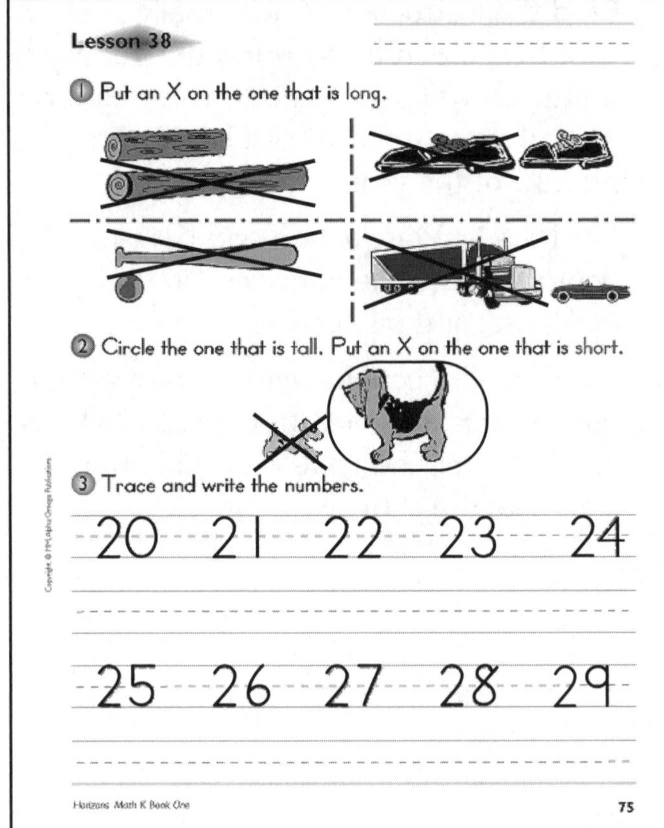

Overview:

- Identify long, short & tall
- Write 20–29
- Count dimes
- Addition 1's family

Material and Supplies:

- Teacher's Guide & Student Workbook
- White board
- Objects for counters
- Number flash cards
- Number chart
- Number line strip
- Count by 10's flash cards

Teaching Tips:

Teach long and short.
Review tall and short.
Review addition 1's.
Review oral counting to 60.

Activities:

① Read the instruction. Explain and give examples of long and short. Have the student(s) write an X on the one that is long in each group.

② Read the instruction. Explain and give examples of tall and short. Have the student(s) circle the one that is tall and write an X on the one that is short.

③ Read the instruction. Count orally 1–30 with the student(s). Have the student(s) complete the activity by tracing the numbers and writing another row of each set of numbers.

④ Read the instruction. Have the student(s) count by 10's to find the number of cents. Instruct the student(s) to draw a line from each box of dimes to the correct amount.

⑤ Read the instruction. Instruct them to color the squares for the numbers in the addition problems with two different colors. The student(s) should complete the activity.

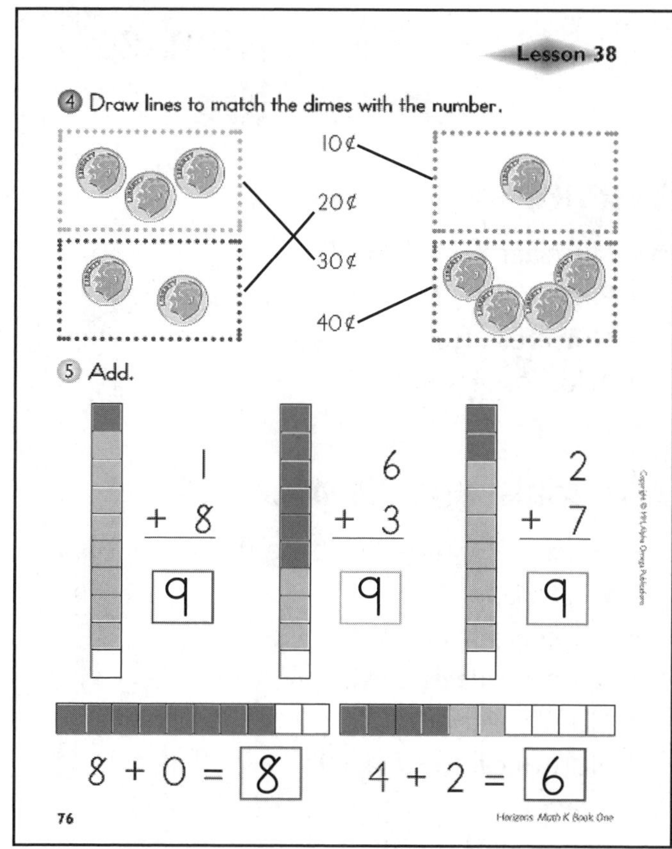

Lesson 39 - Number Between 10's

Overview:

- Number between 10's
- Pictograph, shapes
- Number after 0–9
- Addition 1's family
- Groups of 10

Materials and Supplies:

- Teacher's Guide & Student Workbook
- White board
- Objects for counters
- Number flash cards
- Number chart
- Number line strip 10's
- Crayons
- Shape flash cards
- Tally marks flash cards
- Count by 10's flash cards

Teaching Tips:

Teach number between 10's.
Review pictographs.
Review shapes.
Review number after 1's.
Review addition.
Review tally marks.
Review counting by 10.
Review oral counting to 60.

Activities:

① Read the instruction. Use number line strips to demonstrate the number between. Also point out that number between is counting by 1's. Have the student(s) write their answers.

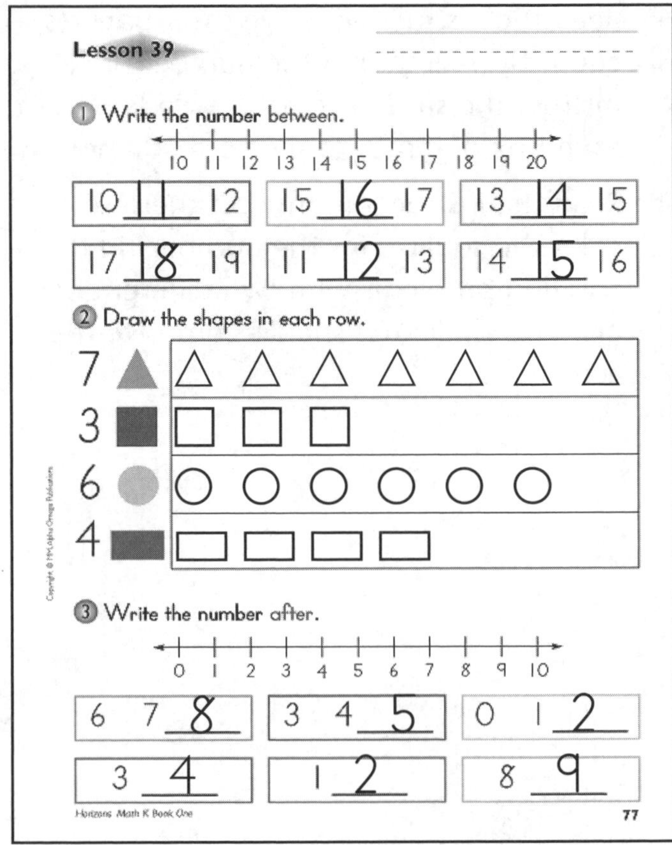

② Read the instruction. The number on the left indicates how many of each shape are to be drawn in the row.

③ Read the instruction. Demonstrate with a number line and/or with counters the number after and have the student(s) complete the activity.

④ Read the instruction. Instruct the student(s) to color the squares for the numbers in the addition problems with two different colors. The student(s) should complete the activity by coloring the squares and writing the answers to the addition problems.

⑤ Read the instruction. Have the student(s) circle groups of 10 tally marks. Then count the number of tens and write it in the box.

Lesson 40 - Count to 40

Overview:

- Count 1–40
- Number between 10's
- Bar graph
- Number after 0–9
- Trace & write 30–39

Material and Supplies:

- Teacher's Guide & Student Workbook
- White board
- Objects for counters
- Number flash cards
- Number chart
- Number line strips
- Worksheet 15 &25

Teaching Tips:

Teach counting objects to 40.
Teach writing numbers 30's.
Review number between 10's.
Review bar graph.
Review number after 10's.
Review oral counting to 60.

Activities:

① Read the instruction. Count the flowers to 40.

② Read the instruction. Use number line strips to demonstrate the number between. Also point out that number between is counting by 1's. Have the student(s) write their answers.

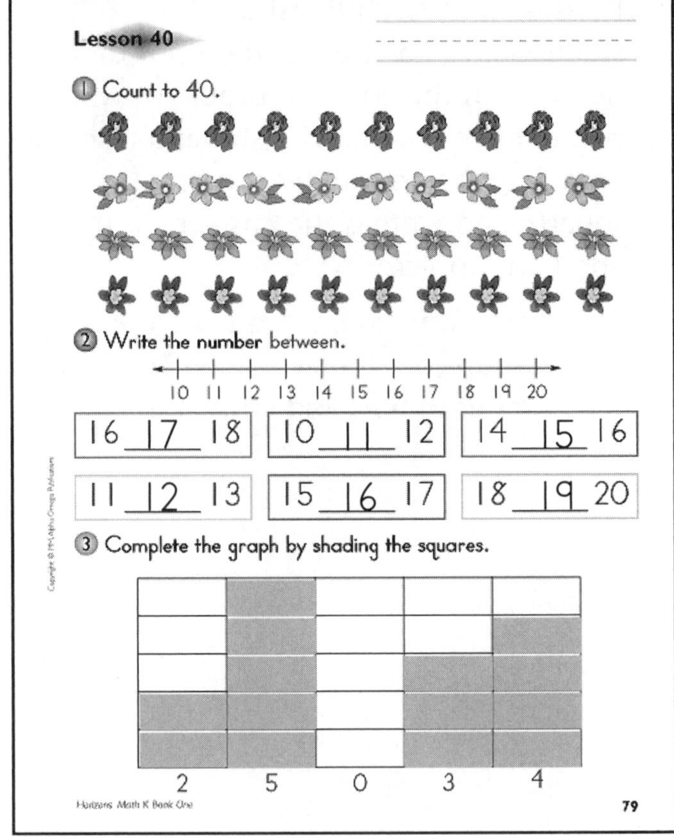

③ Read the instruction to the class. The numbers on the bottom tell how many rectangles are to be colored in each row. Demonstrate this on the white board. Point out that the student(s) are to start on the bottom and color the rectangles for each number given.

④ Read the instruction to the class. Demonstrate with a number line and/or with counters the number after and have the student(s) complete the activity.

⑤ Read the instruction to the class. Count orally 1–40 with the student(s). Have the student(s) complete the activity by tracing the numbers and writing another row of each set of numbers.

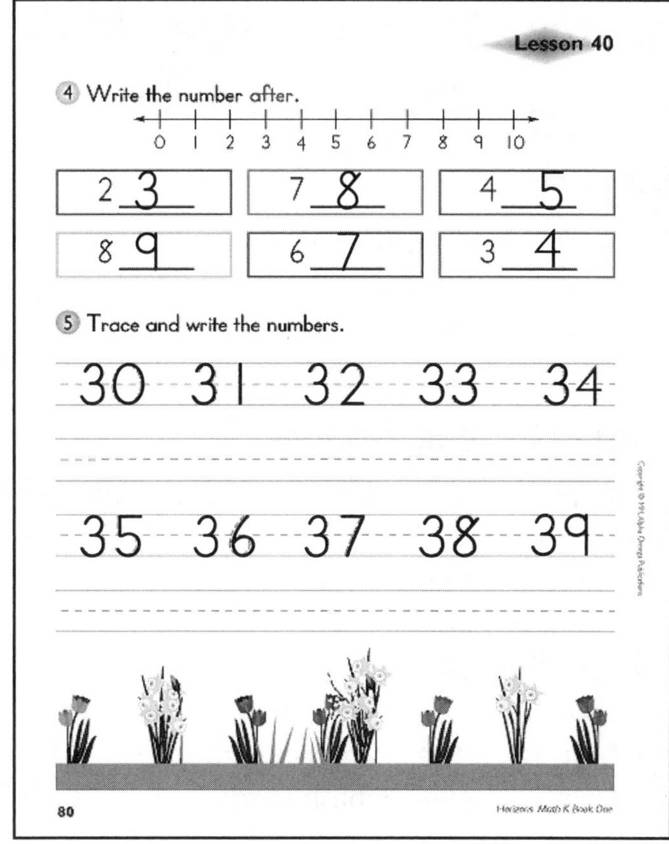

Lesson 41 - Addition With a Number Line 1's

Overview:

- Addition on number line 1's
- Shapes and colors
- Patterns, sequence
- Calendar

Materials and Supplies:

- Teacher's Guide & Student Workbook
- White board
- Objects for counters
- Number flash cards 1–10
- Tally flash cards
- Calendar
- Months of the year flash cards
- Days of the week flash cards
- Color flash cards
- Crayons
- Number chart
- Addition flash cards 1's family
- Dominos

Teaching Tips:

Teach addition with a number line.
Review triangle, circle and square.
Review colors.
Review tally marks.
Review calendar.
Review oral counting to 60.

Activities:

① Use the number line to teach addition facts. Draw lines on the number line to show the process of addition. For example, above the number line draw a line from zero to three and then from three to five. This shows that three plus two equals five. Do several problems like those in

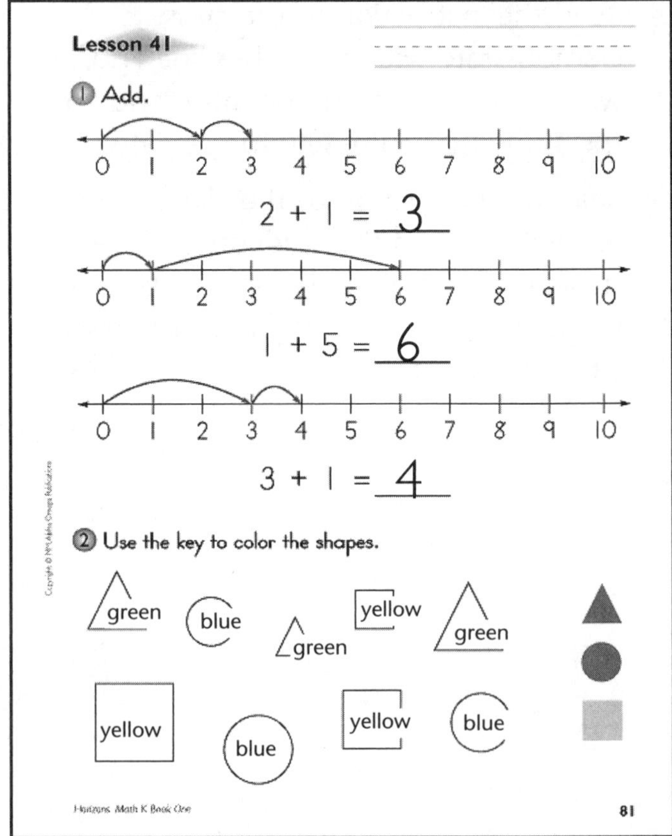

Activity ① orally with the student(s). Write the addition fact. The student(s) need to understand that addition is "putting together." Carefully check each student's progress as they complete the activity.

② Review shapes and colors. Read and review the instruction with the student(s). Give them time to complete the activity.

③ Use shape flash cards to go through a pattern of alternating shapes and ask what comes next in the pattern. Use number flash cards to go though a pattern of alternating numbers and ask what comes next in the pattern. Point out the dotted lines that divide parts of the activity. Go through the items in the first box and have the student(s) circle their answer. Do the same for the second box.

④ Orally count to 50. Have the student(s) recite the months of the year as you point to them on the white board, displayed by flash cards or on the flannel board. Do the same for the days of the week. Read the instruction and have the student(s) complete the activity.

Lesson 41

3 What comes next?

4 Complete the calendar.

October

Sunday	Monday	Tuesday	Wednesday	Thursday	Friday	Saturday
1	2	3	4	5	6	7
8	9	10	11	12	13	14
15	16	17	18	19	20	21
22	23	24	25	26	27	28
29	30	31				

82 Horizons Math K Book One

Lesson 42 - Number Between 20's

Overview:

- Number between 20's
- Addition 1's family
- Trace & write 20–39

Materials and Supplies:

- Teacher's Guide & Student Workbook
- White board
- Objects for counters
- Addition flash cards 1's family
- Number chart
- Number line strips
- Number flash cards

Teaching Tips:

Teach number between 20's.
Review addition with a number line.
Review oral counting to 60.

Activities:

① Direct the student(s) in practicing what comes between two numbers using the number chart. Review 1's and 10's. Practice the 20's. Have them complete the activity using number line strips if necessary.

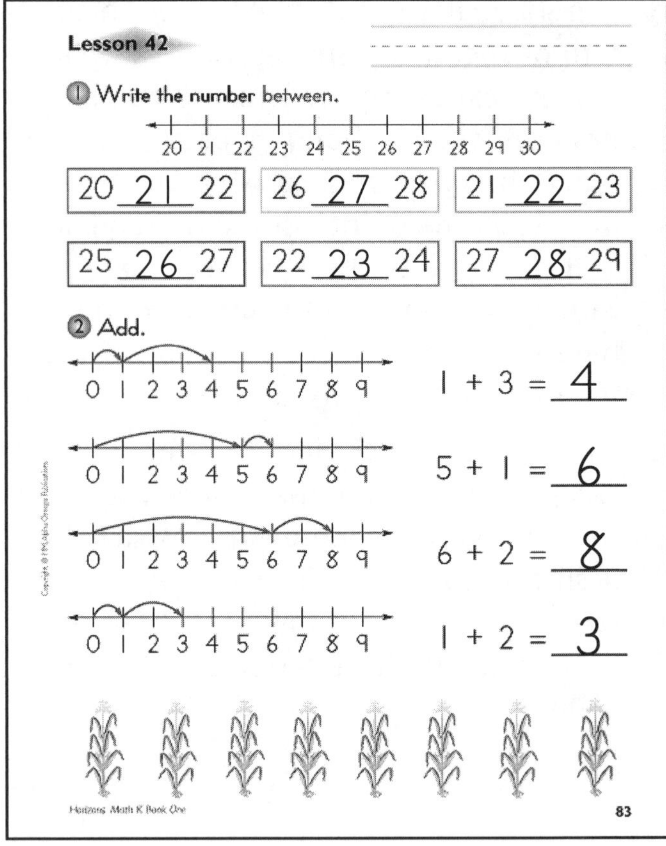

② In preparation for this activity use a number line on the white board to demonstrate several addition facts. Example: 3 + 2 = 5. Have the student(s) find the first number of the addition fact by counting from zero to three. Write three above the line. The second number is found by counting from three to five. Write two above the second line. Five is the answer. Have the student(s) tell you the addition fact, 3 + 2 = 5. Be sure the student(s) follow each step as they do this activity.

③ Have the student(s) count orally to 50. Have them trace and write the numbers in Activity ③.

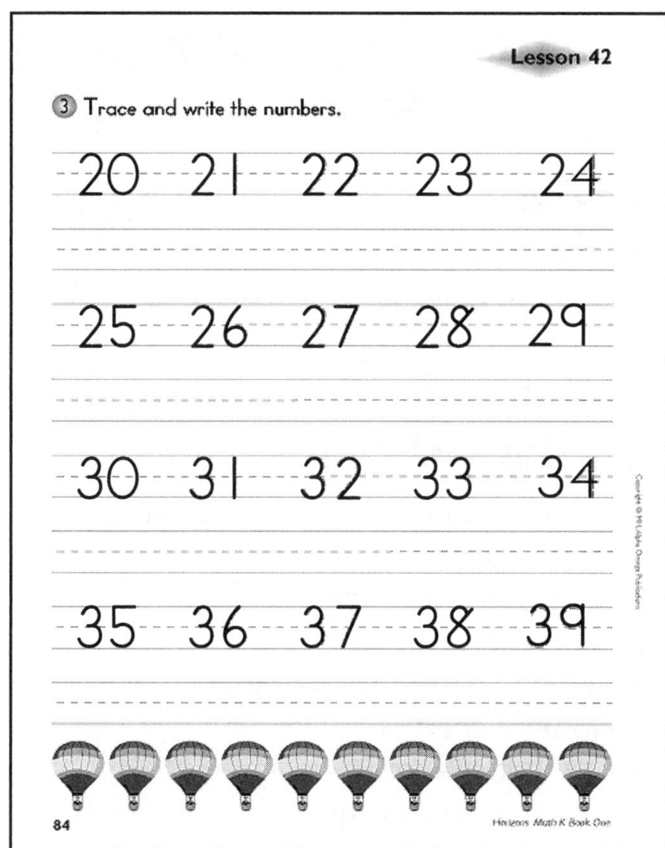

Lesson 43 - Dimes & Pennies

Overview:

- Dimes & pennies
- Number between 20's
- Addition 1's family
- Time – hour

Materials and Supplies:

- Teacher's Guide & Student Workbook
- White board
- Objects for counters
- Pennies & dimes
- Addition flash cards 1's family
- Number chart
- Number line strips
- Number flash cards
- Clocks

Teaching Tips:

Teach counting pennies & dimes.
Review number between 20's.
Review addition with a number line.
Review time – hour.
Review oral counting to 60.

Activities:

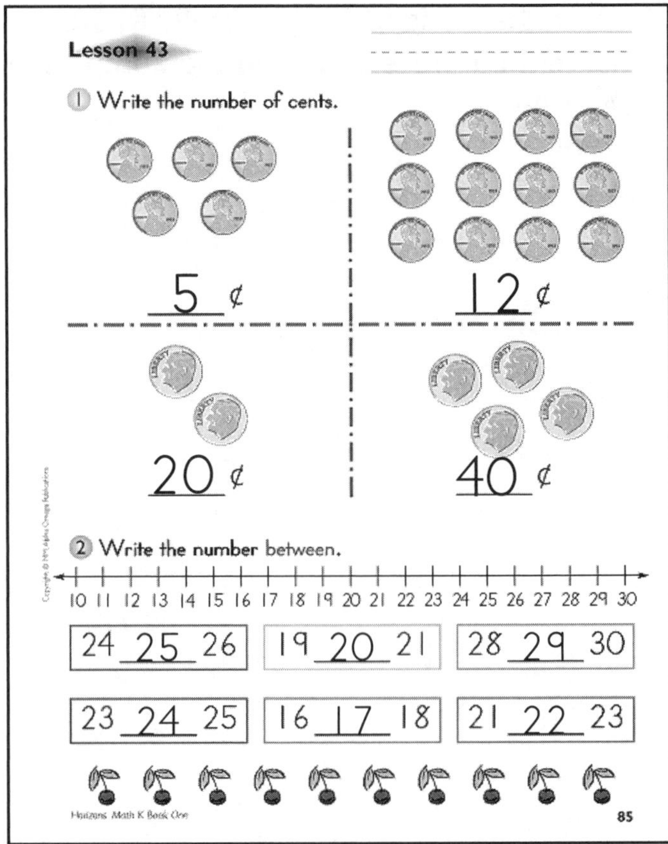

① Use real or play money for the student(s) to see the front and back of a penny. Ask, "What color is the penny?" "Whose picture is on the front of the penny?" (Abraham Lincoln) "What building is on the back of a penny?" (The Lincoln Memorial) Explain that you can write a penny's name in three ways: penny, 1 cent, or 1¢. The ¢ symbol is the short way to write cents. Read the directions to the student(s). Be sure they point to each penny as they count. Point out that any time you count money, you need to use a label to show that you are talking about money. For example, in writing, money must be labeled with the dollar sign or cent sign. When reading money, $4.95 would be read, "four dollars and ninety-five cents."

Show the student(s) a real dime. Ask what color is the dime? Whose picture is on the front? (Franklin D. Roosevelt) What is on the back? (the torch and sprigs of laurel and oak) What is the monetary value? What are three ways of referring to it? (10¢, dime, 10 cents) When counting dimes, count by tens. One dime equals ten cents. Have a student count several sets of dimes and tell how much they are worth. Have the student(s) finish the activity on their own.

② Direct the student(s) in practicing what comes between two numbers using the number chart or a number line. Review 1's and 10's. Practice the 20's. Have them complete the activity using number line strips if necessary.

③ In presenting addition, point out to the student(s) that zero means "nothing." When you add zero to a number you are putting nothing with it. To add zero on the number line means that you add nothing. Zero added to any number is the same number. In preparation for this activity, the student(s) need to be reminded to begin at zero on the number line. They then draw a line to the first number. Next, they count over on the marks to equal the second number. The second line is drawn to this number. They can put a dot on this number before drawing the second line. Where the second line ends is the answer to the addition fact. After the student(s) practice several of these problems have them attempt the activity while you work closely with them.

④ Inform the student that "o'clock" and ":00" are synonymous. Put the hands on the clock model at 8 o'clock. Show two ways of writing time (8 o'clock, 8:00). Do several other times and have the student(s) tell what time it is and write it both ways. Complete the activity.

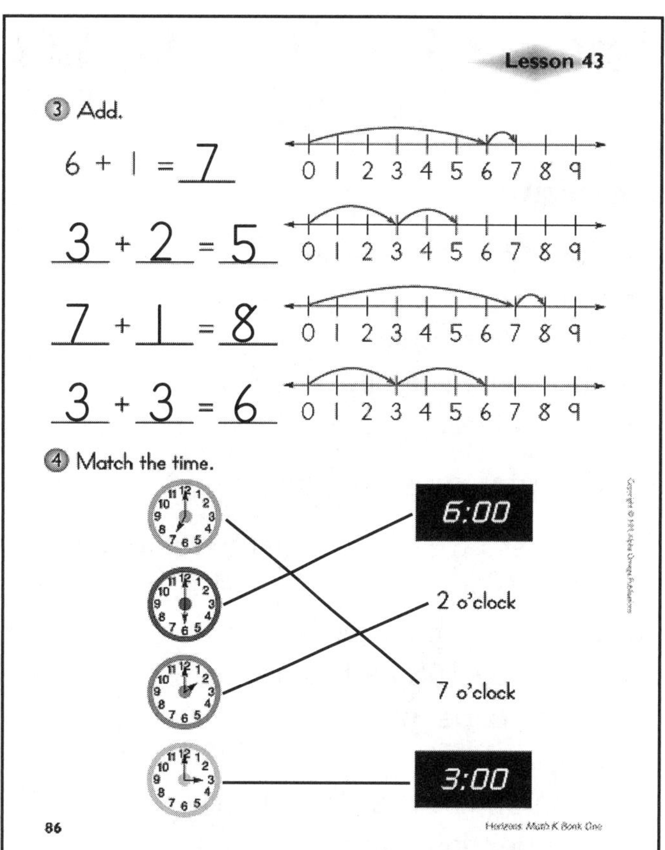
Lesson 43

③ Add.

6 + 1 = 7
0 1 2 3 4 5 6 7 8 9

3 + 2 = 5
0 1 2 3 4 5 6 7 8 9

7 + 1 = 8
0 1 2 3 4 5 6 7 8 9

3 + 3 = 6
0 1 2 3 4 5 6 7 8 9

④ Match the time.

6:00

2 o'clock

7 o'clock

3:00

86

Horizons Math K Book One

Lesson 44 - Count by 10's to 100

Overview:

- Count by 10's to 100
- Trace 10's
- Dimes & pennies
- Addition 1's family
- Time – hour

Materials and Supplies:

- Teacher's Guide & Student Workbook
- White board
- Objects for counters
- Count by 10's flash cards
- Dimes & pennies
- Clock models
- Addition flash cards 1's family
- Number flash cards
- Number chart
- Number line strips

Teaching Tips:

Teach counting by 10's to 100.
Review counting pennies & dimes.
Review addition with a number line.
Review time – hour.
Teach oral counting to 70.

Activities:

① Count by tens to 100 as preparation for this activity. The student(s) should count each row to themselves as they do the activity. Together, read the numbers that should have been circled.

② Trace the 10's.

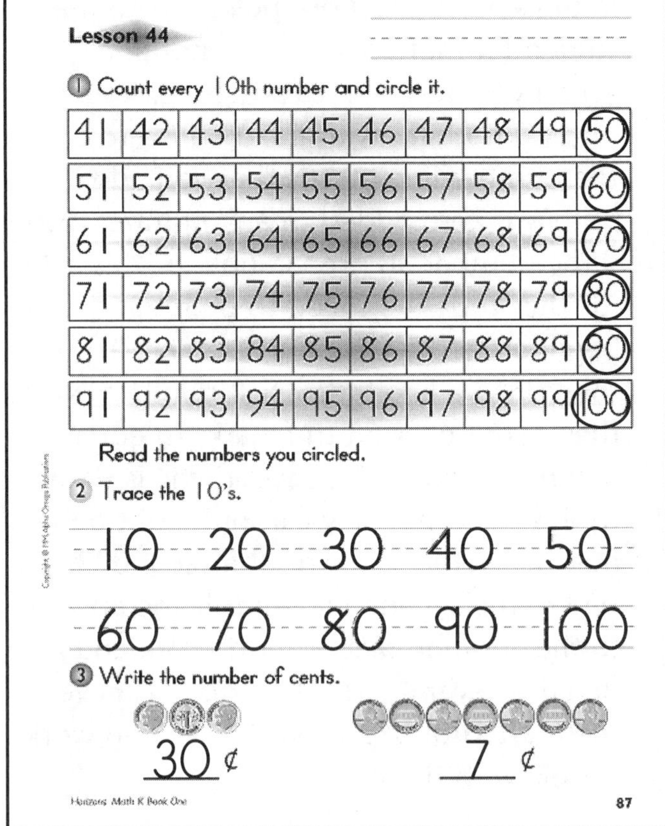

③ Display a set of dimes. Have the student(s) count them by tens to find the value. Do this several times. On the number chart, point to the multiples of 10 and ask how many dimes it will take to equal that number of cents. The ¢ symbol is the short way to write cents.

④ On the white board demonstrate several addition facts (1–9) on the number line. Read the directions to the student(s) in Activity ④. Have them count on the number line to find the first number in the addition fact. Write the number. Then count to find the second and write that number. Write the answer to the addition fact. Do the same for the remaining problems.

⑤ Remind the student(s) of the two ways to write time. Using the clock model, show several times on the hour and have the student(s) tell what time it is and how to write it two ways. Have them do the activity independently.

Lesson 45 - Number Between 30's

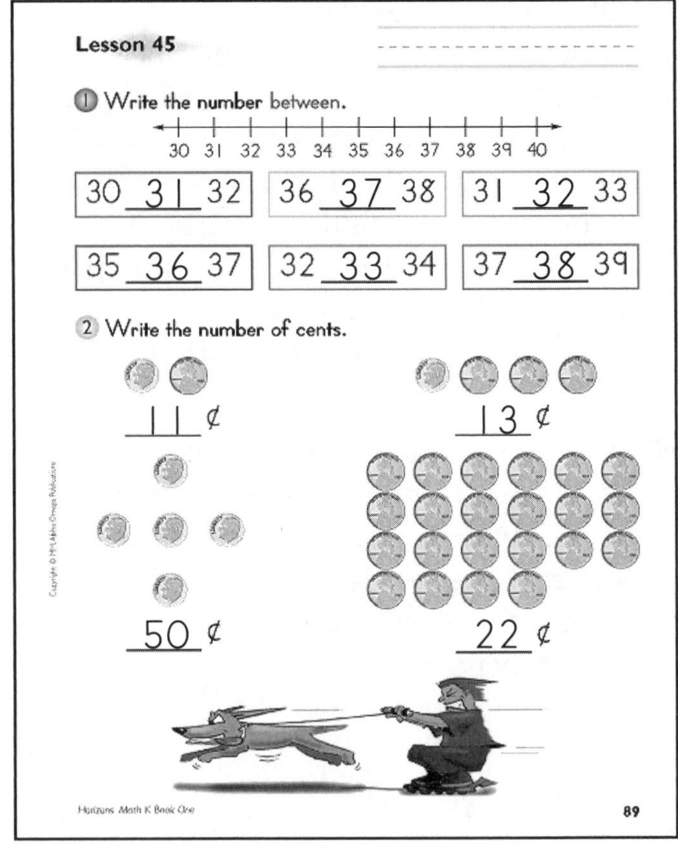

Lesson 45

① Write the number between.

30 31 32 33 34 35 36 37 38 39 40

30 31 32	36 37 38	31 32 33
35 36 37	32 33 34	37 38 39

② Write the number of cents.

11 ¢

13 ¢

50 ¢

22 ¢

Horizons Math K Book One 89

Overview:

- Number between 30's
- Dimes & pennies
- Addition 1's family
- Count by 10's to 100

Materials and Supplies:

- Teacher's Guide & Student Workbook
- White board
- Objects for counters
- Dimes & pennies
- Addition flash cards 1's family
- Number chart
- Count by 10's flash cards
- Shape flash cards
- Number flash cards 1–10

Teaching Tips:

Teach number between 30's.
Review counting by 10's to 100.
Review counting pennies & dimes.
Review addition with a number line.
Review oral counting to 70.

Activities:

① Review counting by ones with the student(s) as a refresher. To do the problems in this activity they need to count by ones to themselves. The number chart may be a help to the student(s).

② Give each student play money (dimes and pennies). Let them set up a group of dimes and a group of pennies. Count the dimes by tens and the pennies by ones to see the value of the money. Two students may work together, one setting up the sets and the other counting them and vice versa. Read the directions to the activity. Do the first problem together, then allow the student(s) to work independently, giving help where it is needed.

③ On the white board demonstrate several addition fact (1–9) on the number line. Read the directions to the student(s) in Activity ④. Have them count on the number line to find the first number in the addition fact. Write the number. Then count to find the second and write that number. Write the answer to the addition fact. Do the same for the remaining problems.

④ Count by tens to 100 as preparation for this activity. The student(s) should count as they trace the numbers.

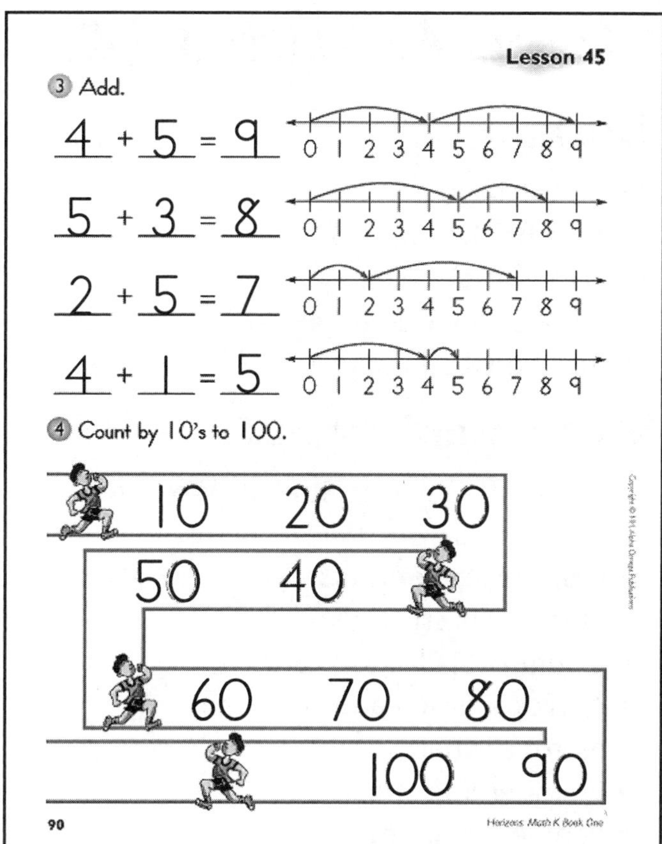
Lesson 45

③ Add.

4 + 5 = 9 0 1 2 3 4 5 6 7 8 9

5 + 3 = 8 0 1 2 3 4 5 6 7 8 9

2 + 5 = 7 0 1 2 3 4 5 6 7 8 9

4 + 1 = 5 0 1 2 3 4 5 6 7 8 9

④ Count by 10's to 100.

10 20 30

50 40

60 70 80

100 90

90

Horizons Math K Book One

Lesson 46 - Count 1-50

Overview:

- Count 1–50
- Number between 30's
- Dimes & pennies
- Trace and write 40–49
- Addition 1's family

Materials and Supplies:

- Teacher's Guide & Student Workbook
- White board
- Objects for counters
- Number flash cards
- Count by 10's flash cards
- Addition flash cards 1's family
- Number chart
- Number line strips
- Pennies & dimes
- Worksheet 16 & 26

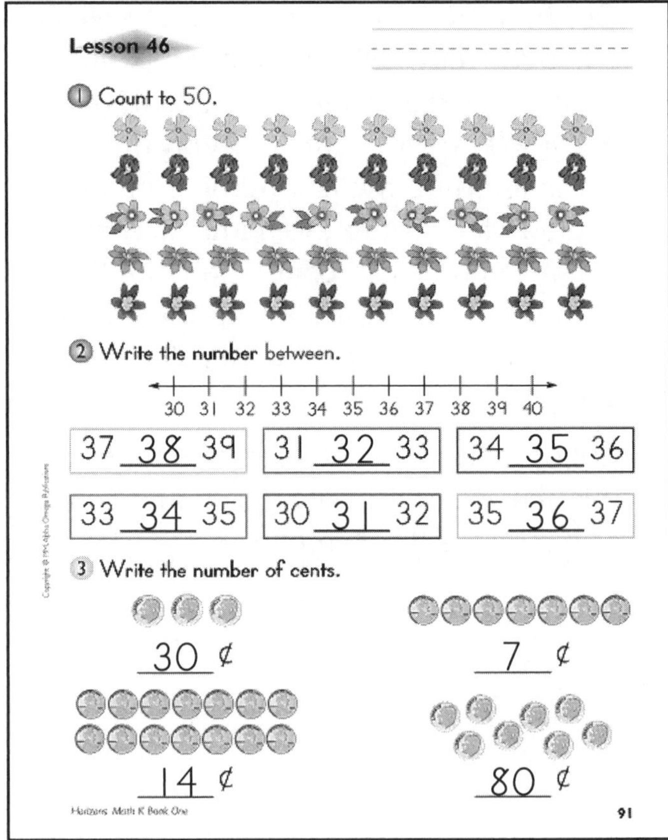
Lesson 46

① Count to 50.

② Write the number between.

30 31 32 33 34 35 36 37 38 39 40

37 38 39 | 31 32 33 | 34 35 36

33 34 35 | 30 31 32 | 35 36 37

③ Write the number of cents.

30 ¢ | 7 ¢

14 ¢ | 80 ¢

Horizons Math K Book One | 91

Teaching Tips:

Teach counting items to 50.
Teach writing numbers 40's.
Review number between 30's.
Review counting by 10's to 100.
Review counting pennies & dimes.
Review addition with a number line.
Review oral counting to 70.

Activities:

① Count out loud by ones to 70 using the number chart. Have the student(s) count the flowers 1–50 in the activity.

② Direct the student(s) in practicing what comes between two numbers using the number chart. Review 1's and 10's. Practice the 30's. Have them complete the activity using number line strips if necessary.

③ Give each student play money (dimes and pennies). Let them set up a group of dimes and a group of pennies. Count the dimes by tens and the pennies by ones to see the value of the money. Two students or a parent and a child may work together, one setting up the sets and the other counting them and vice versa. Read the directions to the activity. Do the first problem together, then allow the student(s) to work independently giving help where it is needed.

④ Trace and write the 40's family. Remind the student(s) to use good spacing and penmanship.

⑤ On the white board demonstrate several addition facts (1–9) on the number line. Read the directions to the student(s) in Activity ⑤. Have them count on the number line to find the first number in the addition fact. Then count to find the second and write that number as the answer to the addition fact. Do the same for the remaining problems. Some student(s) might need to use counters for this activity.

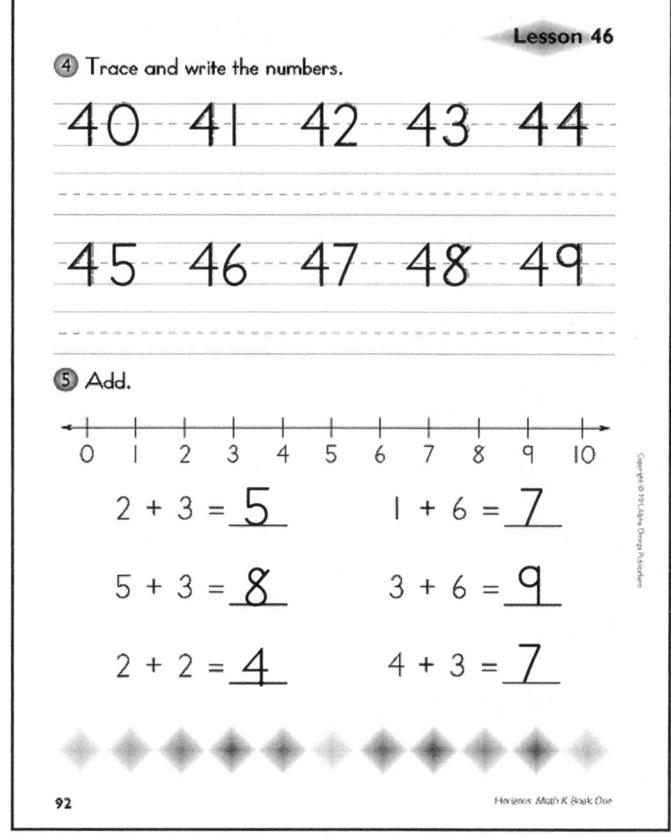

Lesson 47 - Place Value 1's

Overview:

- Place value 1's
- Count 1–50
- Trace 41–50
- Ordinals first–tenth
- Addition 1's family

Materials and Supplies:

- Teacher's Guide & Student Workbook
- White board
- Objects for counters
- Number flash cards
- Addition flash cards 1's
- Ordinal number flash cards
- Place value chart
- Number chart
- Number line strips

Teaching Tips:

Teach place value.
Review counting items to 50.
Review writing numbers 41–50.
Review addition with a number line.
Review oral counting to 70.

Activities:

① Make a place value chart from a piece of cardboard or poster board. It should look like the place value chart in the student book. Use red colors for the tens and blue for the ones. Put a hook on the top or a pocket on the bottom to "hang" a number flash card in the tens' or ones' places. Before doing this activity, discuss the number of places a single-digit numeral (such as 4) takes. Using the numbers chart, ask what the largest number is that takes only one place (9). Discuss how

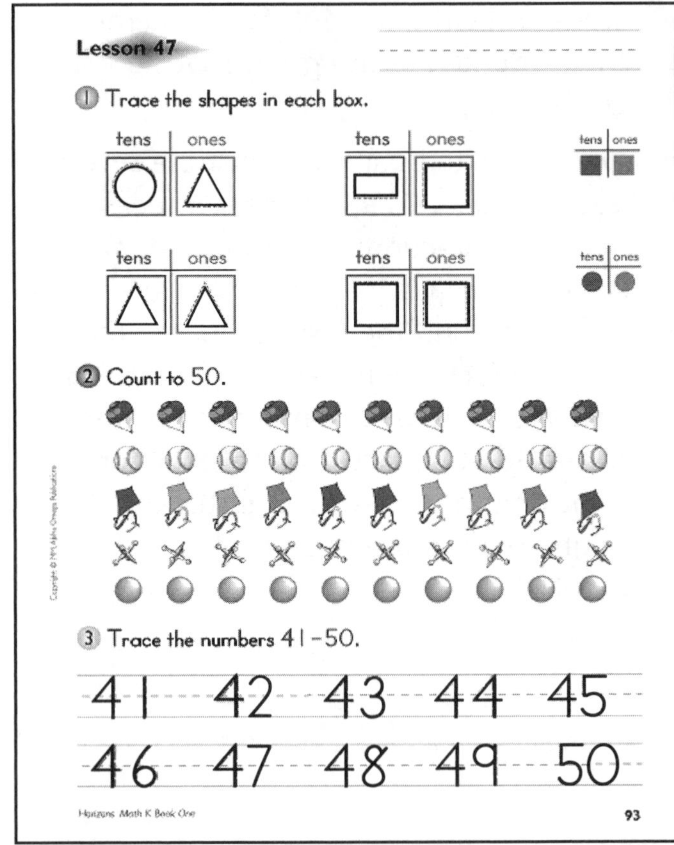

Lesson 47

① Trace the shapes in each box.

tens	ones

② Count to 50.

③ Trace the numbers 41–50.

41 42 43 44 45

46 47 48 49 50

Horizons Math K Book One 93

many ones are in this number (9). Discuss the next number (10). How many places does it take? What is in the tens' place? What is in the ones' place? Read over the instruction with the student(s). Have them trace the shapes to illustrate that different numbers or the same number can be in both the tens' and in the ones' place.

② Count out loud by ones to 70 using the number chart. Have the student(s) count the toys, 1–50, in the activity.

③ Trace 41–50. Remind the student(s) to use good penmanship.

④ Read the instruction and have the student(s) complete the activity.

⑤ On the white board demonstrate several addition facts (1–9) on the number line. Read the directions to the student(s) in Activity ⑤. On the number line have them trace the dotted line for first number in the addition fact. Then have them trace the dotted line for the second. The number the second line points to is the answer. Write the answer to the addition problem. Do the same for the remaining problems.

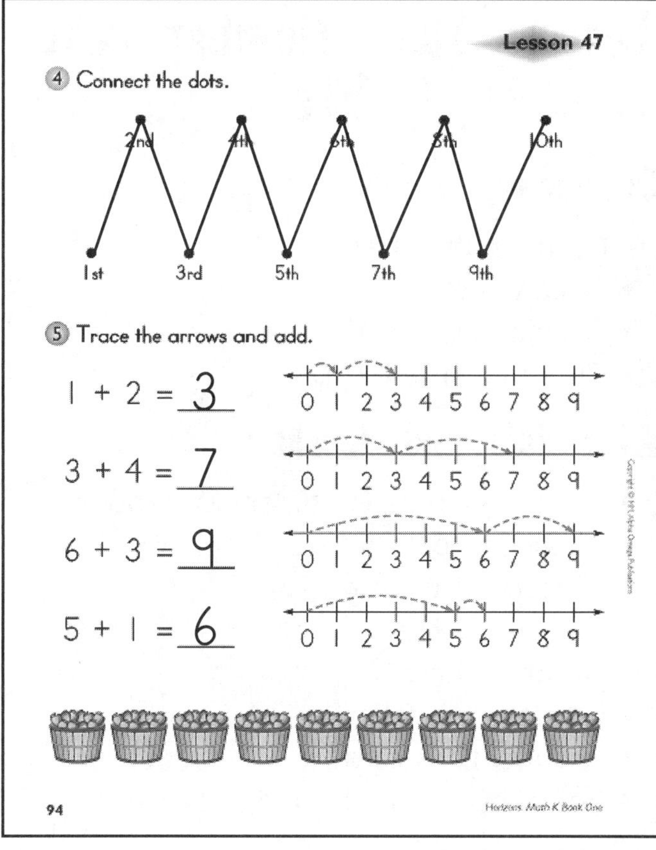

Lesson 48 - Number After 10's

Overview:

- Number after 10's
- Place value 1's
- Ordinals first–tenth
- Count & write by 10's

Materials and Supplies:

- Teacher's Guide & Student Workbook
- White board
- Objects for counters
- Place value chart
- Number chart
- Number line strips
- Number flash cards
- Count by 10's flash cards

Teaching Tips:

Teach number after 1's and 10's.
Review place value.
Teach sequence of events.
Review counting by 10's to 100.
Review oral counting to 70.

Activities:

① The student(s) may refer to the pages in one of their textbooks or a library book to see what number comes after a given number. They should be able to do the activity independently.

Lesson 48

① Write the number after.

9 10 11 12 13 14 15 16 17 18 19

9 10	14 15	18 19
12 13	16 17	10 11

② Trace the numbers.

place value: tens | ones

tens	ones	tens	ones	tens	ones
	0		1		2
	3		4		5
	6		7		8
			9		

Horizons Math K Book One — 95

② Before doing this activity, discuss the number of places a single-digit numeral (such as 4) takes. Using the numbers chart, ask what the largest number is that takes only one place (9). Discuss how many ones in this number (9). Discuss the next number (10). How many places does it take? What is in the tens' place? What is in the ones' place? Read over the instructions with the student(s). Trace the numbers 0–9 that can be in the ones' place.

③ To aid in the teaching of the sequence of events, ask the student(s) which is the correct sequence. Do they get dressed and then get out of bed or do they get out of bed and then get dressed? Do they put their shirt on and then their coat or do they put their coat on and then their shirt? Do they drink their milk and then pour it or do they pour their milk and then drink it? Have the student(s) look at the activity. Ask them to point to the picture that comes first and circle it. Then have them point to the picture that comes last. Now let them tell you the sequence that the three pictures should be in.

④ Count by tens to 100 as preparation for this activity. The student(s) should count as they trace the numbers.

⑤ Read the instruction and allow the students to work independently.

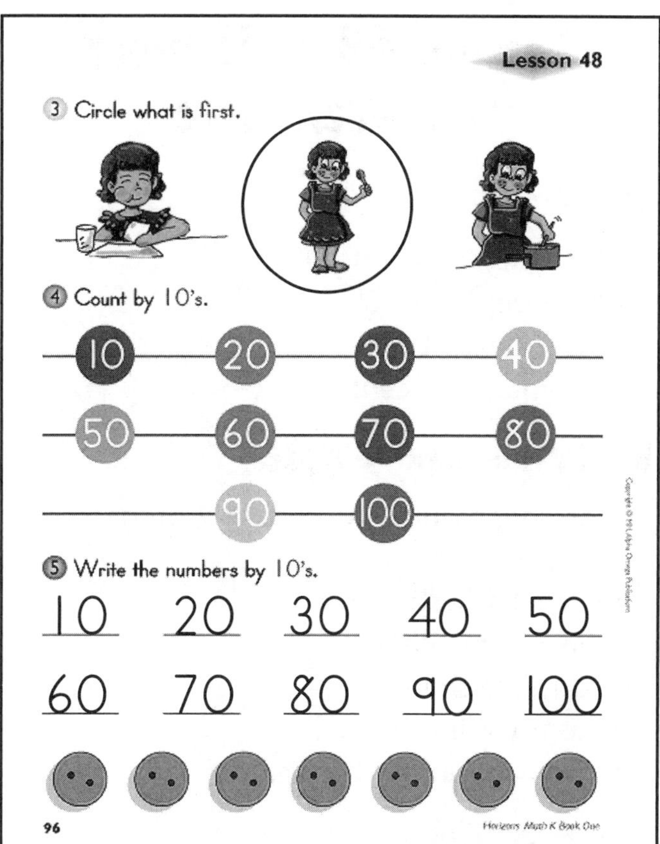

Lesson 49 - Number Between 40's

Overview:

- Number between 40's
- Number after 10's
- Place value 1's
- Ordinals first–tenth

Materials and Supplies:

- Teacher's Guide & Student Workbook
- White board
- Number flash cards
- Place value chart
- Number chart
- Number line strips
- Ordinal number flash cards

Teaching Tips:

Teach number between 40's.
Review number after 1's and 10's.
Review place value.
Review ordinal numbers.
Review oral counting to 70.

Activities:

① Choose three consecutive whole number flash cards 39–50. Arrange the cards out of order. Have the student(s) put them in correct order. Repeat this four times with different sets of three numbers. Read the instruction and have the student(s) complete the activity.

② Drill number after by holding up a flash card and asking the student(s) to say the next number. The student(s) may refer to the pages in one of their textbooks or a library book to see what number comes after a given number. They should be able to do the activity independently.

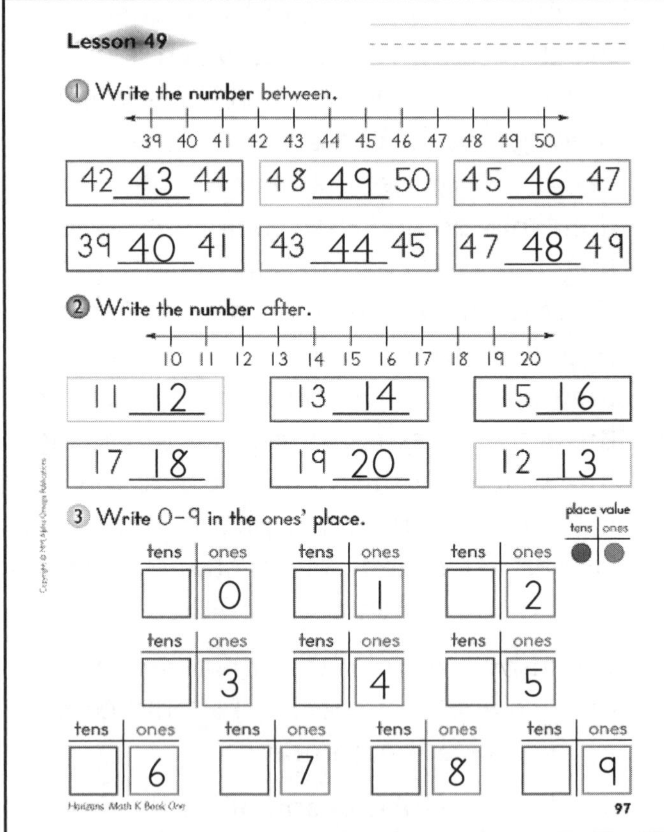
Lesson 49

① Write the number between.

39 40 41 42 43 44 45 46 47 48 49 50

42 43 44	48 49 50	45 46 47
39 40 41	43 44 45	47 48 49

② Write the number after.

10 11 12 13 14 15 16 17 18 19 20

11 12	13 14	15 16
17 18	19 20	12 13

③ Write 0–9 in the ones' place.

place value: tens | ones

tens	ones	tens	ones	tens	ones
	0		1		2
	3		4		5

tens	ones	tens	ones	tens	ones	tens	ones
	6		7		8		9

Horizons Math K Book One 97

③ Before doing this activity, discuss the number of places a single-digit numeral (such as 4) takes. Using the numbers chart, ask what the largest number is that takes only one place (9). Discuss how many ones in this number (9). Discuss the next number (10). How many places does it take? What is in the tens' place? What is in the ones' place? Read over the instruction with the student(s). Write the numbers 0–9 in the ones' place.

④ Review with ordinal number flash cards. Read each instruction and have the student(s) circle their choice in each row.

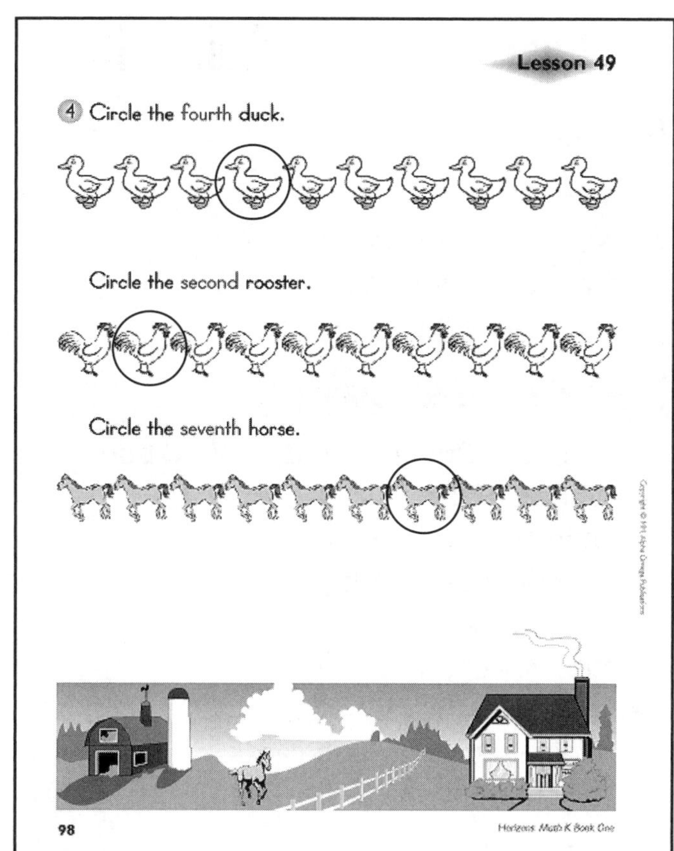

Lesson 50 - Ruler 1"

Overview:

- Ruler 1″
- Number between 40's
- Ordinals first–tenth
- Place value 1's

Materials and Supplies:

- Teacher's Guide & Student Workbook
- White board
- Objects for counters
- Number flash cards
- Place value chart
- Number chart
- Ruler with inches
- Ordinal number flash cards
- Tally mark flash cards

Teaching Tips:

Teach inches.
Review number between 40's.
Review place value.
Review ordinal numbers.
Review oral counting to 70.

Activities:

① Only 1 inch markings will be learned this year. Addition marks will be pictured in the activities to provide a more realistic looking ruler. When measuring with a ruler, always put one end of the object at zero. Where the other end stops is the length of the object expressed in inches. Have the student place their finger on the tip of the pencil and slide up to the ruler to see that the pencil is 5 inches long. Then have them place their finger on the end of the eraser and slide up to the ruler to give them the number to write in the blank. Do the same for the crayon. Remember, measurements are always labeled with the unit of measure.

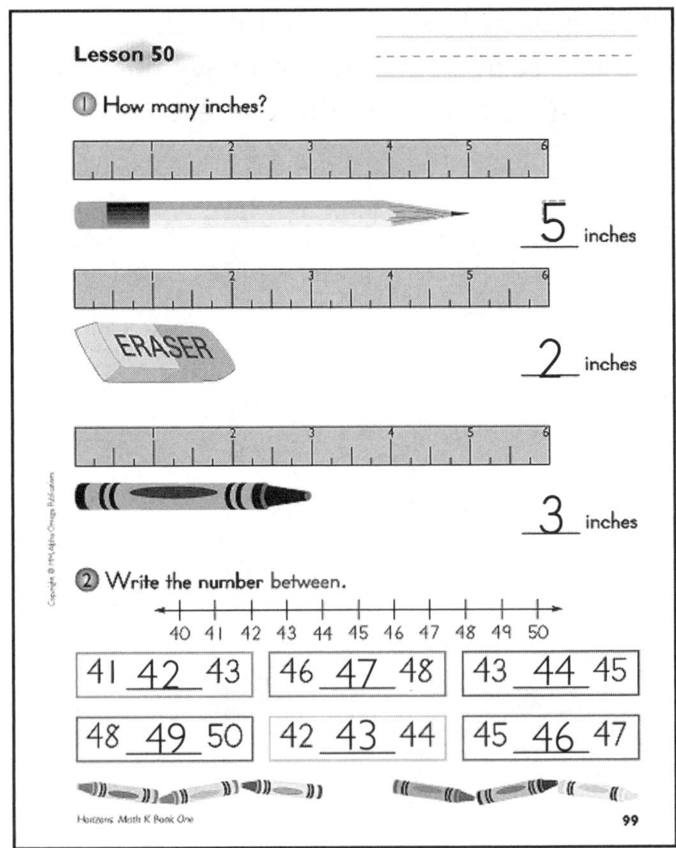
Lesson 50

① How many inches?

5 inches

2 inches

3 inches

② Write the number between.

40 41 42 43 44 45 46 47 48 49 50

41 42 43 | 46 47 48 | 43 44 45

48 49 50 | 42 43 44 | 45 46 47

Horizons Math K Book One 99

② Choose three consecutive whole-number flash cards 39–50. Arrange the cards out of order. Have the student(s) put them in correct order. Repeat this four times with different sets of three numbers. Read the instruction and have the student(s) complete the activity.

③ Before doing this activity, discuss the number of places a single-digit numeral (such as 6) takes. Using the numbers chart, ask what the largest number is that takes only one place (9). Discuss how many ones in this number (9). Discuss the next number (10). How many places does it take? What is in the tens' place? What is in the ones' place? Read over the instruction with the student(s). Count the objects and write the number in the ones' place.

④ Review with ordinal number flash cards. Read each instruction and have the student(s) circle their choice in each row.

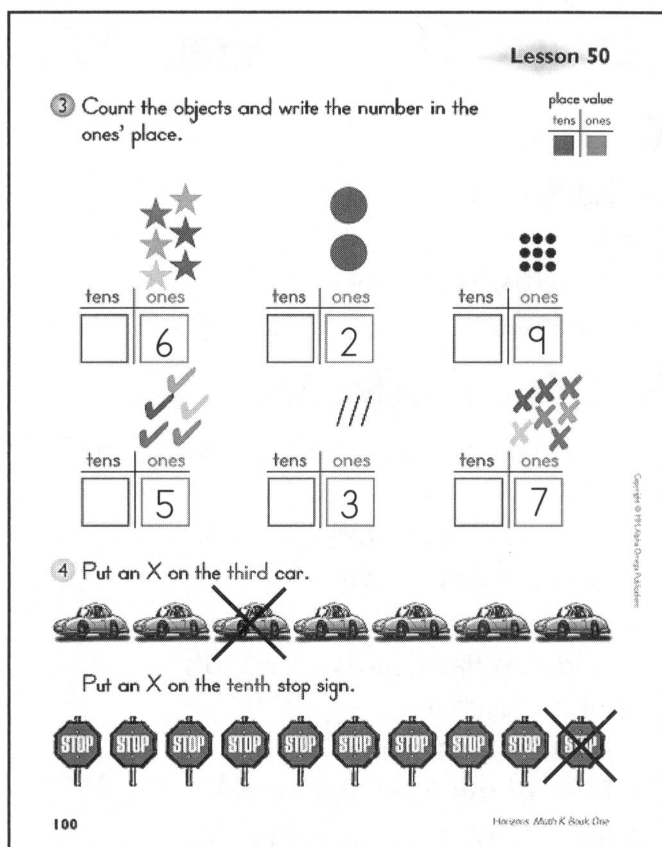

Lesson 51 - Addition 10's

Overview:

- Addition 10's
- Ruler 1″
- Patterns, sequence
- Calendar

Materials and Supplies:

- Teacher's Guide & Student Workbook
- White board
- Objects for counters
- Number flash cards
- Ruler – inches
- Addition flash cards 1's & 10's
- Number chart
- Number line strips
- Days of the week flash cards
- Months of the year flash cards
- Calendar

Teaching Tips:

Teach addition on number line 10's.
Review inches.
Review patterns & sequence.
Review calendar.
Review oral counting to 70.

Activities:

① In preparation for this activity use a number line on the white board to demonstrate several addition facts. Example: 13 + 2 = 15. Using a number line, let the student(s) find the answer to several addition facts 10–19. Go to the first number in the addition fact. Count the number of marks needed for the second number. The mark you end on is the answer to the addition fact. Guide the student(s) through the first problem. Allow them to finish the rest of the activity independently, helping only those who need it.

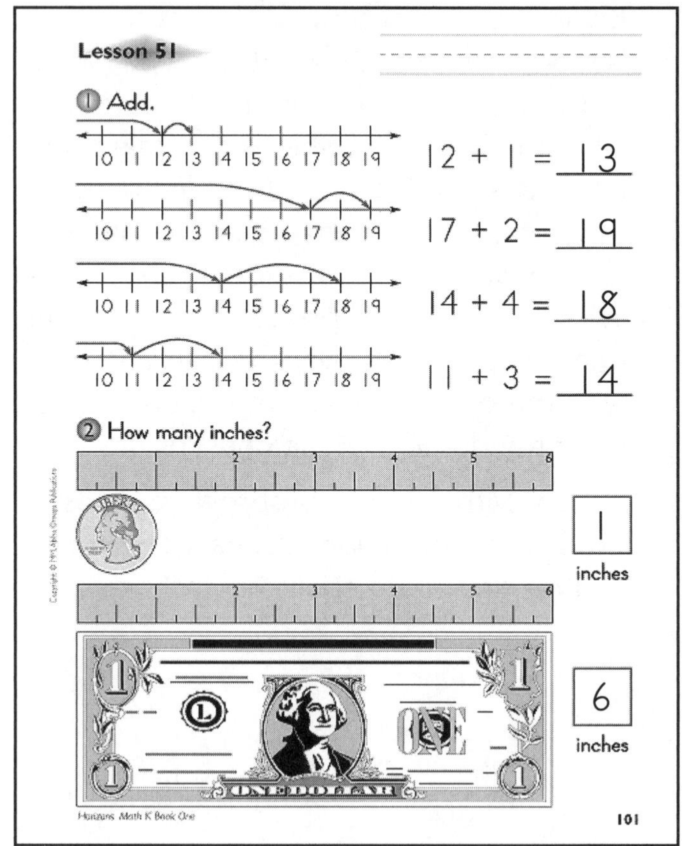

② Before starting this activity, talk with the student(s) about the inch ruler, "What is it used for?" "How long is an inch?" "What do you measure with an inch ruler?" You wouldn't use it to measure the distance from home to the grocery store, but you would use it to find out how long your pencil is. Have the student(s) trace with their finger from the edge of the quarter up to the ruler. This is the length of the quarter. Allow the student(s) to complete the remainder of the activity with as little help as possible.

③ Use shape flash cards to go through a pattern of alternating shapes and ask what comes next in the pattern. Point out the dotted lines that divide parts of the activity. Go through the items in the first box and have the student(s) circle their answer. Do the same for the second box.

④ Go over the months of the year in order with the student(s) using a calendar. Discuss how many days are in each month. Recite with the student(s):

Thirty days hath September,
April, June, and November.
All the rest have thirty-one
Except February alone
Which has twenty-eight
Until leap year gives it twenty-nine.

Have them repeat the first two lines several times. Then go through the verse again. Have them complete the calendar.

Lesson 51

③ What comes next?

④ Complete the calendar.

November

Sunday	Monday	Tuesday	Wednesday	Thursday	Friday	Saturday
			1	2	3	4
5	6	7	8	9	10	11
12	13	14	15	16	17	18
19	20	21	22	23	24	25
26	27	28	29	30		

102 Horizons Math K Book One

Lesson 52 - Dollar Bill

Overview:

- Dollar bill
- Addition 10–19
- More & less
- Dimes & pennies

Material and Supplies:

- Teacher's Guide & Student Workbook
- White board
- Objects for counters
- Number flash cards
- Addition flash cards 1's & 10's
- Dollar bill, dimes, pennies
- Number chart
- Number line strips

Teaching Tips:

Teach dollar bills.
Review addition on number line 10's.
Review more and less.
Review dimes & pennies.
Review oral counting to 70.

Activities:

① Give each student a play money dollar bill. Discuss the color, picture on the front (George Washington), and the word "ONE" on the back with the student(s). Tell them that one dollar can be written as cents (100¢) or it can be written as a dollar ($1). The number by the $ sign means one dollar. Have the student(s) count the dollar bills in the activity and write the value. Encourage the student(s) to be conscious of prices on sales receipts which are printed with the dollar sign and the decimal point separating the dollars and cents.

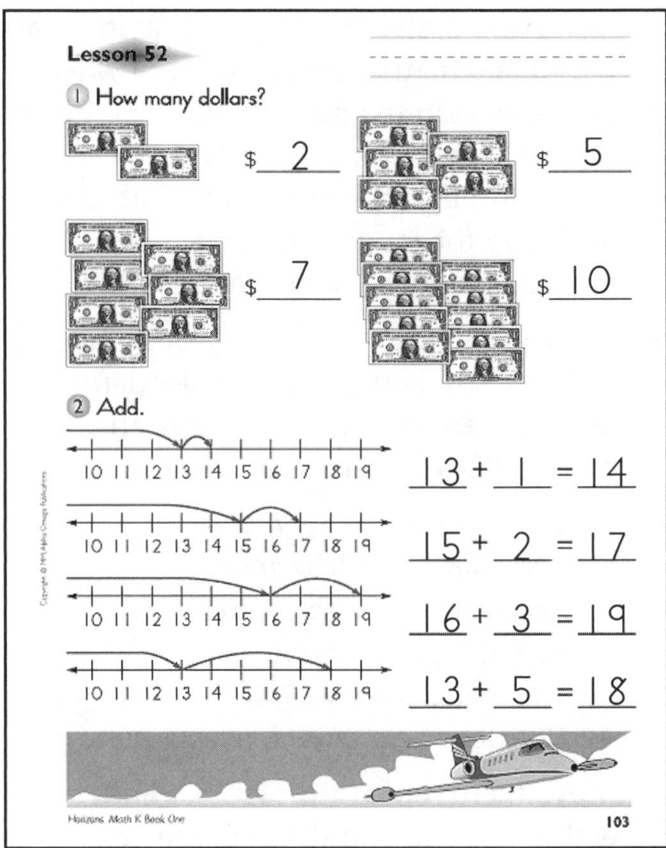

② In preparation for this activity use a number line (0–19) on the white board to demonstrate several addition facts. Example: 15 + 2 = 17. Using the number line, let the student(s) find the answer to several addition facts 10–19. Go to the first number in the addition fact. From that number count the number of marks needed for the number being added. The mark you end on is the answer to the addition fact. Guide the student(s) through the first problem. The line has been shortened to save space. Allow them to finish the rest of the activity independently, helping only those who need it.

③ Before this activity ask a student to choose two number flash cards, 1–20. Locate the two numbers on a number line. Ask a student to tell you which is the greater number. Point out that the larger number is to the right on the number line. Repeat the activity several times. Have the student(s) count the items in Activity ③ and circle which is more. Have them locate the numbers on a number line if they have problems picking the one that is more.

④ Show the students how this activity has the same addition facts as Activity ②. All of the problems are 10 plus something. Show them how to do this with a number line strip. Since they are adding (counting) money, the answer needs to have the ¢ sign.

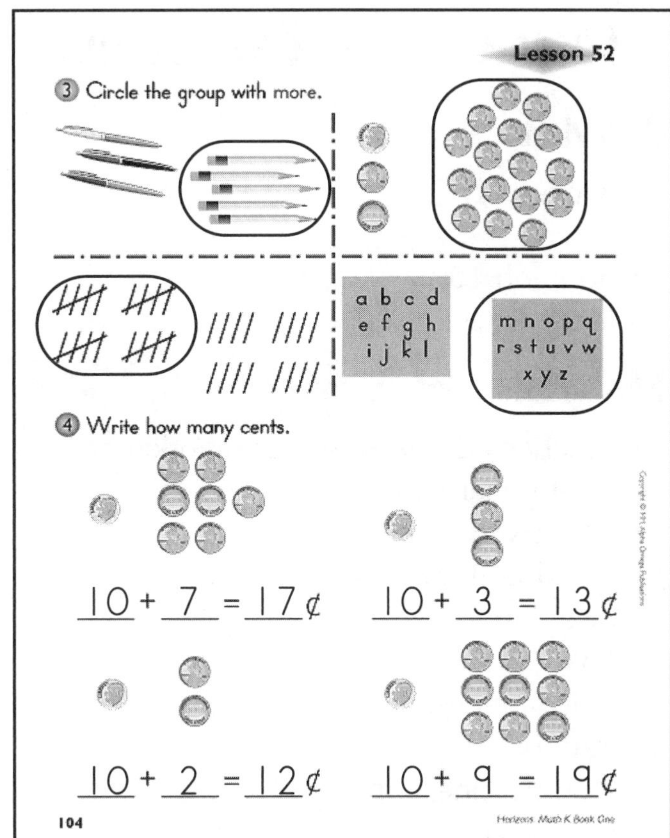
Lesson 52

③ Circle the group with more.

a b c d
e f g h
i j k l

m n o p q
r s t u v w
x y z

④ Write how many cents.

10 + 7 = 17¢ 10 + 3 = 13¢

10 + 2 = 12¢ 10 + 9 = 19¢

104 Horizons Math K Book One

Lesson 53 - Bar Graph

Overview:

- Bar graph
- Ruler 1″
- Addition 10's
- More & less

Materials and Supplies:

- Teacher's Guide & Student Workbook
- White board
- Objects for counters
- Number flash cards
- Addition flash cards 1's & 10's
- Shape flash cards
- Ruler – inches
- Number chart
- Number line strips

Teaching Tips:

Teach bar graph.
Review inches.
Review addition on number line 10's.
Review more and less.
Review oral counting to 70.

Activities:

① Put a completed bar graph on the white board. Tell the student(s) that a bar graph is used to help us count things. Have the student(s) look at the bar graph. Ask them why it is called a bar graph. Help them see that the bars picture the number of objects. Tell them that the bar graph in this activity is going to help them count how many stars, rectangles, letter (b)s and number (3)s they have. If there are 4 blocks colored above the star, that would mean that they have 4 stars. If there are 2 blocks colored in then they have 2 objects, etc. Have them color the same number of blocks in the graph for each of the objects they count.

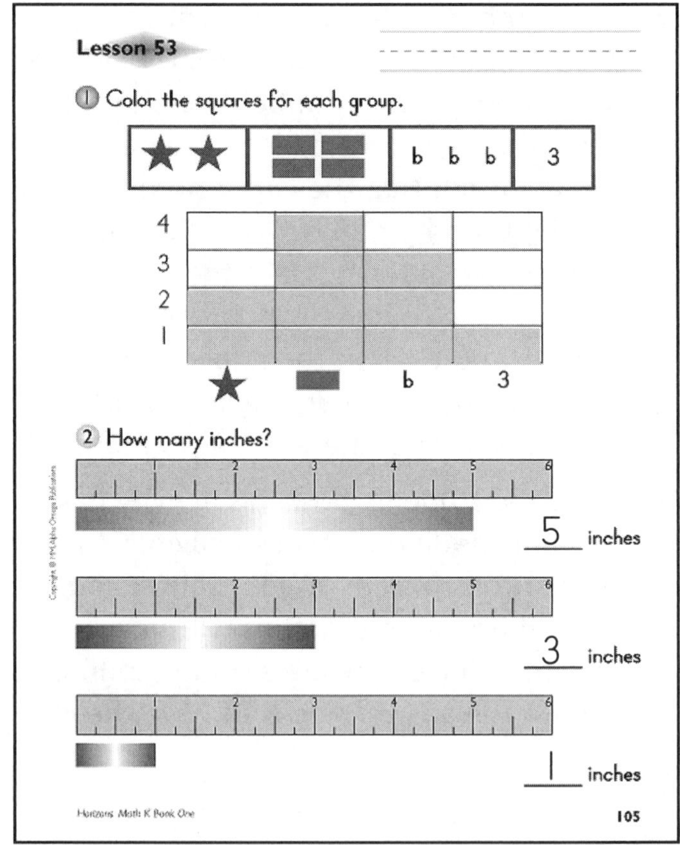

② Have the student(s) trace with their finger from the right edge of the green strip up to the ruler. This is the length of the green strip. Allow the student(s) to complete the remainder of the activity with as little help as possible.

③ Demonstrate adding several combination of the 10's family on the white board. Instruct the student(s) to go to the first number in the addition fact. Count the number of marks needed for the second number. The mark you end on is the answer to the addition fact. Guide the student(s) through the first problem. Allow them to finish the rest of the activity independently, helping only those who need it.

④ Before doing this activity the student(s) orally identify two numerals on the number line. State which is less and which is greater or more. Repeat the activity several times. Have the student(s) count the items in Activity ④ and put an X on the set that is less.

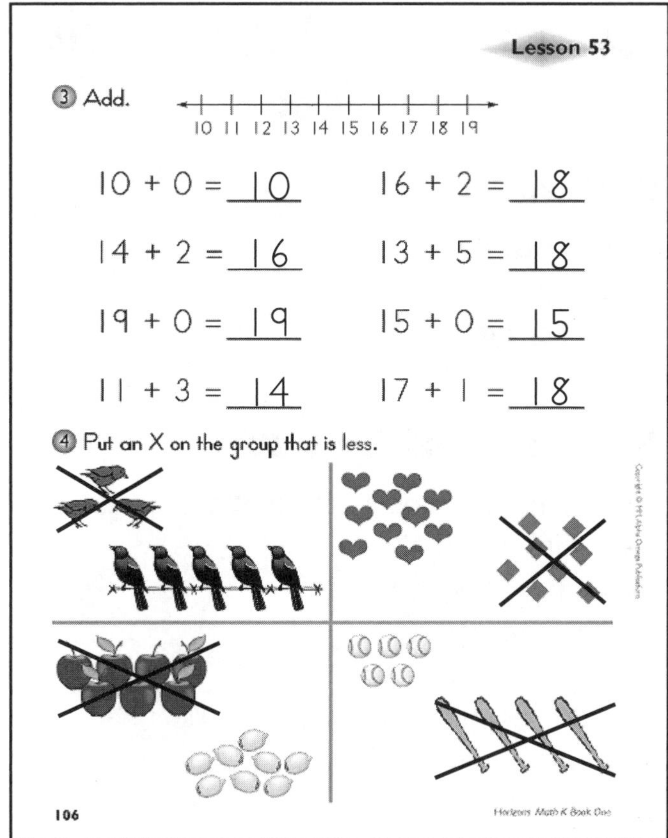

Lesson 54 - Days of the Week

Overview:

- Days of the week
- Bar graph
- Dollar bill
- Addition 10's

Materials and Supplies:

- Teacher's Guide & Student Workbook
- White board
- Objects for counters
- Number chart
- Number flash cards
- Addition flash cards 1's & 10's
- Dollars
- Crayons
- Calendar
- Months flash cards
- Days of the week flash cards
- Ordinal number flash cards
- Dominos & domino flash cards

Teaching Tips:

Teach calendar and days of the week.
Review ordinal numbers.
Review bar graph.
Review dollars.
Review addition on number line 10's.
Teach oral counting to 80.

Activities:

① Recite *Thirty Days Hath September* and the days of the week in order. Using the calendar, discuss with the student(s) what day of the week certain dates fall on. Look at the month given in the student activity. Read the instructions out loud and guide the student(s) through the activity.

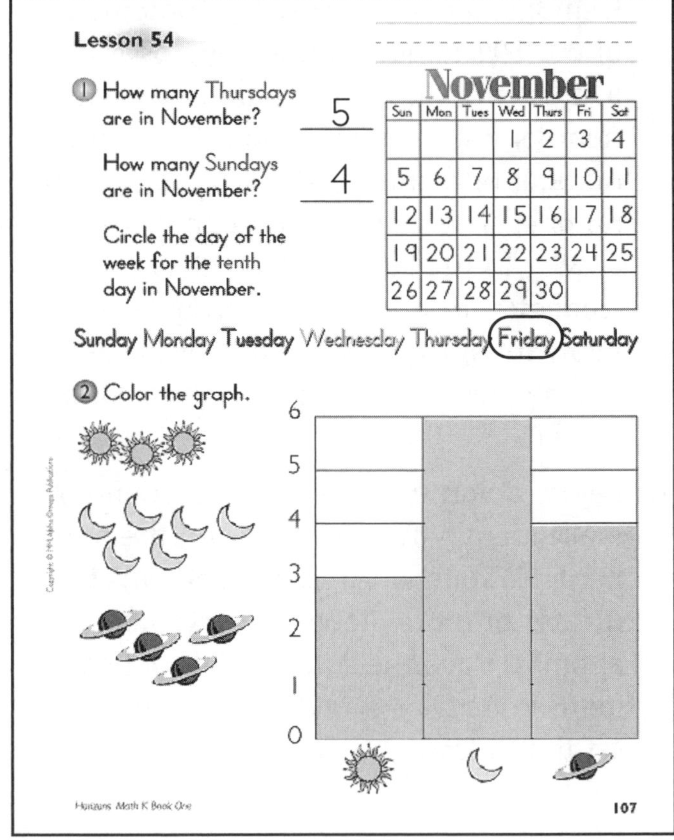

Lesson 54

① How many Thursdays are in November? 5

How many Sundays are in November? 4

Circle the day of the week for the tenth day in November.

November

Sun	Mon	Tues	Wed	Thurs	Fri	Sat
			1	2	3	4
5	6	7	8	9	10	11
12	13	14	15	16	17	18
19	20	21	22	23	24	25
26	27	28	29	30		

Sunday Monday Tuesday Wednesday Thursday (Friday) Saturday

② Color the graph.

Horizons Math K Book One 107

② When starting this activity, tell the student(s) a bar graph is used to help us count things. Have a student count the suns. Have another student count the moons. Have them color three blue blocks above the sun in the bar graph. Have them color 6 green blocks above the moon in the bar graph. Allow the student(s) to complete the last part of the graph for the planets on their own.

③ Give each student a play money dollar bill. Review the color, picture on the front (George Washington), and the word "ONE" on the back with the student(s). Have the student(s) count the dollar bills in the activity and write the value.

④ Review by adding several combination of the 10's family on the white board. Instruct the student(s) to go to the first number in the addition fact. Count the number of marks needed for the second number. The mark you end on is the answer to the addition fact. Discuss with the student(s) the fact that any number added to zero is equal to the same number. Then discuss the fact that the number that comes after a given number is equal to the given number plus 1 (e.g. the number that comes after 15 is equal to 15 + 1). Guide the student(s) through the first problem. Allow them to finish the rest of the activity independently, helping only those who need it.

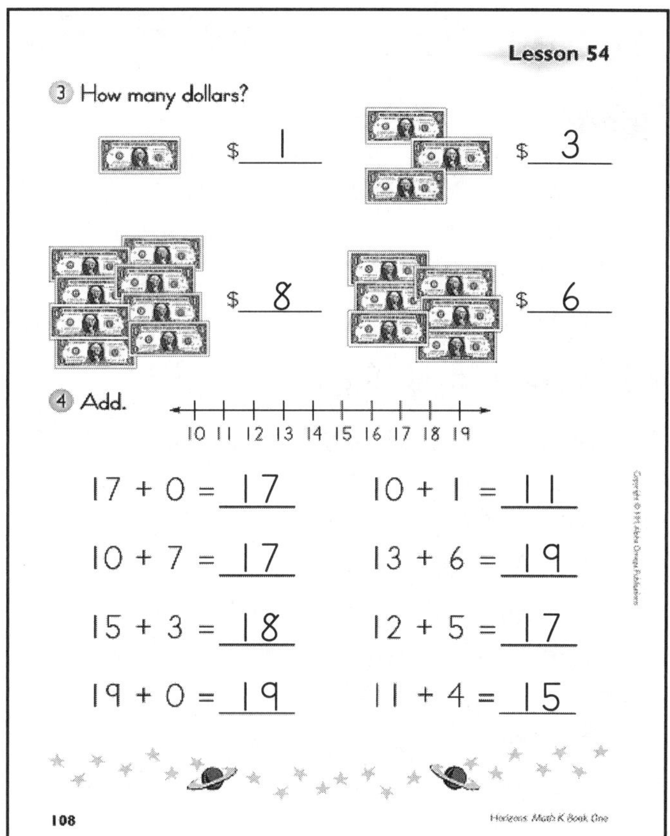

Lesson 54

③ How many dollars?

$ 1 $ 3

$ 8 $ 6

④ Add.

10 11 12 13 14 15 16 17 18 19

17 + 0 = 17 10 + 1 = 11

10 + 7 = 17 13 + 6 = 19

15 + 3 = 18 12 + 5 = 17

19 + 0 = 19 11 + 4 = 15

108 Horizons Math K Book One

Lesson 55 - Count by 5's

Overview:

- Count by 5's
- Dollar bill
- Addition 10's
- Bar graph

Materials and Supplies:

- Teacher's Guide & Student Workbook
- White board
- Objects for counters
- Number flash cards
- Addition flash cards 1's & 10's
- Pennies & nickels
- Number chart
- Crayons
- Worksheet 36

Teaching Tips:

Teach counting by 5's.
Review dollars.
Review addition on number line 10's.
Review bar graph.
Review oral counting to 80.

Activities:

① Count out loud by fives to 100 using a number chart. Discuss with the student(s) that counting by fives means to count over five places on the number chart, to count every fifth number, or to add five to each number. Repeat the activity by having the student(s) follow along with the chart in Activity ①. Instruct them to trace every 5th number.

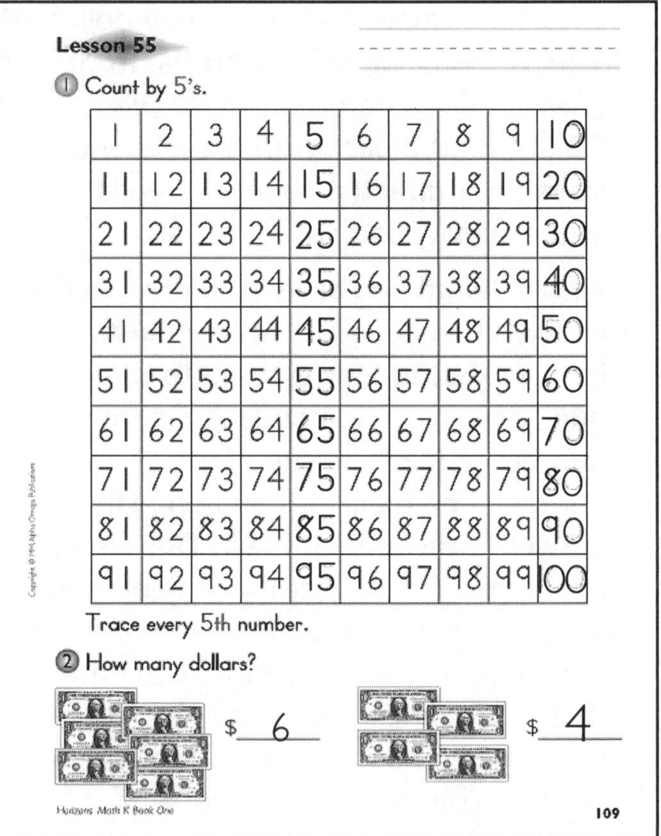

Lesson 55

① Count by 5's.

1	2	3	4	5	6	7	8	9	10
11	12	13	14	15	16	17	18	19	20
21	22	23	24	25	26	27	28	29	30
31	32	33	34	35	36	37	38	39	40
41	42	43	44	45	46	47	48	49	50
51	52	53	54	55	56	57	58	59	60
61	62	63	64	65	66	67	68	69	70
71	72	73	74	75	76	77	78	79	80
81	82	83	84	85	86	87	88	89	90
91	92	93	94	95	96	97	98	99	100

Trace every 5th number.

② How many dollars?

$ 6 $ 4

Horizons Math K Book One 109

② Have the student(s) count the dollar bills in the activity and write the value.

③ Review by adding several combinations of the 10's family on the white board. Instruct the student(s) to go to the first number in the addition fact. Count the number of marks needed for the second number. The mark you end on is the answer to the addition fact. Review with the student(s) the fact that when zero is added to number the answer is equal to the same number. Then discuss the fact that the number that comes after a given number is equal to the given number plus 1 (e.g. the number that comes after 11 is equal to 11 + 1). Guide the student(s) through the first problem. Allow them to finish the rest of the activity independently.

④ Tell the student(s) that a bar graph is used to help us count things. Have the student(s) look at the bar graph in the activity. Ask them why it is called a bar graph. Help them see that the bars picture the number of objects. Tell them that this bar graph is going to help them count how many curve signs, stop signs and Route 66 signs they have. If there are 5 blocks above the curve sign, then they have 5 curve signs. If there are 2 blocks then they have 2 objects, etc. Read the first sign to them. Ask them to count the blocks for each sign represented and write the number on the blank. Then read the second sign. Repeat this for the curve sign.

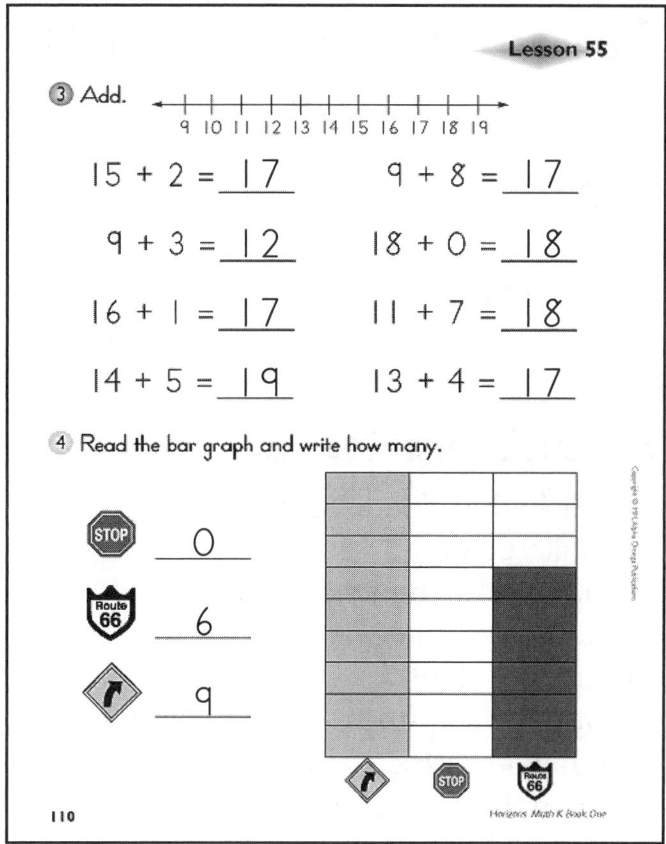

Lesson 55

③ Add.

9 10 11 12 13 14 15 16 17 18 19

15 + 2 = 17   9 + 8 = 17

9 + 3 = 12   18 + 0 = 18

16 + 1 = 17   11 + 7 = 18

14 + 5 = 19   13 + 4 = 17

④ Read the bar graph and write how many.

STOP 0

Route 66 6

9

110   Horizons Math K Book One

Lesson 56 - Number after 20's

Overview:

- Number after 20's
- Count by 5's
- Addition 10's
- Dollar

Materials and Supplies:

- Teacher's Guide & Student Workbook
- White board
- Objects for counters
- Number flash cards
- Number chart
- Number line strips
- Addition flash cards 1's & 10's
- Count by 5's flash cards
- Dollar bills

Teaching Tips:

Teach number after 20's.
Review counting by 5's.
Review dollars.
Review addition on number line 10's.
Review oral counting to 80.

Activities:

① The student(s) may refer to the pages in a book, a number line or to a number chart to see what number comes after a given number. They should be able to do the activity independently.

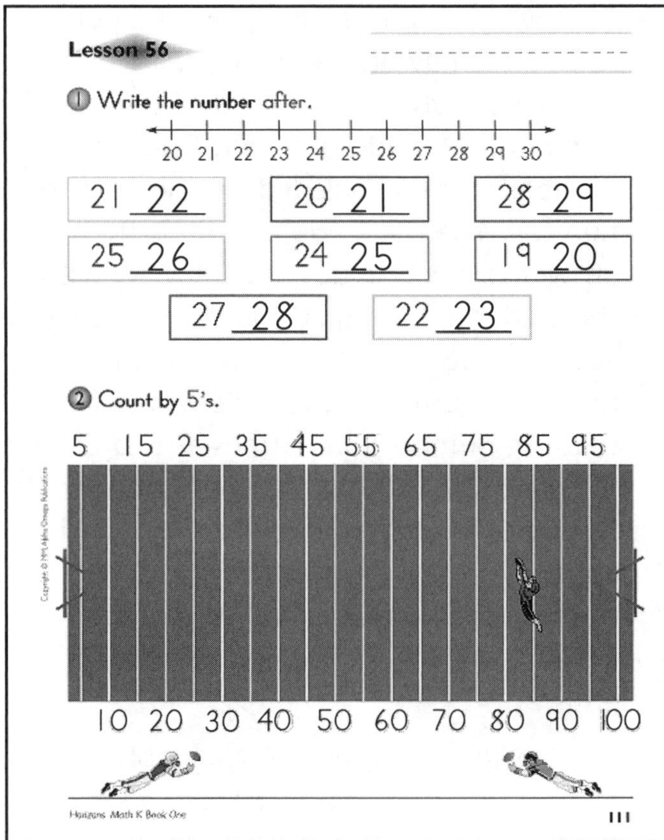

② Count out loud with the student(s) by 5's to 100. Have them trace and count by 5's in Activity ② by tracing the numbers from the top of the football field to the bottom.

③ Review by adding several combination of the 10's family on the white board. Instruct the student(s) to go to the first number in the addition fact. Count the number of marks needed for the second number. The mark you end on is the answer to the addition fact. Review with the student(s) the fact that when zero is added to number the answer is equal to the same number. This activity is vertical addition. Remind them that the bar under the problem is used in place of the equal sign. Guide the student(s) through the first problem. Allow them to finish the rest of the activity independently.

④ Have the student(s) count the dollar bills in the activity and draw a line to match the value.

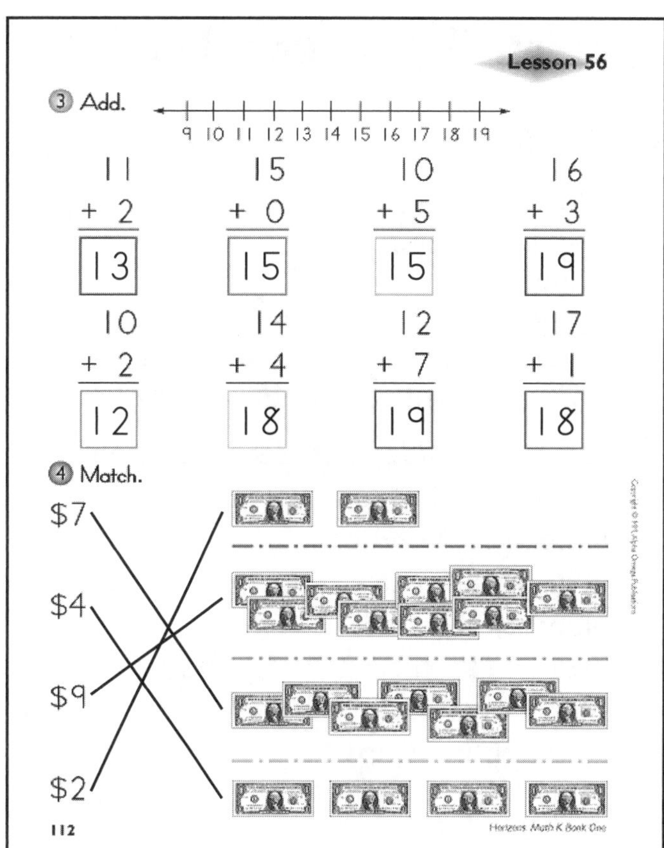

Lesson 57 - Count to 60

Overview:

- Count to 60
- Number after 20's
- Count by 5's
- Horizontal addition 10's

Materials and Supplies:

- Teacher's Guide & Student Workbook
- White board
- Objects for counters
- Number flash cards
- Number chart
- Addition flash cards 1's & 10's
- Count by 5's flash cards
- Number line strips

Teaching Tips:

Teach counting items to 60.
Review number after 20's.
Review counting by 5's.
Review dollars.
Review addition on number line 10's.
Review oral counting to 80.

Activities:

① Count out loud by ones to 60 using the number chart. Have the student(s) count the flowers in the activity.

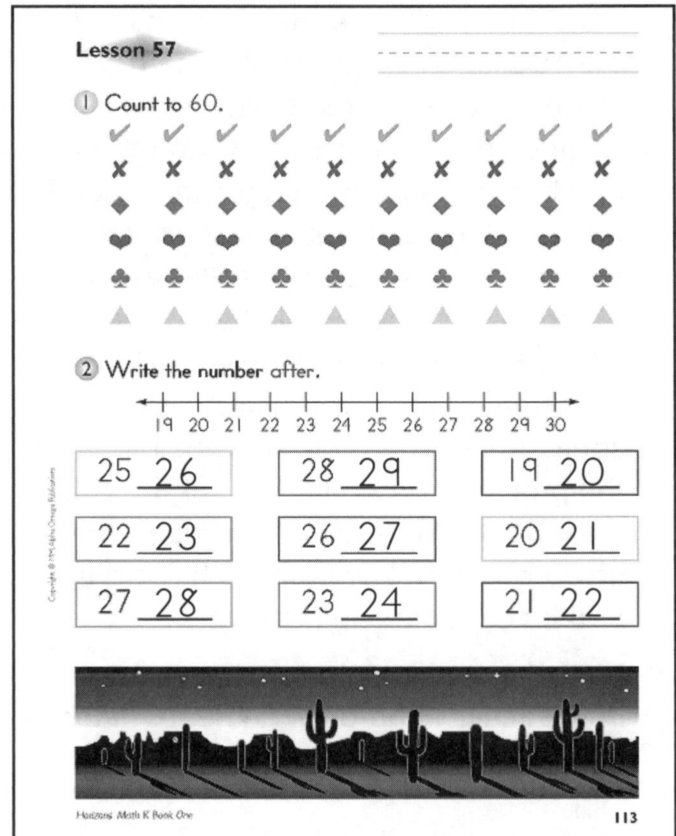

Lesson 57

① Count to 60.

② Write the number after.

19 20 21 22 23 24 25 26 27 28 29 30

25 26	28 29	19 20
22 23	26 27	20 21
27 28	23 24	21 22

Horizons Math K Book One 113

② The student(s) may refer to the pages in a book, a number line or to a number chart to see what number comes after a given number. They should be able to do the activity independently.

③ Count out loud with the student(s) by 5's to 100. Have them count by 5's in Activity ③ by writing the missing numbers. Display the 5's flash cards or a number chart for them to refer to.

④ On the white board demonstrate several addition fact (10–19) on the number line. Do some samples of adding a number to 9. This may be confusing for them since they count past 10 when they add. Read the directions to the student(s) for Activity ④. Have them count on the number line to find the first number in the addition fact. Then count to find the second and write that number as the answer to the addition fact. Do the same for the remaining problems. Some student(s) might need to use counters for this activity.

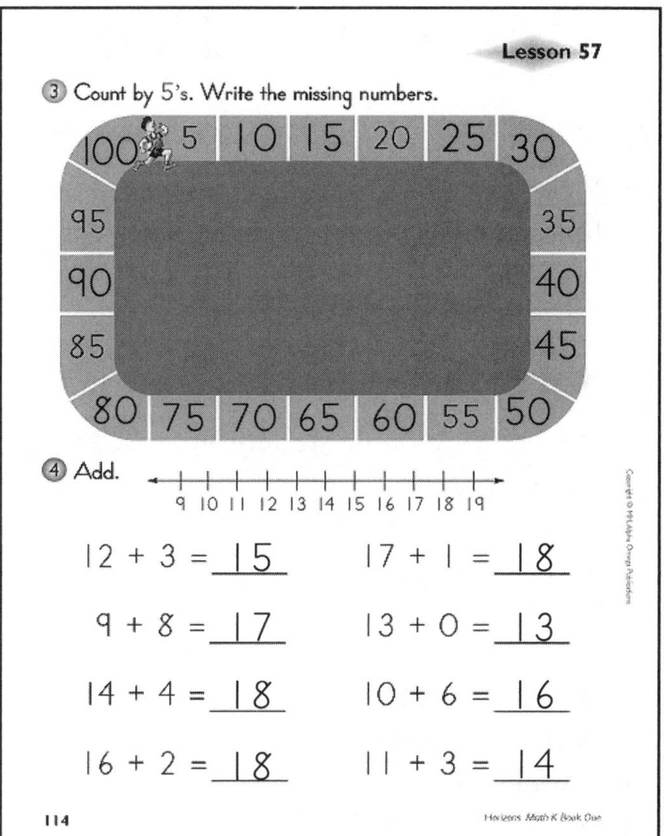
Lesson 57

③ Count by 5's. Write the missing numbers.

100 5 10 15 20 25 30 35 40 45 50 55 60 65 70 75 80 85 90 95

④ Add.

9 10 11 12 13 14 15 16 17 18 19

12 + 3 = 15 17 + 1 = 18

9 + 8 = 17 13 + 0 = 13

14 + 4 = 18 10 + 6 = 16

16 + 2 = 18 11 + 3 = 14

114 Horizons Math K Book One

Lesson 58 - Nickels

Overview:

- Nickels
- Trace & write 50–59
- Time – hour
- Vertical addition 10's

Materials and Supplies:

- Teacher's Guide & Student Workbook
- White board
- Objects for counters
- Number flash cards
- Number chart
- Addition flash cards 1's & 10's
- Nickels & pennies
- Number line strips
- Model clocks
- Worksheet 17 & 27

Teaching Tips:

Teach nickels.
Teach writing numbers 50's.
Review counting items to 60.
Review time – hour.
Review addition on number line 10's.
Review oral counting to 80.

Activities:

① Use play money for the student(s) to see the front and back of the nickel. Discuss the color of the nickel, whose picture is on the front of the nickel (Thomas Jefferson), what is on the back of a nickel (Monticello, Thomas Jefferson's home), and what is the value of a nickel. Point out the two ways to write a nickel's name. 5¢ or 5 cents. Quickly review counting by fives. Put several different sets of nickels on the flannel board or white board and have the student(s) count them by fives to learn their value. Do the first problem together. They should be able to complete the activity on their own.

② Trace and write the 50's family. Remind the student(s) to use good spacing and penmanship.

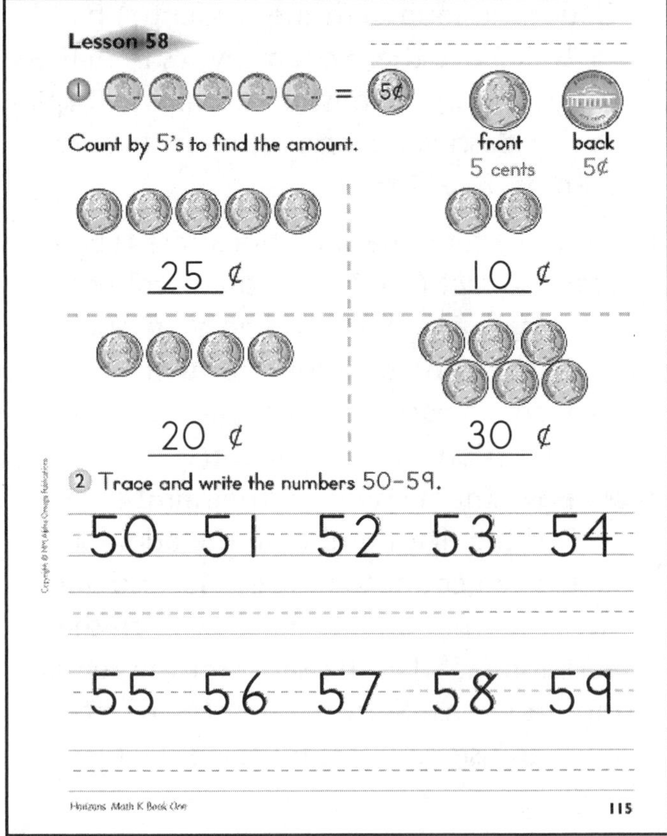

③ Each student will need a small clock model. Have them put the long hand (minute hand) on twelve. As you call out or write on the white board several hour times, have them put the short hand (hour hand) pointing to the correct number. Do a similar activity with a digital clock model. Review writing just the hour number when "o'clock" is used.

④ On the white board demonstrate several addition facts (10–19) on the number line. Do some samples of adding a number to 9. This may be confusing for them since they count past 10 when they add. Read the direction to the student(s) for Activity ④. Have them count on the number line to find the first number in the addition fact. Then count to find the second and write that number as the answer to the addition fact. Do the same for the remaining problems. Some student(s) might need to use counters for this activity.

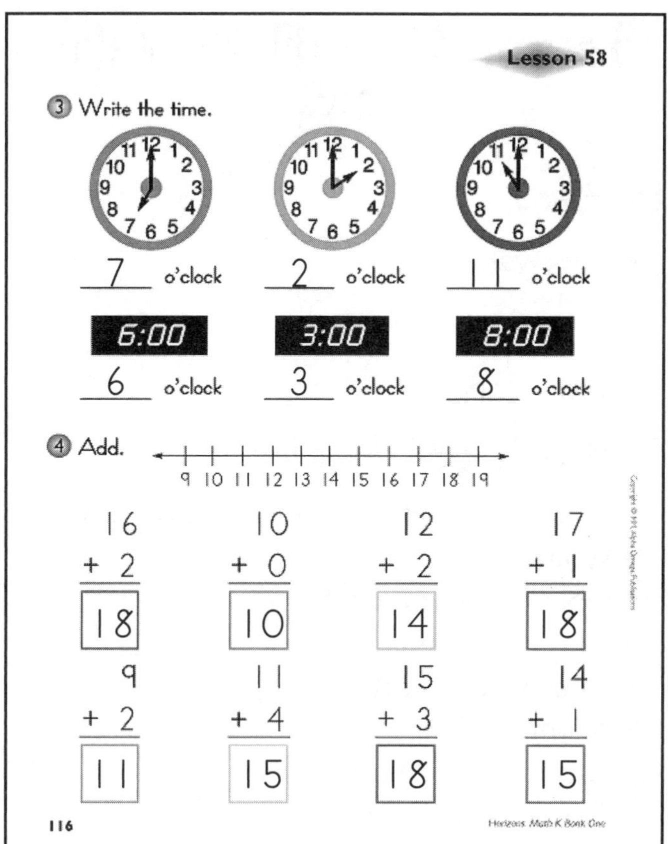

Lesson 58

③ Write the time.

7 o'clock   2 o'clock   11 o'clock

6:00 — 6 o'clock   3:00 — 3 o'clock   8:00 — 8 o'clock

④ Add.

9 10 11 12 13 14 15 16 17 18 19

16 + 2 = 18	10 + 0 = 10	12 + 2 = 14	17 + 1 = 18
9 + 2 = 11	11 + 4 = 15	15 + 3 = 18	14 + 1 = 15

116   Horizons Math K Book One

Lesson 59 - Place Value 10's

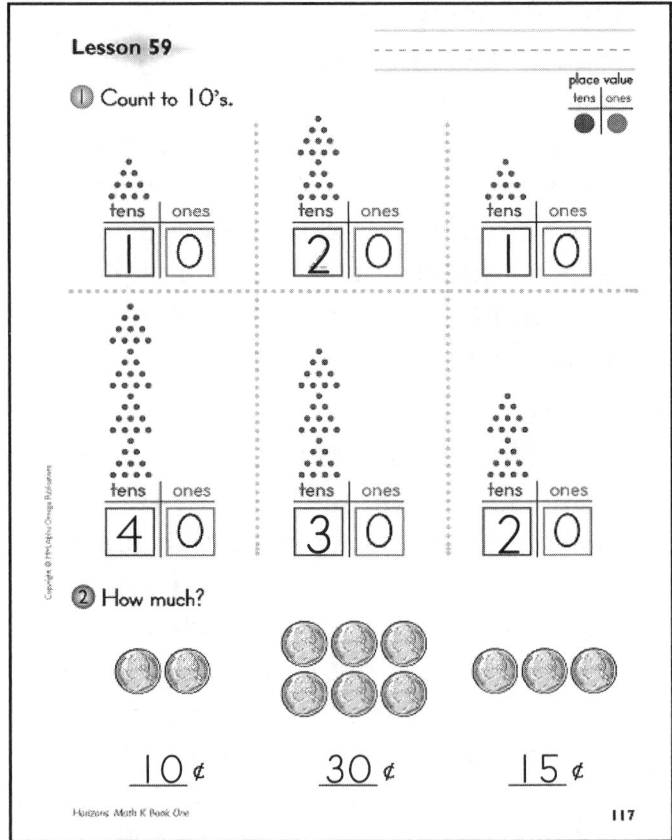
Lesson 59

① Count to 10's.

place value
tens | ones

tens	ones
1	0

tens	ones
2	0

tens	ones
1	0

tens	ones
4	0

tens	ones
3	0

tens	ones
2	0

② How much?

10 ¢ 30 ¢ 15 ¢

Horizons Math K Book One 117

Overview:

- Place value 10's
- Nickels
- Ruler
- Time – hour

Materials and Supplies:

- Teacher's Guide & Student Workbook
- White board
- Objects for counters
- Number flash cards
- Place value chart
- Number chart
- Group of 10's flash cards
- Count by 10's flash cards
- Ruler – inches
- Digital clock flash cards for hours
- Clock model
- Nickels

Teaching Tips:

Teach place value 10's.
Review counting by 10's.
Review nickels.
Review counting items to 60.
Review time – hour.
Review ruler – inches.
Review oral counting to 80.

Activities:

① Using place value materials for groups of ten and then counting them by tens will increase the student's understanding as they start the tens' place. Display 5 groups of ten and have the student(s) count them by tens. Example: 10, 20, 30, 40, 50. Therefore, the value of 5 groups of ten is 50. Make flash cards of the bowling pin pattern (red dots) used in this activity for review and practice. Have them trace the first 2 answers and count the other sets and write the number in the place value box.

② Use play money for the student(s) to see the front and back of the nickel. Review, "What is the color of the nickel?" "Whose picture is on the front of the nickel?" (Thomas Jefferson) "What is on the back of a nickel?" (Monticello, Thomas Jefferson's home) "What is the value of a nickel?" Point out the three ways to write a nickel's name: 5¢, nickel or 5 cents. Quickly review counting by fives. Put several different sets of nickels on the white board and have the student(s) count them by fives to learn their value. They should be able to complete the activity on their own.

③ Review with the student(s) the inch ruler, "What is it used for?" "How long is an inch?" "What do you measure with an inch ruler?" "You wouldn't use it to measure long distances." Have the student(s) trace with their finger from the edge of the comb up to the ruler. This is the length of the comb. Allow the student(s) to complete the remainder of the activity.

④ Each student will need a small clock model. Have them put the long hand (minute hand) on twelve. As you call out or write on the white board several hour times, have them put the short hand (hour hand) pointing to the correct number. Have the student(s) point to where the short hand (hour hand) is to be drawn for each clock in this activity. Then, draw the hour hand making sure it is shorter than the long hand. Do a similar activity with a digital clock model by having the student(s) choose number flash cards for the hour that you call out. Have them place the flash card on the digital clock model.

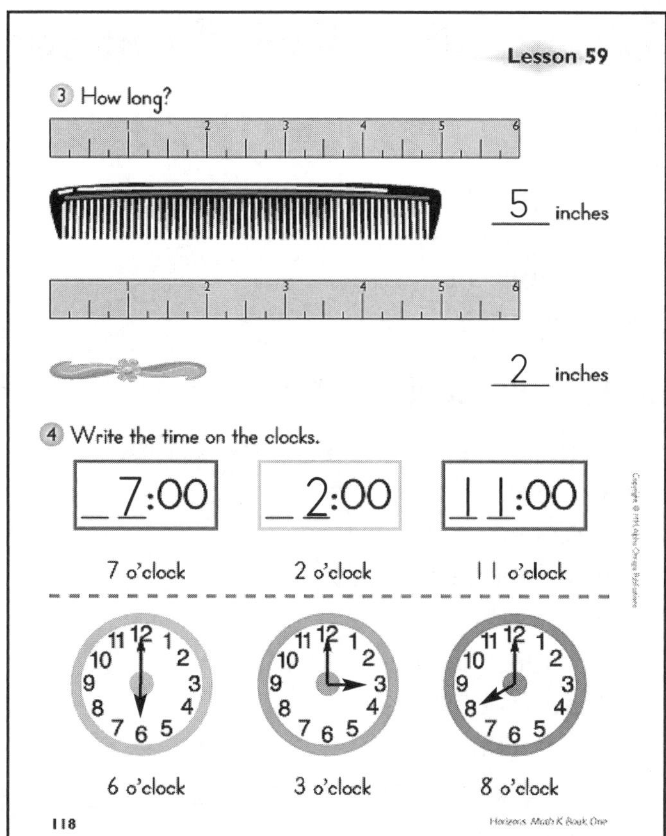

Lesson 60 - Find Perimeter

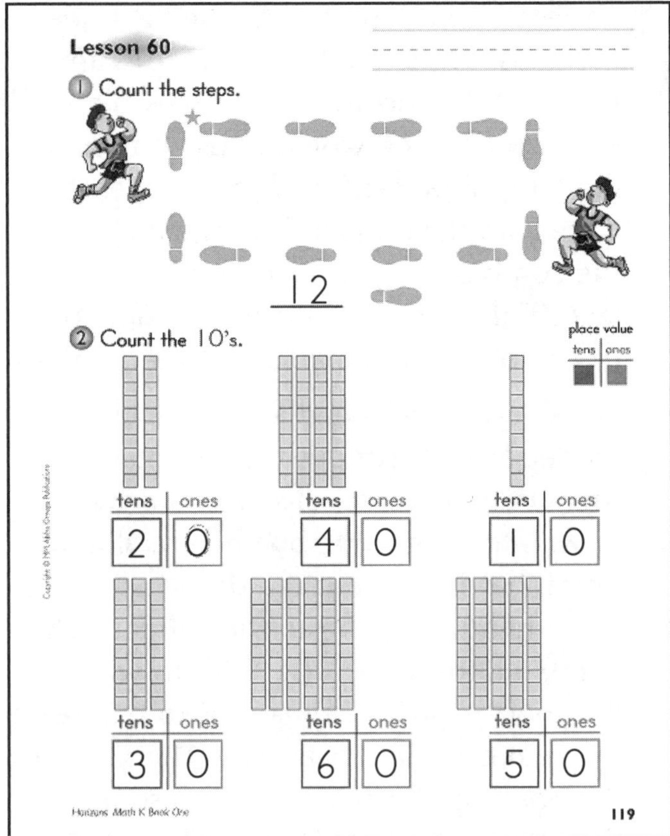

Overview:

- Find perimeter
- Place value 10's
- Number after 20's
- Addition 10's

Materials and Supplies:

- Teacher's Guide & Student Workbook
- White board
- Objects for counters
- Number flash cards
- Number chart
- Addition flash cards 1's & 10's
- Base 10 blocks
- Place value chart
- Group of 10's flash cards
- Count by 10's flash cards
- Number line strips

Teaching Tips:

Teach perimeter.
Review place value 10's.
Review counting by 10's.
Review number after.
Review oral counting to 80.

Activities:

① The perimeter activities in this material will be counting practice. In this activity the student(s) are counting shoe prints in a rectangle shape. Have them practice this on the playground by counting the steps that they make as they walk around a table or another object. Instruct them to begin at the star and count the shoe prints. This number is a measurement, so when they write the number on the blank it is labeled with a shoe print.

② Using place value materials for groups of ten and then counting them by tens will increase the students' understanding as they continue the tens' place. Display 5 groups of ten and have the student(s) count them by tens. Example: 10, 20, 30, 40, 50. Therefore, the value of 5 groups of ten is 50. Instruct the student(s) to write a zero in the ones' place as a place holder. You cannot be the second person in a line if no one is first in the line. A 1 cannot represent 10 unless there is a 0 for a place holder. Many place value materials are available for purchase. To make them yourself, look at the student book to see how they should look. Cut ten 1" or 2" cardboard squares to represent the ones' place. Color them blue. For the tens' place cut ten stacks of ten squares. Color them red. Glue a magnet on the back of each piece to allow you to display place value concepts on any magnetic surface.

③ Drill number after by holding up a flash card and asking the student(s) to say the next number. The student(s) may refer to the pages in a book, a number chart or a number line strip to see what number comes after a given number. They should be able to do the activity independently.

④ On the white board demonstrate several addition facts (10–19) on the number line. Have a student read the direction. Have them count on the number line to find the first number in the addition fact. Then count to find the second and write that number as the answer to the addition fact. Do the same for the remaining problems. Some student(s) might need to use counters for this activity.

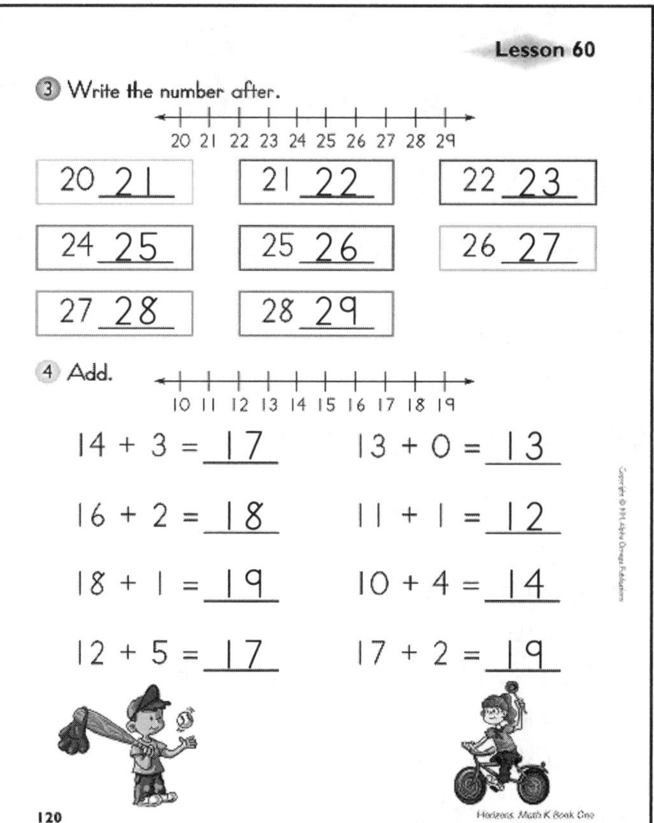
Lesson 60

3 Write the number after.

20 21 22 23 24 25 26 27 28 29

20 21 | 21 22 | 22 23
24 25 | 25 26 | 26 27
27 28 | 28 29

4 Add.

10 11 12 13 14 15 16 17 18 19

14 + 3 = 17 | 13 + 0 = 13
16 + 2 = 18 | 11 + 1 = 12
18 + 1 = 19 | 10 + 4 = 14
12 + 5 = 17 | 17 + 2 = 19

120 | Horizons Math K Book One

Lesson 61 - Number Between 50's

Overview:

- Number between 50's
- Find perimeter
- Addition 1's
- Time – hour

Materials and Supplies:

- Teacher's Guide & Student Workbook
- Objects for counters
- Number flash cards
- Number chart
- Addition flash cards 1's family
- Clock models
- Number line strips

Teaching Tips:

Teach number between 50's.
Review perimeter.
Review addition 1's.
Review time – hour.
Review oral counting to 80.

Activities:

① Choose three consecutive whole number flash cards 50–60. Arrange the cards out of order. Have the student(s) put them in correct order. Repeat this four times with different sets of three numbers. Choose two flash cards with a number missing between them. Have the student(s) give you the missing number. Read the instruction and have the student(s) complete the activity.

② The perimeter activities in this material will be counting practice. In this activity the student(s) are counting footprints in a rectangle shape. Have them practice this by counting the steps that they make as they walk around the classroom or another object. Instruct them to begin at the star and count the footprints. This number is a measurement, so when they write the number on the blank it is labeled with a footprint.

③ This activity is for addition drill work for the ones' family. Construct a set of flash cards for ones' family addition to use for regular classroom drill and review. Try to get the student(s) to memorize these facts but counters or a number line may be used if necessary.

④ Each student will need a small clock model. Have them put the long hand (minute hand) on twelve. As you call out or write on the white board several hour times, have them put the short hand (hour hand) pointing to the correct number. Do a similar activity with a digital clock model by having the student(s) choose number flash cards for the hour that you call out. Have them place the flash card on the digital clock model.

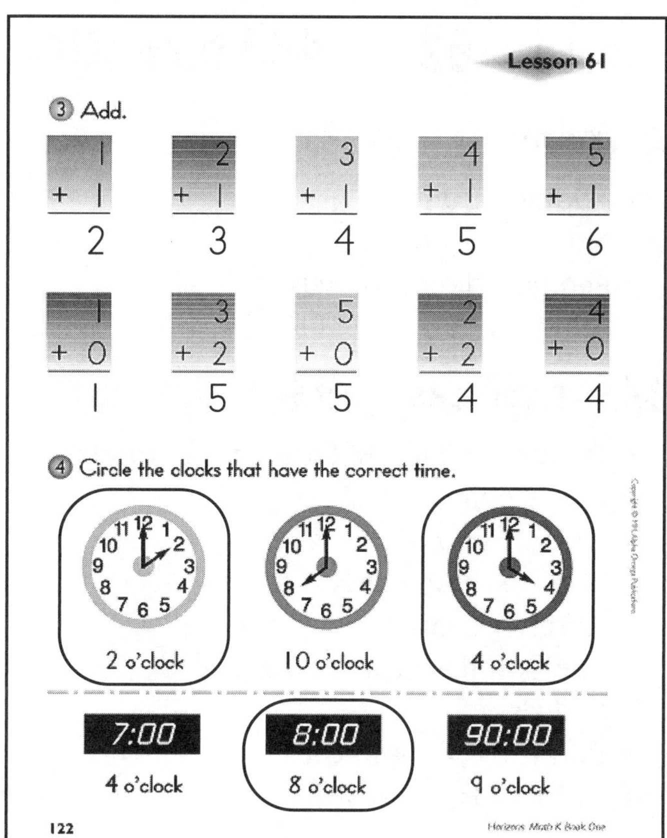

Lesson 62 - Addition 20's

Overview:

- Addition 20's
- Number between 50's
- Pennies, dimes, nickels
- Addition 10's

Materials and Supplies:

- Teacher's Guide & Student Workbook
- White board
- Objects for counters
- Number flash cards
- Number chart
- Addition flash cards 20's
- Nickels
- Count by 5's flash cards
- Number line strips

Teaching Tips:

Teach addition 20's.
Review number between 50's.
Review nickels.
Review addition 1's & 10's.
Review oral counting to 80.

Activities:

① Using a number line, let the student(s) find the answer to several addition problems 20–29. Start at the first number in the addition fact. Count the number of marks needed for the second number. The mark you end on is the answer to the addition fact. Guide the student(s) through the first activity. Allow them to finish the rest of the activity independently, helping only those who need it.

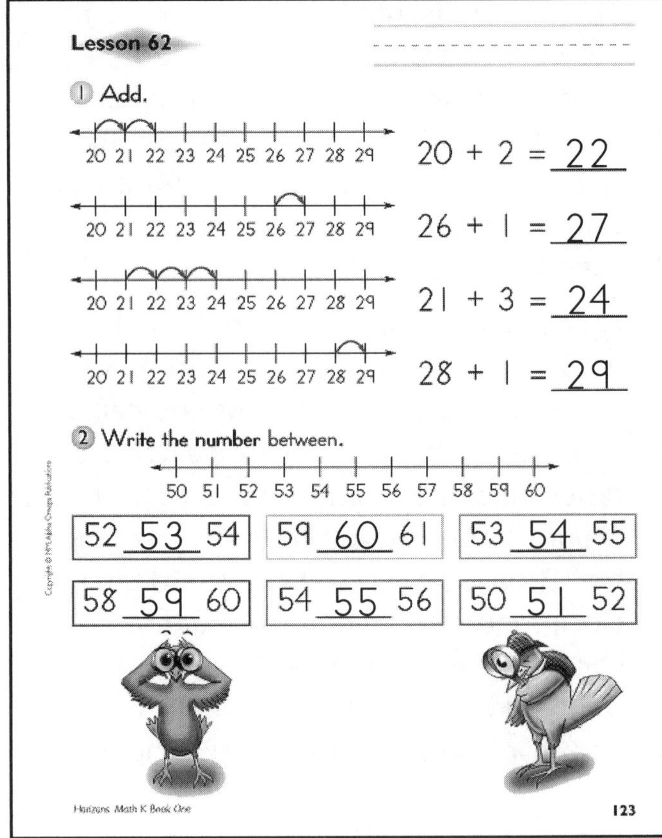

Lesson 62

① Add.

20 21 22 23 24 25 26 27 28 29 — 20 + 2 = 22

20 21 22 23 24 25 26 27 28 29 — 26 + 1 = 27

20 21 22 23 24 25 26 27 28 29 — 21 + 3 = 24

20 21 22 23 24 25 26 27 28 29 — 28 + 1 = 29

② Write the number between.

50 51 52 53 54 55 56 57 58 59 60

52 53 54	59 60 61	53 54 55
58 59 60	54 55 56	50 51 52

Horizons Math K Book One — 123

② Choose two flash cards 50–60 with a number missing between them. Have the student(s) give you the missing number. Repeat this four times with different sets of two numbers. Read the instruction and have the student(s) complete the activity using a number chart or number line strip if necessary.

③ Use play money for the student(s) to see the front and back of the nickel. Review the nickel and the value of a nickel. Quickly review counting by fives. Put several different sets of nickels on the white board and have the student(s) count them by fives to learn their value. They should be able to complete the activity on their own.

④ Using a number line 0–19, find the answers to several addition facts. Start at zero and count over the number of marks equal to the first number in the addition fact. Continue counting over the number of marks to equal the second number in the addition fact. Where you stop is the answer to the addition fact. Instruct the student(s) to do activity independently. If the student(s) have the addition fact memorized, they may write the answer without using the number line.

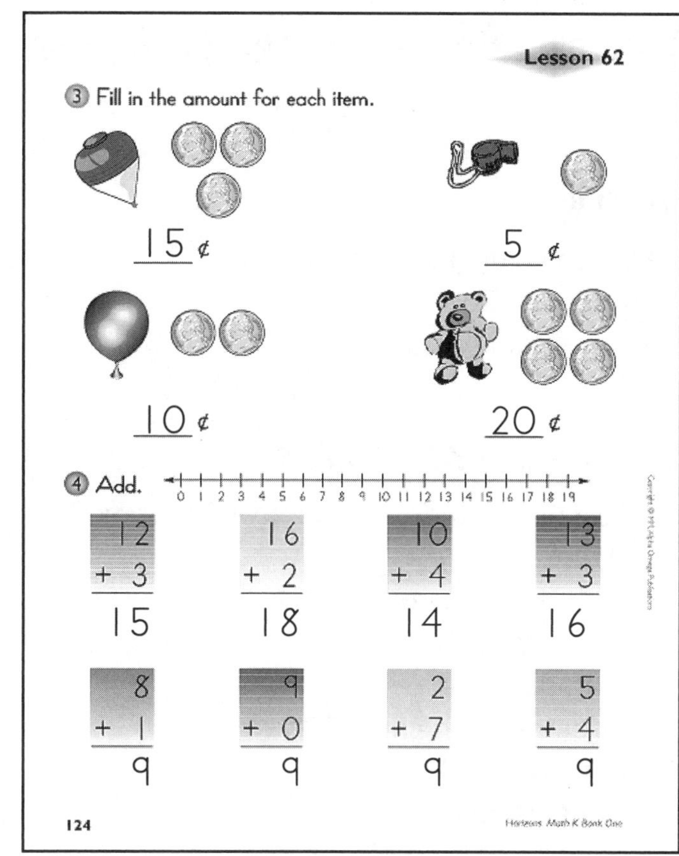
Lesson 62

③ Fill in the amount for each item.

15 ¢ 5 ¢

10 ¢ 20 ¢

④ Add.

0 1 2 3 4 5 6 7 8 9 10 11 12 13 14 15 16 17 18 19

12 + 3	16 + 2	10 + 4	13 + 3
15	18	14	16

8 + 1	9 + 0	2 + 7	5 + 4
9	9	9	9

124 Horizons Math K Book One

Lesson 63 - Place Value 1's & 10's

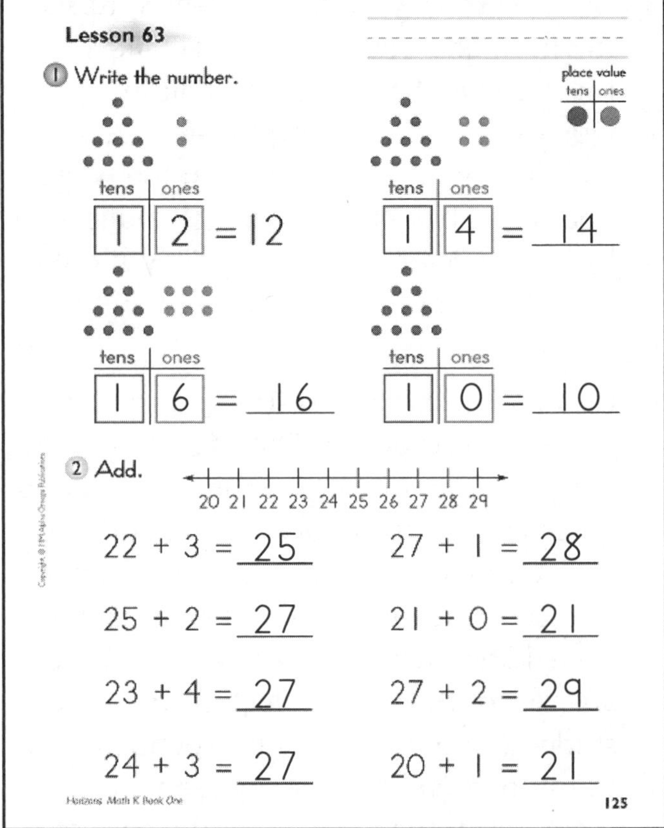
Lesson 63

① Write the number.

place value
tens | ones

tens | ones
1 | 2 = 12

tens | ones
1 | 4 = 14

tens | ones
1 | 6 = 16

tens | ones
1 | 0 = 10

② Add.

20 21 22 23 24 25 26 27 28 29

22 + 3 = 25
27 + 1 = 28
25 + 2 = 27
21 + 0 = 21
23 + 4 = 27
27 + 2 = 29
24 + 3 = 27
20 + 1 = 21

Horizons Math K Book One
125

Overview:

- Place value 1's & 10's to 19
- Addition 20's
- Place value 10's
- Pictograph

Materials and Supplies:

- Teacher's Guide & Student Workbook
- White board
- Objects for counters
- Number flash cards
- Number chart
- Addition flash cards 20's
- Base 10 blocks
- Place value chart
- Group of 10's flash cards
- Count by 10's flash cards
- Number line strips

Teaching Tips:

Teach place value 1's & 10's.
Review addition 20's.
Review counting by 10's.
Review pictograph.
Review oral counting to 80.

Activities:

① Before Activity ①, discuss the number of places a single-digit numeral (such as 4) takes. Using the numbers chart, ask what the largest number is that takes only one place (9). Discuss how many ones in this number (9). Discuss the next number (10). How many places does it take? What is in the tens' place? What is in the ones' place? Read over the instructions with the student(s). Do other examples using place value materials for the student(s). The student(s) should tell you how many groups of ten and write them in the place value box; then, how many ones and write them in the place value box.

② Using a number line, let the student(s) find the answer to several addition problems 20–29. Start at the first number in the addition fact. Count the number of marks needed for the second number. The mark you end on is the answer to the addition fact. Guide the student(s) through the first activity as they count from the first number the correct number of marks. Allow them to finish the rest of the activity independently, helping only those who need it.

③ Quickly review counting by tens. Put several different sets of tens on the flannel board or white board and have the student(s) count them by tens. They should be able to complete the activity on their own.

④ Review bar and pictographs. The student(s) should be able to count the objects on the graph and write their answer on the blanks independently.

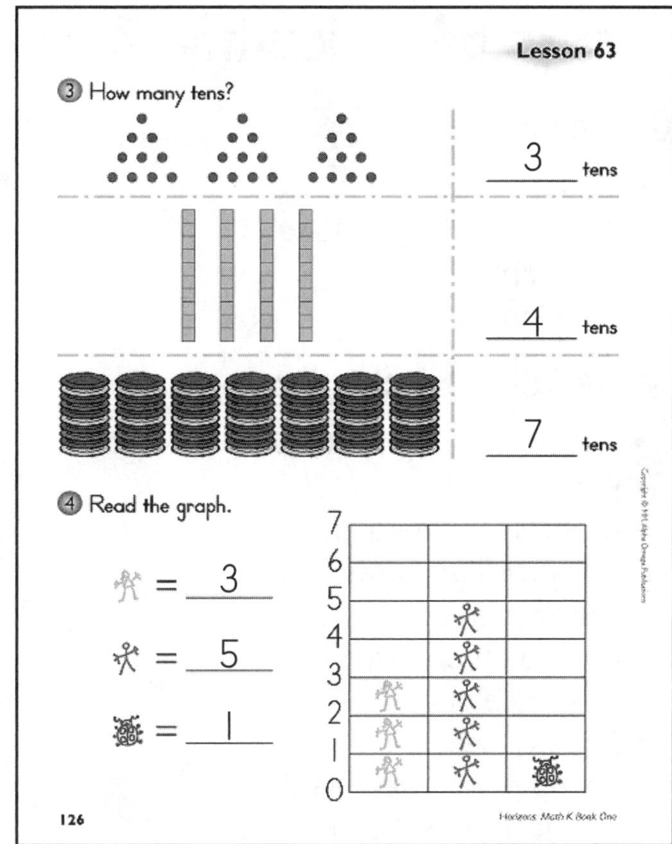

Lesson 64 - Identify Pairs

Overview:

- Identify pairs
- Place value 1's & 10's to 19
- Bar graph
- Addition 20's

Materials and Supplies:

- Teacher's Guide & Student Workbook
- White board
- Objects for counters
- Number flash cards
- Number chart
- Addition flash cards 20's
- Base 10 blocks
- Place value chart
- Group of 10's flash cards
- Count by 10's flash cards
- Number line strips

Teaching Tips:

Teach pairs.
Review place value 1's & 10's.
Review addition 20's.
Review counting by 10's.
Review bar graph.
Review oral counting to 80.

Activities:

① Ask the student(s) to give you examples of things that are pairs: gloves, shoes, hands, arms, legs, socks, pants (two legs), eye glasses. Discuss with them that pairs do not have to be identical. For example the tops are two different colors. Twins will be covered later. Have them circle the pairs and count them to answer the question.

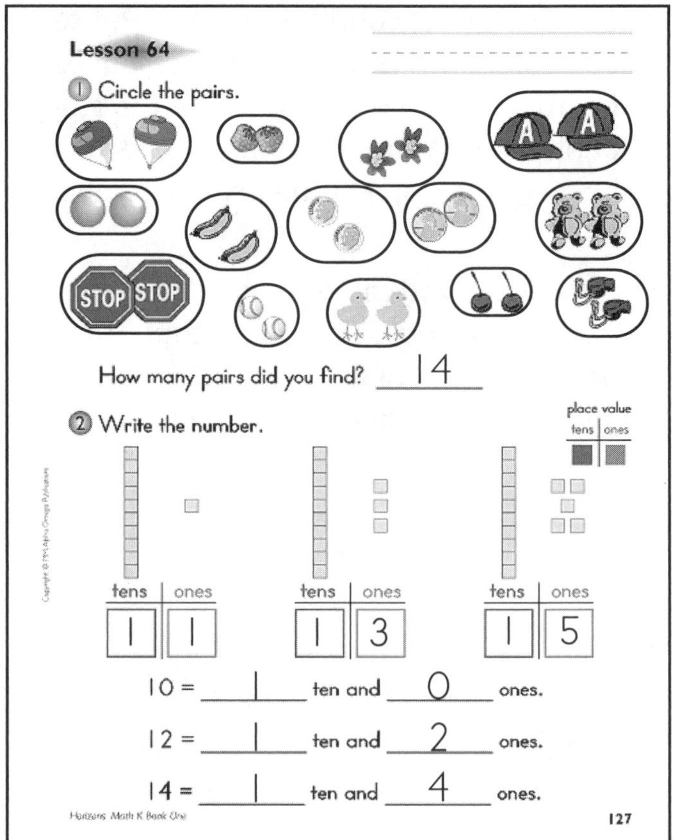
Lesson 64

① Circle the pairs.

How many pairs did you find? 14

② Write the number.

place value
tens | ones

tens	ones
1	1

tens	ones
1	3

tens	ones
1	5

10 = 1 ten and 0 ones.

12 = 1 ten and 2 ones.

14 = 1 ten and 4 ones.

Horizons Math K Book One 127

② Before doing this activity, discuss the number of places a single-digit numeral (such as 4) takes. Using the numbers chart, ask what the largest number is that takes only one place (9). Discuss how many ones in this number (9). Discuss the next number (10). How many places does it take? What is in the tens' place? What is in the ones' place? Read over the instructions with the student(s). Do other examples using place value materials for the student(s). The student(s) should tell you how many groups of ten and write them in the place value box; then, how many ones and write them in the place value box. Choose a flash card from the 10's family. Ask the student(s) to tell you how many tens the number has and how many ones. Guide them as they do the first horizontal place value activity.

③ Review bar and pictographs.The student(s) should be able to independently color the bars on the graph in the proper column.

④ Using a number line, let the student(s) find the answer to several addition problems 20–29. Start at the first number in the addition fact. Count the number of marks needed for the second number. The mark you end on is the answer to the addition fact. Guide the student(s) through the first activity as they count from the first number the correct number of marks. Allow them to finish the rest of the activity independently, helping only those who need it.

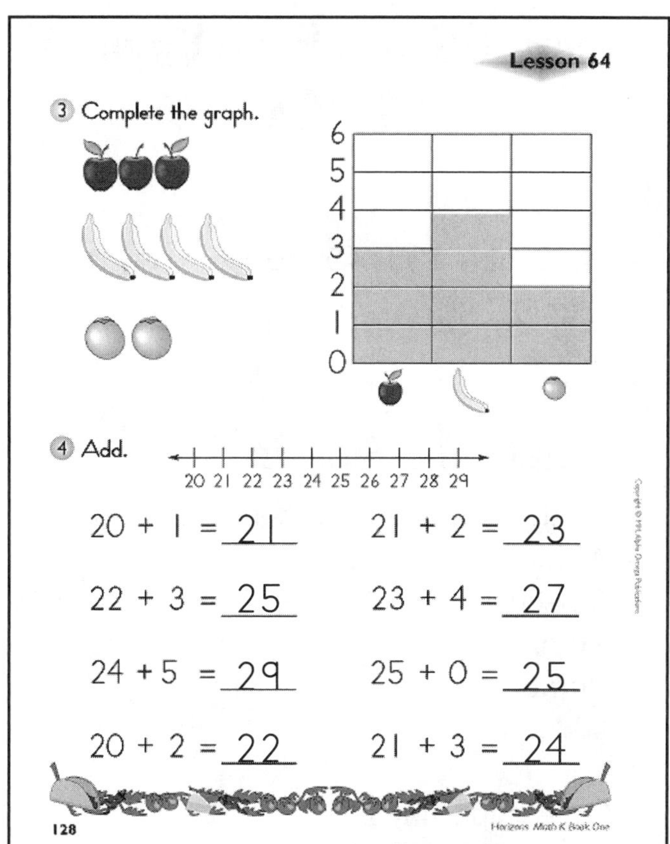

Lesson 65 - Place Value 1's & 10's

Overview:

- Place value 1's & 10's to 19
- Identify pairs
- Inch
- Addition 20's

Materials and Supplies:

- Teacher's Guide & Student Workbook
- White board
- Objects for counters
- Number flash cards
- Number chart
- Addition flash cards 20's
- Base 10 blocks
- Place value chart
- Group of 10's flash cards
- Count by 10's flash cards
- Ruler – inches
- Number line strips

Teaching Tips:

Teach place value 1's & 10's.
Review pairs.
Review inches.
Review addition 20's.
Teach oral counting to 90.

Activities:

① In the first set in this activity, have the student(s) count the tens and write the number. Then have them count the ones and write the number. This is the number 14. Write it down (place value materials may be a help). The student(s) may need the teacher's guidance through each of these sets.

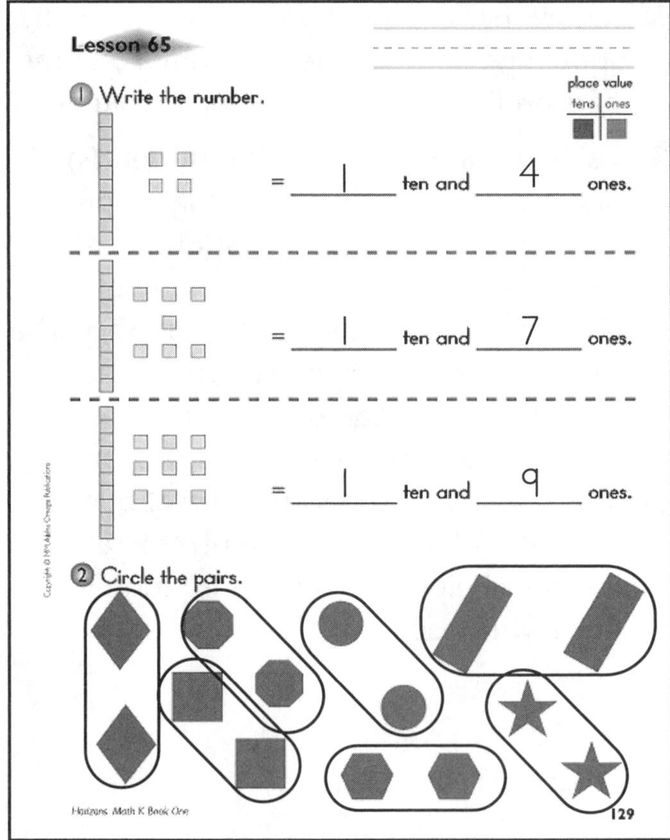

② Ask the student(s) to give you some more examples of things that are pairs. Review with them that pairs do not have to be identical. For example, these figures are two different colors. Have them circle the pairs and count them.

③ Review measurement with a ruler. Have the student(s) count the inches for each object.

④ Using a number line, let the student(s) find the answer to several addition problems 20–29. Start at the first number in the addition fact. Count the number of marks needed for the second number. The mark you end on is the answer to the addition fact. Guide the student(s) through the first activity as they count from the first number the correct number of marks. Allow them to finish the rest of the activity independently, helping only those who need it.

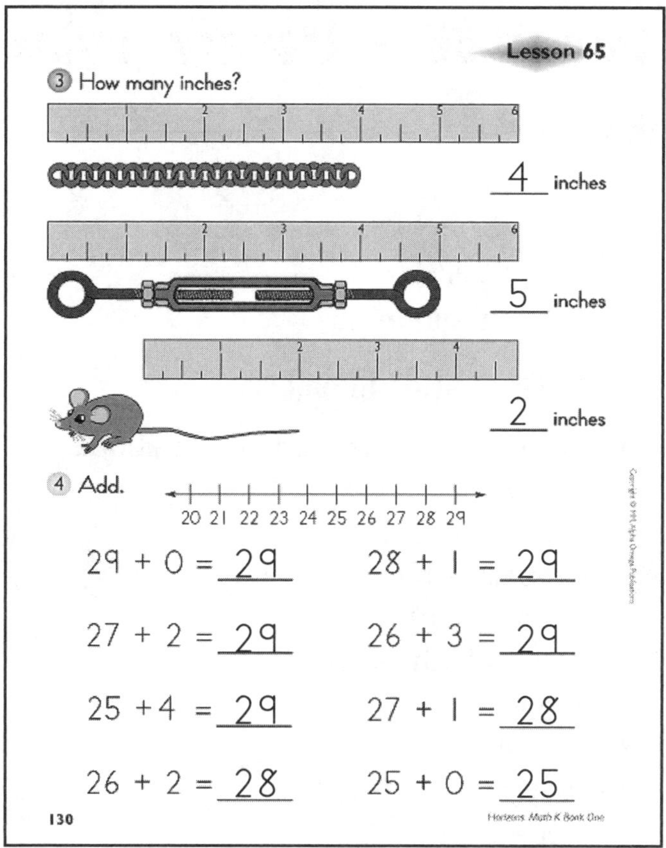

Lesson 66 - Identify Twins

Overview:

- Identify twins
- Inch
- Count by 5's
- Vertical addition 20's

Materials and Supplies:

- Teacher's Guide & Student Workbook
- White board
- Objects for counters
- Number flash cards
- Number chart
- Addition flash cards 20's
- Nickels
- Crayons
- Count by 5's flash cards
- Ruler – inches
- Number line strips

Teaching Tips:

Teach twins.
Review inches.
Review counting by 5's.
Review addition 20's.
Review oral counting to 90.

Activities:

① Ask the student(s) to give you some examples of things that are twins. Twins, like pairs, correlate with the number 2. Twins would be 2 people or animals born at the same time that have the same mother. Read the instruction and have the student(s) complete the activity.

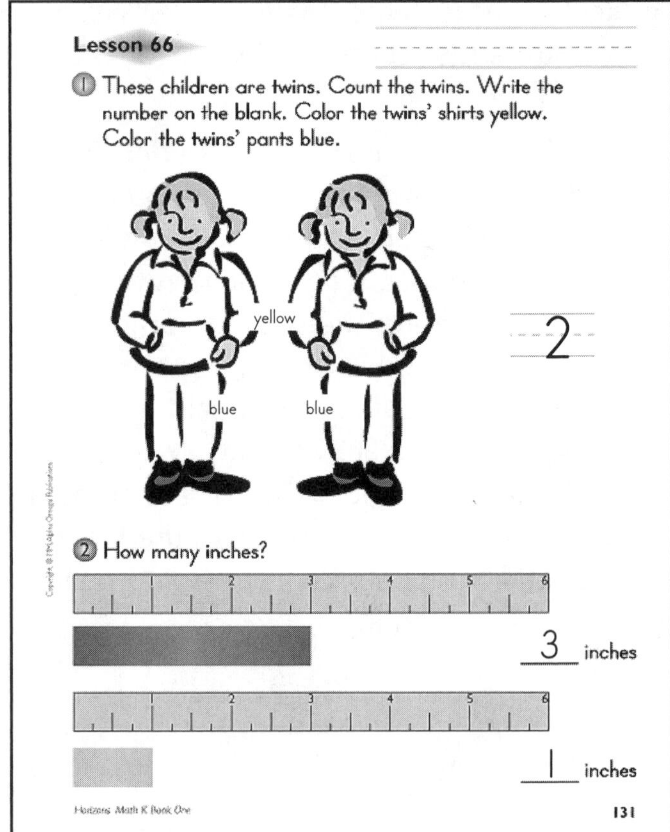

② Review measurement with a ruler. Have the student(s) count the inches for each object.

③ Review counting by 5's to 100 with flash cards, a number chart or nickels. Hold up random cards and ask for the next number by 5's. Some student(s) may need to look at a number chart to complete this activity.

④ Using a number line, let the student(s) find the answer to several addition problems 20–29. Start at the first number in the addition fact. Count the number of marks needed for the second number. The mark you end on is the answer to the addition fact. Guide the student(s) through the first activity as they count from the first number the correct number of marks. Allow them to finish the rest of the activity independently, helping only those who need it.

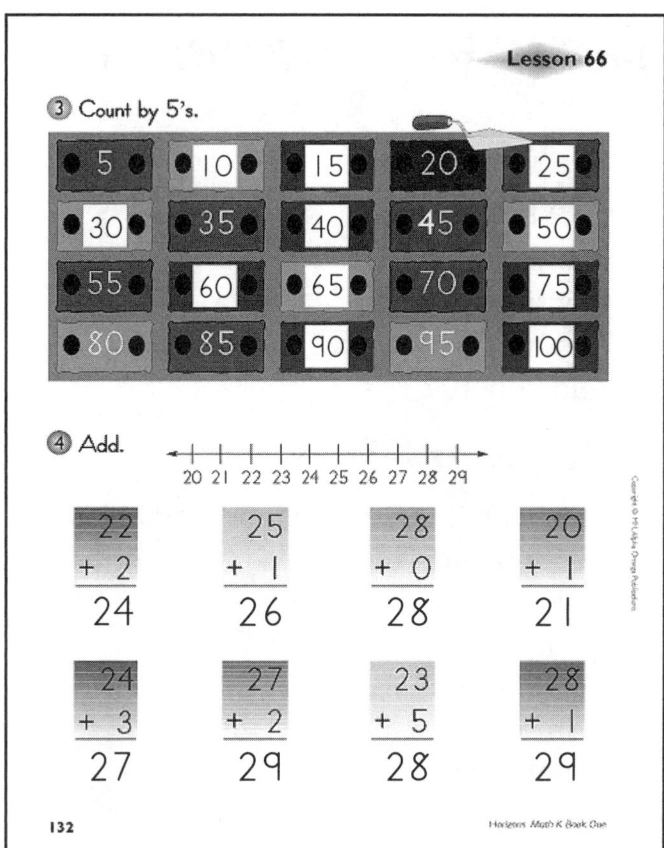

Lesson 67 - Number After 30's

Overview:

- Number after 30's
- Identify twins
- Ordinals first–tenth
- Addition 10's

Materials and Supplies:

- Teacher's Guide & Student Workbook
- White board
- Objects for counters
- Number flash cards
- Addition flash cards 10's
- Number chart
- Number line strips
- Ordinal number flash cards

Teaching Tips:

Teach number after 30's.
Review twins.
Review ordinals.
Review addition 10's.
Review counting orally to 90.

Activities:

① Use number line strips or a number chart to demonstrate the number after. Practice number recognition by holding up three number cards. Ask the student(s) to tell you which card is a particular number. Left, right or middle? Top, bottom middle? Have the student(s) write their answers for the activity.

② Ask the student(s) to give you some additional examples of things that are twins. Twins for this activity are two children that look exactly the same. In some of the pairs the children look enough alike to be twins but tell the student(s) that the twins faces and hair must match. Clothing color can be different. With this definition read the instruction and have the student(s) complete the activity.

③ Review ordinal numbers with several coins. Have a student pick the 4th coin that you lay out on a table. Have them tell you the name of the coin and the value. To do the activity, read each instruction twice and have the student(s) mark their answer.

④ Drill the 1's family, sums to 9, addition facts with flash cards. Do several 20's family addition problems with the class. Allow the student(s) to complete Activity ④ by going to the first number on the number line and counting the number added to it.

Lesson 68 – Identify Inside & Outside

Overview:

- Identify *inside* & *outside*
- Number after 30's
- Identify twins & pairs
- Ordinals first–tenth

Materials and Supplies:

- Teacher's Guide & Student Workbook
- White board
- Objects for counters
- Number flash cards
- Number chart
- Number line strips
- Color flash cards
- Crayons
- Ordinal number flash cards

Teaching Tips:

Teach inside and outside.
Review number after 30's.
Review twins.
Review ordinals.
Review counting orally to 90.

Activities:

① Your student(s) might already know *inside* and *outside* since they are very common direction words. If they need introduction and practice with the concept, talk about going *outside* the room for recess. When you return to the classroom you say you are going *inside*. Draw a triangle or rectangle on the white board. Draw some objects both inside and outside the shape. Ask what the shape is and which of the objects are inside the shape and which objects are outside the shape.

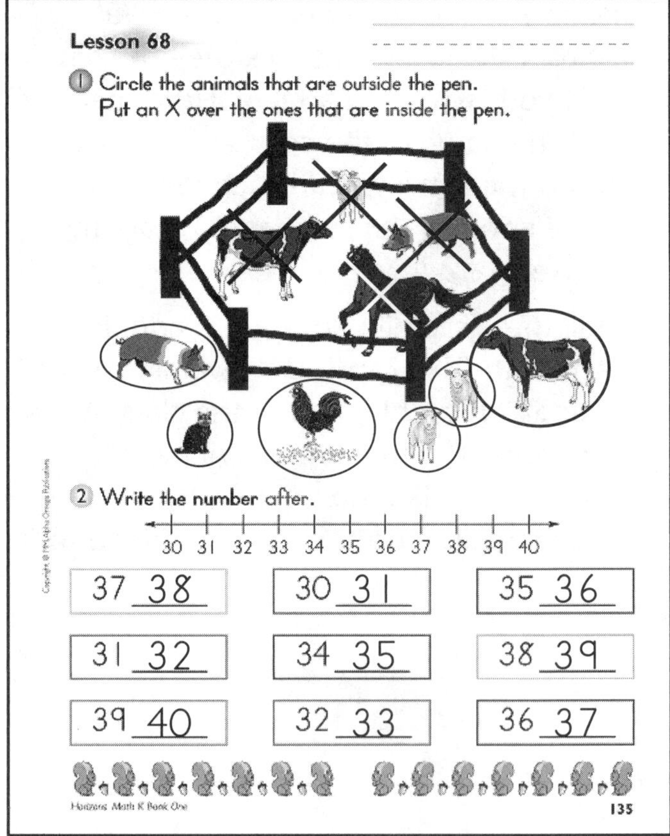

Lesson 68

① Circle the animals that are outside the pen.
Put an X over the ones that are inside the pen.

② Write the number after.

30 31 32 33 34 35 36 37 38 39 40

37 38	30 31	35 36
31 32	34 35	38 39
39 40	32 33	36 37

Horizons Math K Book One 135

② Use number line strips or a number chart to review the number after. Practice number recognition by holding up three number cards. Ask the student(s) to tell you which card is a particular number: the *left*, *right* or *middle* card? *Top*, *bottom*, or *middle*? Have the student(s) write their answers for the activity using a number chart if necessary.

③ Review pairs and twins. Twins are exactly alike for this activity and pairs are two things that go together. Both are different ways to refer to two items. Ask the student(s) if they can tell you how many people are in a trio or quartet. What is a triple, a deuce, a pentathelete, a triad, etc.? Perhaps they can think of other examples.

④ This is a puzzle. If the student(s) colors it correctly it will make a shape. Read the directions one at a time giving them time to color the squares they have chosen.

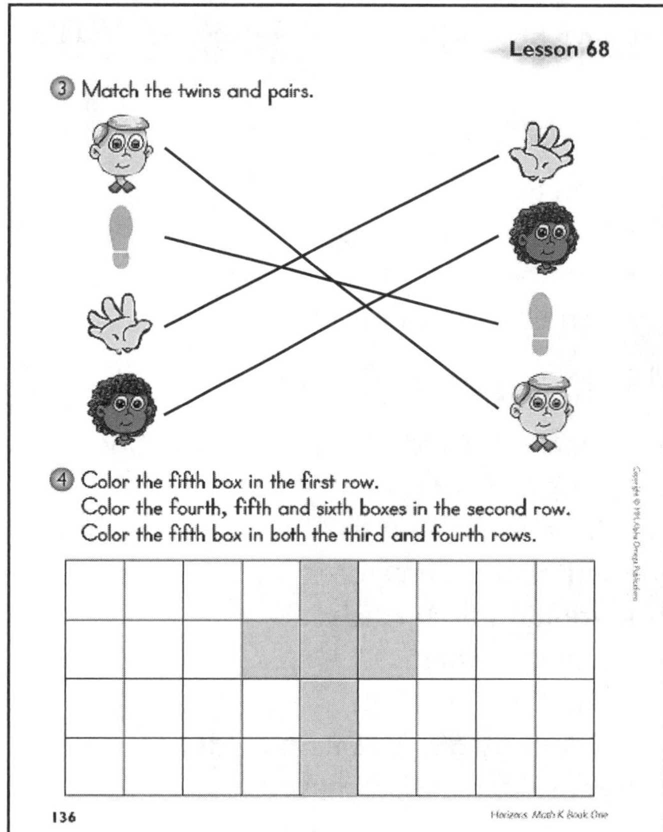
Lesson 68

③ Match the twins and pairs.

④ Color the fifth box in the first row.
Color the fourth, fifth and sixth boxes in the second row.
Color the fifth box in both the third and fourth rows.

136

Horizons Math K Book One

Lesson 69 - Addition 30's

Overview:

- Addition 30's
- Identify *inside* & *outside*
- Number after 30's
- Pennies, dimes, nickels

Materials and Supplies:

- Teacher's Guide & Student Workbook
- White board
- Objects for counters
- Number flash cards
- Addition flash cards
- Number chart
- Number line strips
- Count by 5's, 10's flash cards
- Pennies, nickel, dimes

Teaching Tips:

Teach addition 30's.
Review inside and outside.
Review number after 30's.
Review coins.
Review addition facts 1's.
Review counting orally to 90.

Activities:

① This is the first time that the students are asked to add to the 30's family. In this activity they are adding either a 1 or a 2 to a number in the 30's family. Do several examples on the white board using either a number line strip or a number chart. Ask the student(s) where they might see the number 30 in everyday activities. Possible answers might be a speed limit sign, number of students in a classroom, money, candy pieces in a bag.

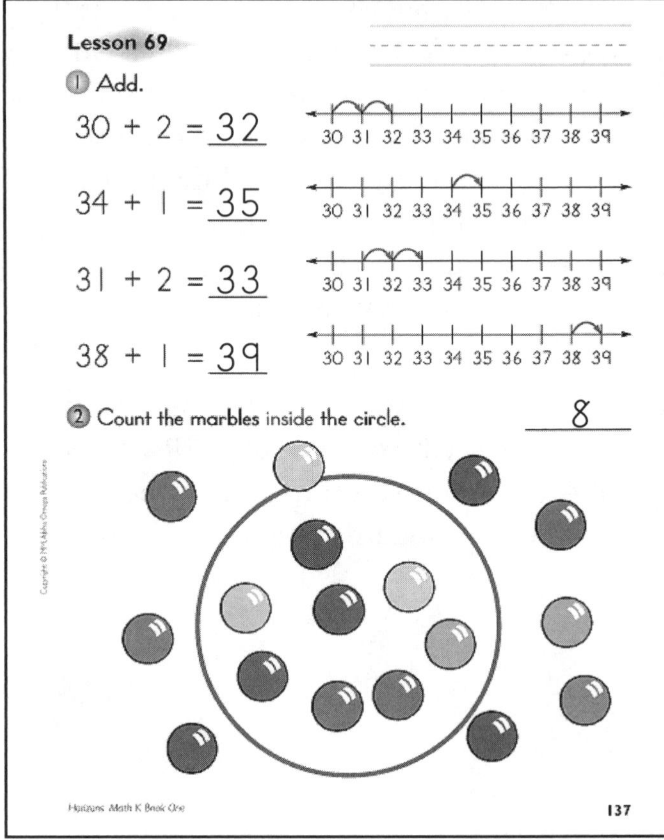

② Review *inside* and *outside*. Ask for some more examples of inside and outside from the student(s). Draw a triangle or rectangle on the white board. Draw some objects both inside and outside the shape. Ask what the shape is and which of the objects are inside the shape and which objects are outside the shape.

③ Use number line strips or a number chart to review the number after. Have the student(s) write their answers for the activity using a number chart if necessary.

④ Review counting by 1's, 5's and 10's. Remind the student(s) that they are counting coins in this activity and that the answer blank has a ¢ sign.

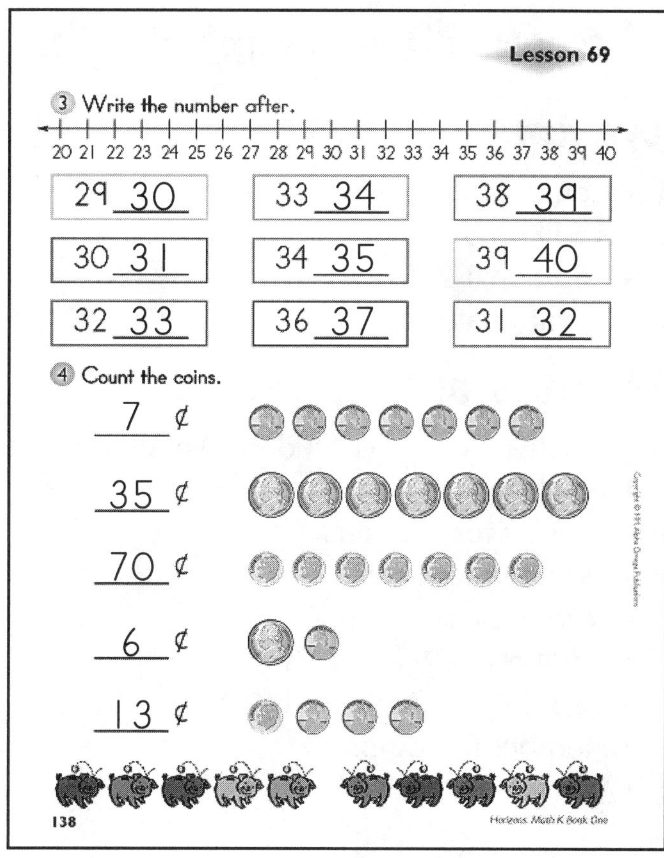

Lesson 70 - Count to 70

Overview:

- Count to 70
- Addition 30's
- Addition 1's
- Number after 30's

Materials and Supplies:

- Teacher's Guide & Student Workbook
- White board
- Objects for counters
- Number flash cards
- Number chart
- Addition flash cards 1's
- Count by 5's flash cards
- Number line strips
- Worksheet 18 & 28

Teaching Tips:

Teach counting items to 60.
Review addition 30's.
Review addition facts 1's.
Review number after 30's.
Review oral counting to 90.

Activities:

① Count out loud by ones to 70 using the number chart. Have the student(s) count the objects in the activity. Ask them for the name of each shape and the color of the shapes in each row. Review ordinal numbers by asking what shape or color is in the 4th row, etc.

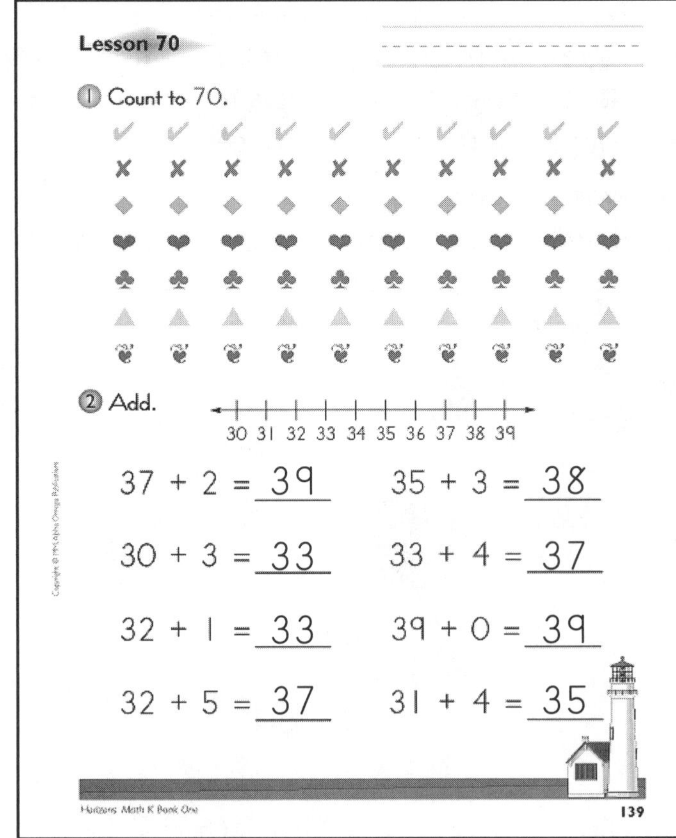

② Review addition of the 30's family. In this activity they are adding 0–5 to a number in the 30's family. Do several examples on the white board using either a number line strip or a number chart. Remind them that when 0 is added to a number the number stays the same. The student(s) should be able to complete this activity without additional help.

③ Drill addition of the 1's family with flash cards. Play a game by having the student(s) form two lines. Flash an addition card to the people in the front of the lines. The first person to answer the addition fact stays at the front. The other goes to the back of the line.

④ Use number line strips or a number chart to review the number after. Have the student(s) write their answers for the activity using a number chart or number line if necessary.

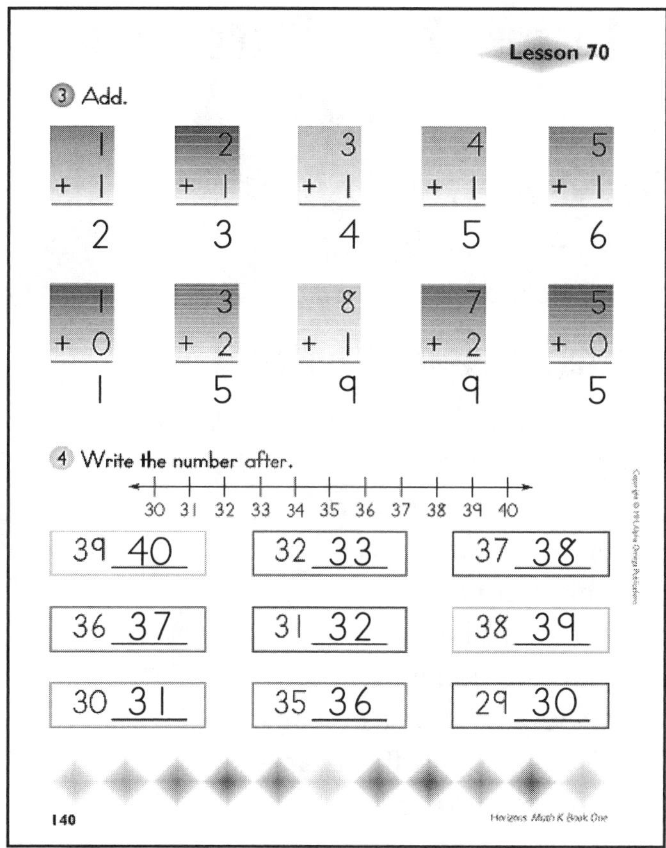

Lesson 70

③ Add.

1 + 1 = 2	2 + 1 = 3	3 + 1 = 4	4 + 1 = 5	5 + 1 = 6
1 + 0 = 1	3 + 2 = 5	8 + 1 = 9	7 + 2 = 9	5 + 0 = 5

④ Write the number after.

30 31 32 33 34 35 36 37 38 39 40

39 40	32 33	37 38
36 37	31 32	38 39
30 31	35 36	29 30

140 Horizons Math K Book One

Lesson 71 - Place Value 20's

Overview:

- Place value 20's
- Vertical addition 30's

Materials and Supplies:

- Teacher's Guide & Student Workbook
- White board
- Objects for counters
- Number flash cards
- Number chart
- Base 10 blocks
- Place value chart
- Group of 10's flash cards
- Count by 10's flash cards
- Number line strips

Lesson 71

① Write the numbers.

place value: tens | ones

tens	ones	
2	1	= 21
2	3	= 23
2	8	= 28
2	5	= 25
2	7	= 27
2	2	= 22
2	9	= 29

Horizons Math K Book One 141

Teaching Tips:

Teach place value 20's.
Review addition 30's.
Review oral counting to 90.

Activities:

① Look at the 20's family with a number chart or number line strip. In the 20's family there is always a 2 in the tens' place. Ask what numbers can be in the ones' place. If a student correctly counts 0–9 have the class count 0–9 together. They are to count the dots: the red dots by 10's and the blue dots by 1's. The ten number is to be written in the tens' box and the one number in the ones' place. Finally they write the number as they would normally see it. If you have not made place value blocks, this would be a good time to make them yourself. Look at the student book to see how they should look. Cut ten 1" or 2" cardboard squares to represent the ones' place. Color them blue. For the tens' place cut ten stacks of ten squares. Color them red. Glue a magnet on the back of each piece to allow you to display place value concepts on any magnetic surface.

② This is a review activity. Go over the 30's with a number line chart. Add 1 to each of the numbers. (30 + 1 =) (31 + 1 =) (32 + 1 =) etc. Start over again adding 2, 3, 4, etc. Practice on the white board if student(s) need extra practice.

Lesson 72 - Number Before 1's

Overview:

- Number before 1's
- Place value 20's
- Vertical addition 30's
- Perimeter

Materials and Supplies:

- Teacher's Guide & Student Workbook
- White board
- Objects for counters
- Number flash cards
- Number chart
- Count by 10's flash cards
- Base 10 blocks
- Place value chart
- Group of 10's flash cards
- Count by 10's flash cards
- Shape flash cards
- Number line strips

Teaching Tips:

Teach number before 1's.
Review counting by 10's.
Review place value 20's.
Review shapes.
Review addition 30's.
Review oral counting to 90.

Activities:

① Have the student(s) put four crayons on their desk. Ask them to take one of them away and put it on their lap. Tell them to count the crayons that they have left. This is the number before. Point to a number on the number chart or a number line strip 1's. Ask the student(s) to say the number before. This activity is to help the student(s) prepare for subtraction problems. A number line strip or number chart can be used by the student(s) if necessary.

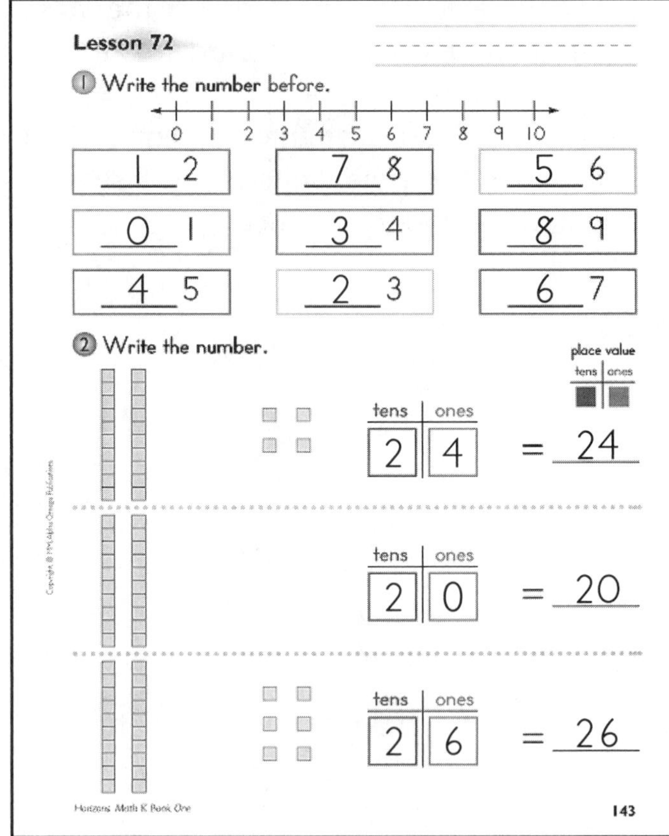

Lesson 72

① Write the number before.

0 1 2 3 4 5 6 7 8 9 10

1 2	7 8	5 6
0 1	3 4	8 9
4 5	2 3	6 7

② Write the number.

place value: tens | ones

tens	ones	
2	4	= 24
2	0	= 20
2	6	= 26

Horizons Math K Book One 143

② Review the 20's family with a number chart or number line strip. In the 20's family there is always a 2 in the tens' place. Ask what numbers can be in the ones' place. If a student correctly counts 0–9 have the class count 0–9 together. They are to count the 10 blocks and the ones blocks. The red blocks by 10's and the blue blocks by 1's. The ten number is to be written in the tens' box and the one number in the ones' place. After the (=) sign they write the number as they would normally see it. Do one problem as a class activity and have them complete the activity on their own.

③ This is a review activity. Go over the 30's with a number line chart. Add all of the ones to each of the numbers in the 30's family. (30 + 1 =) (30 + 2 =) (30 + 3 =) etc. Start over again with 31 and add all the ones to it, etc. Only do sums to 40. Practice on the white board if student(s) need extra practice.

④ Review rectangle. Review perimeter. It is the distance around the outside of an object. In this activity they are to count the links of chain that make the rectangle. Instruct them to pick a starting point so they count each link only once. This is a measurement, so the answer blank is labeled with a chain link.

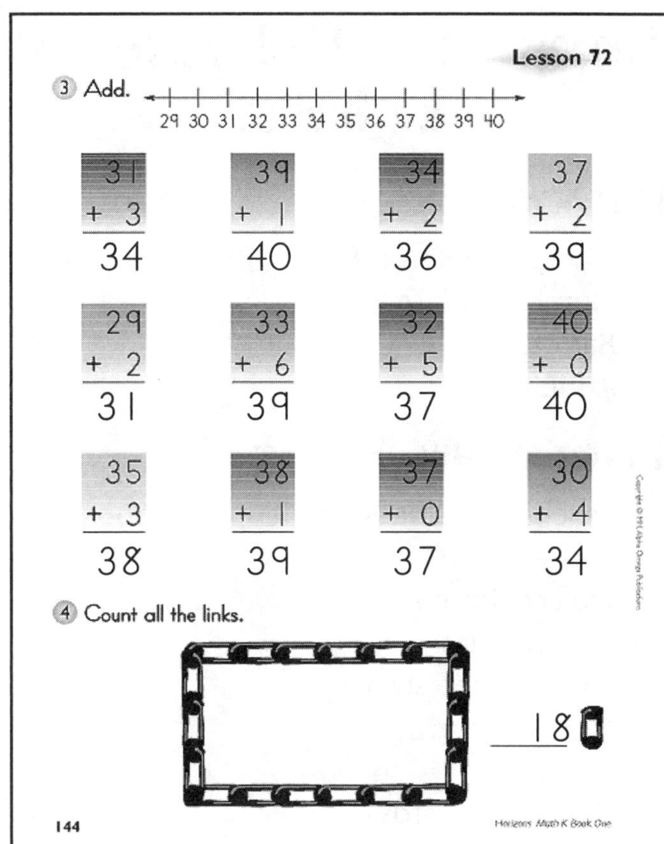
Lesson 72

③ Add.

29 30 31 32 33 34 35 36 37 38 39 40

31 + 3 = 34	39 + 1 = 40	34 + 2 = 36	37 + 2 = 39
29 + 2 = 31	33 + 6 = 39	32 + 5 = 37	40 + 0 = 40
35 + 3 = 38	38 + 1 = 39	37 + 0 = 37	30 + 4 = 34

④ Count all the links.

18

144

Horizons Math K Book One

Lesson 73 - Find Perimeter in Inches

Overview:

- Find perimeter in inches
- Number before 1's
- Bar graph
- Addition 30's

Materials and Supplies:

- Teacher's Guide & Student Workbook
- White board
- Objects for counters
- Number flash cards
- Number line strip
- Number chart
- Crayons
- Color flash cards
- Ruler – inches

Teaching Tips:

Teach perimeter.
Review ruler inches.
Review number before 1's.
Review bar graph.
Review colors.
Review addition 30's.
Review oral counting to 90.

Activities:

① Read the instruction. Talk about perimeter as being the distance around an object. Have a student pace off the number of steps it takes to walk around a desk or a table. Have another student do the same but have them take short steps or long steps. Since they will get a different number of steps, talk about the inch marks on a ruler. Every ruler with inch markings is the same. It doesn't matter who measures an object, the measurement will be the same. This is really just a counting activity but will introduce the concept of perimeter. Have the student(s) count the inches around the rectangle. Remind them to pick a starting point so they do not count the same side twice. If your student(s) have difficulty with this, have them place counters over each ruler for the number of inches on each side. Then if they count the counters they will have the correct answer.

② The number before is taking away 1. Have each student count out 8 counters. Have them take away 1. How many are left? See if the student(s) can do this if you hold up a flash card 1's and ask for the number before. Some student(s) may be counting up to the number before. For example you hold up a 4 card. They may count 1, 2, 3 and say 3 is the number before 4. Have them complete the activity.

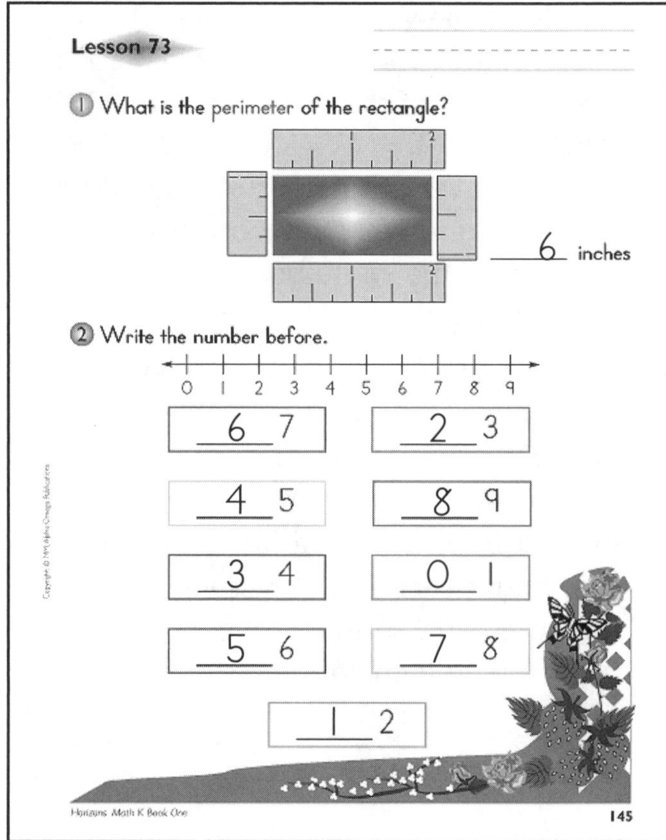

③ Read the instruction. Review bar graphs. Demonstrate this on the white board by using several types of counters. Have a student count one of the sets of counters and color in the correct number of blocks on the bar graph that you have drawn on the board. have them complete the activity.

④ Count orally 1–40 with the student(s). Review addition with the number line as needed for your student(s).

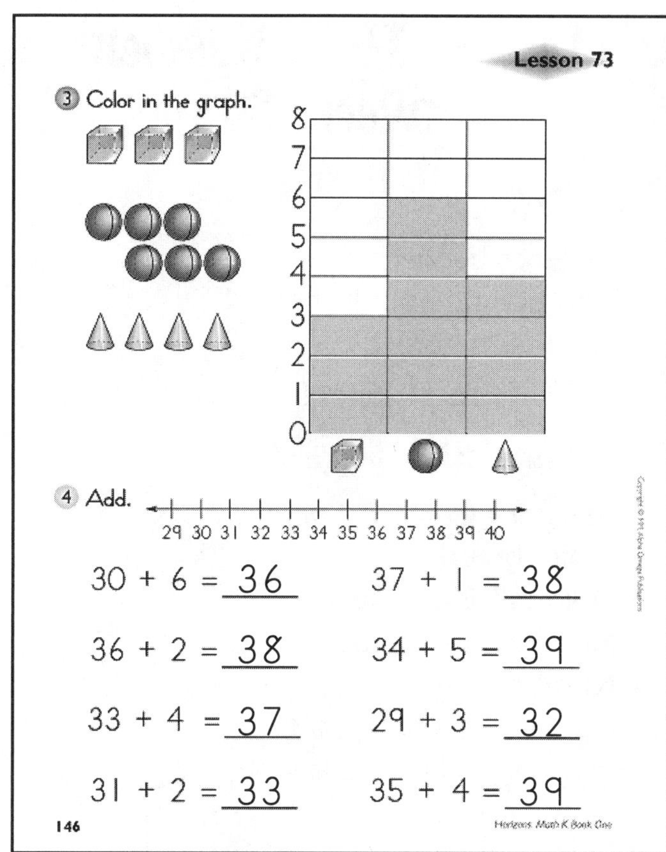

Lesson 74 - Number Between 60's

Overview:

- Number between 60's
- Find perimeter in inches
- Number before 1's
- Pennies, nickels, dollar

Materials and Supplies:

- Teacher's Guide & Student Workbook
- White board
- Objects for counters
- Number flash cards
- Number chart
- Count by 5's flash cards
- Pennies, nickels, dollars
- Number line strip
- Ruler – inches

Teaching Tips:

Teach number between 60's.
Review perimeter.
Review inches.
Review number before 1's.
Review money.
Review oral counting to 90.

Activities:

① Choose three consecutive whole number flash cards 60–70. Arrange the cards out of order. Have the student(s) put them in correct order. Repeat this four times with different sets of three numbers. Read the instruction and have the student(s) complete the activity. They may use a number line or number chart if needed.

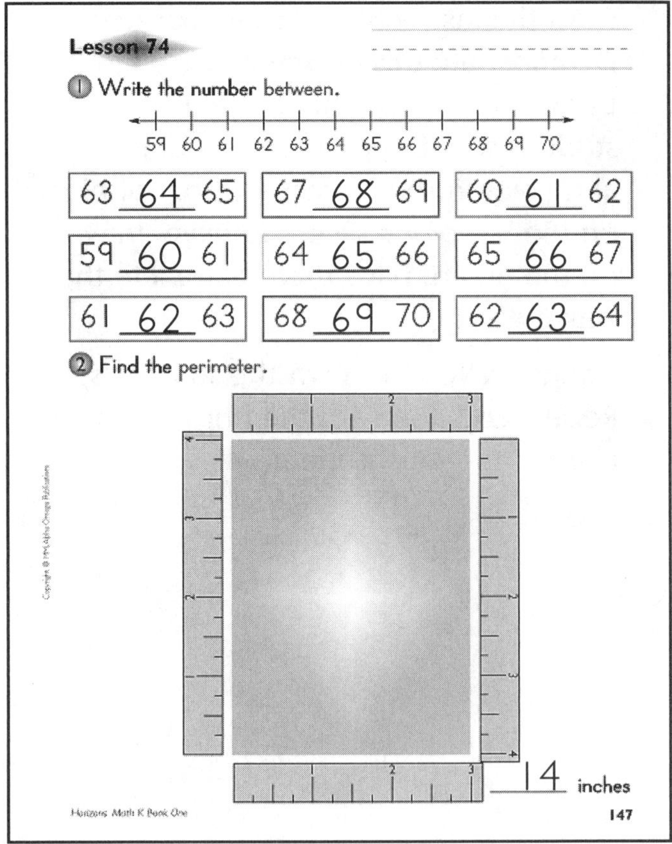

② Review inches and perimeter. This is a larger rectangle. If needed, have the student(s) place counters for the correct number over each ruler. After doing this they should count all of the counters and write the answer on the blank.

③ The number before is counting backward. Have the student(s) count backwards from 10. Point to a number line if necessary. Practice this during games or activities where you can do a countdown before starting: 10, 9, 8, 7, 6, 5, 4, 3 ,2 ,1–go! Sing the *Countdown* song. Have them complete the activity.

④ Review money with flash cards or coins and $1 bills. Review counting by 5's. Talk about things that are equal. Demonstrate this with a balance used in science labs or make a simple hanging pan balance. Emphasize that amounts on both sides of the balance must be equal in weight. The coins in this activity are equal only if they have the same value. Read the instruction and work the first problem with the student(s).

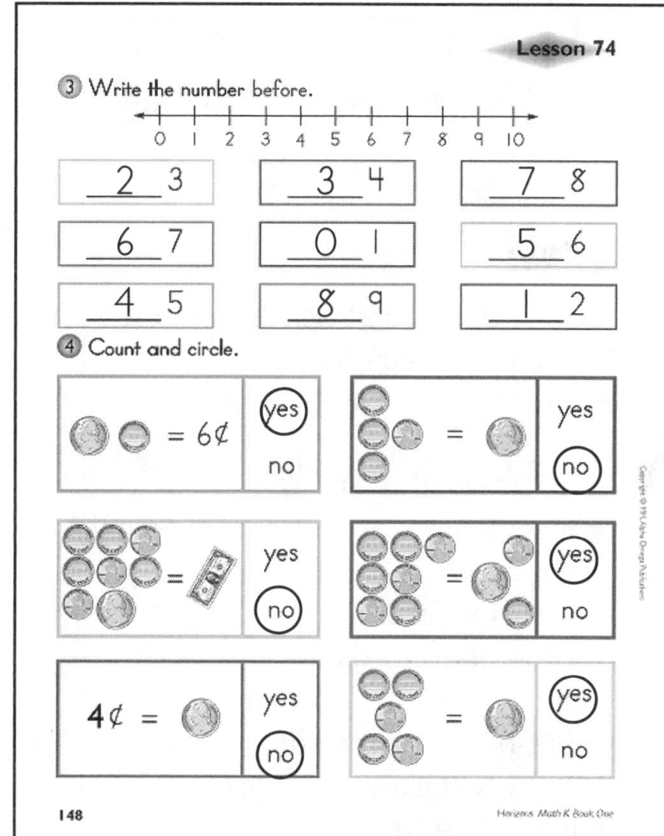
Lesson 74

③ Write the number before.

0 1 2 3 4 5 6 7 8 9 10

2 3 | 3 4 | 7 8
6 7 | 0 1 | 5 6
4 5 | 8 9 | 1 2

④ Count and circle.

= 6¢ yes no
= yes no
= yes no
= yes no
4¢ = yes no
= yes no

148 Horizons Math K Book One

Lesson 75 - Identify Things That Belong Together

Overview:

- Identify things that belong together
- Number between 60's
- Perimeter

Materials and Supplies:

- Teacher's Guide & Student Workbook
- White board
- Objects for counters
- Number flash cards
- Number chart
- Count by 5's flash cards
- Pennies & dollars
- Number line strip
- Ruler – inches

Teaching Tips:

Teach things that go together
Review number between 60's.
Review perimeter.
Review inches.
Teach oral counting to 100.

Activities:

① Ask the student(s) if they can think of food items that go together. (hot dog–catsup, hamburger–bun, lettuce–dressing, etc.) Ask for other items that go together. (pencil–paper, table–chair, bicycle–rider) They will bring up some interesting combinations if given the opportunity. Read the directions. Go through each item in the activity. After reading the directions again have them complete the activity.

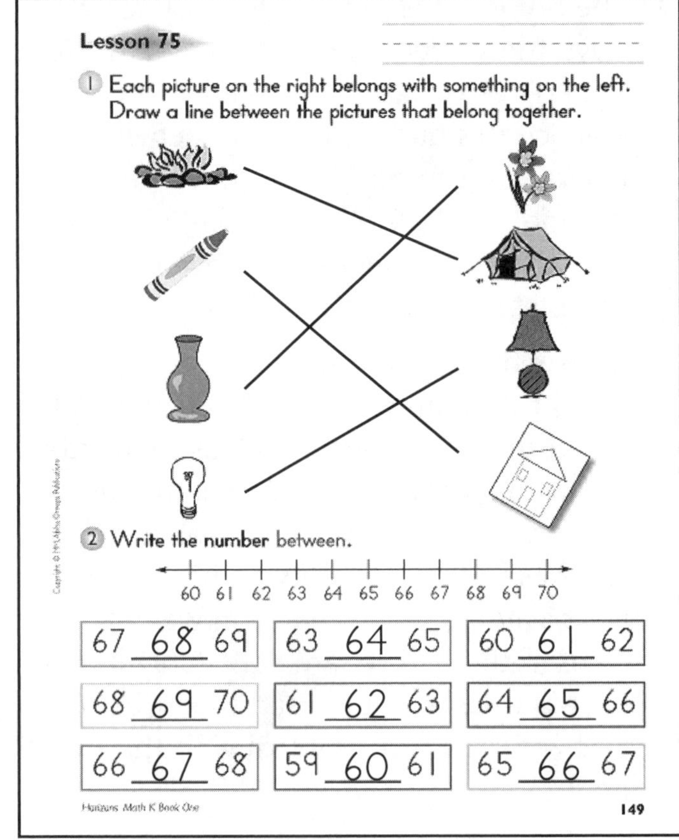

② Choose three consecutive whole-number flash cards 60–70. Hold up two cards with the number between missing. Have the student(s) tell you what number is missing. Repeat this four times with different sets of two numbers. Have the student(s) complete the activity. They may use a number line or number chart if needed.

③ Review inches and perimeter. This is another large rectangle. If the student(s) get confused counting around for the inches, have them place counters for the correct number over each ruler. After doing this they should count all of the counters and write the answer on the blank.

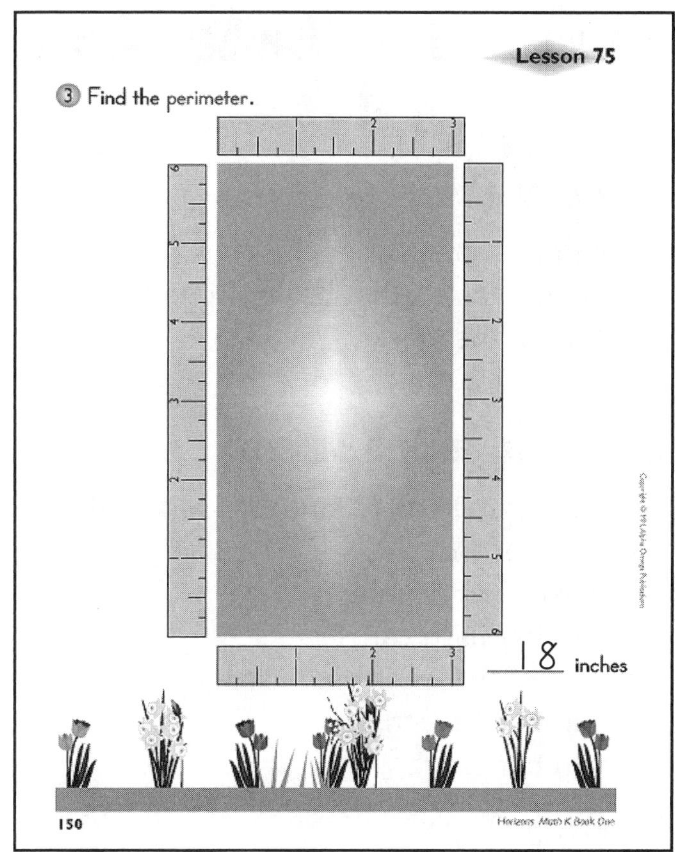

If this is the first time your student(s) have counted orally by 1's to 100, make a big deal out of it. This is a major accomplishment and a necessary requirement for beginning 1st grade math.

Lesson 76 - Number After 40's

Overview:

- Number after 40's
- Identify things that belong together
- Days of the week
- Addition 20's

Materials and Supplies:

- Teacher's Guide & Student Workbook
- White board
- Objects for counters
- Number flash cards
- Days of the week flash cards
- Number line strips
- Number chart

Teaching Tips:

Teach number after 40's.
Review things that go together.
Review days of the week.
Review addition 10's & 20's.
Review counting orally to 100.

Activities:

① Read the numbers in the chart together with the student(s). Point out that these are the odd numbers and are something that will be covered a little later. Count orally to 50 by 1's. Have the student(s) fill in the missing numbers using a number chart if needed. After writing the numbers, read the numbers written together with the class. Explain that these are the even numbers and that counting by every two numbers is called skip counting.

Lesson 76

① Write the number after.

1	2	3	4	5	6	7	8	9	10
11	12	13	14	15	16	17	18	19	20
21	22	23	24	25	26	27	28	29	30
31	32	33	34	35	36	37	38	39	40
41	42	43	44	45	46	47	48	49	50

② Draw a line between the pictures that belong together.

Horizons Math K Book One 151

② Ask the student(s) for additional items that go together. Read the directions. Go through each item in the activity. After reading the directions again have them complete the activity.

③ Review the days of the week several times with flash cards and/or a calendar. Read the instructions and read through each list once, then read them again.

④ Drill the 1's family, sums to 9, addition facts with flash cards. Do several 20's family addition problems with the class. Allow the student(s) to complete Activity ④ by going to the first number on the number line and counting the number added to it.

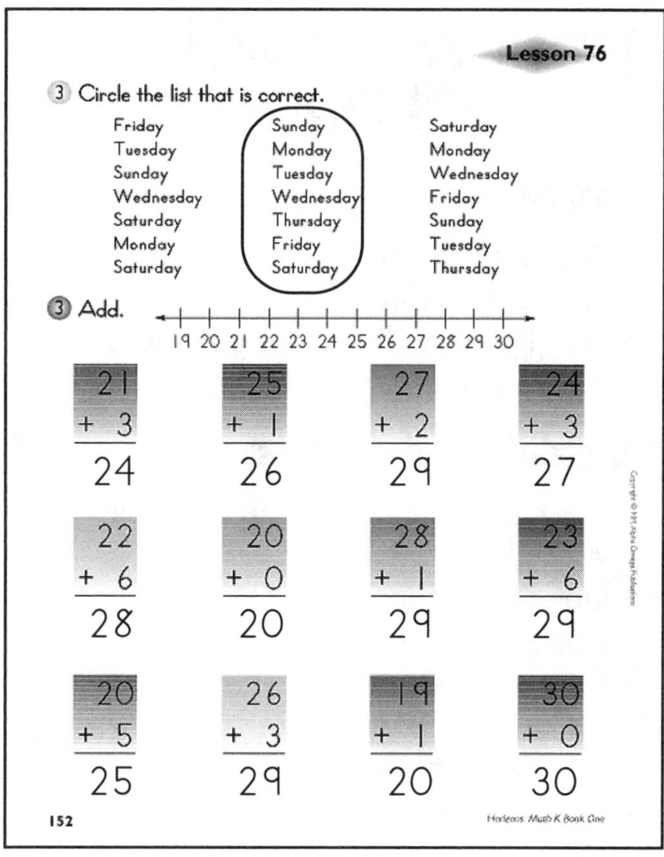

Lesson 77 - Digital Clock, Minutes

Overview:

- Digital clock, minutes
- Number after 40's
- Identify things that belong together
- Place value 20's

Materials and Supplies:

- Teacher's Guide & Student Workbook
- White board
- Objects for counters
- Number flash cards
- Number chart
- Place value chart
- Place value blocks
- Clock models
- Number line strips

Teaching Tips:

Teach time – 10 minutes.
Review number after 40's.
Review things that go together.
Review number after 1–50.
Review counting orally to 100.

Activities:

① Give each student a small digital clock model. Explain that a digital clock is like the place value chart. The numbers before the dots are hours. The first number place after the dots is 10 minutes, and the last place is minutes. Show them the numbers on a circular clock. The numbers 1–12 are for hours, so the numbers that can be placed in the hours' place are 1–12. Count around the clock by 10's to demonstrate that 0–5 are the numbers that can be used in the 10 minutes' place.

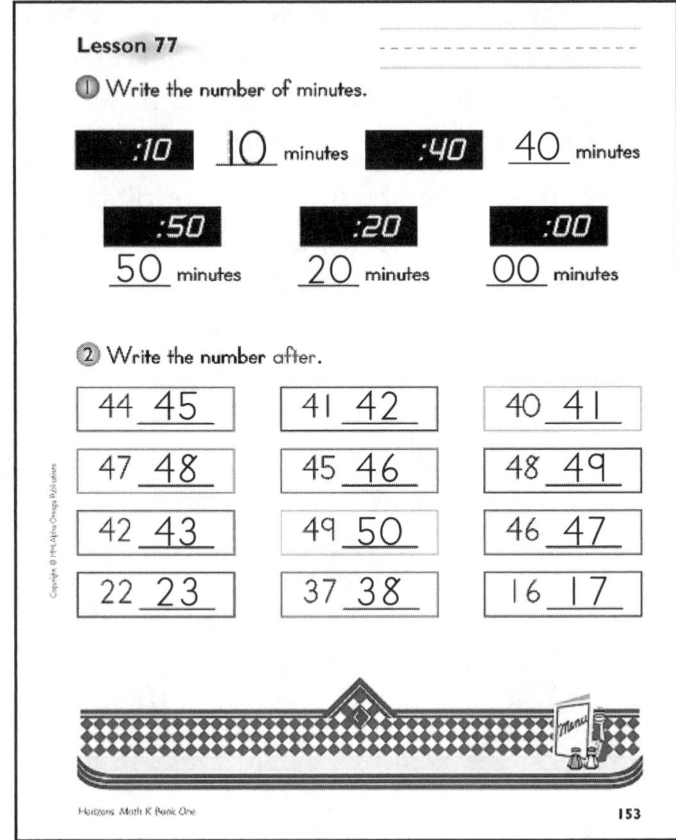

Lesson 77

① Write the number of minutes.

:10 10 minutes　:40 40 minutes

:50 50 minutes　:20 20 minutes　:00 00 minutes

② Write the number after.

44 45	41 42	40 41
47 48	45 46	48 49
42 43	49 50	46 47
22 23	37 38	16 17

Horizons Math K Book One 153

Explain that instead of getting to 60 minutes that the digital clock moves to the next hour. Count by ones to 10 to show that 0–9 are the numbers that can be in the last place. Read the instruction to Activity ①. Review the sample problem and have them trace the 10. After this practice, they should be able to complete the rest of the activity independently.

② Orally review the 40's and number after. Caution the student(s) that this activity includes numbers other than 40's.

③ Continue to ask the student(s) for items that go together. Read the directions. Go through each item in the activity. After reading the directions again have them complete the activity.

④ Do some place value review with flash cards and the place value chart. Review several examples with 10's and 1's blocks. Help the student(s) only as necessary in completing this activity.

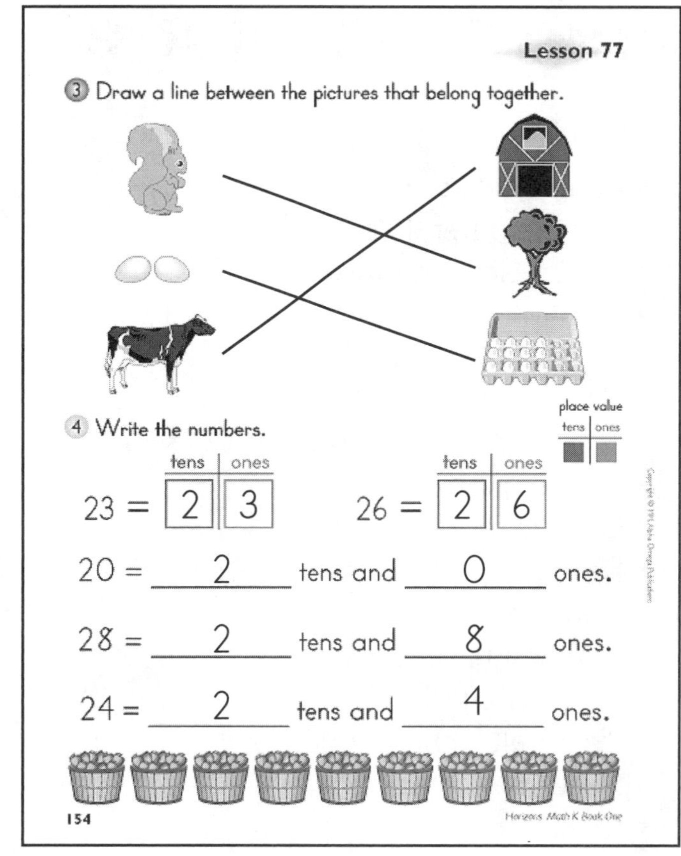

Lesson 77

③ Draw a line between the pictures that belong together.

④ Write the numbers.

place value: tens | ones

	tens	ones
23 =	2	3
26 =	2	6

20 = 2 tens and 0 ones.

28 = 2 tens and 8 ones.

24 = 2 tens and 4 ones.

154 Horizons Math K Book One

Lesson 78 - Addition 40's

Overview:

- Addition 40's
- Number after 40's
- Digital clock, minutes
- Addition 1's

Material and Supplies:

- Teacher's Guide & Student Workbook
- White board
- Objects for counters
- Number flash cards
- Count by 10's flash card
- Addition flash cards 1's
- Number chart
- Place value chart
- Place value blocks
- Clock models
- Number line strips

Teaching Tips:

Teach addition 40's.
Review number after 1–50.
Review time – 10 minutes.
Review addition 1's.
Review counting orally to 100.

Activities:

① This is the first time that the students are asked to add to the 40's family. In this activity they are adding a 0, 1, 2 or a 3 to a number in the 40's family. Do several examples on the white board using either a number line strip or a number chart. Ask the student(s) where they might see the number 40 in everyday activities. Possible answers might be a speed limit sign, yardage markers in football, money, birthday cards.

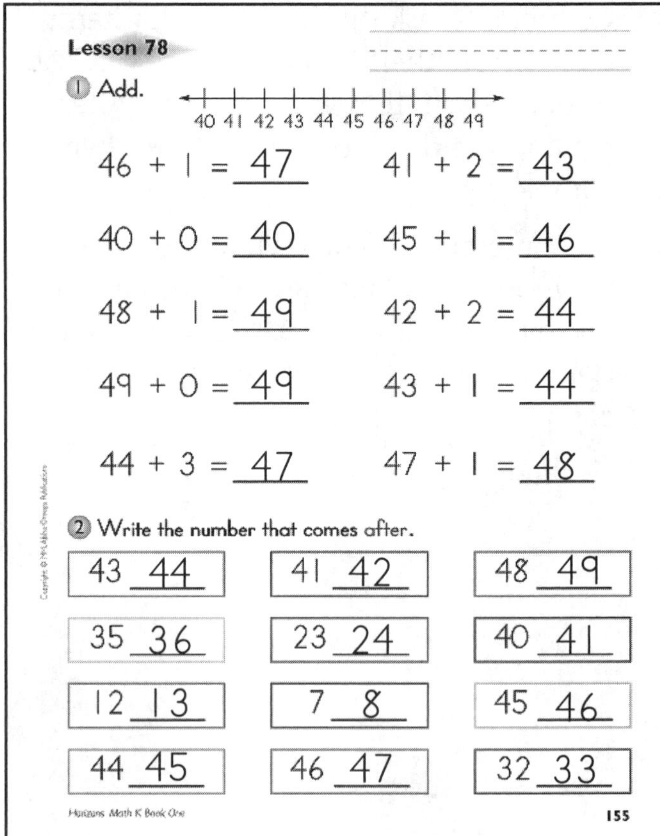

Lesson 78

① Add.

40 41 42 43 44 45 46 47 48 49

46 + 1 = 47	41 + 2 = 43
40 + 0 = 40	45 + 1 = 46
48 + 1 = 49	42 + 2 = 44
49 + 0 = 49	43 + 1 = 44
44 + 3 = 47	47 + 1 = 48

② Write the number that comes after.

43 44	41 42	48 49
35 36	23 24	40 41
12 13	7 8	45 46
44 45	46 47	32 33

Horizons Math K Book One 155

② Orally review the 40's and number after. Caution the student(s) that this activity includes numbers 1–50.

③ Give each student a small digital clock model. Review that a digital clock is like the place value chart. The numbers before the dots are hours. The first number place after the dots is 10 minutes and the last place is minutes. Show them the numbers on a circular clock. The numbers 1–12 are for hours so the numbers that can be placed in the hours' place are 1–12. Count around the clock by 10's to demonstrate that 0–5 are the numbers that can be used in the 10 minutes' place. Explain that instead of getting to 60 minutes that the digital clock moves to the next hour. Count by ones to 10 to show that 0–9 are the numbers that can be in the last place. Count by 10 to 60 several times. Read the instruction to Activity ③. Review the sample problem and have them trace the 10. After this practice, they should be able to complete the rest of the activity independently.

④ Do some oral review of addition facts ones' family. Have them complete the activity.

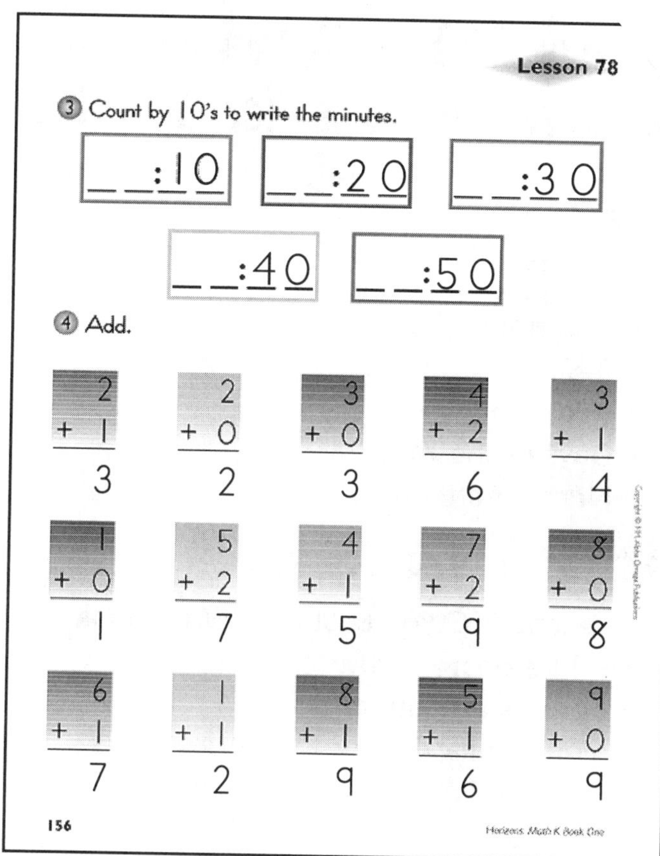

Lesson 79 - Determine the Greater or Smaller Number 0-9

Overview:

- Determine the greater or smaller number 0–9
- Addition 40's
- Days of the week
- Number after 40's

Materials and Supplies:

- Teacher's Guide & Student Workbook
- White board
- Objects for counters
- Number flash cards
- Number line strips
- Calendar
- Months of the year flash cards
- Days of the week flash cards
- Number chart

Teaching Tips:

Teach greater of two numbers 1's.
Review addition 40's.
Review calendar.
Review number after 1–50.
Review counting orally to 100.

Activities:

① Have each student count out a set of 4 counters and a set of 6 counters. Ask them which set has the most counters. Which number is greater: 4 or 6? Do this with the number chart and with a number line pointing out that the numbers get bigger as you move left to right because they represent more items. Read the instruction for Activity ①. Have them count out counters for each pair of numbers to give them a visual image of which number is greater.

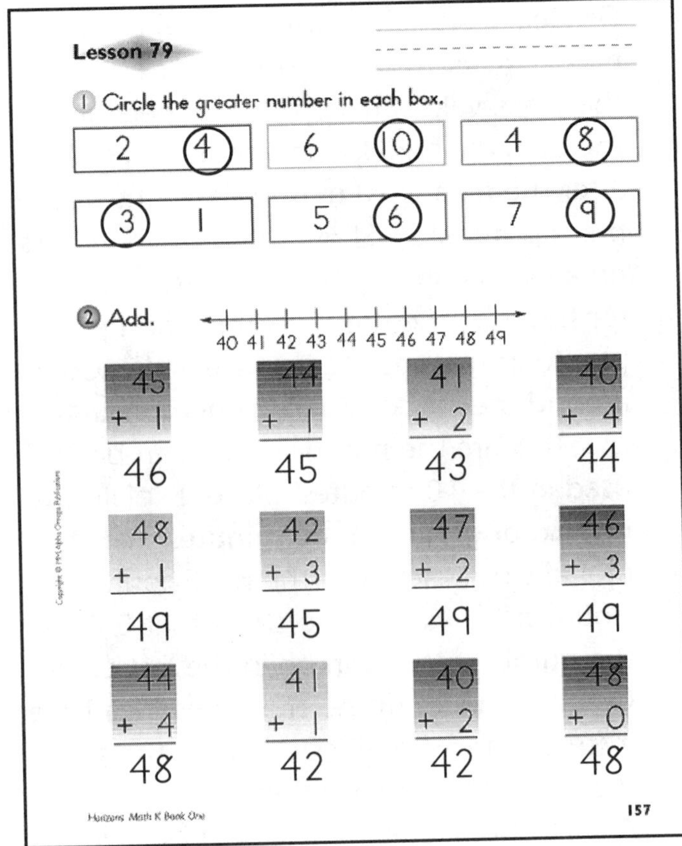

Lesson 79

① Circle the greater number in each box.

2 (4)	6 (10)	4 (8)
(3) 1	5 (6)	7 (9)

② Add.

40 41 42 43 44 45 46 47 48 49

45 + 1 = 46	44 + 1 = 45	41 + 2 = 43	40 + 4 = 44
48 + 1 = 49	42 + 3 = 45	47 + 2 = 49	46 + 3 = 49
44 + 4 = 48	41 + 1 = 42	40 + 2 = 42	48 + 0 = 48

Horizons Math K Book One 157

② This is the second time that the students are asked to add to the 40's family. In this activity they are adding a 0, 1, 2, 3 or a 4 to a number in the 40's family. Do several examples on the white board using either a number line strip or a number chart. Ask the student(s) for some more examples of where they might see the number 40 in everyday activities.

③ Review days of the week and months of the year with flash cards. Review the *Thirty Days Hath September* poem. Read the questions for Activity ③ and have the student(s) write their answers.

④ Orally review the 40's and number after. Caution the student(s) that this activity includes numbers 1–50.

Lesson 80 - Count to 80

Overview:

- Count to 80
- Pennies, dimes, nickels
- Addition 40's
- Determine the greater or smaller number 0–9

Material and Supplies:

- Teacher's Guide & Student Workbook
- White board
- Objects for counters
- Number flash cards
- Number line strips
- Nickels & pennies
- Count by 5's flash cards
- Number chart
- Worksheet 19 & 29

Teaching Tips:

Teach counting objects to 80.
Teach smaller of two numbers.
Review addition 40's.
Review pennies & nickels.
Review counting orally to 100.

Activities:

① Count out loud by ones to 80 using the number chart. Have the student(s) count the objects in the activity. Ask them for the name of each shape and the color of the shapes in each row. Review ordinal numbers by asking what shape or color is in the 4th row, etc.

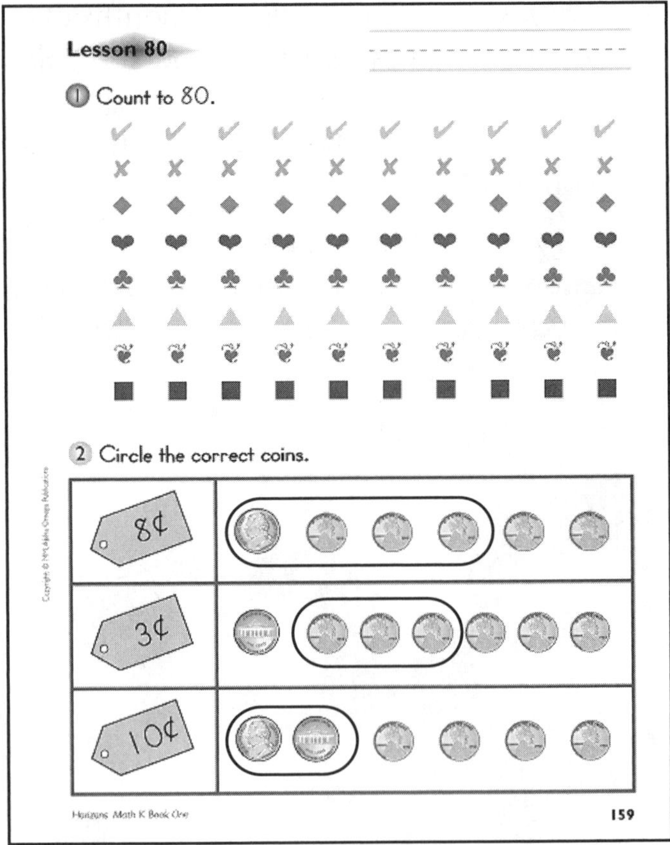

② Review counting by 5's. Show several nickel and penny combinations asking the student(s) if they are equal or different. Read the instruction for Activity ②. The student(s) should be able to complete the activity independently.

③ Do several examples of addition of 40's on the white board using either a number line strip or a number chart.

④ Have each student count out a set of 3 counters and a set of 7 counters. Ask them which set is the smaller. Which number is smaller: 3 or 7? Do this with the number chart and with a number line, pointing out that the numbers get smaller as you move right to left because they represent fewer items. Read the instruction for Activity ④. Have them count out counters for each pair of numbers to give them a visual image of which number is smaller.

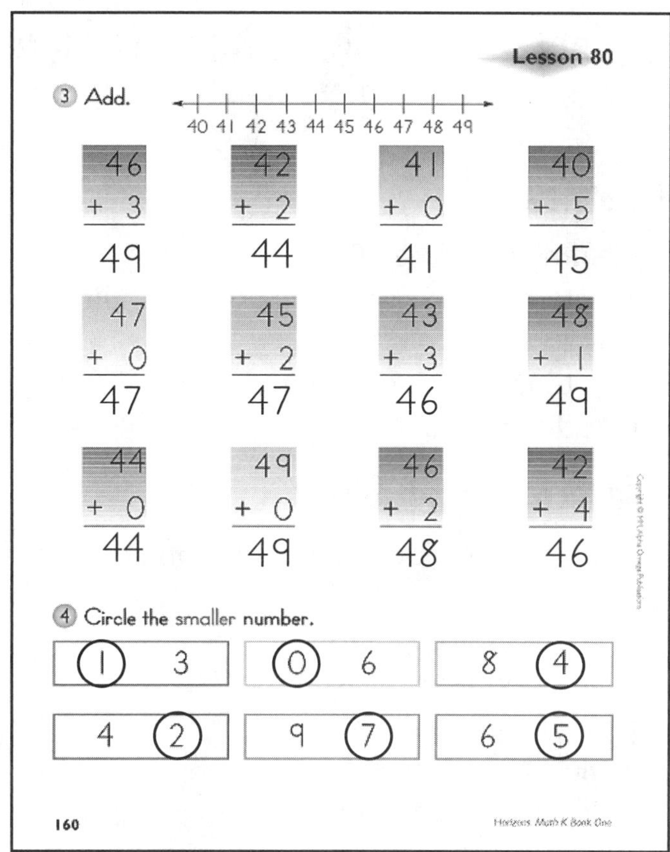

Lesson 80

③ Add.

40 41 42 43 44 45 46 47 48 49

46 + 3 = 49	42 + 2 = 44	41 + 0 = 41	40 + 5 = 45
47 + 0 = 47	45 + 2 = 47	43 + 3 = 46	48 + 1 = 49
44 + 0 = 44	49 + 0 = 49	46 + 2 = 48	42 + 4 = 46

④ Circle the smaller number.

(1) 3	(0) 6	8 (4)
4 (2)	9 (7)	6 (5)

160 Horizons Math K Book One

Lesson 81 - Number Before 10's

Overview:

- Number before 10's
- Determine the greater or smaller number 0–20
- Determine the smaller number 0–20
- Addition 40's

Materials and Supplies:

- Teacher's Guide & Student Workbook
- White board
- Objects for counters
- Number flash cards 1–20
- Number line strips
- Nickels & pennies
- Count by 5's flash cards
- Number chart

Teaching Tips:

Teach number before 10's.
Review counting objects to 80.
Review greater & smaller of two numbers.
Review addition 40's.
Review counting orally to 100.

Activities:

① Use a number chart to point to numbers in the 10s' family. Have the student(s) tell what number comes before the one you are pointing to. Demonstrate that they are moving back one number to find the number before. If you have practiced the countdown from 10 to 0, try starting at 20 and do the same. It may be necessary to point to a number chart as you do this until the student(s) no longer need to see the numbers.

② Have each student count out a set of 11 counters and a set of 15 counters. Ask them which set has the greater number of counters. Which number is greater: 11 or 15? Do this with the number chart and with a number line, pointing out that the numbers get larger as you move to the right because they represent more items. Read the instruction for Activity ②. Have them count out counters for each pair of numbers to give them a visual image of which number is the greater.

③ Have each student count out a set of 8 counters and a set of 16 counters. Ask them which set has the least counters. Which number is smaller 8 or 16? Do this with the number chart and with a number line, pointing out that the numbers get smaller as you move to the left because they represent fewer items. Read the instruction for Activity ③. Have them count out counters for each pair of numbers to give them a visual image of which number is smaller.

④ Do several examples of addition of 40's on the white board using either a number line strip or a number chart.

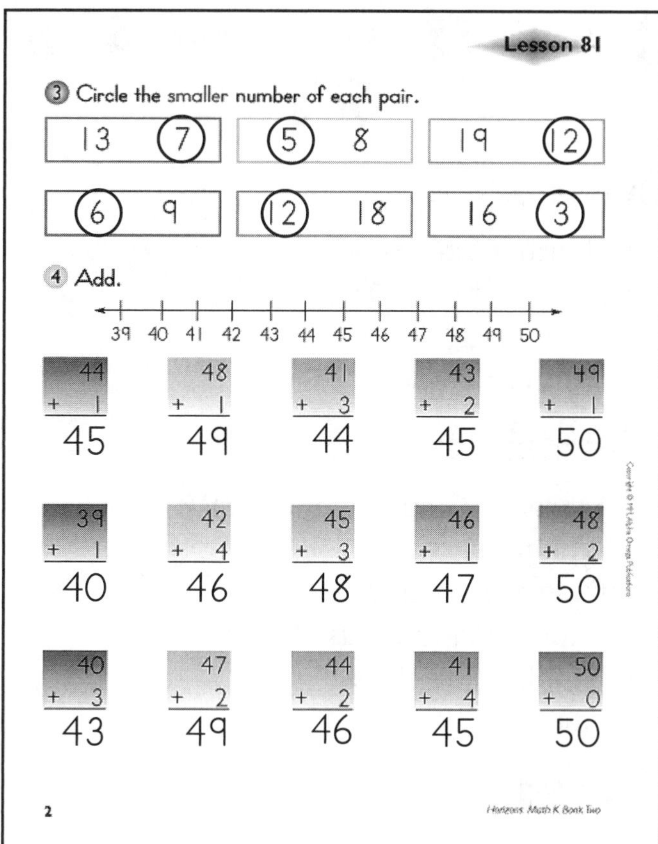

Lesson 82 - Number After 50's

Overview:

- Number after 50's
- Number before 10's
- Addition 30's & 40's
- Smaller number 0–20

Materials and Supplies:

- Teacher's Guide & Student Workbook
- White board
- Objects for counters
- Addition flash cards 1's family
- Number line strips
- Number chart

Teaching Tips:

Teach number after 50's.
Review number before 10's.
Review greater & smaller of two numbers.
Review addition 40's.
Review counting orally to 100.

Activities:

① Review number sequence by pointing to a number chart and asking the student(s) to say the number after 50's. The numbers in this activity are from the 50's family. (50–59) Read the instruction and have the student(s) complete the activity.

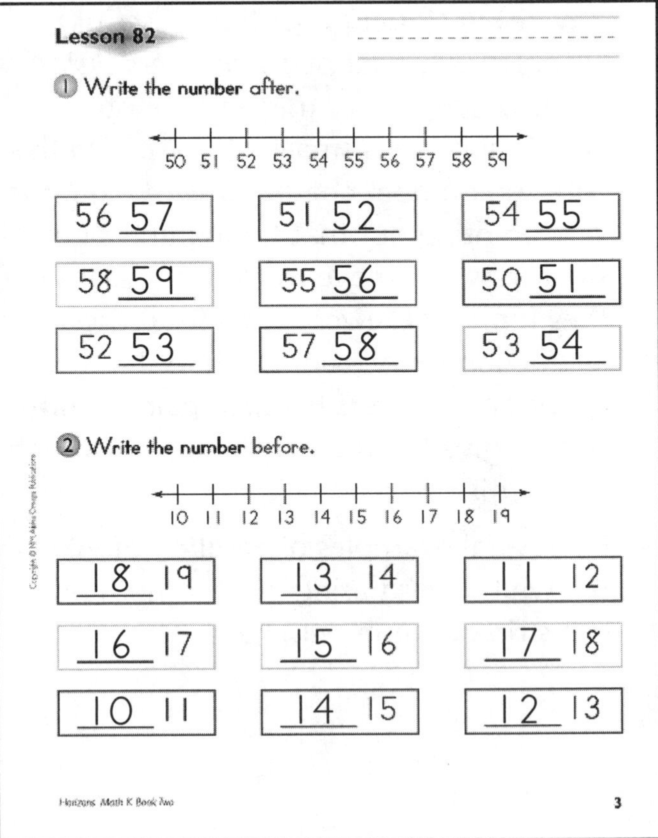

② Use a number chart to point to numbers in the 10's family. Have the student(s) tell what number comes before the one you are pointing to. Demonstrate that they are moving back one number to find the number before. Try counting backward from 20 with the student(s). It may be necessary to point to a number chart as you do this until the student(s) no longer need to see the numbers.

③ Drill the 1's family, sums to 9, addition facts with flash cards. Do several 30's and 40's family addition problems with the class. Allow the student(s) to complete Activity ③ by going to the first number on the number line and counting the number added to it. Alert them that the problems in this activity are from both the 30's and the 40's family.

④ Review greater and smaller number as you feel is necessary. Do some review with the number chart or number line pointing out the larger or the smaller of two numbers. Read the instruction for the activity. If necessary have them count out counters for each pair of numbers to give them a visual image of which number is smaller.

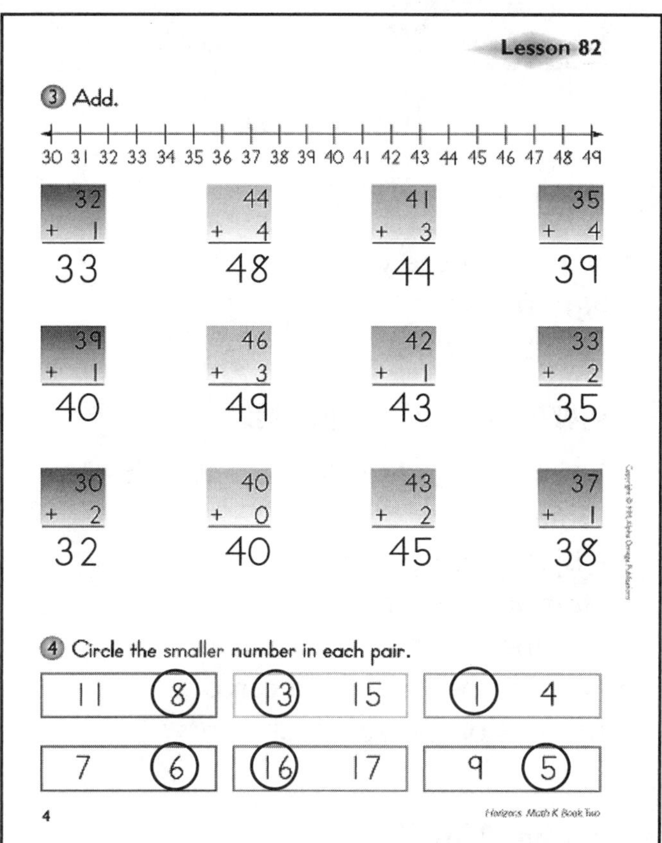

Lesson 83 - Months of the Year

Overview:

- Months of the year
- Number after 50's
- Number before 10's

Materials and Supplies:

- Teacher's Guide & Student Workbook
- White board
- Objects for counters
- Number line strips
- Number chart
- Days of the week flash cards
- Months of the year flash cards
- Calendars

Teaching Tips:

Teach calendar months.
Review days of the week.
Review number after 50's.
Review number before 10's.
Review oral counting to 100.

Activities:

① Review the use of a calendar. Discuss months, days, weeks and year. Have the student(s) repeat the months after you or say them as you point to them on a calendar. Ask them if they know what month it is? Do they know the date? The day of the week? The year? The century? Discuss any of these that the student(s) do not know. Recite with the student(s) *Thirty Days Hath September.* Review the days of the week by having the student(s) repeat them after you or say them as you point to them on a calendar. Show them different types of calendars. Read each question in Activity ① and give the student(s) time to count and write their answers.

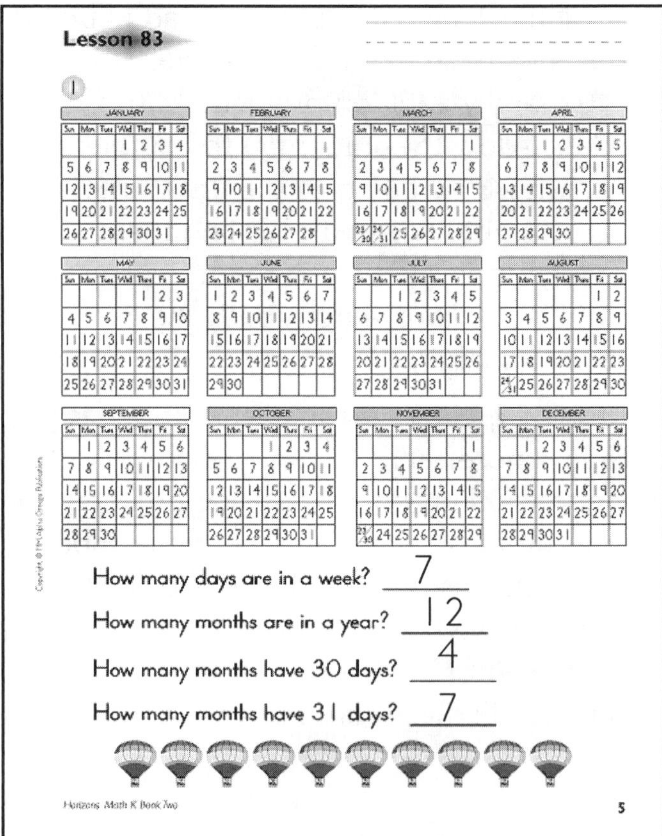

Lesson 83

①

JANUARY

Sun	Mon	Tues	Wed	Thurs	Fri	Sat
			1	2	3	4
5	6	7	8	9	10	11
12	13	14	15	16	17	18
19	20	21	22	23	24	25
26	27	28	29	30	31	

FEBRUARY

Sun	Mon	Tues	Wed	Thurs	Fri	Sat
						1
2	3	4	5	6	7	8
9	10	11	12	13	14	15
16	17	18	19	20	21	22
23	24	25	26	27	28	

MARCH

Sun	Mon	Tues	Wed	Thurs	Fri	Sat
						1
2	3	4	5	6	7	8
9	10	11	12	13	14	15
16	17	18	19	20	21	22
23/30	24/31	25	26	27	28	29

APRIL

Sun	Mon	Tues	Wed	Thurs	Fri	Sat
		1	2	3	4	5
6	7	8	9	10	11	12
13	14	15	16	17	18	19
20	21	22	23	24	25	26
27	28	29	30			

MAY

Sun	Mon	Tues	Wed	Thurs	Fri	Sat
				1	2	3
4	5	6	7	8	9	10
11	12	13	14	15	16	17
18	19	20	21	22	23	24
25	26	27	28	29	30	31

JUNE

Sun	Mon	Tues	Wed	Thurs	Fri	Sat
1	2	3	4	5	6	7
8	9	10	11	12	13	14
15	16	17	18	19	20	21
22	23	24	25	26	27	28
29	30					

JULY

Sun	Mon	Tues	Wed	Thurs	Fri	Sat
		1	2	3	4	5
6	7	8	9	10	11	12
13	14	15	16	17	18	19
20	21	22	23	24	25	26
27	28	29	30	31		

AUGUST

Sun	Mon	Tues	Wed	Thurs	Fri	Sat
					1	2
3	4	5	6	7	8	9
10	11	12	13	14	15	16
17	18	19	20	21	22	23
24/31	25	26	27	28	29	30

SEPTEMBER

Sun	Mon	Tues	Wed	Thurs	Fri	Sat
	1	2	3	4	5	6
7	8	9	10	11	12	13
14	15	16	17	18	19	20
21	22	23	24	25	26	27
28	29	30				

OCTOBER

Sun	Mon	Tues	Wed	Thurs	Fri	Sat
			1	2	3	4
5	6	7	8	9	10	11
12	13	14	15	16	17	18
19	20	21	22	23	24	25
26	27	28	29	30	31	

NOVEMBER

Sun	Mon	Tues	Wed	Thurs	Fri	Sat
						1
2	3	4	5	6	7	8
9	10	11	12	13	14	15
16	17	18	19	20	21	22
23/30	24	25	26	27	28	29

DECEMBER

Sun	Mon	Tues	Wed	Thurs	Fri	Sat
	1	2	3	4	5	6
7	8	9	10	11	12	13
14	15	16	17	18	19	20
21	22	23	24	25	26	27
28	29	30	31			

How many days are in a week? 7

How many months are in a year? 12

How many months have 30 days? 4

How many months have 31 days? 7

Horizons Math K Book Two 5

② Review number sequence by pointing to a number chart and asking the student(s) to say the number after 50's. Read the instruction and have the student(s) complete the activity.

③ Use a number chart to point to numbers in the 10's family. Have the student(s) tell what number comes before the one you are pointing to. Also review numbers in the 1's family. Demonstrate that they are moving back one number to find the number before. Try counting backward from 20 with the student(s). It may be necessary to point to a number chart as you do this until the student(s) no longer needs to see the numbers.

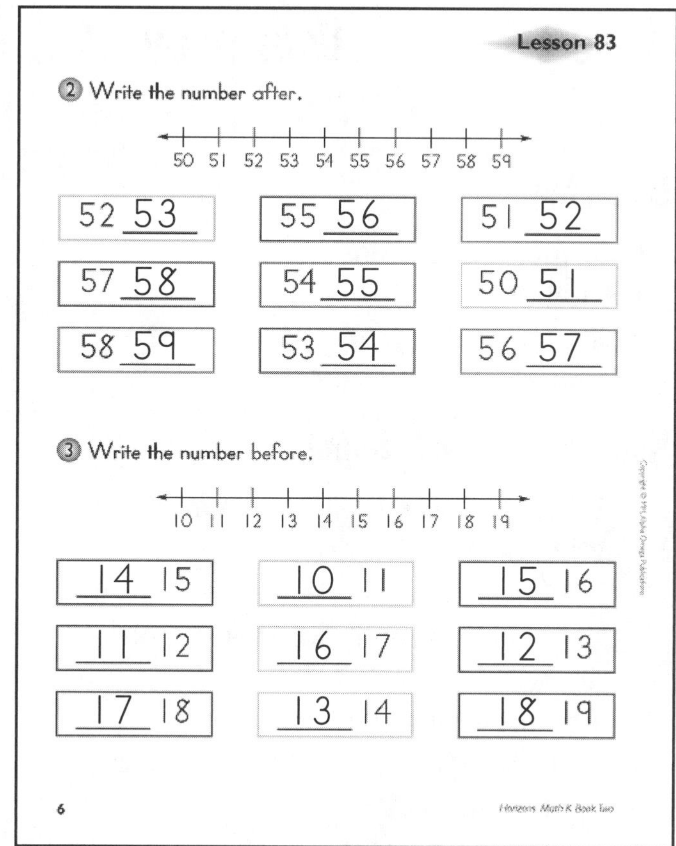

Lesson 84 - Count by 2's, Evens

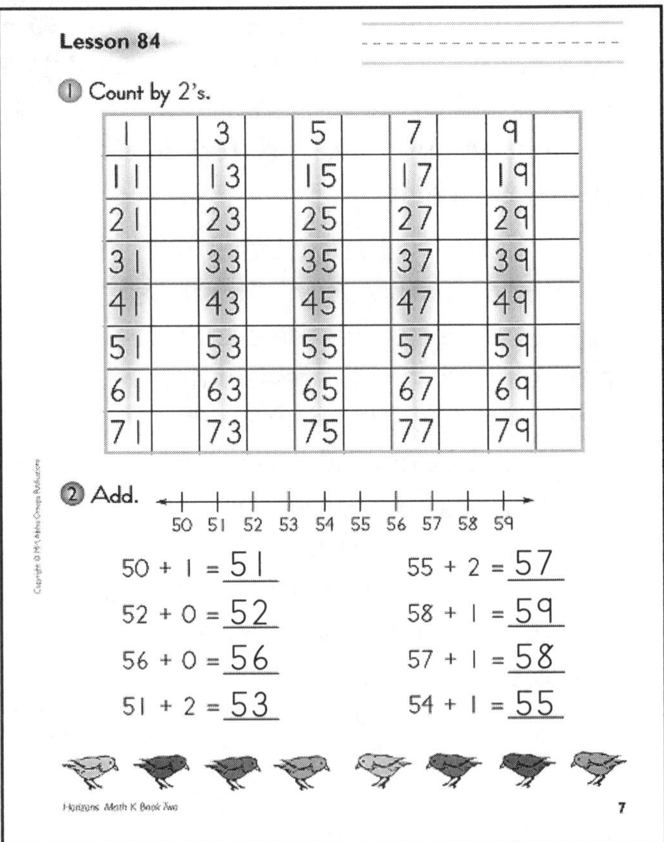

Lesson 84

① Count by 2's.

1		3		5		7		9	
11		13		15		17		19	
21		23		25		27		29	
31		33		35		37		39	
41		43		45		47		49	
51		53		55		57		59	
61		63		65		67		69	
71		73		75		77		79	

② Add.

50 + 1 = 51 55 + 2 = 57

52 + 0 = 52 58 + 1 = 59

56 + 0 = 56 57 + 1 = 58

51 + 2 = 53 54 + 1 = 55

Horizons Math K Book Two 7

Overview:

- Count by 2's, evens
- Addition 50's
- Months of the year, ordinal numbers
- Pennies, dimes, nickels

Materials and Supplies:

- Teacher's Guide & Student Workbook
- White board
- Objects for counters
- Dimes, nickels, half dollar & pennies
- Calendar
- Ordinal number flash cards
- Count by 5's and 10's flash cards
- Addition flash cards 1's family
- Number flash cards
- Number chart
- Number line strips
- Worksheet 32

Teaching Tips:

Teach even and odd numbers.
Teach counting by 2's.
Review addition 50's.
Review calendar and months of the year.
Review ordinal numbers.
Review coins.
Drill addition 1's family.
Review oral counting to 100.

Activities:

① Count orally to 80 by 1's. Then read the numbers in the chart together with the student(s). Point out that these are the odd numbers. Discuss with the student(s) that counting by twos means to count every other number, to count every second number, or to add two to each number. Explain that counting by every two numbers is called skip counting. Play a game at recess or on the playground of *Simon Says*. Have the students line up single file. Number them off or give each student a flash card of their number. Give instructions like the following: Simon says odd numbers move forward 1 step. Simon says the number before 5 move forward one step. Simon says the number after 9 move forward one step. Simon says the answer to 4 plus 2 move forward one step. Be creative and review several concepts. Instruct the student(s) to complete the chart. The numbers that they write on the chart are even numbers. Read the even numbers after the student(s) have written them in.

② This is the first time that the students are asked to add to the 50's family. In this activity they are adding a 0, 1, or 2 to a number in the 50's family. Do several examples on the white board using either a number line strip or a number chart. Do additional practice of the 50's family with a half dollar and pennies.

③ Review the use of a calendar. Review ordinal numbers. Read each instruction for Activity ③ and have the student(s) write their answers.

④ Review counting by 5's and 10's. Have the student(s) count the coins in the activity and write their answers.

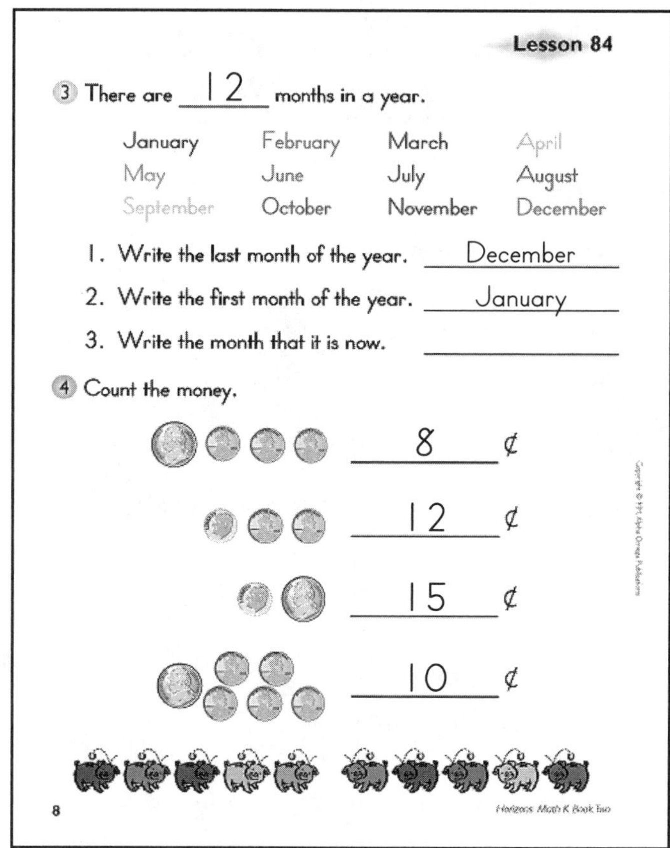
Lesson 84

③ There are 12 months in a year.

January	February	March	April
May	June	July	August
September	October	November	December

1. Write the last month of the year. December
2. Write the first month of the year. January
3. Write the month that it is now. ______

④ Count the money.

8 ¢

12 ¢

15 ¢

10 ¢

8

Horizons Math K Book Two

Lesson 85 - Number Between 70's

Overview:

- Number between 70's
- Count by 2's, evens
- Months of the year
- Addition 50's

Materials and Supplies:

- Teacher's Guide & Student Workbook
- White board
- Objects for counters
- Number flash cards
- Number chart
- Number line strips
- Calendar
- Addition flash cards 1's family

Teaching Tips:

Teach number between 70's.
Review even numbers.
Review counting by 2's.
Review calendar.
Review addition 50's.
Drill addition 1's family.
Review oral counting to 100.

Activities:

① Choose three consecutive whole number flash cards 70–80. Arrange the cards out of order. Have the student(s) put them in correct order. Repeat this four times with different sets of three numbers. Read the instruction and have the student(s) complete the activity. They may use a number line or number chart if needed.

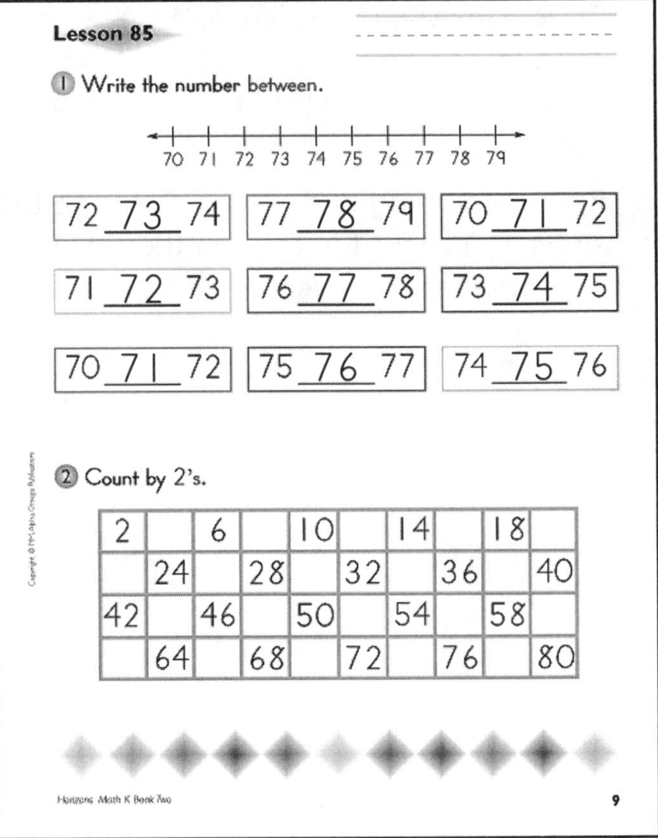

② Count orally to 80 by 1's. Discuss with the student(s) that counting by twos means to count every other number, to count every second number, or to add two to each number. Explain that counting by every two numbers is called *skip counting*. Count by 2's to 80, even numbers, with a number chart. Instruct the student(s) to complete the chart in Activity ②. After they have finished, read the numbers in the chart together with the student(s). Point out that these are the even numbers. Add even numbers to the game *Simon Says* mentioned before. Include even numbers with the instructions for the game.

③ Review the use of a calendar. Read each question for Activity ③ and have the student(s) write their answers.

④ This is the second time that the students are asked to add to the 50's family. In this activity they are adding a 0, 1, 2 or 3 to a number in the 50's family. Do several examples on the white board using either a number line strip or a number chart.

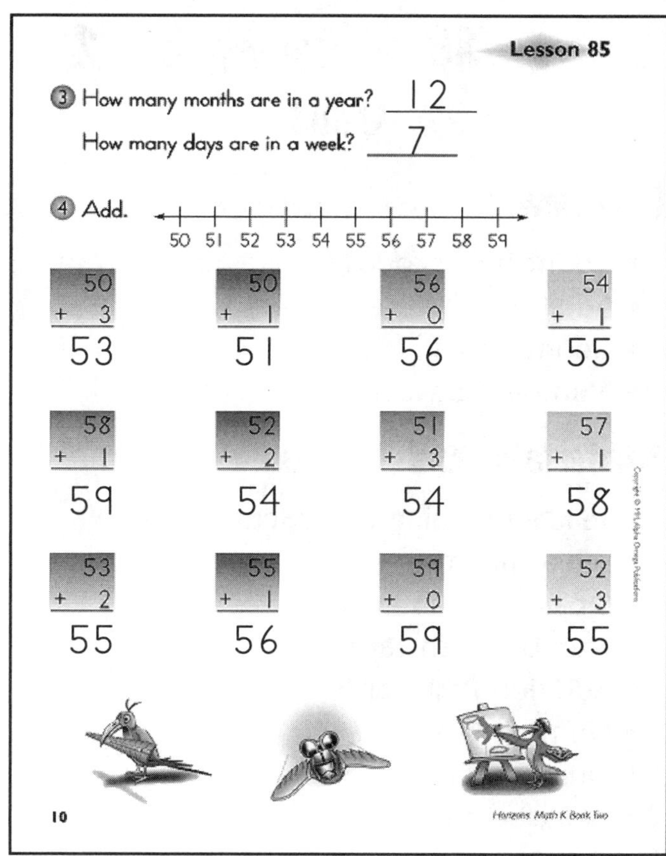

Lesson 86 - Count by 2's, Odds

Overview:

- Count by 2's, odds
- Addition 50's
- Count by 2's
- Number between 70's

Materials and Supplies:

- Teacher's Guide & Student Workbook
- White board
- Objects for counters
- Number flash cards
- Addition flash cards 1's family
- Number line strips
- Number chart
- Worksheet 33

Teaching Tips:

Teach odd numbers to 80.
Review even numbers to 80.
Review counting by 2.
Review addition 50's.
Review number between 70's.
Drill addition 1's family.
Review oral counting to 100.

Activities:

① Read the numbers in the chart together with the student(s). Point out that these are the even numbers. Count orally to 80 by 1's. Have the student(s) fill in the missing numbers using a number chart if needed. After writing the numbers, read the numbers written in together with the class. Explain that these are the odd numbers and that counting by every two numbers is called skip counting.

Lesson 86

① Count by 2's.

	2		4		6		8		10
	12		14		16		18		20
	22		24		26		28		30
	32		34		36		38		40
	42		44		46		48		50
	52		54		56		58		60
	62		64		66		68		70
	72		74		76		78		80

② Add.

50 51 52 53 54 55 56 57 58 59

52 + 2 = 54	56 + 3 = 59	54 + 4 = 58	50 + 3 = 53
55 + 3 = 58	53 + 2 = 55	52 + 3 = 55	57 + 2 = 59

Horizons Math K Book Two 11

② This is the third time that the students are asked to add to the 50's family. In this activity they are adding a 2, 3 or 4 to a number in the 50's family. Do several examples on the white board using either a number line strip or a number chart. Have one student in the class call out a 50's number. Have a different student spin a spinner with numbers 0–4 to add to the number given by the first student.

③ Count orally to 80 by 1's. Then together with the student(s) look at the numbers in the chart. Point out that this is an even number chart. Have the student(s) complete the chart by looking back at Activity ① if needed.

④ Lay flash cards 70–80 face down on a table or desk in front of the class. Flip up two of the cards that have a number between them and call on a student to give the number between. Repeat this several times with different sets of three numbers. Read the instruction and have the student(s) complete the activity. They may use a number line or number chart if needed.

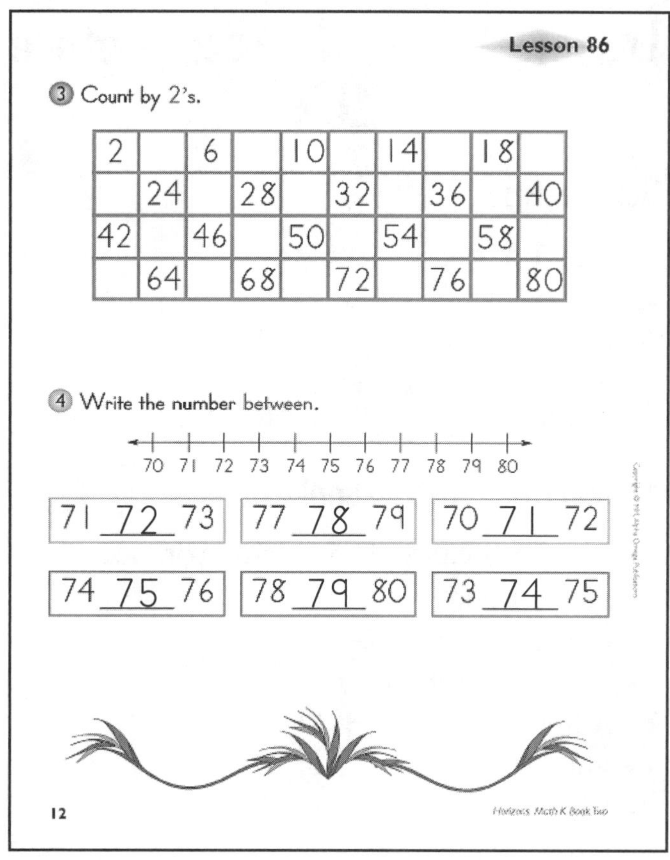

Lesson 87 - Number Before 20's

Overview:

- Number before 20's
- Count by 2's, odds
- Perimeter, inches
- Pennies, dimes, nickels
- Addition 50's

Materials and Supplies:

- Teacher's Guide & Student Workbook
- White board
- Objects for counters
- Number flash cards
- Addition flash cards 1's
- Ruler – inches
- Dice
- Number chart
- Pennies, nickels, dimes
- Number line strips

Teaching Tips:

Teach number before 20's.
Review odd numbers to 80.
Review counting by 2's
Review ruler – inches.
Review perimeter.
Review coins.
Review addition 50's.
Drill addition 1's family.
Review oral counting to 100.

Activities:

① Read the numbers in the 20's family from a number chart or line. Discuss that the words "number before" means to count backward. Count backwards from 29 by looking at a number chart. Pick random numbers from the 20's family and call on student(s) to give you the answer. Have the student(s) complete the activity.

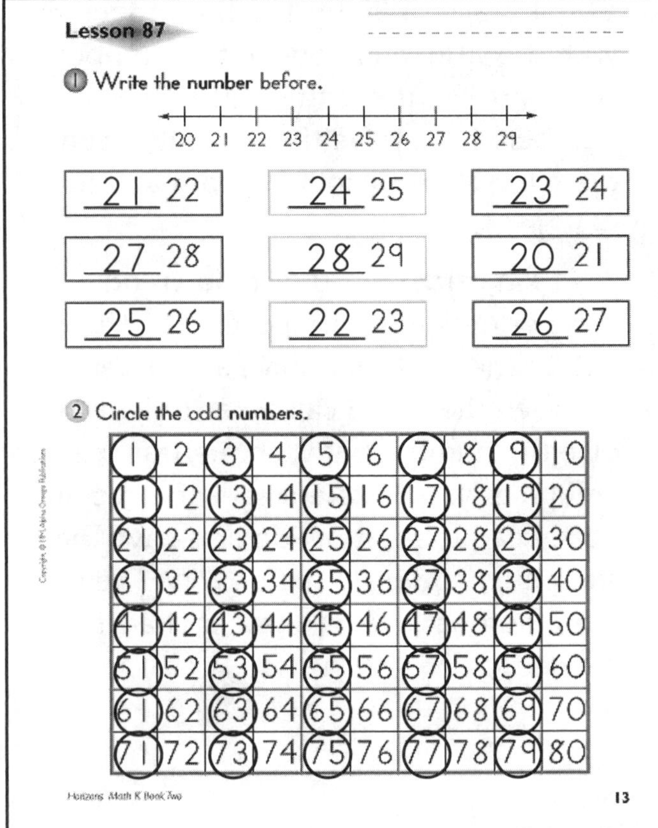

Lesson 87

① Write the number before.

20 21 22 23 24 25 26 27 28 29

21 22	24 25	23 24
27 28	28 29	20 21
25 26	22 23	26 27

② Circle the odd numbers.

1	2	3	4	5	6	7	8	9	10
11	12	13	14	15	16	17	18	19	20
21	22	23	24	25	26	27	28	29	30
31	32	33	34	35	36	37	38	39	40
41	42	43	44	45	46	47	48	49	50
51	52	53	54	55	56	57	58	59	60
61	62	63	64	65	66	67	68	69	70
71	72	73	74	75	76	77	78	79	80

Horizons Math K Book Two 13

② Count out loud by ones to 80 using the number chart. Have the student(s) begin with 1 and circle all of the odd numbers. This is also counting by 2's or skip counting.

③ Review inches and perimeter. Ask them what the shape is. (rectangle) Remind the student(s) to choose a starting point so they do not count the same side twice. If the student(s) get confused counting around for the inches, have them place counters for the correct number over each ruler. After doing this they should count all of the counters and write the answer on the blank.

④ Review counting by 5's and 10's. Have the student(s) count the coins in the activity and write their answers.

⑤ In this activity the student(s) are adding a 2, 3 or 4 to a number in the 50's family. Do several examples on the white board using either a number line strip or a number chart. Have one student in the class call out a 50's number. Have a different student roll a die, spin a spinner or use another manipulative to find a number to add to the number given by the first student.

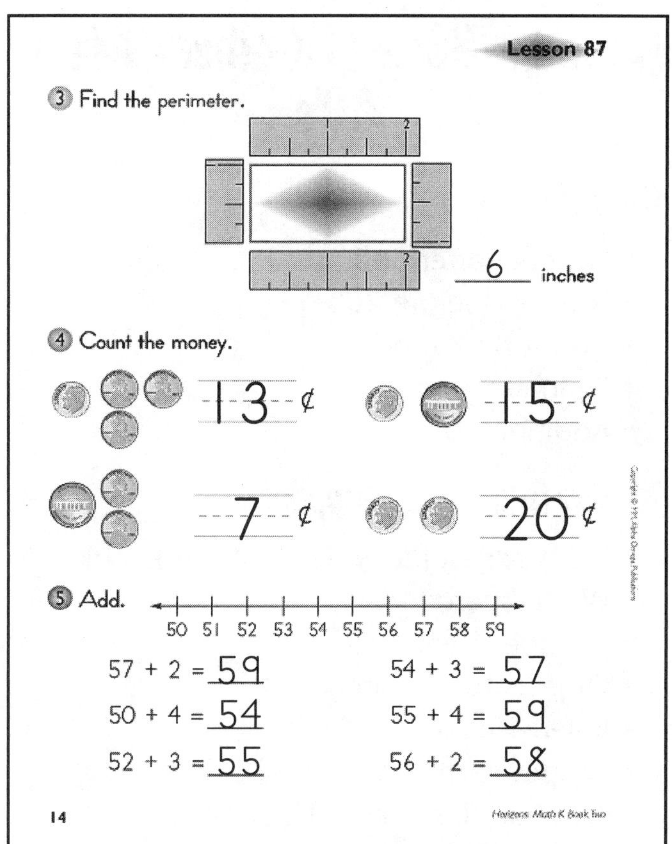
Lesson 87

③ Find the perimeter.

6 inches

④ Count the money.

13 ¢ 15 ¢

7 ¢ 20 ¢

⑤ Add.

50 51 52 53 54 55 56 57 58 59

57 + 2 = 59 54 + 3 = 57

50 + 4 = 54 55 + 4 = 59

52 + 3 = 55 56 + 2 = 58

14 Horizons Math K Book Two

Lesson 88 - Number After 60's

Overview:

- Number after 60's
- Number before 20's
- Count by 2's, odds
- Perimeter, inches
- Addition 20's

Materials and Supplies:

- Teacher's Guide & Student Workbook
- White board
- Number flash cards
- Objects for counters
- Ruler – inches
- Shapes flash cards
- Addition flash cards 1's family
- Number line strips
- Number chart

Teaching Tips:

Teach number after 60's.
Review number before 20's.
Review odd numbers to 35.
Review ruler – inches.
Review perimeter.
Review addition 20's.
Drill addition 1's family.
Review oral counting to 100.

Activities:

① Review number sequence by pointing to a number chart and asking the student(s) to say the number after 60's. The numbers in this activity are from the 60's family. (60–69) Read the instruction and have the student(s) complete the activity. The student(s) may refer to the pages in one of their textbooks or a library book to see what number comes after a given number.

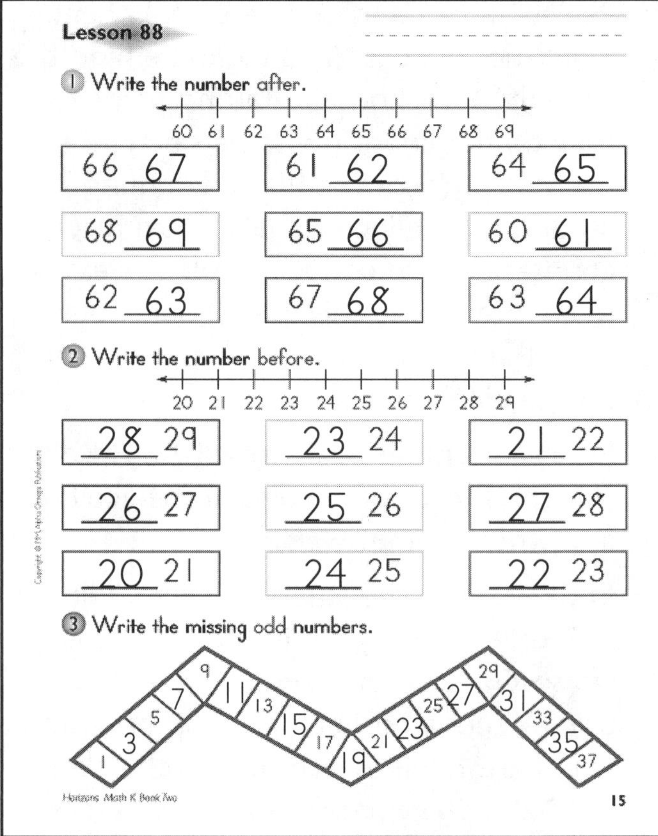

② Review the numbers in the 20's family from a number chart or line. Discuss that the words "number before" means to count backward. Count backwards from 29 by looking at a number chart. Pick random numbers for the 20's family and call on student(s) to give you the number before. Have the student(s) complete the activity.

③ Count out loud by ones to 37. Count again by looking at a number chart and saying only the odd numbers. For the activity have the student(s) begin with 1 and write the missing odd numbers.

④ Review inches and perimeter. Ask them what the shape is. (square) Remind the student(s) to choose a starting point so they do not count the same side twice. If the student(s) get confused counting around for the inches, have them place counters for the correct number over each ruler. After doing this they should count all of the counters and write the answer on the blank.

⑤ Read the instruction and allow the students to work independently. This is a review activity of addition of the 20's family.

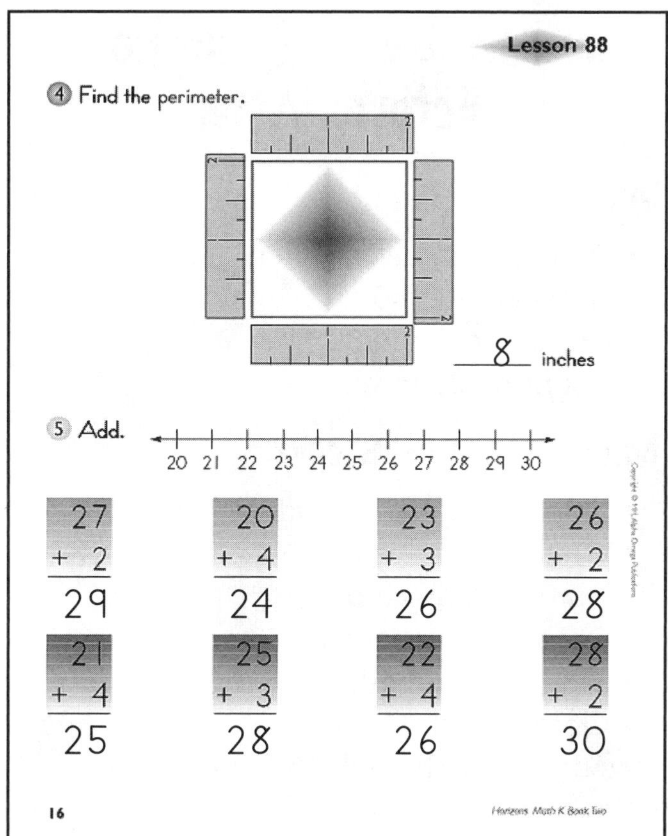

Lesson 88

④ Find the perimeter.

8 inches

⑤ Add.

20 21 22 23 24 25 26 27 28 29 30

27	20	23	26
+ 2	+ 4	+ 3	+ 2
29	24	26	28
21	25	22	28
+ 4	+ 3	+ 4	+ 2
25	28	26	30

16 Horizons Math K Book Two

Lesson 89 - Time-hour, Before, After

Overview:

- Time – hour, *before, after*
- Number after 60's
- Number before 20's
- Count by 2's, evens

Materials and Supplies:

- Teacher's Guide & Student Workbook
- White board
- Number flash cards
- Objects for counters
- Digital clock model
- Clock model
- Addition flash cards 1's family
- Number line strips
- Number chart

Teaching Tips:

Teach time – hour before and after.
Review number after 60's.
Review number before 20's.
Review odd numbers to 37.
Drill addition 1's family.
Review oral counting to 100.

Activities:

① This exercise is an application of the number before and number after concept. Here it is applied to time and the hour before and the hour after a given time. Point out that a clock only has the numbers 1–12 for the hours. After 12 o'clock it starts over again with 1 o'clock. Do several examples using clock models. Help the student(s) with the first 2 activities. They should be able to answer the last two on their own.

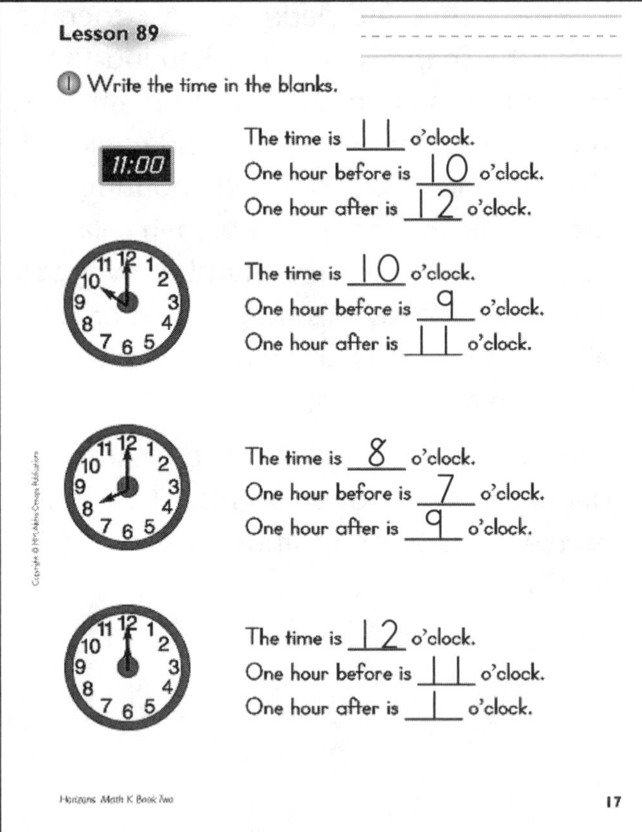

② Review number sequence by pointing to a number chart and asking the student(s) to say the number after 60's. Read the instruction and have the student(s) complete the activity. The student(s) may refer to the pages in one of their textbooks or a library book to see what number comes after a given number.

③ Review the numbers in the 20's family from a number chart or line. Count backwards from 29 by looking at a number chart. Pick random numbers for the 20's family and call on student(s) to give you the number before. Have the student(s) complete the activity. They can refer to the pages in a book to add what number comes before a given number.

④ Count out loud by ones to 38. Count again by looking at a number chart and saying only the even numbers. For the activity have the student(s) begin with 2 and write the missing even numbers.

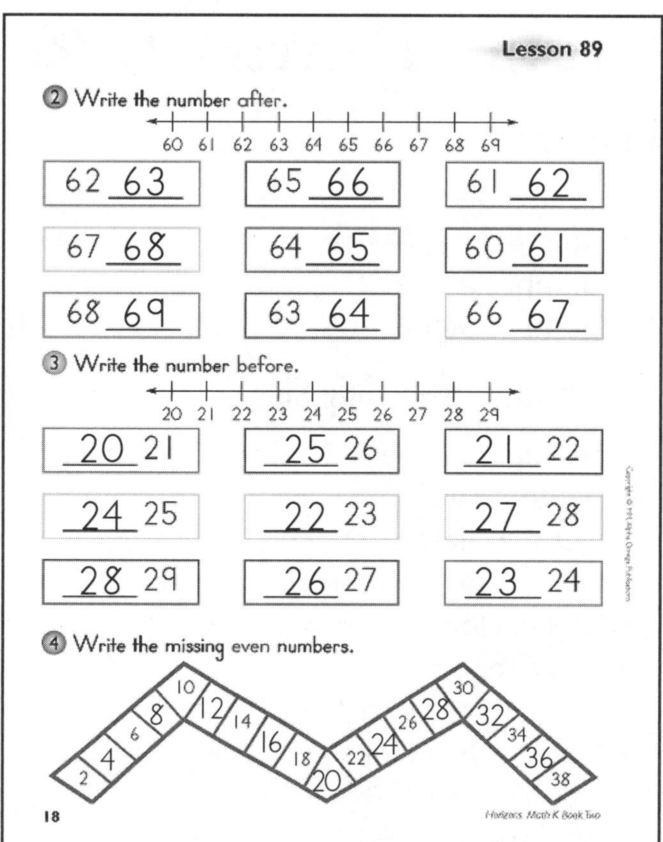

Lesson 90 - Count to 90

Overview:

- Count to 90
- Time – hour, *before, after*
- Number after 60's
- Number before 20's

Materials and Supplies:

- Teacher's Guide & Student Workbook
- White board
- Number flash cards
- Objects for counters
- Digital clock model
- Clock model
- Addition flash cards 1's family
- Number line strips
- Number chart
- Worksheet 20 & 30

Teaching Tips:

Teach counting objects to 90.
Review time – hour before and after.
Review number after 60's.
Review number before 20's.
Drill addition 1's family.
Review oral counting to 100.

Activities:

① Count out loud by ones to 90 using the number chart. Have the student(s) count the tags in Activity ①. They should be counting left to right and top to bottom. Since the tags are all the same they may need to make a mark by each row as they count it to stay on the correct row.

Lesson 90

① Count to 90.

② Write the time in the blanks.

6:00
The time is 6 o'clock.
One hour before is 5 o'clock.
One hour after is 7 o'clock.

The time is 3 o'clock.
One hour before is 2 o'clock.
One hour after is 4 o'clock.

The time is 7 o'clock.
One hour before is 6 o'clock.
One hour after is 8 o'clock.

The time is 2 o'clock.
One hour before is 1 o'clock.
One hour after is 3 o'clock.

Horizons Math K Book Two 19

② This activity continues to apply the before and after concept to time. Do several examples of one hour before and one hour after using clock models. Help the student(s) with the first 2 activities. They should be able to answer the last two on their own.

③ Review number sequence by pointing to a number chart and asking the student(s) to say the number after 60's. Read the instruction and have the student(s) complete the activity. The student(s) may refer to the pages in one of their textbooks or a library book to see what number comes after a given number.

④ Review the numbers in the 20's family from a number chart or line. Count backwards from 29 by looking at a number chart. Pick random numbers for the 20's family and call on student(s) to give you the number before. Have the student(s) complete the activity. They can refer to the pages in a book to find what number comes before a given number.

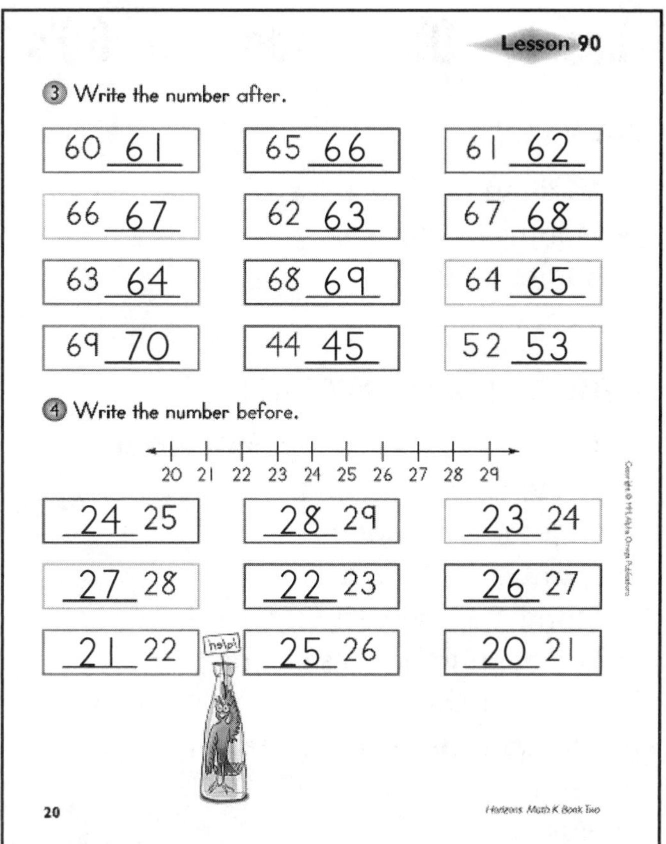
Lesson 90

③ Write the number after.

60 61	65 66	61 62
66 67	62 63	67 68
63 64	68 69	64 65
69 70	44 45	52 53

④ Write the number before.

20 21 22 23 24 25 26 27 28 29

24 25	28 29	23 24
27 28	22 23	26 27
21 22	25 26	20 21

20 Horizons Math K Book Two

Lesson 91 - Addition 60's

Overview:

- Addition 60's
- Months of the year
- Addition 30's
- Inches

Materials and Supplies:

- Teacher's Guide & Student Workbook
- White board
- Objects for counters
- Number flash cards
- Months of the year flash cards
- Ordinal number flash cards
- Ruler – inches
- Addition flash cards 1's family
- Number line strips
- Number chart

Teaching Tips:

Teach addition 60's.
Review months of the year.
Review ordinal numbers
Review addition 50's.
Review ruler – inches.
Drill addition 1's family.
Review oral counting to 100.

Activities:

① This is the first time that the students are asked to add to the 60's family. In this activity they are adding a 0, 1, or 2 to a number in the 60's family. Do several examples on the white board using either a number line strip or a number chart. Review number after 60's. Remind the student(s) to go to the first number and count the number being added to find the answer.

Lesson 91

① Add.

60 61 62 63 64 65 66 67 68 69

60 + 1	65 + 2	62 + 0	68 + 1
61	67	62	69
66 + 0	67 + 1	61 + 2	64 + 1
66	68	63	65

② How many months are in a year? 12

What is the third month in a year? March

In which month is your birthday? ____________

What month is it today? ____________

Horizons Math K Book Two 21

② Review the use of a calendar. Review ordinal numbers. Read each question for Activity ② and have the student(s) write their answers. Have the names of the months available for the student(s) to use in writing the names for the months.

③ This is a review in which the students are asked to add to the 30's family. In this activity they are adding a 2, 3, 4, 5 or 6 to a number in the 30's family. Do several examples on the white board using either a number line strip or a number chart.

④ Review measurement with a ruler. Have the student(s) count the inches for each object.

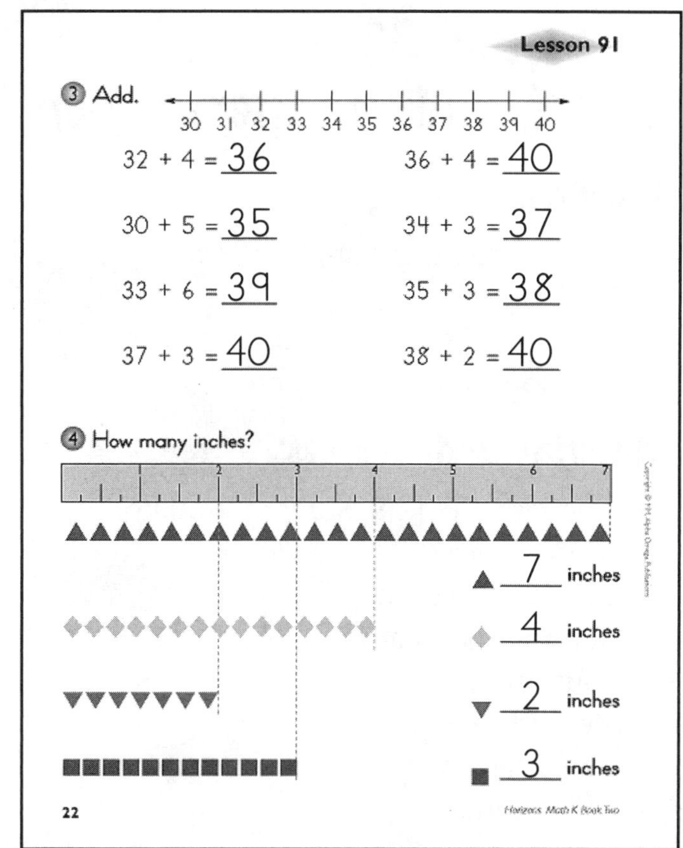

Lesson 92 - Identify Quart, Gallon, Liter & Cup

Overview:

- Identify quart, gallon, liter & cup
- Addition 60's
- Count by 2's, evens
- Addition 40's

Material and Supplies:

- Teacher's Guide & Student Workbook
- White board
- Objects for counters
- Number flash cards
- Count by 2's flash cards
- Measuring cup
- Quart carton or bottle
- Gallon jug
- Liter bottle
- Addition flash cards 1's family
- Number line strips
- Number chart

Teaching Tips:

Teach cup, quart, gallon & liter.
Review addition 60's.
Review counting by 2's.
Review addition 40's.
Drill addition 1's family.
Review oral counting to 100.

Activities:

① Display a one cup measuring cup, a quart milk carton or bottle, a one liter soft drink bottle and a gallon milk jug for the student(s) to examine. Explain that they are used to measure a given amount of liquid. Ask which of the four they are most familiar with, which is the largest, and which is the smallest. Using flash cards for each unit of measure, have the student(s) tell you which container goes with which name. Spend several minutes with the student(s) learning to name each container correctly. As you call out the name of the different containers, have the student(s) point to the correct container in the activity. The work with these units of measure will be for counting practice. There is no need to discuss converting units because the student(s) will not be asked to convert one volume to the other. Instruct the student(s) to count the number of each volume in the activity and write their answers on the blank. Each answer has been labeled because these are units of measure.

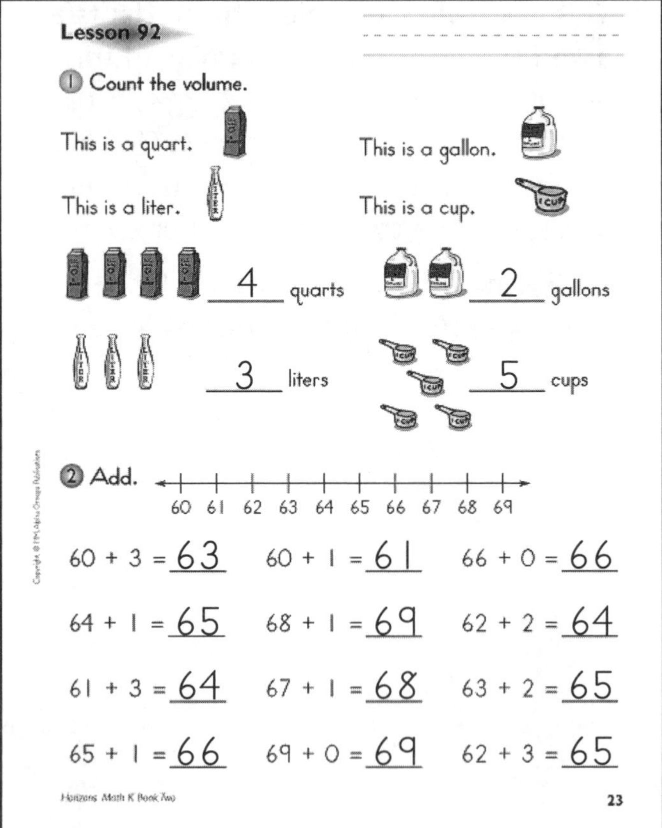

② This is the second time that the students are asked to add to the 60's family. In this activity they are adding a 0, 1, 2 or 3 to a number in the 60's family. Do several examples on the white board using either a number line strip or a number chart.

③ Count orally to 90 by 1's. Count orally to 90 by 2's. Instruct the student(s) to complete the chart using a number chart if necessary.

④ This is a review in which the students are asked to add to the 40's family. In this activity they are adding a 0–7 to a number in the 40's family. Do several examples on the white board using either a number line strip or a number chart.

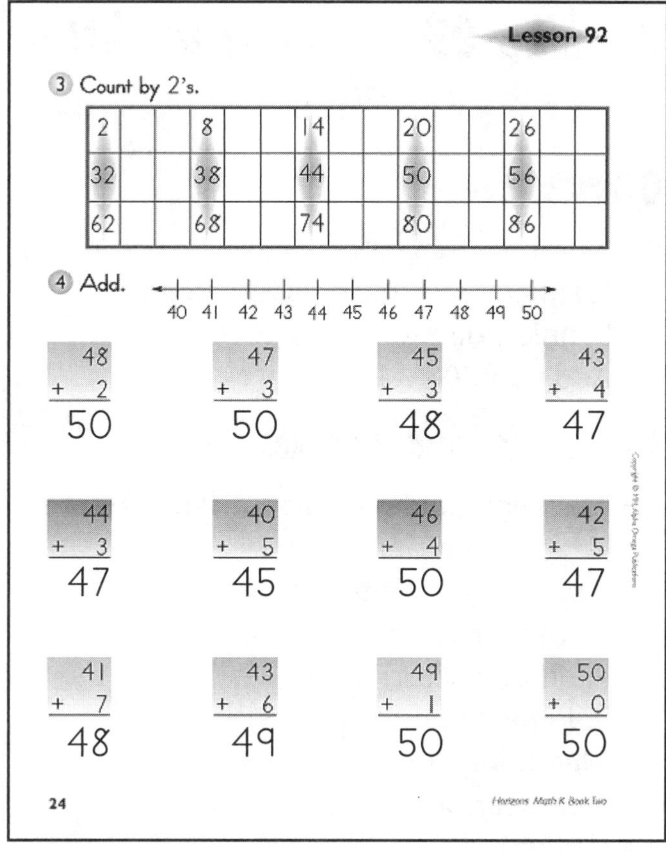

Lesson 93 - Number After 70's

Overview:

- Number after 70's
- Identify quart, gallon, liter & cup
- Pennies, dimes, nickels
- Addition 60's

Materials and Supplies:

- Teacher's Guide & Student Workbook
- White board
- Objects for counters
- Number flash cards
- Pennies, nickels, dimes
- Volume name flash cards
- Measuring cup
- Quart carton or bottle
- Gallon jug
- Liter bottle
- Addition flash cards 1's family
- Number line strips
- Number chart

Teaching Tips:

Teach number after 70's.
Review cup, quart, gallon & liter.
Review money.
Review addition 60's.
Drill addition 1's family.
Review oral counting to 100.

Activities:

① Review number sequence by pointing to a number chart and asking the student(s) to say the number after 70's. The numbers in this activity are from the 70's family. (70–79) Read the instruction and have the student(s) complete the activity. The student(s) may refer to a number chart to see what number comes after a given number.

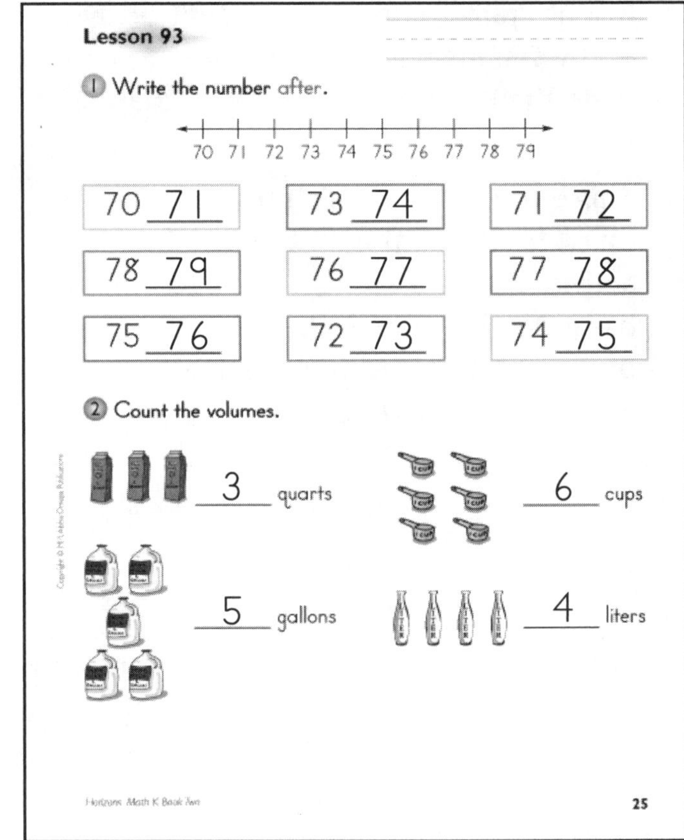
Lesson 93

① Write the number after.

70 71 72 73 74 75 76 77 78 79

70 71	73 74	71 72
78 79	76 77	77 78
75 76	72 73	74 75

② Count the volumes.

3 quarts

6 cups

5 gallons

4 liters

Horizons Math K Book Two 25

② Display the cup, quart, liter and gallon containers. Practice the names of each container using the flash cards. Have a student read the directions for the activity. Read each of the names and have the student(s) count the corresponding containers.

③ Review counting by 5's and 10's to 100. Demonstrate with a number chart the addition of money. Have the student(s) complete the activity.

④ This is the third time that the students are asked to add to the 60's family. In this activity they are adding a 0, 1, 2, 3, 4 or 6 to a number in the 60's family. Do several examples on the white board using either a number line strip or a number chart. Have one student in the class call out a 60's number. Have a different student spin a spinner with numbers 0–7 to add to the number given by the first student. Call on another student to give the answer.

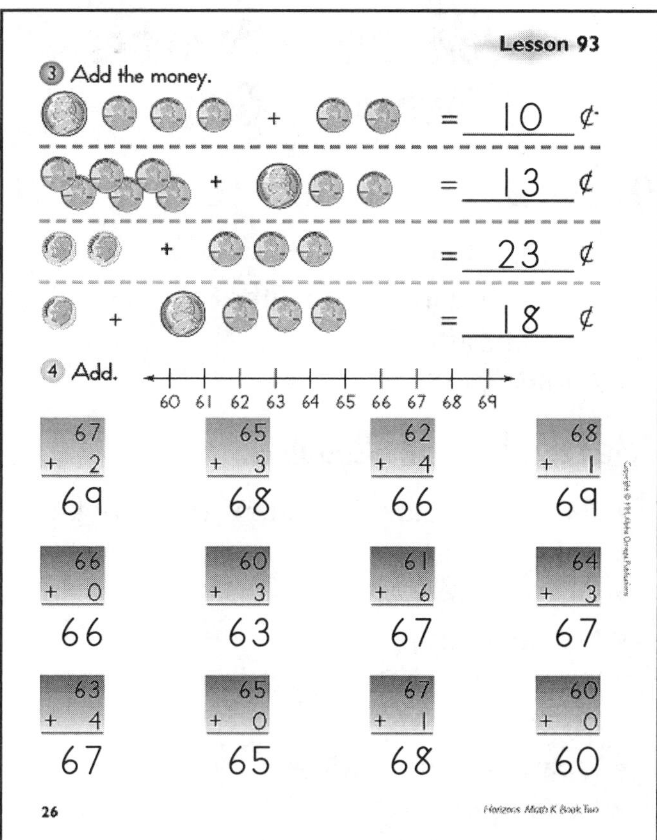

Lesson 93

③ Add the money.

+ = 10 ¢

+ = 13 ¢

+ = 23 ¢

+ = 18 ¢

④ Add.

60 61 62 63 64 65 66 67 68 69

67 + 2	65 + 3	62 + 4	68 + 1
69	68	66	69
66 + 0	60 + 3	61 + 6	64 + 3
66	63	67	67
63 + 4	65 + 0	67 + 1	60 + 0
67	65	68	60

26 Horizons Math K Book Two

Lesson 94 - Number Between 80's

Overview:

- Number between 80's
- Identify quart, gallon, liter & cup
- Number after 70's
- Addition 60's

Materials and Supplies:

- Teacher's Guide & Student Workbook
- White board
- Objects for counters
- Number flash cards
- Volume name flash cards
- Measuring cup
- Quart carton or bottle
- Gallon jug
- Liter bottle
- Addition flash cards 1's family
- Number line strips
- Number chart

Teaching Tips:

Teach number between 80's.
Review cup, quart, gallon & liter.
Review number after 70's.
Review addition 60's.
Drill addition 1's family.
Review oral counting to 100.

Activities:

① Choose three consecutive whole number flash cards 80–90. Arrange the cards out of order. Have the student(s) put them in correct order. Repeat this four times with different sets of three numbers. Read the instruction and have the student(s) complete the activity. They may use a number line or number chart if needed.

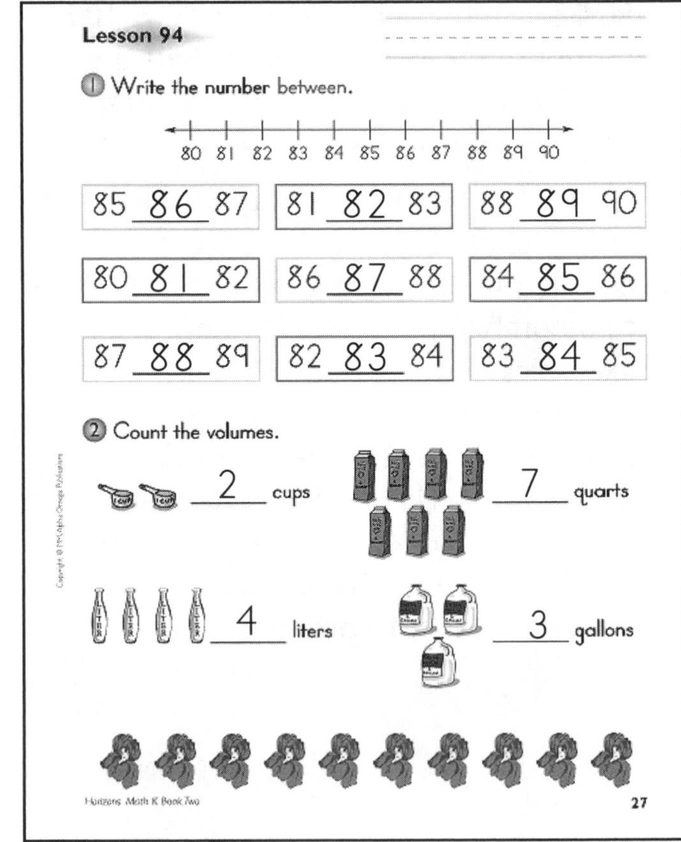

② Display the cup, quart, liter and gallon containers. Practice the names of each container using the flash cards. Discuss that the cup, quart and gallon are English units of measurement and the the liter is a metric unit of measure. When people in many other countries put gasoline in their cars they use metric units of measure. Read each of the names and have the student(s) count the corresponding containers.

③ Review number sequence by pointing to a number chart and asking the student(s) to say the number after 70's. Read the instruction and have the student(s) complete the activity. The student(s) may refer to a number chart to see what number comes after.

④ This is the third time that the students are asked to add to the 60's family. In this activity they are adding a 2, 3, 4, 5, 6 or 7 to a number in the 60's family. Do several examples on the white board using either a number line strip or a number chart. Have one student in the class call out a 60's number. Have a different student spin a spinner with numbers 0–7 to add to the number given by the first student. Call on another student to give the answer.

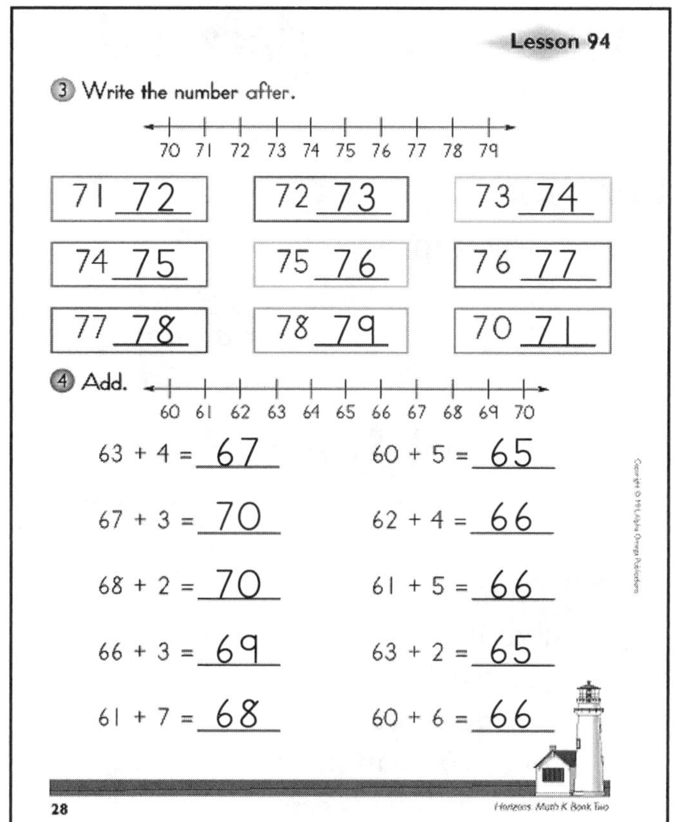
Lesson 94

③ Write the number after.

70 71 72 73 74 75 76 77 78 79

71 72	72 73	73 74
74 75	75 76	76 77
77 78	78 79	70 71

④ Add.

60 61 62 63 64 65 66 67 68 69 70

63 + 4 = 67 | 60 + 5 = 65
67 + 3 = 70 | 62 + 4 = 66
68 + 2 = 70 | 61 + 5 = 66
66 + 3 = 69 | 63 + 2 = 65
61 + 7 = 68 | 60 + 6 = 66

28 Horizons Math K Book Two

Lesson 95 - Place Value 30's

Overview:

- Place value 30's
- Number between 80's
- Identify quart, gallon, liter & cup
- Number after 70's

Materials and Supplies:

- Teacher's Guide & Student Workbook
- White board
- Objects for counters
- Number flash cards
- Base 10 blocks
- Place value chart
- Group of 10's flash cards
- Count by 10's flash cards
- Liquid measure flash cards
- Addition flash cards 1's
- Number chart

Teaching Tips:

Teach place value 30's.
Review number between 80's.
Review cup, quart, gallon & liter.
Review number after 70's.
Drill addition 1's family.
Review oral counting to 100.

Activities:

① Look at the 30's family with a number chart or number line strip. In the 30's family there is always a 3 in the tens' place. Ask what numbers can be in the ones' place. If a student correctly counts 0–9 have the class count 0–9 together.

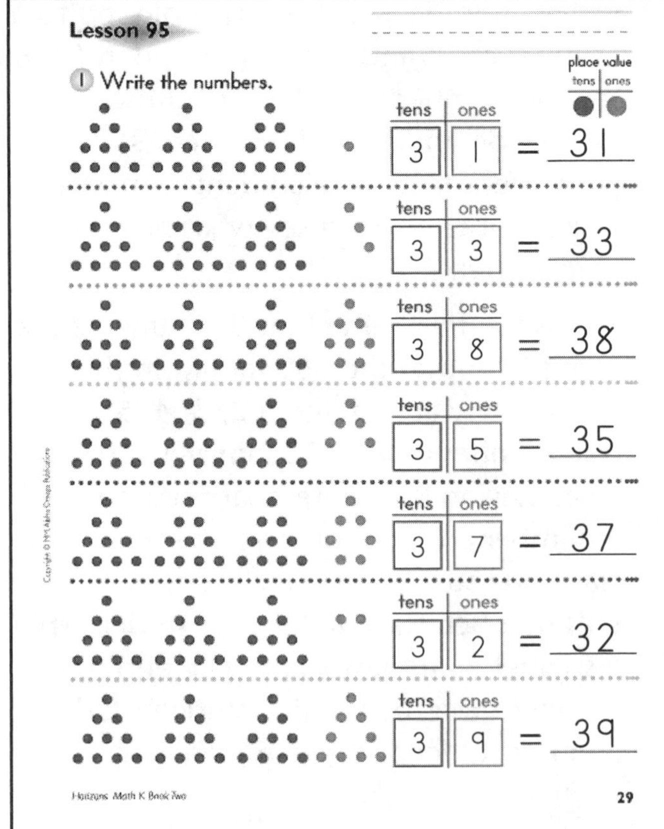

They are to count the dots: the red dots by 10's and the blue dots by 1's. The ten number is to be written in the tens' box and the one number in the ones' box. Finally they write the number as they would normally see it.

② Lay flash cards 80–90 face down on a table or desk in front of the class. Flip up two of the cards that have a number between them and call on a student to give the number between. Repeat this several times with different sets of three numbers. Read the instruction and have the student(s) complete the activity. They may use a number line or number chart if needed.

③ Discuss with the student(s) the units of measure used for liquids by pointing to each container and having them name it. Display the liquid measure flash cards on the white board rail to aid the student(s) in completing Activity ③.

④ Review number sequence by pointing to a number chart and asking the student(s) to say the number after 70's. Read the instruction and have the student(s) complete the activity. The student(s) may refer to the pages in one of their textbooks or a library book to see what number comes after a given number.

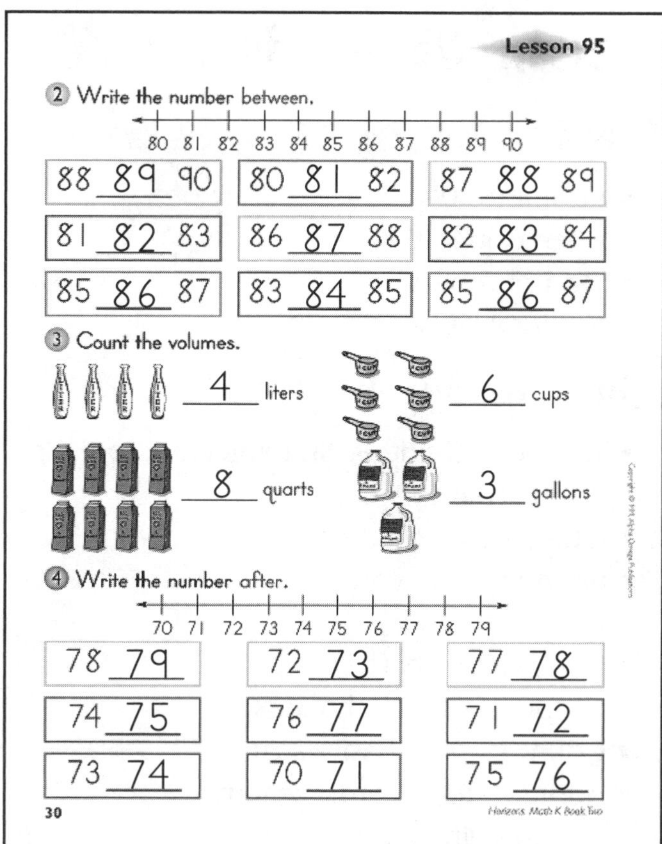
Lesson 95

② Write the number between.

80 81 82 83 84 85 86 87 88 89 90

88 89 90	80 81 82	87 88 89
81 82 83	86 87 88	82 83 84
85 86 87	83 84 85	85 86 87

③ Count the volumes.

4 liters

6 cups

8 quarts

3 gallons

④ Write the number after.

70 71 72 73 74 75 76 77 78 79

78 79	72 73	77 78
74 75	76 77	71 72
73 74	70 71	75 76

30

Horizons Math K Book Two

Lesson 96 - Addition 70's

Overview:

- Addition 70's
- Place value 30's
- Odd numbers
- Addition 60's

Materials and Supplies:

- Teacher's Guide & Student Workbook
- White board
- Objects for counters
- Number flash cards
- Base 10 blocks
- Place value chart
- Group of 10's flash cards
- Count by 10's flash cards
- Addition flash cards 1's family
- Number line strips
- Number chart

Teaching Tips:

Teach addition 70's.
Review place value 30's.
Review odd numbers.
Review addition 60's.
Drill addition 1's family.
Review oral counting to 100.

Activities:

① This is the first time that the students are asked to add to the 70's family. In this activity they are adding a 0, 1, 2, 3 or 4 to a number in the 70's family. Do several examples on the white board using either a number line strip or a number chart. Review number after 70's. Remind the student(s) to go to the first number and count the number being added to find the answer. Be sure they are using the number line and not just guessing.

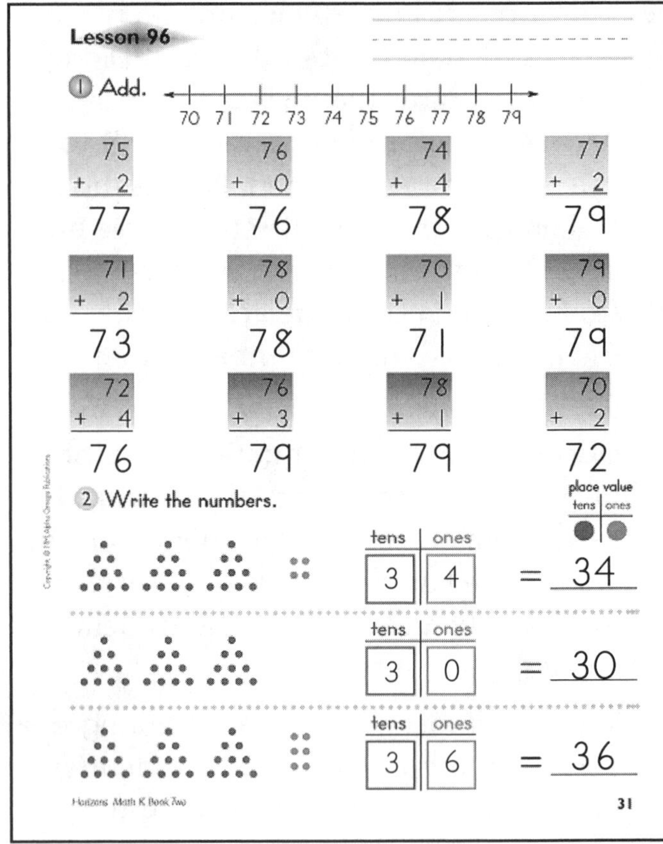
Lesson 96

① Add. 70 71 72 73 74 75 76 77 78 79

75 + 2 = 77	76 + 0 = 76	74 + 4 = 78	77 + 2 = 79
71 + 2 = 73	78 + 0 = 78	70 + 1 = 71	79 + 0 = 79
72 + 4 = 76	76 + 3 = 79	78 + 1 = 79	70 + 2 = 72

② Write the numbers. place value tens ones

tens	ones	
3	4	= 34
3	0	= 30
3	6	= 36

Horizons Math K Book Two 31

② Review the 30's family with a number chart or number line strip. In the 30's family there is always a 3 in the tens' place. Ask what numbers can be in the ones' place. Have the class count 30–39 together. They are to count the tens' dots and the ones' dots: the red dots by 10's and the blue dots by 1's. The ten number is to be written in the tens' box and the one number in the ones' box. After the (=) sign they write the number as they would normally see it. Do one problem as a class activity and have them complete the activity on their own.

③ Count out loud by ones to 89. Count again by looking at a number chart and saying only the odd numbers. For the activity have the student(s) begin with 1 and write the missing odd numbers.

④ In this activity the student(s) are adding a 2, 3, 4, 5, 6 or 7 to a number in the 60's family. Do several examples on the white board using either a number line strip or a number chart. Have one student in the class call out a 60's number. Have a different student draw a flash card 0–7 to add to the number given by the first student. Call on another student to give the answer.

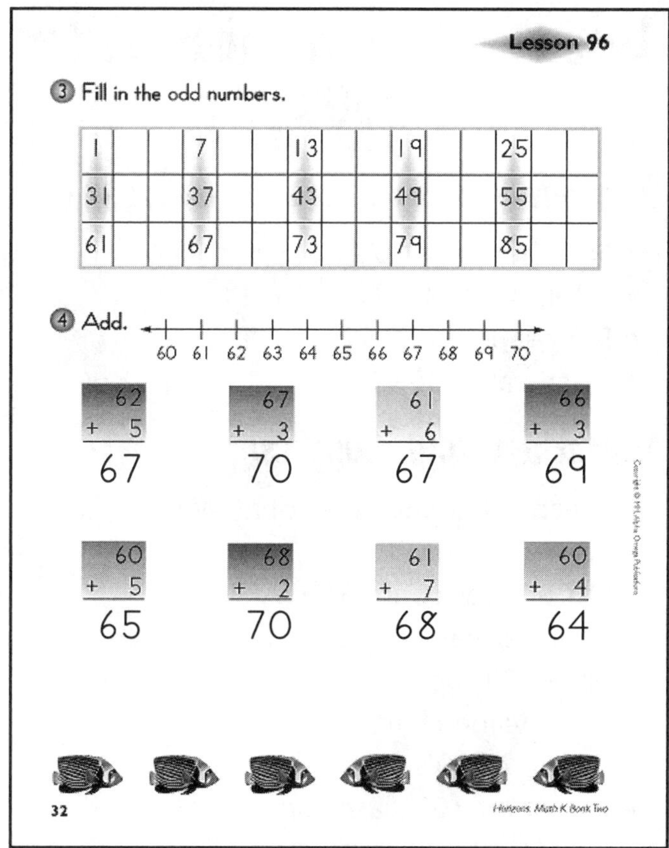

Lesson 96

③ Fill in the odd numbers.

1			7			13			19			25		
31			37			43			49			55		
61			67			73			79			85		

④ Add.

62 + 5 = 67	67 + 3 = 70	61 + 6 = 67	66 + 3 = 69
60 + 5 = 65	68 + 2 = 70	61 + 7 = 68	60 + 4 = 64

32 Horizons Math K Book Two

Lesson 97 - Number After 80's

Overview:

- Number after 80's
- Addition 70's
- Bar graph
- Place value 30's

Materials and Supplies:

- Teacher's Guide & Student Workbook
- White board
- Objects for counters
- Number flash cards
- Base 10 blocks
- Place value chart
- Group of 10's flash cards
- Count by 10's flash cards
- Addition flash cards 1's family
- Number line strips
- Number chart

Teaching Tips:

Teach number after 80's.
Review addition 70's.
Review bar graph
Review place value 30's.
Drill addition 1's family.
Review oral counting to 100.

Activities:

① Review number sequence by pointing to a number chart and asking the student(s) to say the number after 80's. The numbers in this activity are from the 80's family. (80–89) Read the instruction and have the student(s) complete the activity. The student(s) may refer to a number chart to see what number comes after a given number.

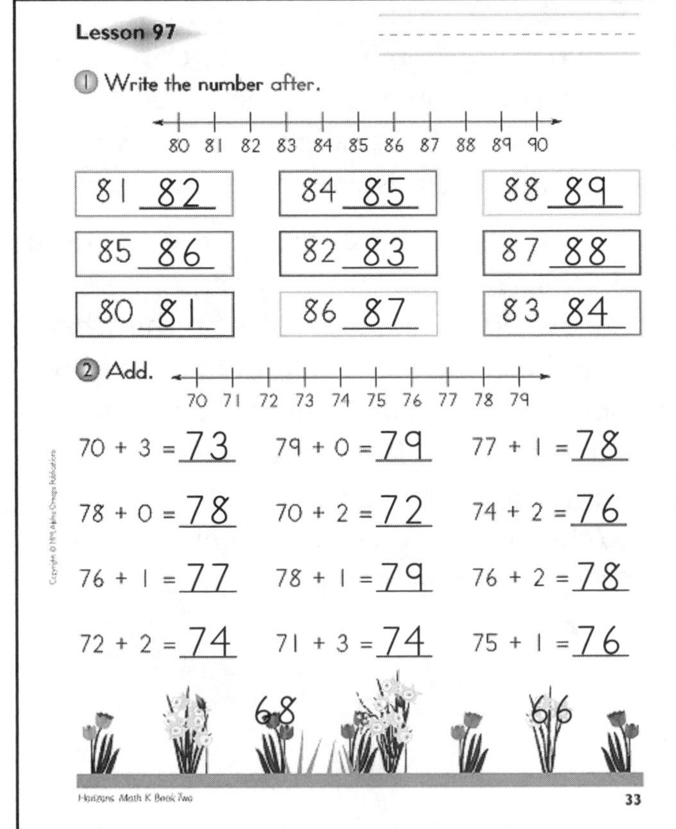

② This is the second time that the students are asked to add to the 70's family. In this activity they are adding a 0, 1, 2 or 3 to a number in the 70's family. Do several examples on the white board using either a number line strip or a number chart.

③ Do a warmup for this activity with some pencils, pens, chalk, crayons, etc. Ask a student to count one of the items. Demonstrate how to color in the same number of blocks on a bar graph.

④ Review the 30's family with a number chart or number line strip. In the 30's family there is always a 3 in the tens' place. Have the student(s) repeat as you say, "30 has 3 tens and 0 ones, 31 has 3 tens and 1 one, 32 has 3 tens and 2 ones, etc. Point to a flash card of each number as you say the phrase. Do one problem as a class activity and have them complete the activity on their own.

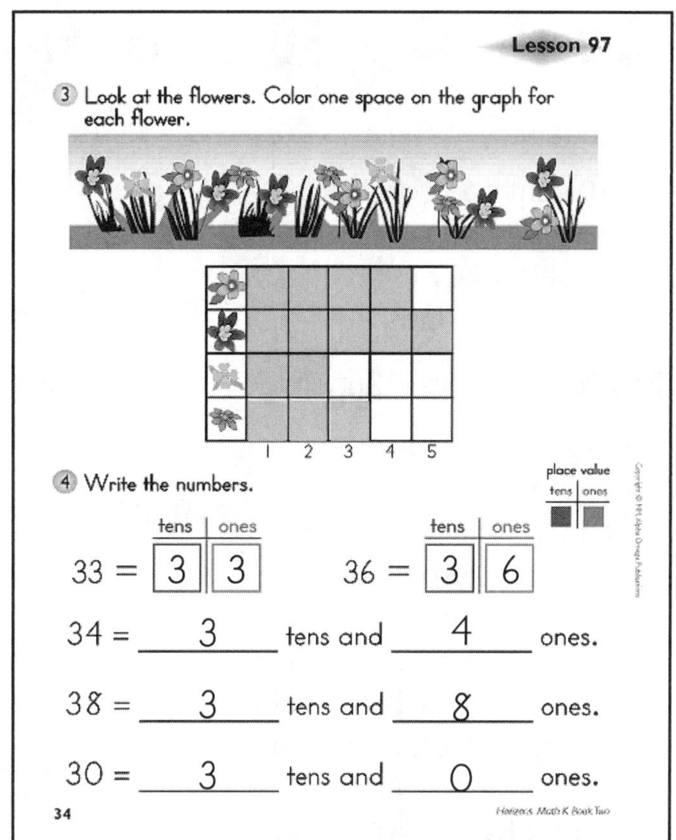
Lesson 97

③ Look at the flowers. Color one space on the graph for each flower.

1 2 3 4 5

④ Write the numbers.

place value: tens | ones

33 = tens 3 | ones 3

36 = tens 3 | ones 6

34 = 3 tens and 4 ones.

38 = 3 tens and 8 ones.

30 = 3 tens and 0 ones.

34

Horizons Math K Book Two

Lesson 98 - 50 cents, $1

Overview:

- 50 cents, $1
- Number after 80's
- Addition 70's
- Match first–tenths

Materials and Supplies:

- Teacher's Guide & Student Workbook
- White board
- Objects for counters
- Number flash cards
- Number chart
- Addition flash cards 1's
- Half dollar, $1 bill or coin
- Dimes, nickels & pennies
- Count by 10's flash cards
- Count by 5's flash cards
- Number line strips
- Ordinal number flash cards

Teaching Tips:

Teach half dollars.
Review pennies, nickels and dimes.
Review number after 80.
Review addition 70's.
Review ordinals.
Drill addition 1's family.
Review oral counting to 100.

Activities:

① Show the student(s) a real half dollar. Allow them to hold it and feel the imprint as well as talk about the texture of the edge. Discuss the size, the man on the front (John F. Kennedy), the picture on the back (presidential seal), color and value of the half dollar. Half dollars are not very common but they work well as a teaching aid for 1/2 of a whole. Show them a dollar bill or dollar coin. Two half dollars equal one dollar bill. Draw a circle on the white board. Divide the circle into halves and into quarters. In Activity ① the student(s) will count other sets of coins that equal 50¢ or are equal to a half dollar. Review counting by 5's and 10's. Have the student(s) count each group of coins and write the amount.

② Review number sequence by pointing to a number chart and asking the student(s) to say the number after 80's. Read the instruction and have the student(s) complete the activity. The student(s) may refer to a number chart see what number comes after.

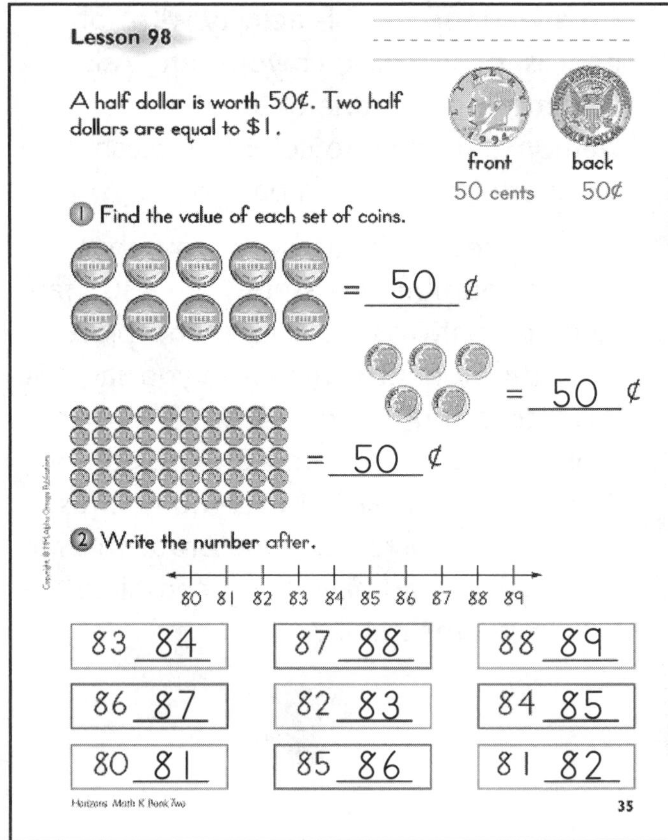
Lesson 98

A half dollar is worth 50¢. Two half dollars are equal to $1.

front 50 cents | back 50¢

① Find the value of each set of coins.

= 50 ¢

= 50 ¢

= 50 ¢

② Write the number after.

80 81 82 83 84 85 86 87 88 89

83 84	87 88	88 89
86 87	82 83	84 85
80 81	85 86	81 82

Horizons Math K Book Two 35

③ This is the third time that the students are asked to add to the 70's family. In this activity they are adding a 0, 1, 2, 3 or 4 to a number in the 70's family. Do several examples on the white board using either a number line strip or a number chart. Randomly select a 70's flash card and a 1's flash card for the student(s) to add together. Don't ask them to do sums beyond the 70's.

④ Review ordinal numbers with flash cards. Have a race or contest at recess where someone can be in 1st place, 2nd place, etc. Demonstrate on the white board how they are to draw lines from the ordinal number to the race cars.

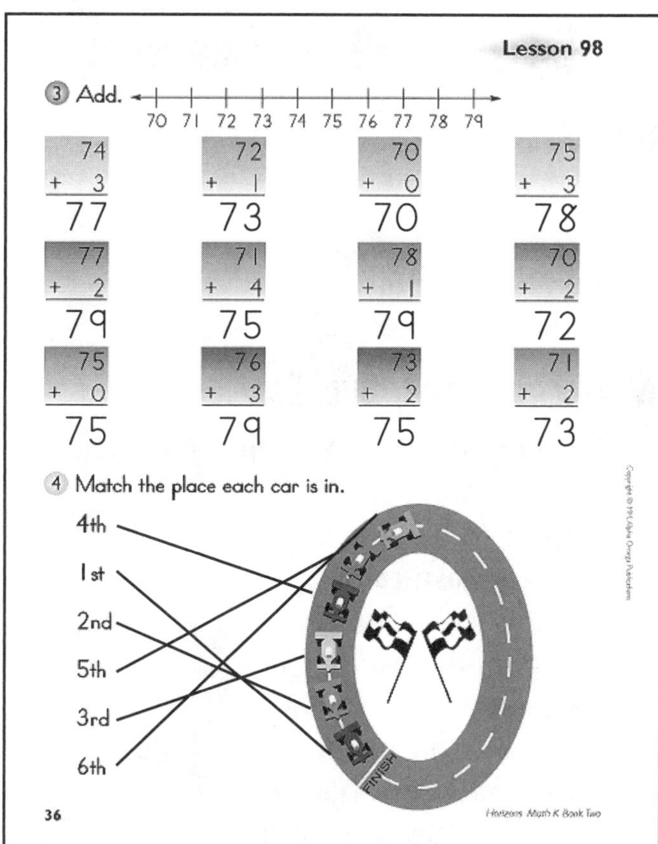

Lesson 99 - Seasons

Overview:

- Seasons
- 50 cents, 1$
- Number after 80's
- Addition 70's

Materials and Supplies:

- Teacher's Guide & Student Workbook
- White board
- Objects for counters
- Number flash cards
- Number chart
- Addition flash cards 1's
- Calendar
- Half dollar, $1 bill or coin
- Dimes, nickels & pennies
- Count by 10's flash cards
- Count by 5's flash cards
- Number line strips

Teaching Tips:

Teach seasons.
Review calendar and months.
Review half dollars.
Review nickels and dimes.
Review number after 80.
Review addition 70's.
Drill addition 1's family.
Review oral counting to 100.

Activities:

① Show the student(s) a calendar. Discuss the seasons. Ask them for characteristics of each season. Write the names of the seasons on the white board. Discuss the pictures in Activity ① but do not say the season. Talk about the snow, the new green leaves, the sunshine on the beach and the falling leaves. Read the first season to the student(s) and have them draw a line to the picture that they choose. Do the same for the other seasons.

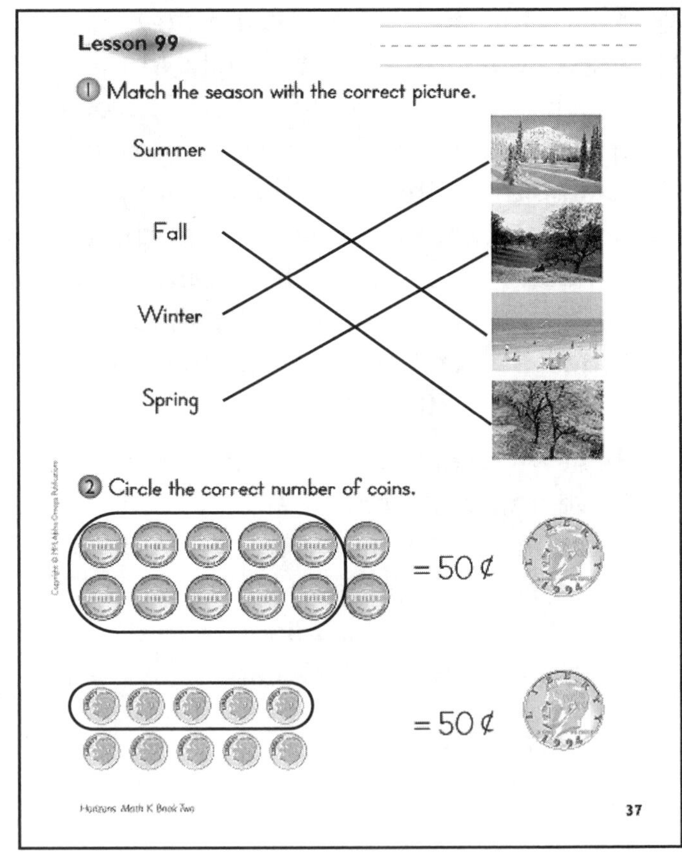

② Give the student(s) 2 half dollars, ten dimes and 20 nickels in play money. Have them put the coins in groups by type in the top center of their desks. Count the dimes by 10's and the nickels by 5's. Have the students divide the set of dimes into two equal groups. They can slide one dime to one side of their desk and another to the other side. Have them count each set to see if they have the same number in each set. Do the same for the nickels and the half dollars. Have them count each half set of coins. Each set should be 50¢. Demonstrate several samples problems like the ones in Activity ②. Instruct the student(s) to complete the activity.

③ Review number sequence by pointing to a number chart and asking the student(s) to say the number after 80's. Read the instruction and have the student(s) complete the activity.

④ This is the fourth time that the students are asked to add to the 70's family. In this activity they are adding a 2, 3, 4, 5, 6 or 7 to a number in the 70's family. Do several examples on the white board using either a number line strip or a number chart.

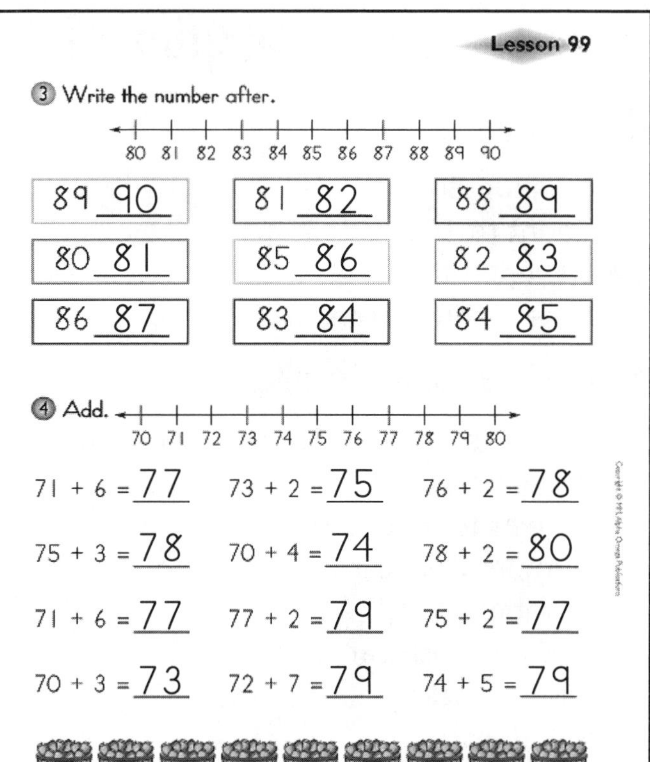
Lesson 99

③ Write the number after.

80 81 82 83 84 85 86 87 88 89 90

89 90	81 82	88 89
80 81	85 86	82 83
86 87	83 84	84 85

④ Add.

70 71 72 73 74 75 76 77 78 79 80

71 + 6 = 77	73 + 2 = 75	76 + 2 = 78
75 + 3 = 78	70 + 4 = 74	78 + 2 = 80
71 + 6 = 77	77 + 2 = 79	75 + 2 = 77
70 + 3 = 73	72 + 7 = 79	74 + 5 = 79

38 Horizons Math K Book Two

Lesson 100 - Addition 80's

Overview:

- Addition 80's
- Count to 100
- 50 cents, 1$
- Time – hour, *before, after*

Materials and Supplies:

- Teacher's Guide & Student Workbook
- White board
- Objects for counters
- Number flash cards
- Number chart
- Addition flash cards 1's
- Model clocks
- Half dollar
- Dimes, nickels & pennies
- Count by 10's flash cards
- Count by 5's flash cards
- Number line strips
- Worksheet 21 & 31

Teaching Tips:

Teach addition 80's.
Teach counting objects to 100.
Review half dollar.
Review pennies, nickels & dimes.
Review time – hour, *before* & *after.*
Drill addition 1's family.
Review oral counting to 100.

Activities:

① This is the first time that the students are asked to add to the 80's family. In this activity they are adding a 1, 2 or 3 to a number in the 80's family. Do several examples on the white board using either a number line strip or a number chart. Review number after 80's. Remind the student(s) to go to the first number and count the number being added to find the answer.

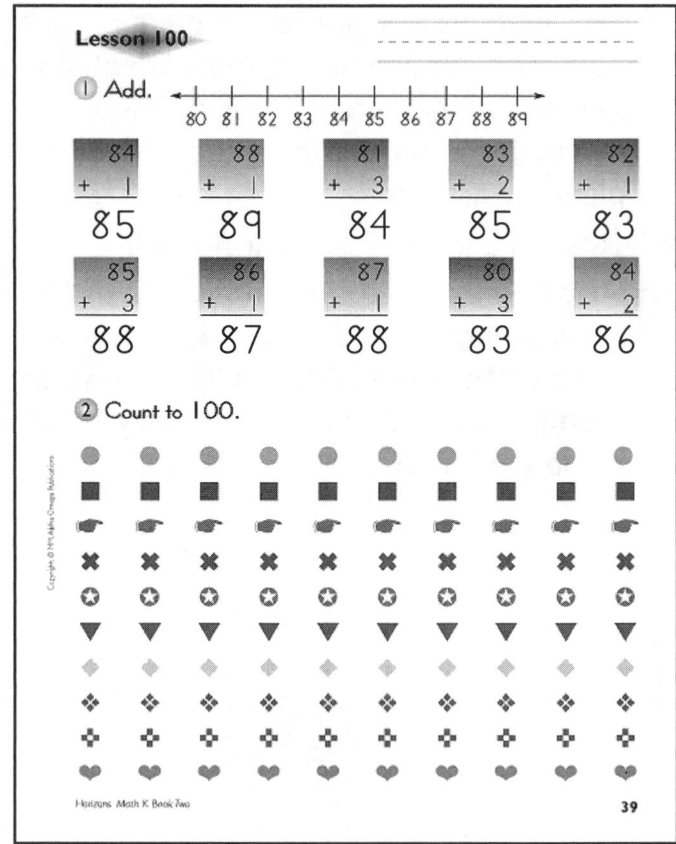

② Count orally to 100 several times. Then ask the students to count the objects in activity. Review ordinal numbers, shapes and colors by asking questions about the 2nd row or another row. This is another major milestone for your student(s). Give the student(s) inexpensive prizes that contain 100 items for them to take home as a reward. Call it the "century day," the day they have completed 100 lessons, 100 days of school and have counted to 100.

③ Practice counting from 50 several times with the student(s). They may need counters, a number line or number chart to count these coins.

④ Do several time examples with the student(s). Ask for the hour, the hour before and the hour after. Have them write the hour as you read each line of the activity.

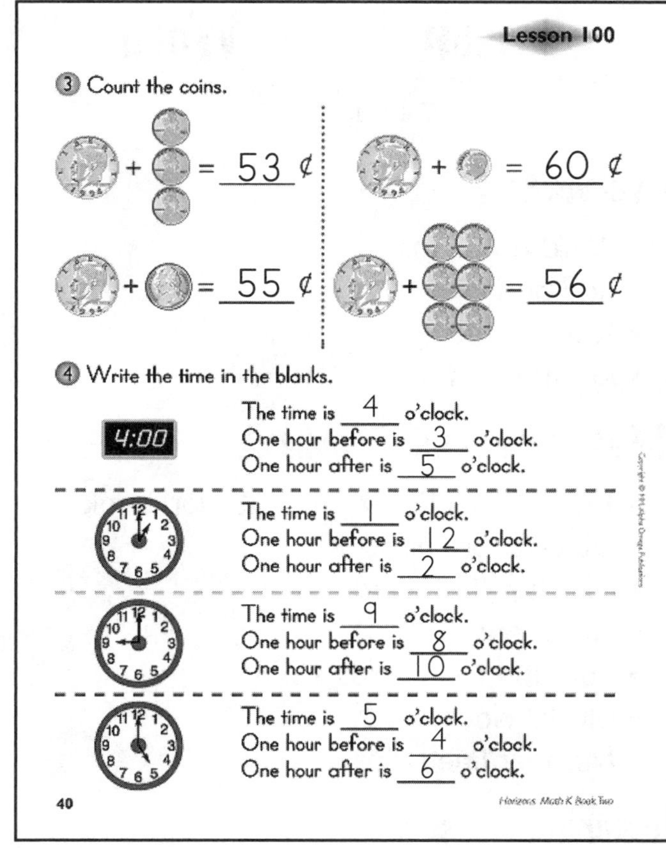

Lesson 101 - Word Problems

Overview:

- Word problems
- Addition 80's
- Time – hour
- Addition 1's

Materials and Supplies:

- Teacher's Guide & Student Workbook
- Objects for counters
- Number flash cards
- Number chart
- Addition flash cards 1's
- Model clocks
- Number line strips

Teaching Tips:

Teach word problems.
Review addition 80's.
Review time – hour.
Drill addition 1's family.
Review oral counting to 100.

Activities:

① Word problems will be given occasionally through the rest of the lessons. The student(s) will not be expected to do a word problem on their own. To begin Activity ① read the word problem to the student(s) as they follow along. Emphasize that the word, "altogether," means to put together or add. Instruct the student(s) to write a 2 in the first blank for the number of cars that Bob has. Have them write a 3 in the second blank for the number of cars that Jim has. Use counters, a number line or a number chart to see how many cars the boys have "altogether." Follow the same procedure for the next two word problems. Show them a calendar for the third problem.

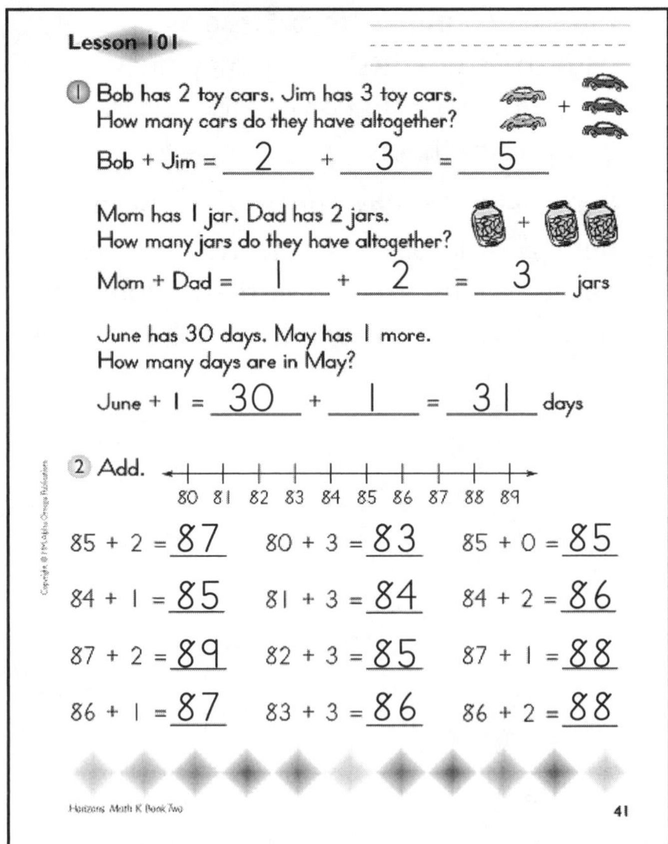

Lesson 101

① Bob has 2 toy cars. Jim has 3 toy cars.
How many cars do they have altogether?
Bob + Jim = 2 + 3 = 5

Mom has 1 jar. Dad has 2 jars.
How many jars do they have altogether?
Mom + Dad = 1 + 2 = 3 jars

June has 30 days. May has 1 more.
How many days are in May?
June + 1 = 30 + 1 = 31 days

② Add.

80 81 82 83 84 85 86 87 88 89

85 + 2 = 87	80 + 3 = 83	85 + 0 = 85
84 + 1 = 85	81 + 3 = 84	84 + 2 = 86
87 + 2 = 89	82 + 3 = 85	87 + 1 = 88
86 + 1 = 87	83 + 3 = 86	86 + 2 = 88

Horizons Math K Book Two 41

② This is the second time that the students are asked to add to the 80's family. In this activity they are adding a 0, 1, 2 or 3 to a number in the 80's family. Do several examples on the white board using either a number line strip or a number chart.

③ Each student will need a small clock model. Review the numbers on a clock face. The numbers 1–12 tell the hour. Also talk about the small marks and that there are 60 of them on the clock face. The small marks are used for minutes. Instruct the student(s) to fill in the hour numbers on the clock in Activity ③.

④ This activity is for addition drill work for the ones' family. Review these facts with flash cards before having the student(s) complete the activity. Try to get the student(s) to memorize these facts, but counters or a number line may be used if necessary.

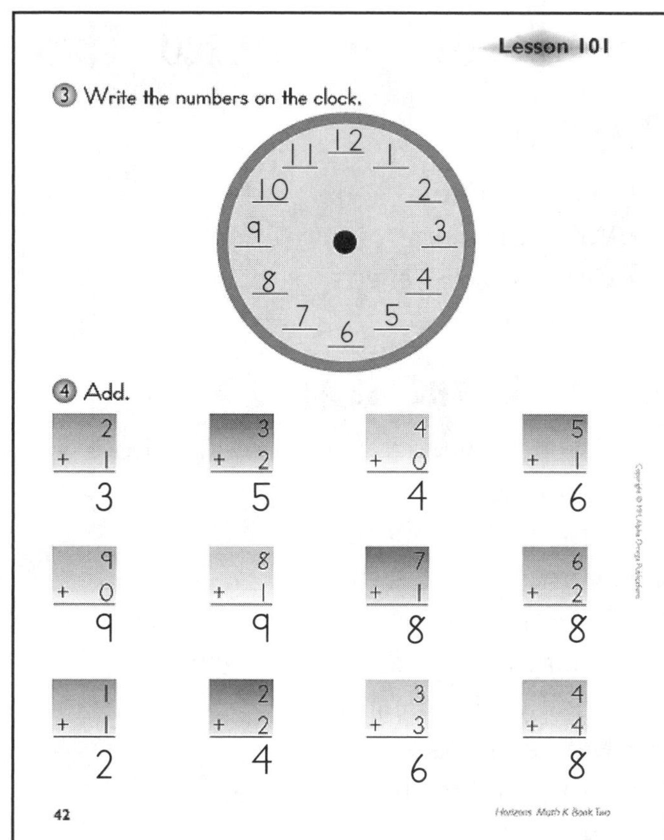

Lesson 102 - Elapsed Time

Overview:

- Elapsed time
- Word problems
- Count by 2's, evens
- Addition 80's

Materials and Supplies:

- Teacher's Guide & Student Workbook
- White board
- Objects for counters
- Number flash cards
- Number chart
- Count by 2's flash cards, evens
- Addition flash cards 1's
- Model clocks
- Number line strips

Teaching Tips:

Teach elapsed time – hours.
Review time – hour.
Review word problems.
Review counting even numbers by 2's to 100.
Review addition 80's.
Drill addition 1's family.
Review oral counting to 100.

Activities:

① Discuss with the student(s) that the short hand is the hour hand and points to the hour in the day (24 hours in a day). The long hand points to the minutes in an hour and is called the minute hand (60 minutes in an hour). The long hand is on 12 when the short hand tells the hour. Demonstrate 1 o'clock, 3 o'clock, 7 o'clock, etc. using a clock model. When starting Activity ①, tell the student(s) that the long hand is on 12 and that the hour hand has moved from 12 to the end of the shaded area. Have the student(s) count how many hours have passed if the short hand moved though the shaded area of each clock.

② Read the first word problem with the student(s). Emphasize that the word "altogether" means to put together or add. Have the student(s) write a 5 for the number of minutes that Bill rode his bike in the first blank. Write a 3 in the second blank for the numbers of minutes that Jim rode his bike in the second blank. Then, have the student(s) write the number of minutes ridden "altogether." Do the same for the rest of the activity.

③ Review counting by twos. Have the student(s) complete the count by 2's arrows in Activity ③ and then orally count by 2's again with the student(s) as they point to the numbers at the ends of their arrows.

④ This is the third time that the students are asked to add to the 80's family. In this activity they are adding a 1, 2, 3, 4, 5, 6 or 7 to a number in the 80's family. Do several examples on the white board using either a number line strip or a number chart. Randomly select an 80's flash card and a 1's flash card for the student(s) to add together. Don't ask them to do sums beyond the 80's.

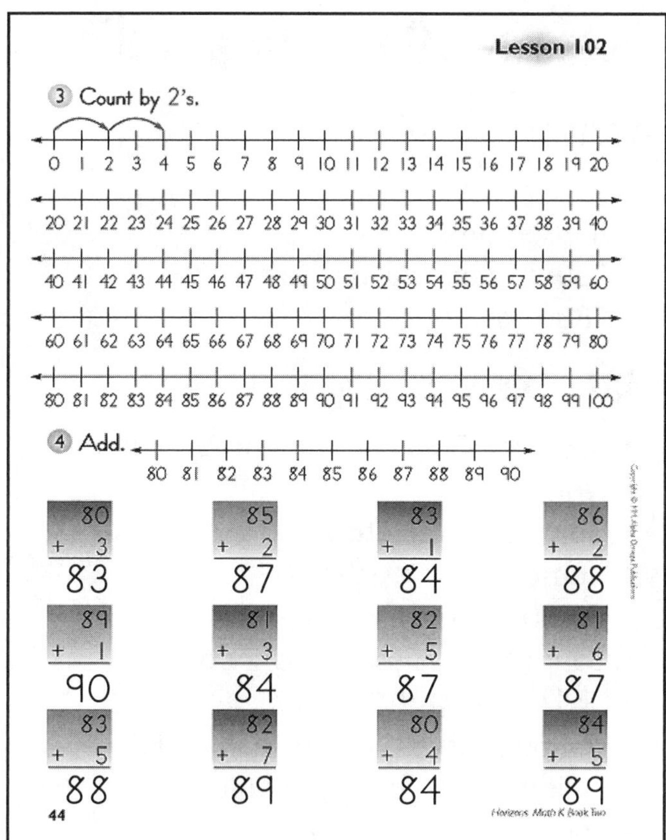

Lesson 103 - One Dollar

Overview:

- $1
- Elapsed time
- Count quart, gallon, cup & liter
- Count by 2's, odds

Materials and Supplies:

- Teacher's Guide & Student Workbook
- White board
- Objects for counters
- Number flash cards
- Number chart
- Count by 2's flash cards, odds
- Dollar bills and $1 coins
- Pennies, nickels, dimes, half dollars
- Gallon, quart, cup, liter volumes
- Addition flash cards 1's
- Model clocks
- Number line strips

Teaching Tips:

Teach 1 dollar bill and $1 coin.
Review penny, nickel, dime and 50¢.
Review elapsed time – hours.
Review time – hour.
Review volumes.
Review counting odd numbers by 2's to 100.
Drill addition 1's family.
Review oral counting to 100.

Activities:

① Using play money, have the student(s) identify each piece of money (front and back) they have studied and tell its value. Show the student(s) a 1 dollar coin. Talk about the color, size and the pictures on each side. Discuss the chart of coins that shows how many of each coin are equal to $1. Instruct the student(s) to use the chart as they write the number of each coin needed to equal $1 on the blanks.

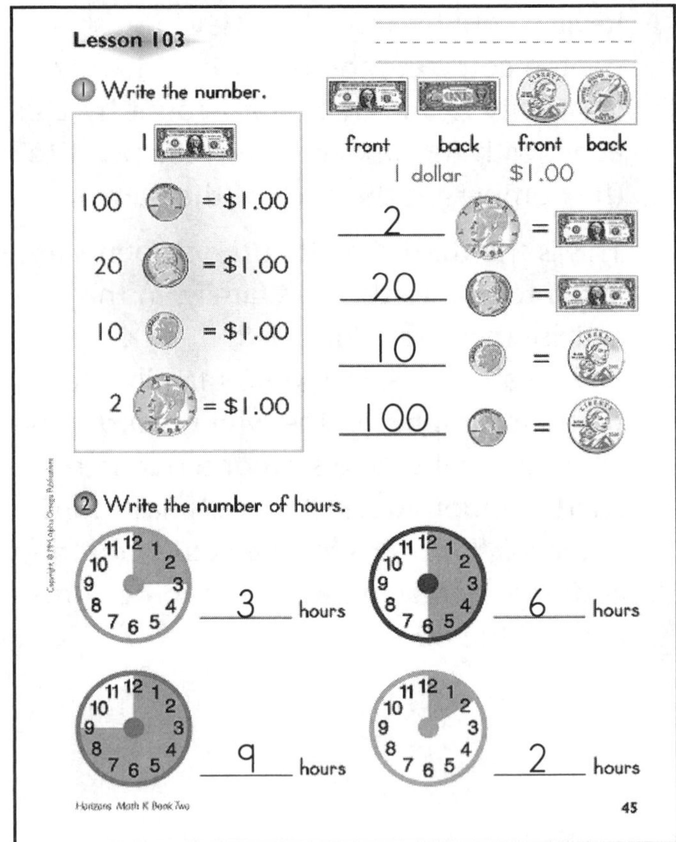

② Give each student a small clock model. Tell them to set the hands at 12:00. Then tell them that 4 hours have passed and ask them to set the hands of the clock correctly. When they are finished, have them hold their clock up so you can check the accuracy of their work. Do several examples before letting them complete the activity independently.

③ With samples or pictures review the names of the volumes. (quarts, cups, gallons, liters) Instruct the student(s) to count the number of each volume in the activity and write the correct number on the blank.

④ Review counting odd numbers by twos. Have the student(s) complete the count by 2's arrows in Activity ④ and then orally count by 2's again with the student(s) as they point to the numbers at the ends of their arrows. Help them as they go from one number line to the next.

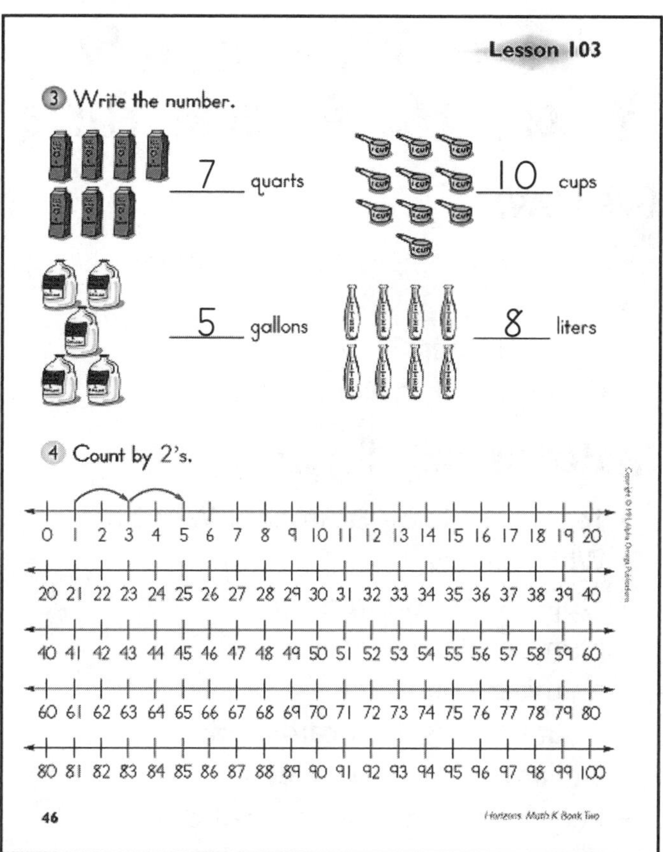

Lesson 104 - Identify Whole, 1/2 & Equal Parts

Overview:

- Identify whole, 1/2 & equal parts
- $1
- Odd numbers
- Count quart, gallon, cup & liter

Materials and Supplies:

- Teacher's Guide & Student Workbook
- White board
- Objects for counters
- Number flash cards
- Number chart
- Count by 2's flash cards, odds
- Dollar bills and $1 coins
- Pennies, nickels, dimes, half dollars
- Gallon, quart, cup, liter volumes
- Crayons
- Addition flash cards 1's
- Shape flash cards
- Number line strips

Teaching Tips:

Teach one half.
Review 1 dollar bill and $1 coin.
Review penny, nickel, dime and 50¢.
Review counting odd numbers by 2's to 100.
Review volumes.
Drill addition 1's family.
Review oral counting to 100.

Activities:

① Using flannel board or other fraction materials, demonstrate to the student(s) several halves that equal a whole when put together. Draw several geometric shapes on the white board and call the student(s) to come up and draw a line that will divide the shape into two equal

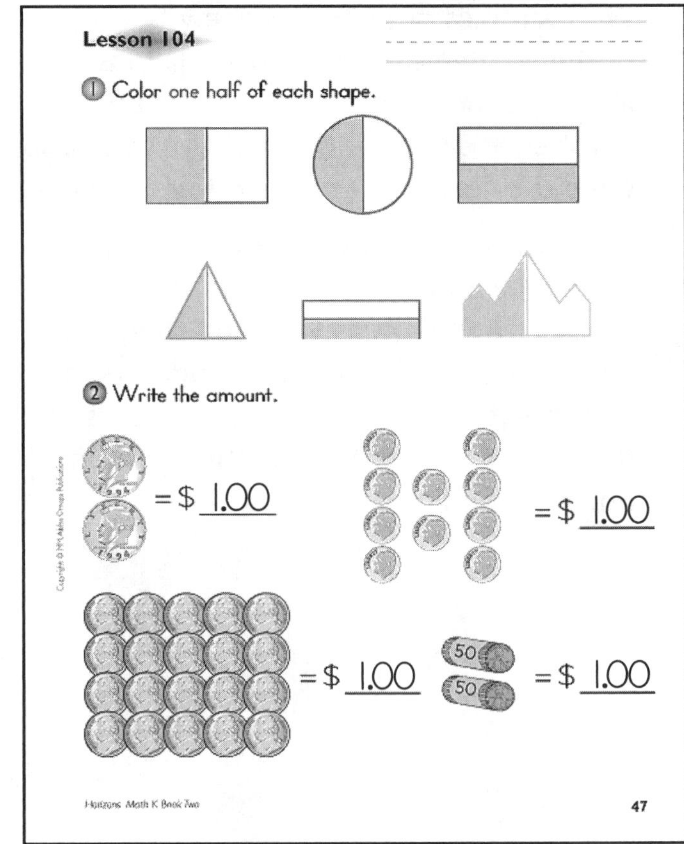

parts or halves. Review the shapes as you draw them. Read the directions for the activity then have the student(s) complete the activity.

② Using play money have the student(s) identify each piece of money (front and back) they have studied and tell its value. Show the student(s) a 1 dollar coin. Talk about the color, size and the pictures on each side. Relate the discussion of one half in the first activity to your review of 50¢. Talk about the rolls of pennies and that each roll has 50 pennies and is worth 50¢. Review counting by 5's and 10's before asking the student(s) to complete the activity. Allow them to use the money chart from *Lesson 103* if needed.

③ Review counting odd numbers by twos. Instruct the student(s) to circle the odd numbers in each flower. Allow them to use the odd number chart from *Lesson 103* if needed.

④ Review the volumes covered in previous lessons. Talk about the quart and the gallon. Tell them that if you take a gallon and divide it into 4 equal parts that you will have 4 quarts. Demonstrate the concept by pouring a gallon of water into 4 quarts. Then pour the 4 quarts back into the gallon. Instruct the student(s) to count the quarts in each group and to write the number on the blank in front of the word quarts. Then they should count the gallons and write the number on the blank for gallons. All of these are equal amounts. The student(s) will not be converting units in this level of material.

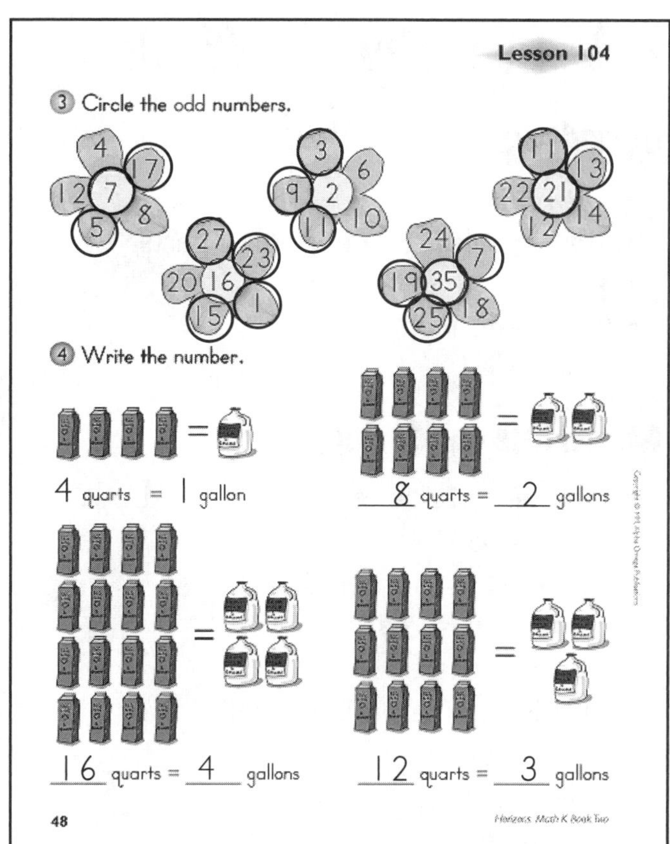

Lesson 105 - 1/2 Hour

Overview:

- 1/2 hour
- Identify whole, 1/2 & equal parts
- $1
- Perimeter, inches
- Months

Materials and Supplies:

- Teacher's Guide & Student Workbook
- White board
- Objects for counters
- Number flash cards
- Number chart
- Pennies, nickels, dimes, half dollars
- Clock models
- Ruler – inches
- Ordinal number flash cards
- Months of the year flash cards
- Addition flash cards 1's
- Shape flash cards
- Number line strips

Teaching Tips:

Teach half past the hour.
Review one half.
Review penny, nickel, dime and 50¢.
Review perimeter.
Review ordinals.
Review calendar.
Drill addition 1's family.
Review oral counting to 100.

Activities:

① When starting this activity, talk about cutting the clock into two half-hours as in the picture of the second clock in the box. Explain how the minutes can be found by counting by fives. Each half-hour is 30 minutes. When the time is on the hour, the long hand is on the 12 (first picture). When 30 minutes have passed on the clock, the long hand is then on the 6 (second picture). Point out that the short hand is halfway between the 8 and the 9. Show on a clock model the distance the two hands move with the passage of 30 minutes. To help the student(s) begin finding the clocks that show the half hour, ask the following questions: "Where is the long hand?" (It must be on 6 for half past) "Where is the short hand?" "What hour is that?"

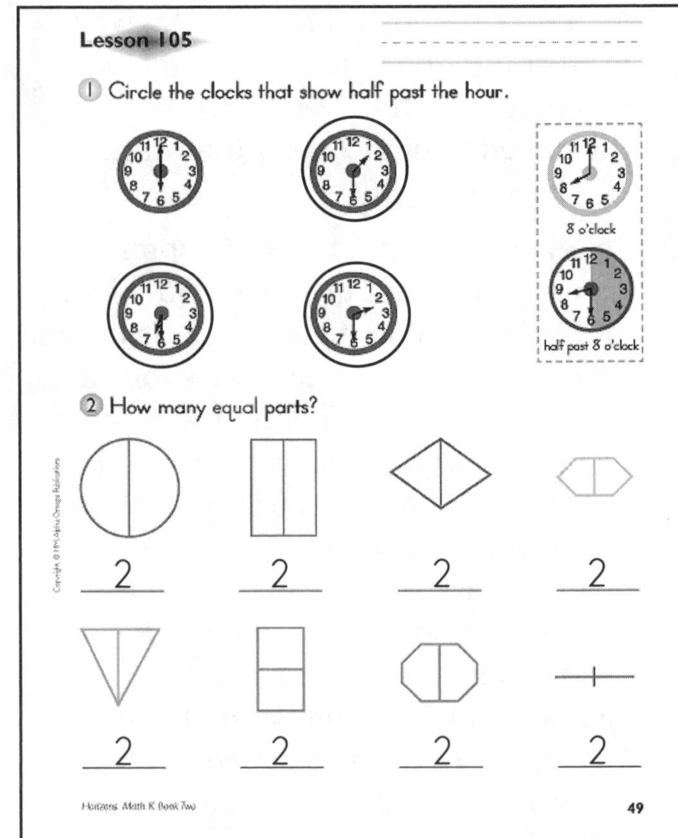

② On the flannel board or white board, show the student(s) a whole. Now show the object cut into two equal halves. Draw several shapes on the white board. Have student(s) come to the board and draw a line that cuts the shape into two equal parts. In Activity ② have the student(s) count the number of equal parts in the figures.

③ Review counting from 50 by 1's, 5's, and 10's. Instruct the student(s) to write the correct amount of money on the blanks.

④ Review the meaning of the word "perimeter." It means the distance around. Remind the student(s) how they previously found the perimeter around a table by counting the number of steps they walked. Explain that distance is labeled in inches in this activity. Instruct the student(s) to count the inches for the perimeter.

⑤ Review ordinal numbers. Review the months of the year by pointing to them on a calendar. Read each instruction and instruct the student(s) to mark their answers correctly.

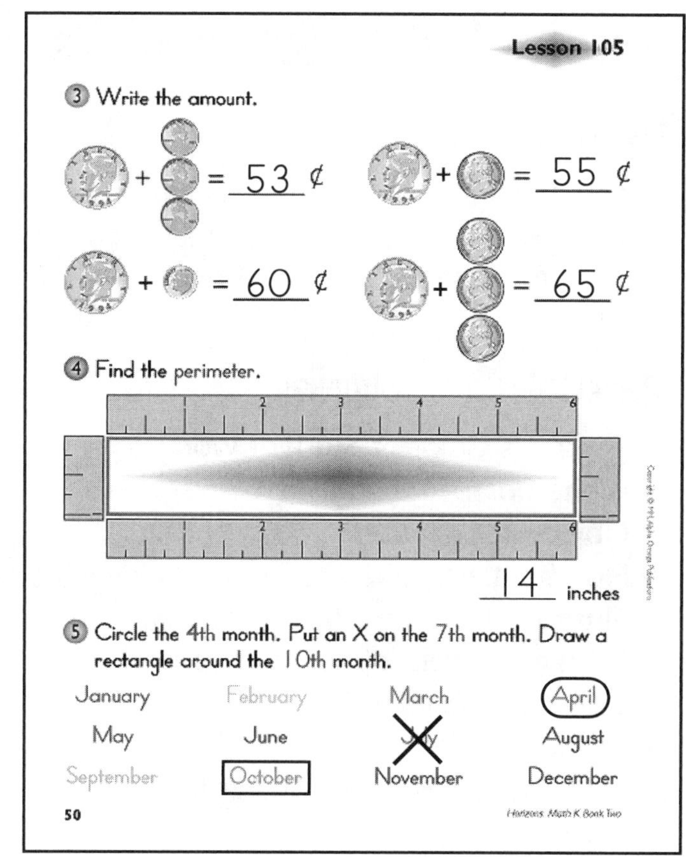

Lesson 106 - Subtract 1's

Overview:

- Subtract 1's
- 1/2 hour
- Identify whole, 1/2 & equal parts
- $1

Materials and Supplies:

- Teacher's Guide & Student Workbook
- White board
- Objects for counters
- Number flash cards
- Number chart
- Pennies, nickels, dimes, half dollars
- Dollar bills & coins
- Clock models
- Count by 5's & 10's flash cards
- Crayons
- Addition flash cards 1's
- Shape flash cards
- Number line strips

Teaching Tips:

Teach subtraction using counters or objects.
Review half past the hour.
Review one half.
Review 1 dollar bill and $1 coin.
Review penny, nickel, dime and 50¢.
Drill addition 1's family.
Review oral counting to 100.

Activities:

① To introduce subtraction, teach the student(s) that the answer is always going to be the same or less. Subtraction is taking away. Have the student(s) put three crayons on their desk. Write "3" on the white board. Show them the symbol (–) used to tell you to subtract. Now tell them to take away one crayon. Write a "1" after the minus sign followed by the (=) sign. Ask them to count the crayons to

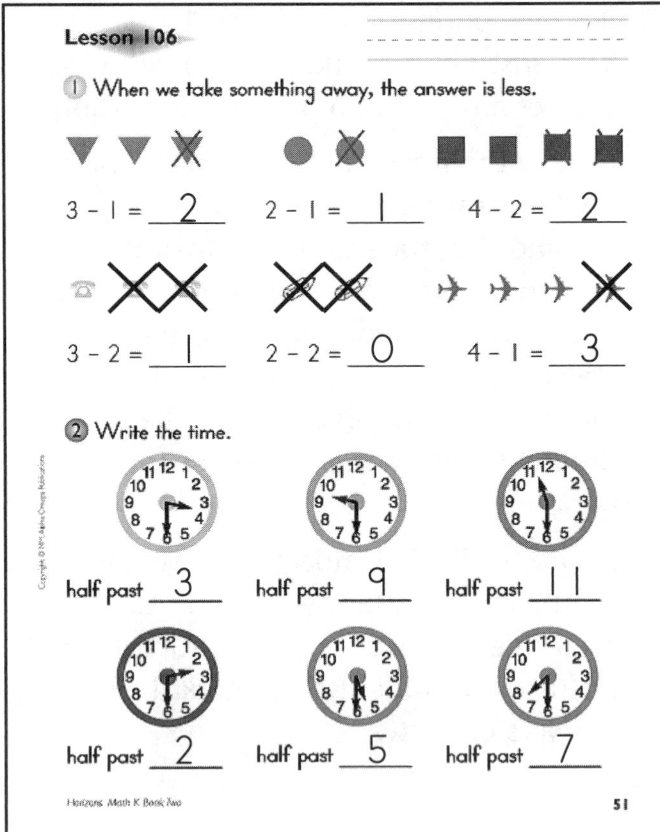

see how many they have left (2) and write "2" on the white board. "3 – 1 = 2" is a subtraction problem. Show how this can be written both horizontally and vertically. Do several other examples using crayons following the same procedure. In Activity ① have the student(s) actually count the objects that are left to arrive at their answer. For the second row they will need to cross out the number being subtracted. They will need your guidance throughout this activity.

② Remind the student(s) that a half-hour is 30 minutes. When the clock is at the half-hour, the long hand is on the 6. The short hand will be halfway between two numbers because it is half past the hour. The hour is indicated by the number the short hand just passed. Give the student(s) a small clock model. Write several times on the white board and have them put the hands in the correct position, placing the long (minute) hand first and then the short (hour) hand. Then have them hold up the clock so it can be checked. Have them do Activity ② by determining where the long hand is and then where the short hand is.

③ Show the student(s) a whole. Now show the object cut into two equal halves. Draw duplicates of several shapes on the white board. Have a student come to the board and draw a line that cuts one of the shapes into two equal parts. Have a second student come up and cut the duplicate shape into two equal parts with a different line. Repeat for the other shapes you have drawn. Have the student(s) complete the activity.

④ Review half dollar. Review counting by 5's and 10's. Review counting from 50 by 1's, 5's and 10's. Instruct the student(s) to write the correct amount of money on the blanks.

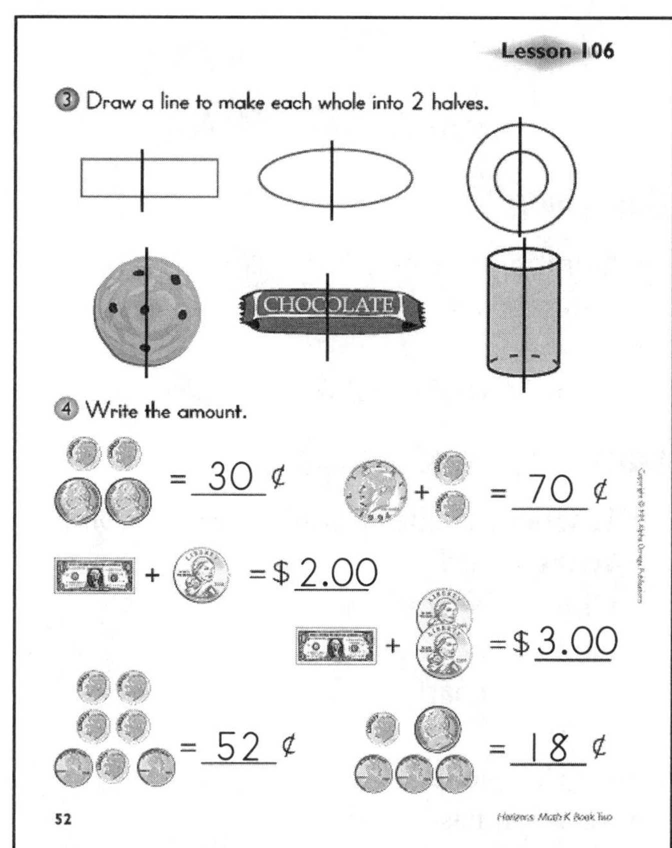

Lesson 107 - Number Between 90's

Overview:

- Number between 90's
- Subtract 1's
- 1/2 hour
- Identify whole, 1/2 & equal parts

Materials and Supplies:

- Teacher's Guide & Student Workbook
- White board
- Objects for counters
- Number flash cards
- Number chart
- Coins
- Clock models
- Addition flash cards 1's
- Shape flash cards
- Number line strips

Teaching Tips:

Teach number between 90's.
Review subtraction using counters or objects.
Review half past the hour.
Review one-half.
Drill addition 1's family.
Review oral counting to 100.

Activities:

① Choose three consecutive whole number flash cards 90–100. Arrange the cards out of order. Have the student(s) put them in correct order. Repeat this four times with different sets of three numbers. Read the instruction and have the student(s) complete the activity. They may use a number line or number chart if needed.

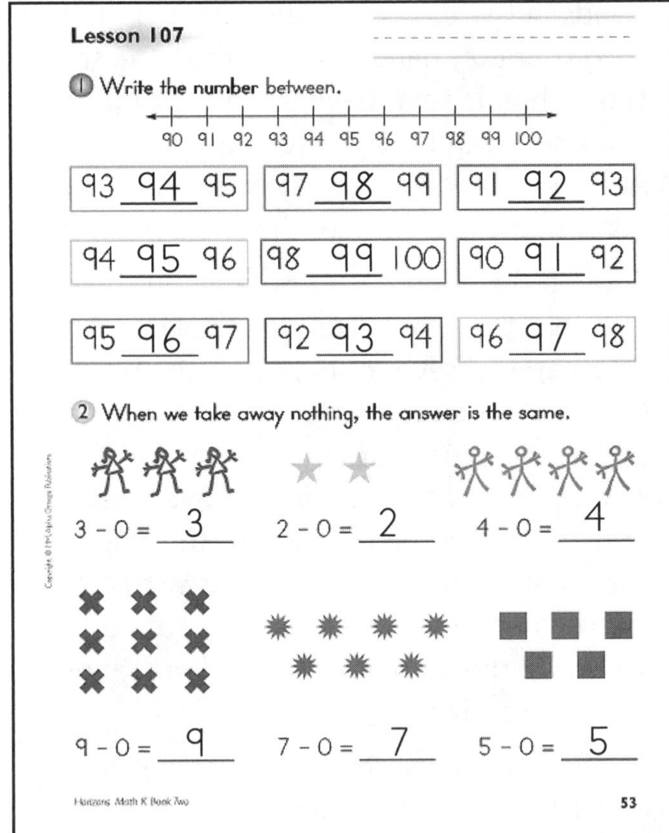

② Review subtraction, remind the student(s) that the answer is always going to be the same or less. Subtraction is taking away. Have the student(s) put three counters on their desk. Write "3" on the white board. Show them the symbol (–) used to tell you to subtract. Now tell them to take away zero counters. Write a "0" after the minus sign followed by the (=) sign. Ask them to count the counters to see how many they have left (3) and write "3" on the white board. "3 – 0 = 3" is a subtraction problem. Do several other examples using counters following the same procedure. In Activity ② have the student(s) count the objects then cross out zero objects to find the answer. They may need your guidance throughout this activity.

③ Remind the student(s) that a half-hour is 30 minutes. When the clock is at the half-hour, the long hand is on the 6. The short hand will be halfway between two numbers because it is half past the hour. The hour is indicated by the number the short hand just passed. Give the student(s) a small clock model. Write several half-hour times on the white board and have them put the hands in the correct position, placing the long (minute) hand first and then the short (hour) hand. Then have them hold up the clock so it can be checked. Have them do Activity ③ by determining where the long hand is, then where the short hand is and which digital clock matches the time.

④ Lay several different figures that have been cut in halves on a table. Have student(s) come to the table and match a pair of halves like a puzzle. Have them tell you how many halves it takes to make a whole. Point out the first shape in the activity. Instruct the students(s) to circle the correct number of halves. Do the same for the other shapes.

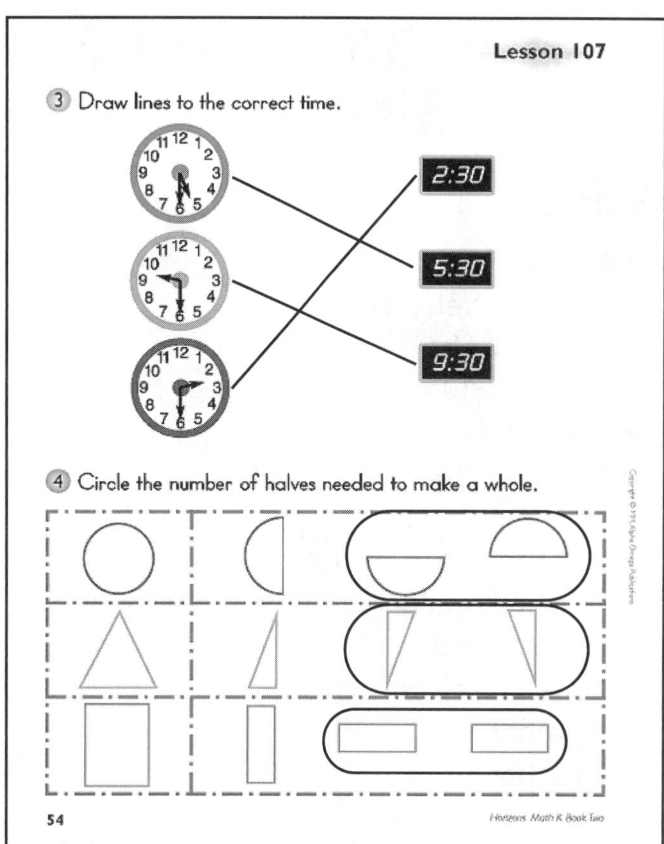

Lesson 108 – Number After 90's

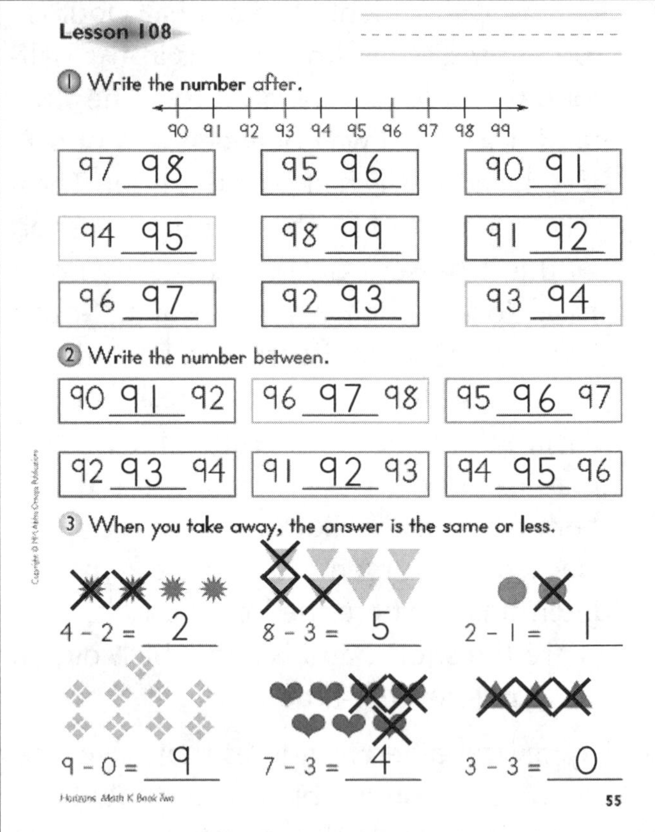
Lesson 108

① Write the number after.

90 91 92 93 94 95 96 97 98 99

97 98 | 95 96 | 90 91
94 95 | 98 99 | 91 92
96 97 | 92 93 | 93 94

② Write the number between.

90 91 92 | 96 97 98 | 95 96 97
92 93 94 | 91 92 93 | 94 95 96

③ When you take away, the answer is the same or less.

4 - 2 = 2 | 8 - 3 = 5 | 2 - 1 = 1
9 - 0 = 9 | 7 - 3 = 4 | 3 - 3 = 0

Horizons Math K Book Two 55

Overview:

- Number after 90's
- Number between 90's
- Subtract 1's
- Addition 80's
- Place Value 30's
- Ordinals, first–tenth

Materials and Supplies:

- Teacher's Guide & Student Workbook
- White board
- Objects for counters
- Number flash cards
- Number chart
- Place value chart
- Ordinal number flash cards
- Addition flash cards 1's
- Number line strips

Teaching Tips:

Teach number after 90's.
Review number between 90's.
Review subtraction 1's.
Review addition 80's.
Review place value 30's.
Review ordinals.
Drill addition 1's family.
Review oral counting to 100.

Activities:

① Review number sequence by pointing to a number chart and asking the student(s) to say the number after 90's. The numbers in this activity are from the 90's family. (90–99) Read the instruction and have the student(s) complete the activity.

② Use number line strips or a number chart to review the number between. Practice number recognition by holding up three number cards. Ask the student(s) to tell you which card is a particular number. The left, right or middle card? Hold them vertically and have them answer top, bottom or middle. Have the student(s) write their answers for the activity using a number chart if necessary.

③ Give each student seven pennies, nickels, or dimes (play money). Tell them to form a set of five. On a clean sheet of paper have them write "5." Ask them to take two away. Have them write "– 2" on their paper. Tell them to count the ones that are left (3). Write "= 3" on their paper. Now read the subtraction fact together. Do this with several other sets of seven or less. The student(s) will need your guidance for each problem in Activity ③. They must count how many items they start with, how many are taken away, (cross them out) and how many are left.

④ This is a review activity. Only help the student(s) if they need it.

⑤ This is a review exercise. Review if necessary.

⑥ Review ordinal numbers. Instruct the student(s) to trace the dotted line and to complete the activity.

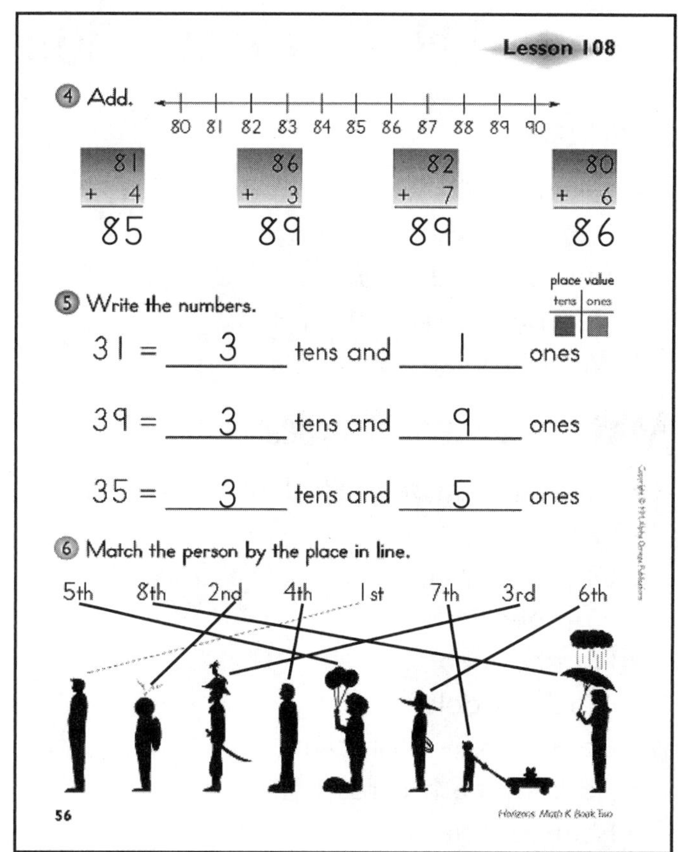

Lesson 109 - Subtract 10's

Overview:

- Subtract 10's
- Count by 3's
- Number after 90's
- Number between 90's
- Word problems

Materials and Supplies:

- Teacher's Guide & Student Workbook
- White board
- Objects for counters
- Number flash cards
- Number chart
- Clock models
- Count by 3's flash cards
- Addition flash cards 1's
- Number line strips
- Worksheet 34

Teaching Tips:

Teach subtraction 10's.
Teach subtraction on a number line.
Review subtraction 1's.
Teach counting by 3's.
Review number after 90's.
Review number between 90's.
Review time – hour.
Drill addition 1's family.
Review oral counting to 100.

Activities:

① Draw a number line on the white board to introduce subtraction facts. Next, write a subtraction fact (19 – 5 = 4) on the white board. Above the number line draw a line starting at zero to 19. This represents how many you have at the beginning. Since you are taking away 5, you want to start counting back five marks from 19 toward zero. Draw a second line under the first one from 19 to 14 (5 marks back). The point where you end up is the answer (14). Do this with several subtraction facts using the number line. When starting Activity ①, have the student(s) state how many there are at the beginning, how many were taken away, and how many are then left. The point where the second line ends moving toward zero is how many are left. Do each subtraction problem together.

② Orally count to 100. Orally count by 3's to 100 with flash cards, a number chart or number line. Instruct the student(s) to complete the activity.

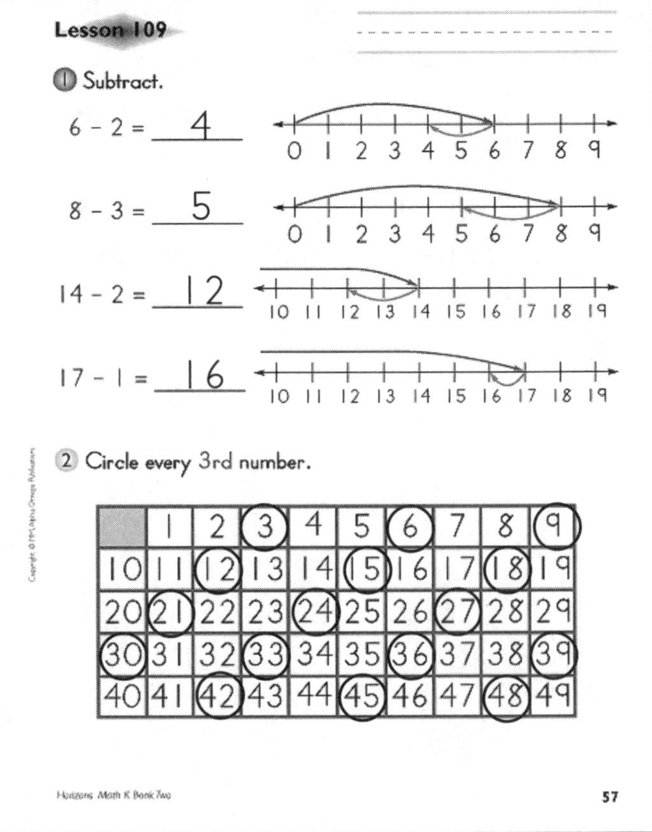

③ Review number after 90's as is needed.

④ Review number between 90's as is needed.

⑤ Discuss the time of the day when the student(s) are involved in a particular activity. Make a chart of the times that some of them go to bed similar to the chart in Activity ⑤. Help them to read the questions in Activity ⑤ and to write the answer on the blanks.

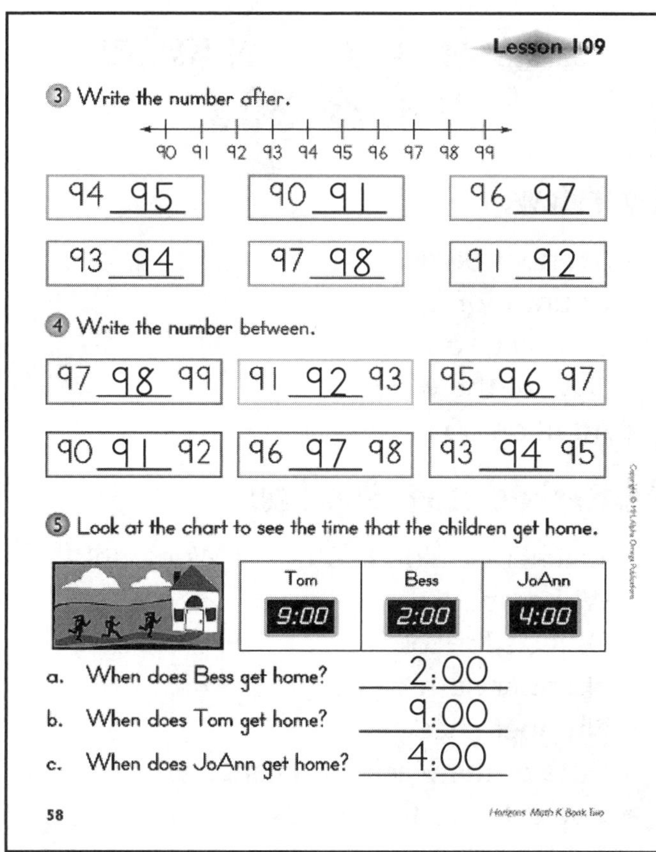

Lesson 110 - Number Before 30's

Overview:

- Number before 30's
- Count by 3's
- Subtract 10's
- Days of the week
- Addition 80's

Materials and Supplies:

- Teacher's Guide & Student Workbook
- White board
- Objects for counters
- Number flash cards
- Number chart
- Days of the week flash cards
- Count by 3's flash cards
- Subtraction flash cards 1's
- Addition flash cards 1's
- Number line strips

Teaching Tips:

Teach number before 30's.
Review counting by 3's.
Review subtraction 1's & 10's.
Review subtraction on a number line.
Review days of the week.
Review addition 80's.
Drill addition 1's family.
Review oral counting to 100.

Activities:

① Read the numbers in the 30's family from a number chart or line. Discuss that the words "number before" means to count backward. Count backwards from 39 by looking at a number chart. Pick random numbers for the 30's family and call on student(s) to give you the number before. Have the student(s) complete the activity.

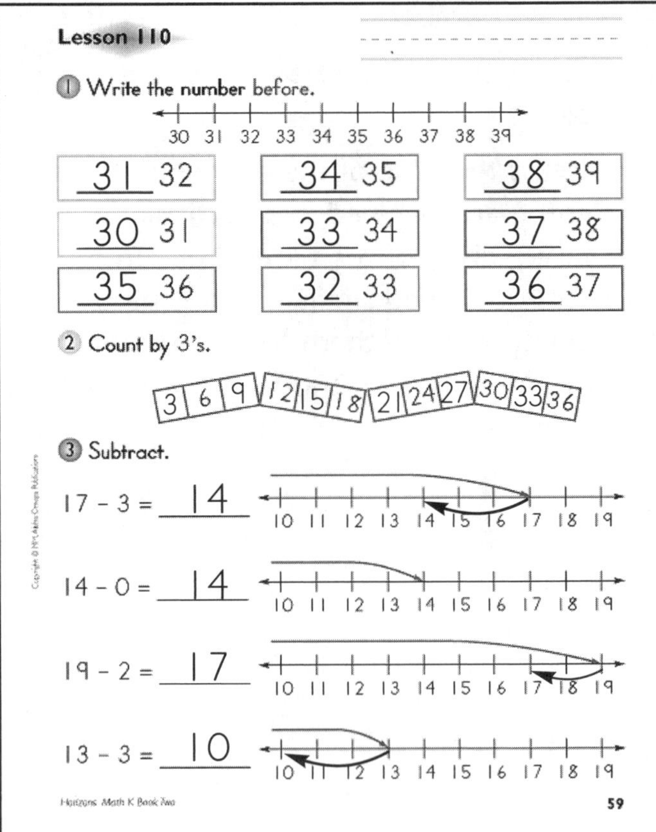

② Orally count to 100. Orally count by 3's to 100 with flash cards, a number chart or number line. Instruct the student(s) to complete the activity.

③ Using a number line on the white board, demonstrate several subtraction facts similar to those in Activity ③. Have the student(s) write the subtraction fact on a piece of paper. Much practice may be needed for the student(s) to think "take away" instead of adding. Have a "backward" day or activity where the student(s) walk backwards or do things backwards to reinforce the concept of counting backwards to subtract. When doing Activity ③, work the first two subtraction facts together and then allow them to continue without help if possible.

④ Review the days of the week as is needed. Read each list to the student(s). Have them circle the list they feel is correct.

⑤ This is a review exercise. Review if necessary.

Lesson 110

④ Circle the correct order for the days of the week.

Saturday Monday Wednesday Friday Sunday Tuesday Thursday

(Sunday Monday Tuesday Wednesday Thursday Friday Saturday)

Saturday Friday Thursday Wednesday Tuesday Monday Sunday

⑤ Add.

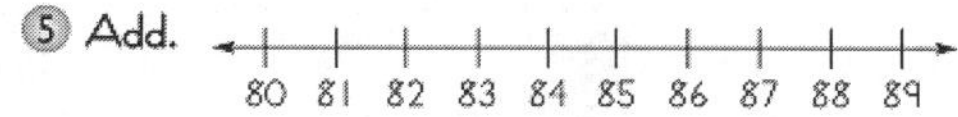

81 + 6 = 87	86 + 3 = 89
85 + 4 = 89	87 + 2 = 89
80 + 7 = 87	81 + 5 = 86
82 + 6 = 88	84 + 4 = 88

60 Horizons Math K Book Two

Lesson 111 - Addition 90's

Overview:

- Addition 90's
- Count by 3's
- Subtract 1's
- Addition 70's
- Subtract 10's
- Number before 30's

Materials and Supplies:

- Teacher's Guide & Student Workbook
- White board
- Objects for counters
- Number flash cards
- Number chart
- Count by 3's flash cards
- Subtraction flash cards 1's
- Addition flash cards 1's
- Number line strips

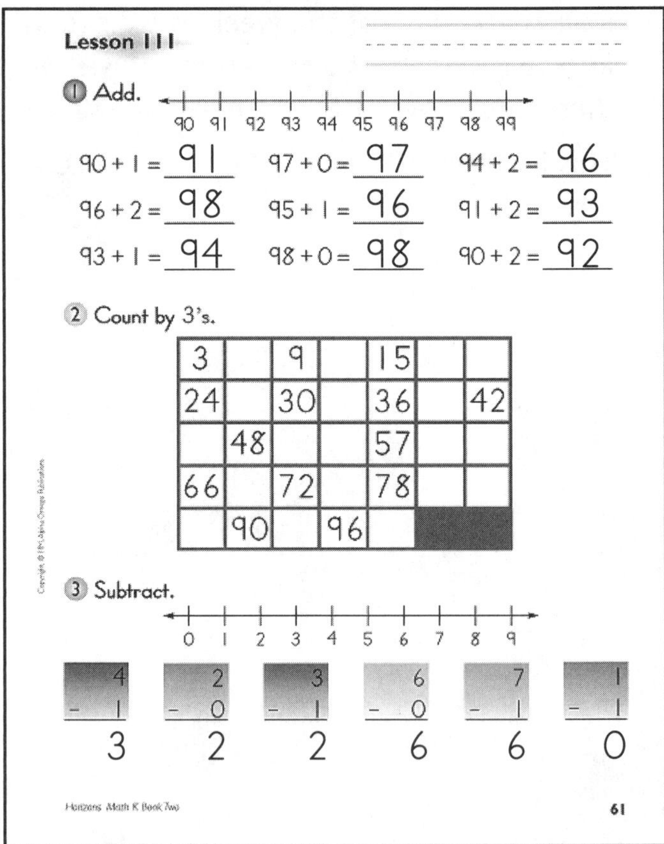

Teaching Tips:

Teach addition 90's.
Review counting by 3's.
Review subtraction on a number line.
Review subtraction 1's & 10's.
Review addition 70's.
Review number before 30's.
Drill addition 1's family.
Review oral counting to 100.

Activities:

① This is the first time that the students are asked to add to the 90's family. In this activity they are adding a 0, 1 or 2 to a number in the 90's family. The 90's are the last family of addition that will be covered in this material. Congratulate the student(s) on their hard work. Encourage them to work hard on subtraction so they can quickly reach subtraction of the 90's family. Do several examples on the white board using either a number line strip or a number chart. Review number after 90's. Remind the student(s) to go to the first number and count the number being added to find the answer.

② Orally count to 100. Orally count by 3's to 100 with flash cards, a number chart or number line. Instruct the student(s) to complete the activity.

③ Write a horizontal subtraction fact on the white board. Discuss that both numerals are one digit and therefore are in the ones' place. When the numerals are then written vertically, they are written straight up and down. The ones always go under the ones' place. Work the first two or three problems in Activity ③ together using the number line and then let the student(s) do the remainder on their own.

④ This is a review exercise. Review if necessary.

⑤ Using a number line on the white board, demonstrate several subtraction facts similar to those in Activity ③. Review counting backward. Instruct the student(s) to complete the activity. Give individual help to those who need it.

⑥ This is a review exercise. Review if necessary.

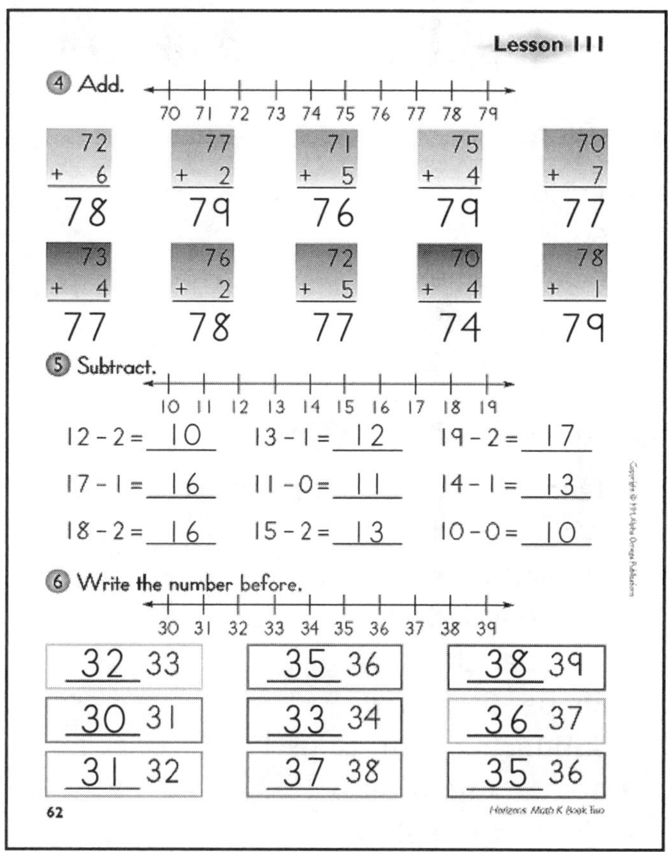
Lesson 111

④ Add.

70 71 72 73 74 75 76 77 78 79

72 + 6	77 + 2	71 + 5	75 + 4	70 + 7
78	79	76	79	77
73 + 4	76 + 2	72 + 5	70 + 4	78 + 1
77	78	77	74	79

⑤ Subtract.

10 11 12 13 14 15 16 17 18 19

12 - 2 = 10 13 - 1 = 12 19 - 2 = 17

17 - 1 = 16 11 - 0 = 11 14 - 1 = 13

18 - 2 = 16 15 - 2 = 13 10 - 0 = 10

⑥ Write the number before.

30 31 32 33 34 35 36 37 38 39

32 33	35 36	38 39
30 31	33 34	36 37
31 32	37 38	35 36

62 Horizons Math K Book Two

Lesson 112 - 1/3 & 1/4

Overview:

- 1/3 & 1/4
- Addition 90's
- Word problems
- Number before 30's
- Subtract 10's

Materials and Supplies:

- Teacher's Guide & Student Workbook
- White board
- Objects for counters
- Number flash cards
- Number chart
- Shapes flash cards
- Subtraction flash cards 1's
- Addition flash cards 1's
- Number line strips

Teaching Tips:

Teach 1/3 & 1/4.
Review addition 90's.
Review word problems.
Review number before 30's.
Review subtraction on a number line.
Review subtraction 10's.
Drill subtraction 1's family.
Drill addition 1's family.
Review oral counting to 100.

Activities:

① On the white board draw different shapes that can be divided into three equal parts (or use fraction materials). Have a student come to the white board and draw lines to divide one shape into three equal parts. Then have them shade 1/3 of the shape with the marker. Follow the same steps for each of the other shapes on the white board. Repeat the activity dividing the shapes into four equal parts. Let a student read the directions for the activity before they complete it on their own. Leave the samples on the white board for them to look at as they do the activity.

② This is the second time that the students are asked to add to the 90's family. In this activity they are adding a 0, 1, 2, 3 or 4 to a number in the 90's family. Do several examples on the white board using either a number line strip or a number chart.

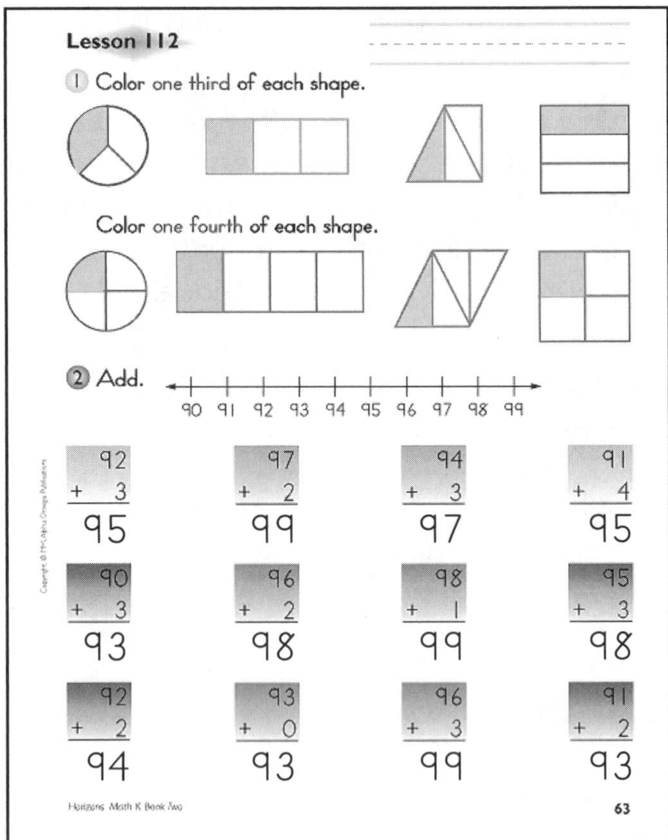

Lesson 112

① Color one third of each shape.

Color one fourth of each shape.

② Add.

90 91 92 93 94 95 96 97 98 99

92 + 3 = 95	97 + 2 = 99	94 + 3 = 97	91 + 4 = 95
90 + 3 = 93	96 + 2 = 98	98 + 1 = 99	95 + 3 = 98
92 + 2 = 94	93 + 0 = 93	96 + 3 = 99	91 + 2 = 93

Horizons Math K Book Two 63

③ Read the first problem to the student(s). "How many pens does Dad have?" "How many pens does Kim have?" "What is the question?" "Say it as an addition problem." "3 + 2 = how many pens." "3 + 2 = 5 pens" Repeat for the other questions. Emphasize the words *altogether* and *in all.*

④ Drill number before 30's family.

⑤ Write several horizontal subtraction facts on the white board. Write them in vertical form and use the number line to determine the answer. The student(s) should then be allowed to do the activity on their own with you giving individual help where it is needed.

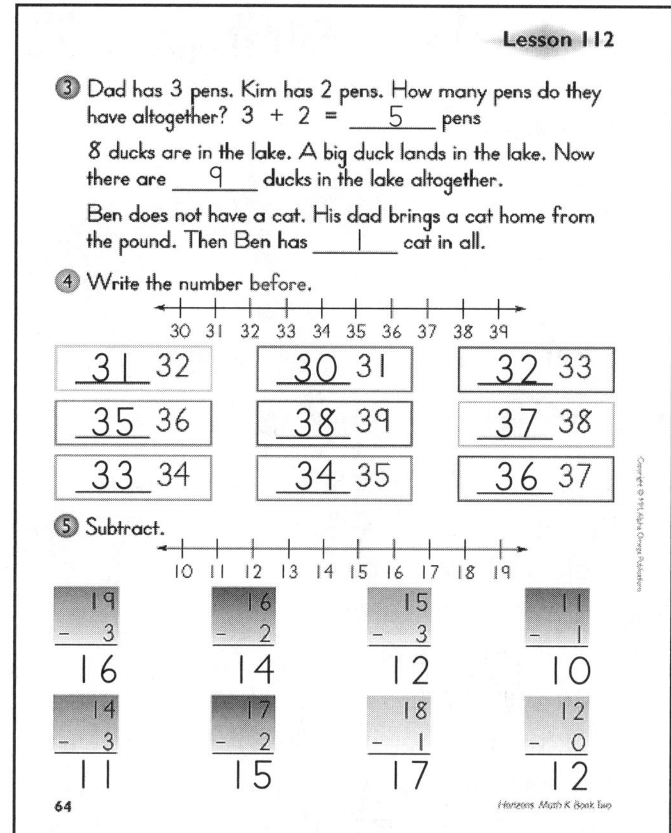

Lesson 112

③ Dad has 3 pens. Kim has 2 pens. How many pens do they have altogether? 3 + 2 = __5__ pens

8 ducks are in the lake. A big duck lands in the lake. Now there are __9__ ducks in the lake altogether.

Ben does not have a cat. His dad brings a cat home from the pound. Then Ben has __1__ cat in all.

④ Write the number before.

30 31 32 33 34 35 36 37 38 39

31 32	30 31	32 33
35 36	38 39	37 38
33 34	34 35	36 37

⑤ Subtract.

10 11 12 13 14 15 16 17 18 19

19 − 3 = 16	16 − 2 = 14	15 − 3 = 12	11 − 1 = 10
14 − 3 = 11	17 − 2 = 15	18 − 1 = 17	12 − 0 = 12

64 Horizons Math K Book Two

Lesson 113 - Subtract 20's

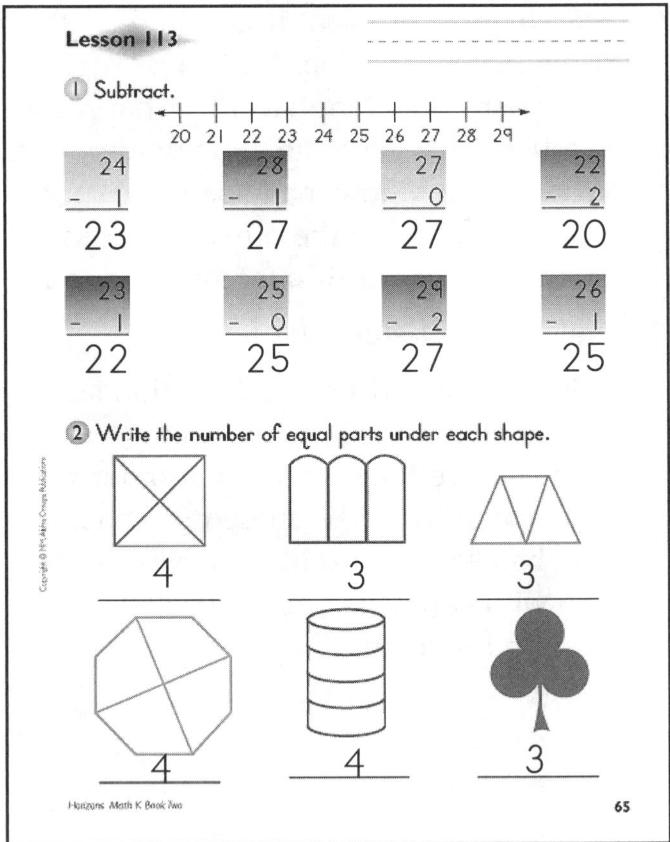

Overview:

- Subtract 20's
- 1/3 & 1/4
- Addition 90's
- Count by 2's & 3's
- Subtract 10's

Materials and Supplies:

- Teacher's Guide & Student Workbook
- White board
- Objects for counters
- Number flash cards
- Number line strip
- Number chart
- Shapes flash cards
- Subtraction flash cards 1's
- Addition flash cards 1's
- Number line strips

Teaching Tips:

Teach subtraction 20's.
Review 1/3 & 1/4.
Review addition 90's.
Review count by 2's.
Review count by 3's.
Review subtraction on a number line.
Review subtraction 10's.
Drill subtraction 1's family.
Drill addition 1's family.
Review oral counting to 100.

Activities:

① Draw a number line on the white board to introduce subtraction facts. Next, write a subtraction fact (26 – 4 =) on the white board. Above the number line draw a line starting at zero to 26. This represents how many you have at the beginning. Since you are taking away 4, you want to start counting back four marks from 26 toward zero. Draw a second line under the first one from 26 to 22 (4 marks back). The point where you end up is the answer (22). Do this with several subtraction facts using the number line. When starting Activity ①, have the student(s) state how many there are at the beginning, how many were taken away, and how many are then left. The point where the second line ends moving toward zero is how many are left. Do each subtraction problem together.

② On the white board repeat the practice activity done in the previous lesson by drawing different shapes that can be divided into three equal parts (or use fraction materials). Have a student come to the white board and draw lines to divide one shape into three equal parts. Then have them shade 1/3 of the shape with the marker. Follow the same steps for each of the other shapes on the white board. Repeat the activity dividing the shapes into four equal parts. Let a student read the directions for the activity before they complete it on their own. Leave the samples on the white board for them to look at as they do the activity.

③ This is the third time that the students are asked to add to the 90's family. In this activity they are adding a 1, 2, 3, 4 or 6 to a number in the 90's family. Do several examples on the white board using either a number line strip or a number chart.

④ This is a review exercise. Review if necessary.

⑤ Write several horizontal subtraction facts on the white board and use the number line to determine the answer. The student(s) should then be allowed to do the activity on their own with you giving individual help where it is needed.

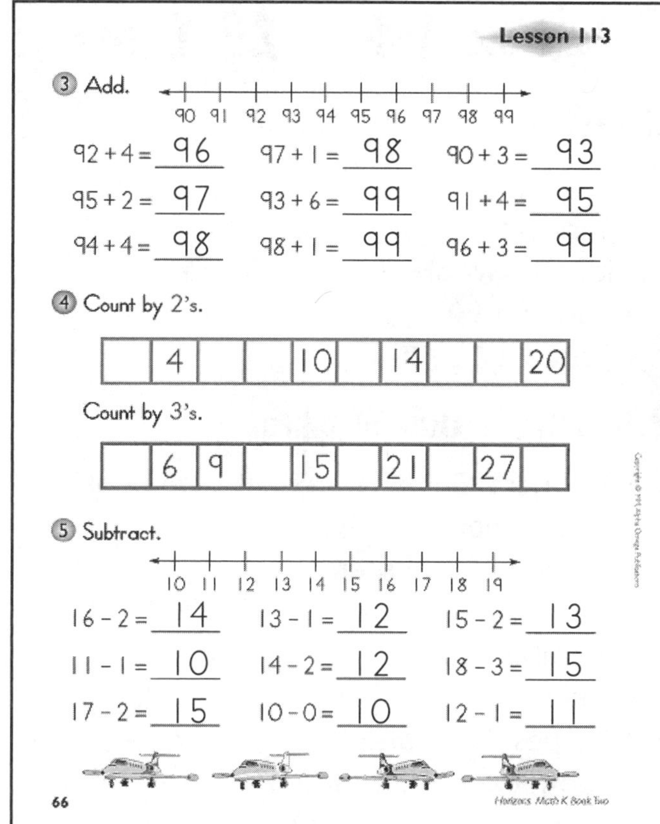
Lesson 113

③ Add.

90 91 92 93 94 95 96 97 98 99

92 + 4 = 96　　97 + 1 = 98　　90 + 3 = 93

95 + 2 = 97　　93 + 6 = 99　　91 + 4 = 95

94 + 4 = 98　　98 + 1 = 99　　96 + 3 = 99

④ Count by 2's.

	4			10		14			20

Count by 3's.

	6	9		15		21		27	

⑤ Subtract.

10 11 12 13 14 15 16 17 18 19

16 - 2 = 14　　13 - 1 = 12　　15 - 2 = 13

11 - 1 = 10　　14 - 2 = 12　　18 - 3 = 15

17 - 2 = 15　　10 - 0 = 10　　12 - 1 = 11

66　　Horizons Math K Book Two

Lesson 114 - 25 Cents

Overview:

- 25 cents
- Subtract 20's
- Identify whole, 1/2, 1/3 & 1/4
- Addition 90's
- Subtract 1's

Materials and Supplies:

- Teacher's Guide & Student Workbook
- White board
- Objects for counters
- Number flash cards
- Number chart
- Quarters
- Shapes flash cards
- Subtraction flash cards 1's
- Addition flash cards 1's
- Number line strips

Teaching Tips:

Teach 25 cents & quarters.
Review subtraction on a number line.
Review subtraction 20's.
Review equal parts.
Review addition 90's.
Drill subtraction 1's family.
Drill addition 1's family.
Review oral counting to 100.

Activities:

① Using play money quarters, have the student(s) count by 25 to determine how many cents there are in 1, 2, 3, and 4 quarters. Draw sets of 1, 2, 3, and 4 circles on the white board and put 25¢ in each circle. Draw a line under each circle. As they count three circles by 25 write "25," "50," "75" on the lines. Three quarters then equal 75¢ Do this for 1, 2, and 4 circles. Guide the student(s) to follow the same counting by 25's in Activity ①.

② Drill subtraction 1's with flash cards. Review subtraction on the number line. Instruct the student(s) to complete the activity.

③ Draw different shapes on the white board that are divided into equal and not equal parts. Have a student come to the board and circle one shape that has equal parts. Continue to call on student(s) until all of the equal shapes have been circled. Read the directions for the activity and let the student(s) complete it on their own.

④ This is a review activity. Only help the student(s) if they need it.

⑤ The student(s) should be allowed to do this activity on their own.

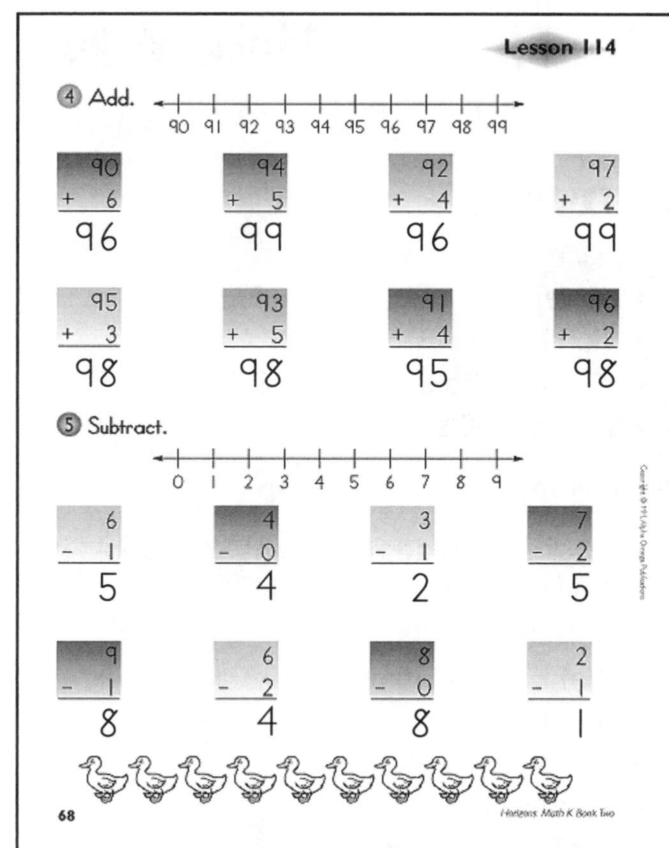

Lesson 114

④ Add.

90 91 92 93 94 95 96 97 98 99

90 + 6	94 + 5	92 + 4	97 + 2
96	99	96	99
95 + 3	93 + 5	91 + 4	96 + 2
98	98	95	98

⑤ Subtract.

0 1 2 3 4 5 6 7 8 9

6 − 1	4 − 0	3 − 1	7 − 2
5	4	2	5
9 − 1	6 − 2	8 − 0	2 − 1
8	4	8	1

68 Horizons Math K Book Two

Lesson 115 - Place Value 40's

Overview:

- Place value 40's
- 25 cents
- Match seasons
- Identify whole, 1/2, 1/3 & 1/4
- Subtract 20's

Materials and Supplies:

- Teacher's Guide & Student Workbook
- White board
- Objects for counters
- Number flash cards
- Number chart
- Quarters, nickels, pennies
- Seasons flash cards
- Shapes flash cards
- Subtraction flash cards 1's
- Addition flash cards 1's
- Number line strips

Teaching Tips:

Teach place value 40's.
Review 25 cents & quarters.
Review seasons.
Review equal parts.
Review subtraction on a number line.
Review subtraction 20's.
Drill subtraction 1's family.
Drill addition 1's family.
Review oral counting to 100.

Activities:

① Review place value with a place value chart or blocks. Practice a few numbers in the 40's family. Instruct the student(s) to complete the activity. Alert them to the two different types of problems in the activity.

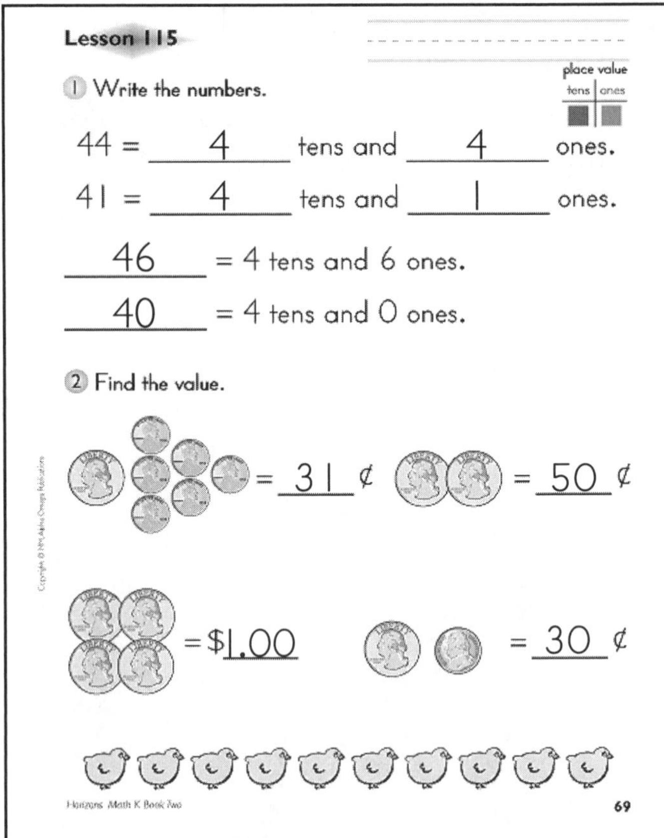

② Count four quarters by 25 to find their value using play money. Do a few combinations of 1 quarter and pennies or nickels. Practice counting by 25 to a number and then continue by 1's, 5's or 10's.

③ Review the words for the seasons. Read the seasons and instruct the student(s) to draw a line from the name to the picture.

④ Draw different shapes on the white board and allow the student(s) to divide them into two and four equal parts (or use fraction materials). Have them color 1/4 of the shapes divided into 4 parts or 1/2 of the shapes divided into 2 parts. Give individual help as the student(s) complete the activity.

⑤ The student(s) should be allowed to do this activity on their own.

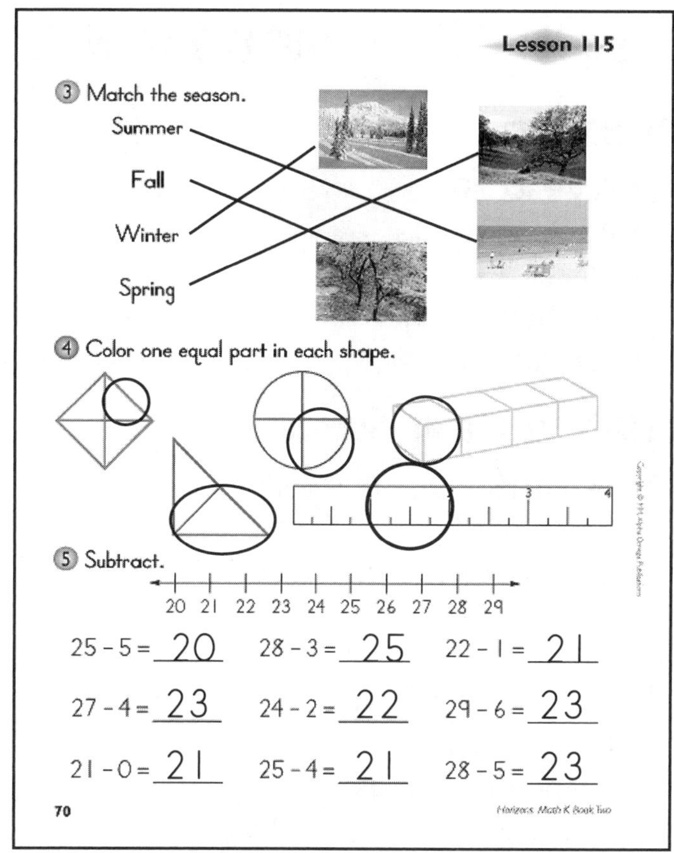

Lesson 116 - Subtract 30's

Overview:

- Subtract 30's
- Place value 40's
- 25 cents
- Perimeter, inches
- Subtract 20's

Materials and Supplies:

- Teacher's Guide & Student Workbook
- White board
- Objects for counters
- Number flash cards
- Number chart
- Quarters, nickels, dimes, pennies
- Ruler – inches
- Shapes flash cards
- Subtraction flash cards 1's
- Addition flash cards 1's
- Number line strips

Teaching Tips:

Teach subtraction 30's.
Review place value 40's.
Review quarters, dimes, nickels & pennies.
Review perimeter.
Review subtraction 20's.
Drill subtraction 1's family.
Drill addition 1's family.
Review oral counting to 100.

Activities:

① Draw a number line on the white board to introduce subtraction facts. Next, write a subtraction fact (33 – 2 =) on the white board. Above the number line draw a line to 33. This represents how many you have at the beginning. Since you are taking away 2, you want to start counting back two marks from 33 toward zero. Draw a second line under the first one from 33 to 31 (2 marks back). The point

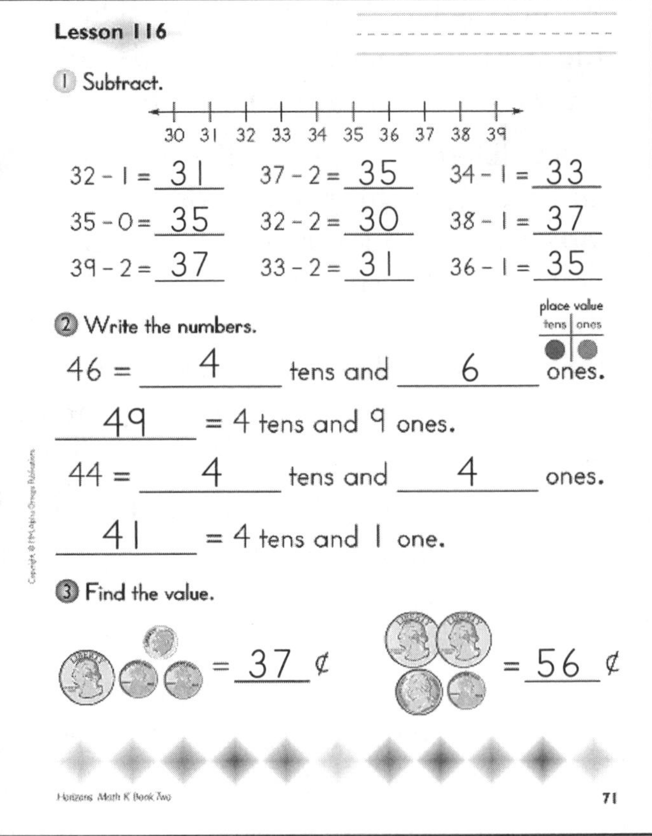

where you end up is the answer (31). Do this with several subtraction facts using the number line. When starting Activity ①, have the student(s) state how many there are at the beginning, how many were taken away, and how many are then left. The point where the second line ends moving toward zero is how many are left. Do each subtraction problem together.

② Review place value by counting the 40's. "40 is 4 tens and 0 ones, 41 is 4 tens and 1 one, 42 is 4 tens and 2 ones, etc."

③ Count four quarters by 25 to find their value using play money. Do a few combinations of 1 quarter and pennies or nickels. Practice counting by 25 to a number and then continue by 1's, 5's or 10's.

④ Review perimeter as distance around an object.

⑤ Drill 1's family subtraction with flash cards. The student(s) should be able to do this activity on their own.

Lesson 117 - Number Before 40's

Overview:

- Number before 40's
- Subtract 30's
- Count by 2's, 3's & 10's
- 25 cents

Materials and Supplies:

- Teacher's Guide & Student Workbook
- White board
- Objects for counters
- Number flash cards
- Number chart
- Quarters, nickels, dimes, pennies
- Subtraction flash cards 1's
- Addition flash cards 1's
- Number line strips

Teaching Tips:

Teach number before 40's.
Review subtraction 30's.
Review count by 2's, 3's and 10's.
Review quarters, dimes, nickels & pennies.
Drill subtraction 1's family.
Drill addition 1's family.
Review oral counting to 100.

Activities:

① Read the numbers in the 40's family from a number chart or line. Discuss that the words "number before" mean to count backward. Count backwards from 49 by looking at a number chart. Pick random numbers for the 40's family and call on student(s) to give you the number before. Have the student(s) complete the activity.

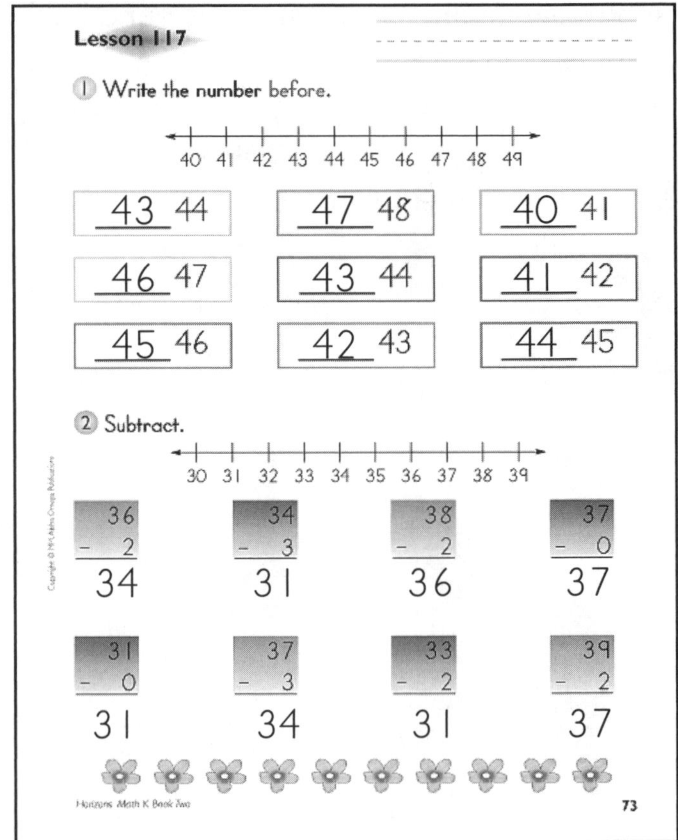

② Drill subtraction 1's with flash cards. Review subtraction on the number line. Instruct the student(s) to complete the activity.

③ Review counting by 2's (even numbers), 3's and 10's. Have the student(s) complete the activity.

④ Review coins and their value. Drill several combinations and the value. Help the student(s) as they complete this activity.

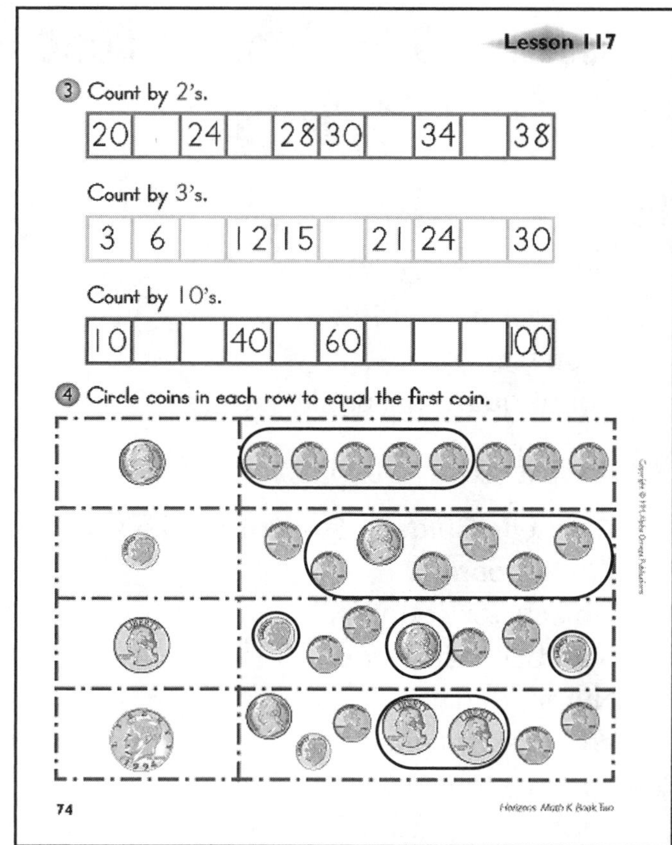

Lesson 117

③ Count by 2's.

20		24		28	30		34		38

Count by 3's.

3	6		12	15		21	24		30

Count by 10's.

10			40		60				100

④ Circle coins in each row to equal the first coin.

74 Horizons Math K Book Two

Lesson 118 - Sphere, Cone & Cylinder

Overview:

- Sphere, cone & cylinder
- Number before 40's
- Subtract 30's
- Count quart, gallon, liter & cup

Material and Supplies:

- Teacher's Guide & Student Workbook
- White board
- Objects for counters
- Number flash cards
- Number chart
- Volume containers
- Sphere, cone, cylinder
- Subtraction flash cards 1's
- Addition flash cards 1's
- Number line strips

Teaching Tips:

Teach sphere, cone & cylinder.
Review number before 40's.
Review subtraction 30's.
Review volumes.
Drill subtraction 1's family.
Drill addition 1's family.
Review oral counting to 100.

Activities:

① Using models (or you may want to use flash cards), show the student(s) the solids, and have them name each of them. Discuss the characteristics of each solid by asking the student(s) to describe them. Ask the class to look for one solid at a time in the activity and circle it. Several shapes have more than one solid shape.

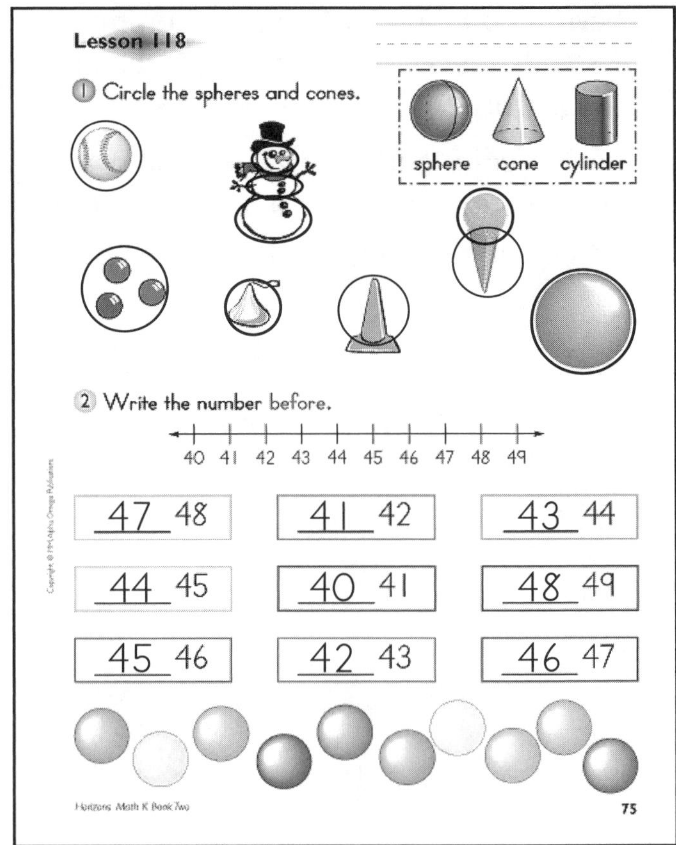

② Orally review the 40's and number before. The student(s) should be able to complete this activity independently.

③ Drill subtraction the 1's family. Review subtraction with a number line. After this practice, they should be able to complete the rest of the activity independently.

④ Review the volume containers and the names. Remind the student(s) that there are 4 quarts in a gallon. The student(s) should be able to complete the activity independently.

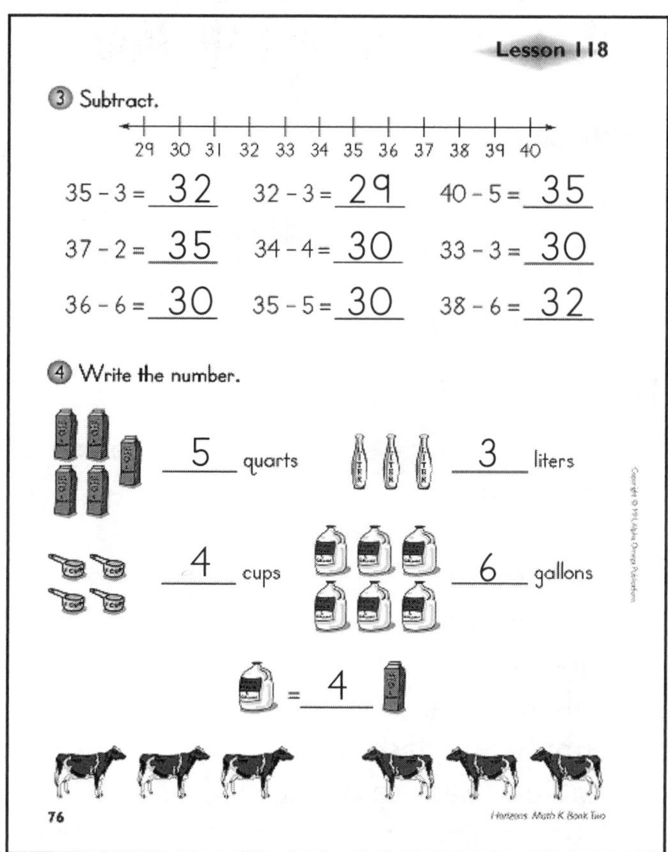

Lesson 119 - 1/4 Hour

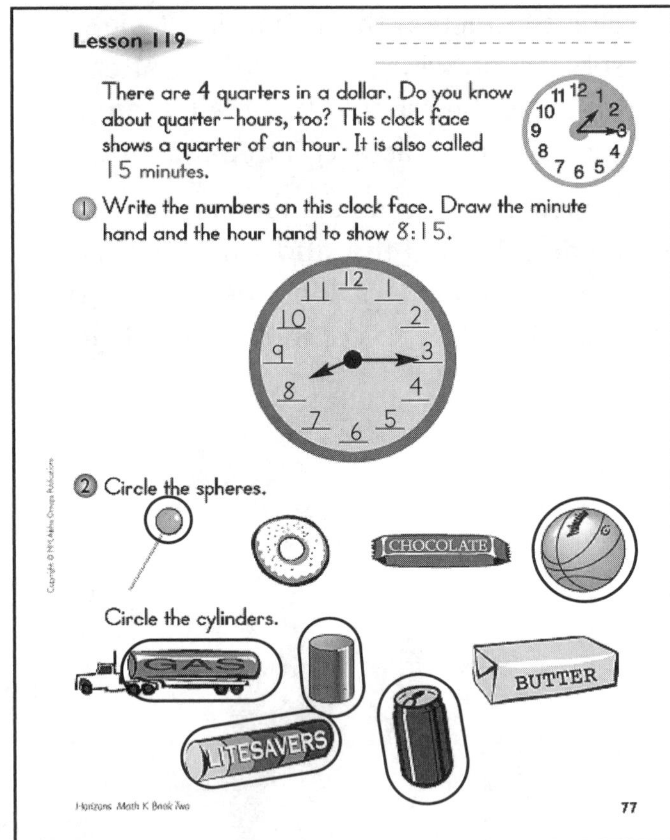
Lesson 119

There are 4 quarters in a dollar. Do you know about quarter-hours, too? This clock face shows a quarter of an hour. It is also called 15 minutes.

① Write the numbers on this clock face. Draw the minute hand and the hour hand to show 8:15.

② Circle the spheres.

Circle the cylinders.

Horizons Math K Book Two 77

Overview:

- 1/4 hour
- Identify sphere, cone & cylinder
- Number before 40's
- Subtract 30's

Materials and Supplies:

- Teacher's Guide & Student Workbook
- White board
- Objects for counters
- Number flash cards
- Number chart
- Clock models
- Sphere, cone, cylinder
- Subtraction flash cards 1's
- Addition flash cards 1's
- Number line strips

Teaching Tips:

Teach time – quarter-hour.
Review sphere, cone & cylinder.
Review number before 40's.
Review subtraction 30's.
Drill subtraction 1's family.
Drill addition 1's family.
Review oral counting to 100.

Activities:

① Review telling time on the hour and half hour. Show the student(s) how to count the minute numbers (in a clockwise direction) by fives using the numbers 1–12 on the clock model. Set the clock for 4:00. Have them read it. Move the minute hand and the hour hand so that the clock represents 4:15. Have them read the short (hour) hand first. The short (hour) hand is read as the number the hand is just past, not what it is nearest to. Tell them that the clock hands always move in the same direction (clockwise) on the face of the clock. To read the long (minute) hand start at 1 and count by fives until you reach the number the hand is pointing to. Do several more examples including 45 minutes past the hour. Have the student(s) look at the top of Activity ① as you explain each clock. Follow the same procedure as above as you guide the student(s) to complete the activity.

② Discuss with the student(s) the names of each of the solids using either flash cards or models, and display all of them in a row. Point to a solid and have them name it. Then name a solid and have the student(s) tell you if it is the first, second, third, etc. one. Read the first instruction in Activity ② and have the student(s) circle the spheres. Do the same for the second instruction.

③ Review number before. This activity includes numbers from several families.

④ The student(s) may use the number line at the top of the page to answer these subtraction problems for the 30's.

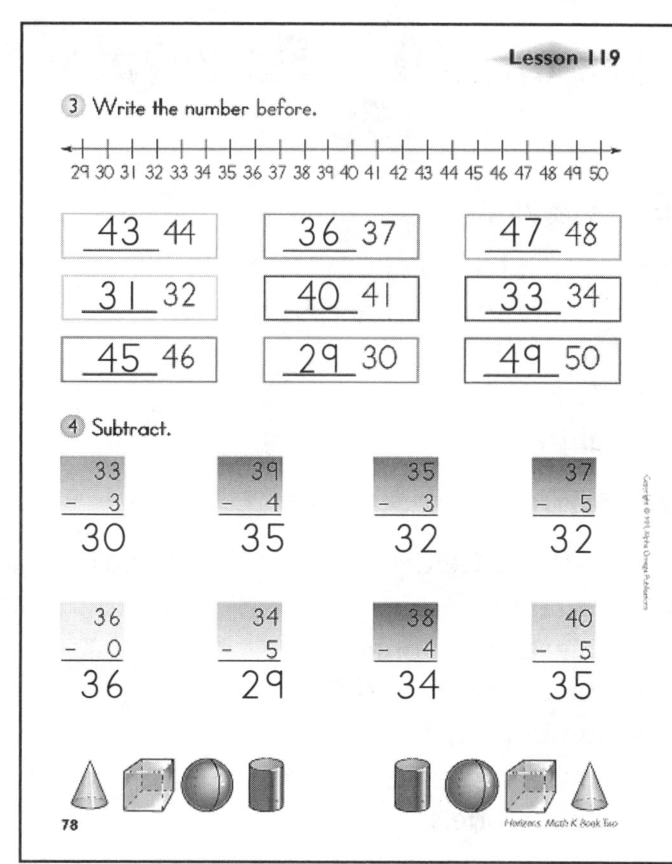

Lesson 120 - Place Value 50's

Overview:

- Place value 50's
- Identify sphere, cone & cylinder
- Bar graph
- 1/4 hour
- Subtract 30's

Material and Supplies:

- Teacher's Guide & Student Workbook
- White board
- Objects for counters
- Number flash cards
- Number chart
- Quarters, nickels, pennies
- Clock models
- Sphere, cone, cylinder
- Subtraction flash cards 1's
- Addition flash cards 1's
- Number line strips

Teaching Tips:

Teach place value 50's.
Review sphere, cone & cylinder.
Review time – quarter-hour.
Review bar graph.
Review number before 40's.
Review subtraction 30's.
Drill subtraction 1's family.
Drill addition 1's family.
Review oral counting to 100.

Activities:

① Review place value with a place value chart or blocks. Practice a few numbers in the 50's family. Instruct the student(s) to complete the activity. Alert them to the two different types of problems in the activity.

② Review the solid shapes with models or flash cards. Instruct the student(s) to circle their answers. Remind them that several have more than one.

③ Review bar graphs and how they tell how many of an item. The items are pictured on the bottom of the graph and the number of blocks colored count how many of the item.

④ Give each student a small clock model. Call out several times, both the hour and the half-hour and have the student(s) set their clocks. Set the hands on the large clock model so they can check their work. Review the placement of the hands for the quarter-hour (15 minutes after the hour). This time, call out several quarter-hour times letting the student(s) place the hands correctly. Check their work. Do the bottom answers for the first clock together with the student(s). Allow them to work the other activity independently after you have reviewed the instructions.

⑤ Drill 1's family subtraction with flash cards. The student(s) should be able to do this activity on their own.

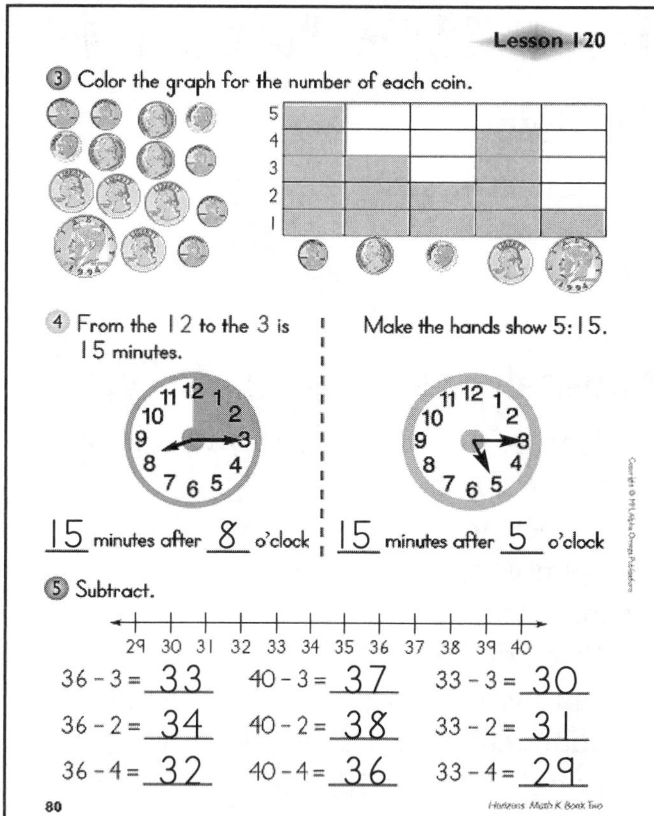

Lesson 121 - Subtract 40's

Overview:

- Subtract 40's
- Place value 50's
- 1/4 hour
- Addition 1's

Materials and Supplies:

- Teacher's Guide & Student Workbook
- White board
- Objects for counters
- Number flash cards
- Number chart
- Clock models
- Place value chart
- Subtraction flash cards 1's
- Addition flash cards 1's
- Number line strips

Teaching Tips:

Teach subtraction 40's.
Review place value 50's.
Review time – quarter-hour.
Review addition 1's.
Drill subtraction 1's family.
Drill addition 1's family.
Review oral counting to 100.

Activities:

① This is the first time the student(s) have subtracted from the 40's family. Review with them using the number line to find the answer to a subtraction problem. Only 0, 1 and 2 are being taken away from the 40's family.

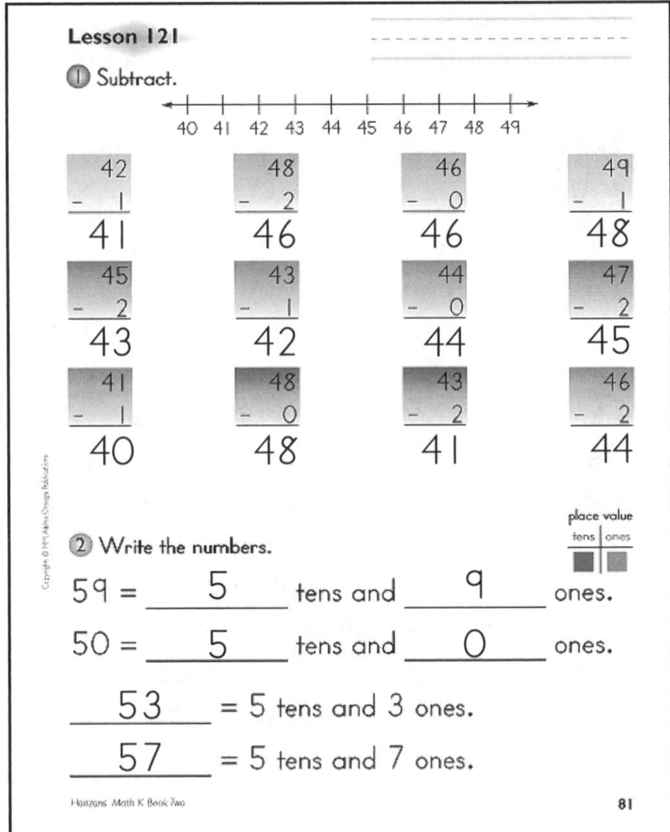

② Review place value by counting the 50's. "50 is 5 tens and 0 ones, 51 is 5 tens and 1 one, 52 is 5 tens and 2 ones, etc." Alert them to the two different types of problems in the activity.

③ Count around the clock by 5's. Display several different times on the clock model for 15 minutes after the hour. Have the student(s) tell you the correct time. Write the answer on the white board to enable the student(s) to see how it is written. Instruct them to make the hands on the clocks in Activity ③ and to write the minutes and the hour under the clock.

④ Drill 1's addition with flash cards. Have the student(s) complete the activity.

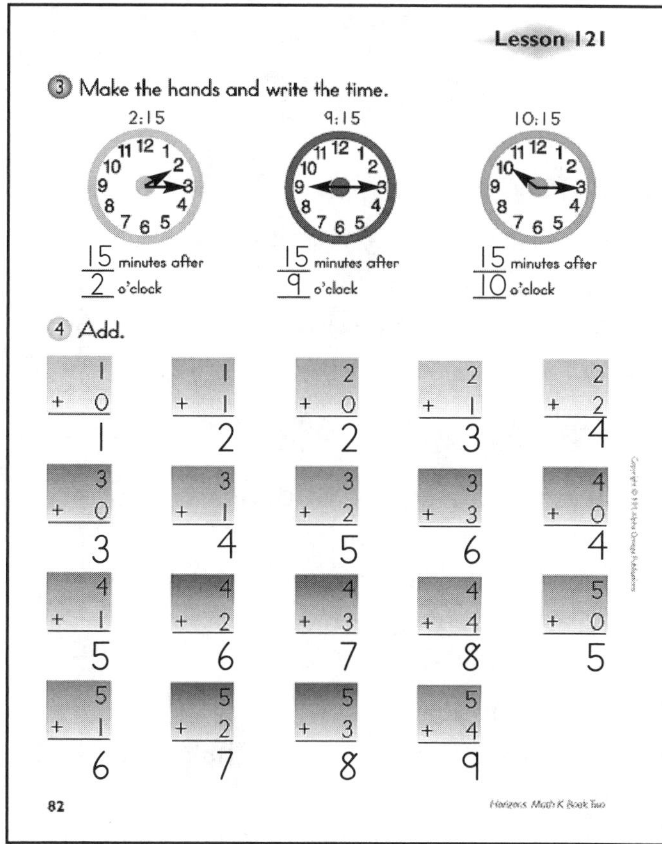
Lesson 121

③ Make the hands and write the time.

2:15 — 15 minutes after 2 o'clock

9:15 — 15 minutes after 9 o'clock

10:15 — 15 minutes after 10 o'clock

④ Add.

1 + 0 = 1	1 + 1 = 2	2 + 0 = 2	2 + 1 = 3	2 + 2 = 4
3 + 0 = 3	3 + 1 = 4	3 + 2 = 5	3 + 3 = 6	4 + 0 = 4
4 + 1 = 5	4 + 2 = 6	4 + 3 = 7	4 + 4 = 8	5 + 0 = 5
5 + 1 = 6	5 + 2 = 7	5 + 3 = 8	5 + 4 = 9	

82 Horizons Math K Book Two

Lesson 122 - Number Before 50's

Overview:

- Number before 50's
- Subtract 40's
- $1, 50 cents, 25 cents, 10 cents, 1 cent
- 1/4 hour

Materials and Supplies:

- Teacher's Guide & Student Workbook
- White board
- Objects for counters
- Number flash cards
- Number chart
- Clock models
- Pennies, nickels, quarters, half dollar & $1 coins
- Place value chart
- Subtraction flash cards 1's
- Addition flash cards 1's
- Number line strips

Teaching Tips:

Teach number before 50's.
Review subtraction 40's.
Review coins and dollar bill.
Review time – quarter-hour.
Drill subtraction 1's family.
Drill addition 1's family.
Review oral counting to 100.

Activities:

① Review number sequence by pointing to a number chart and asking the student(s) to say the number before 50's. The numbers in this activity are from the 50's family. (50–59) Read the instruction and have the student(s) complete the activity.

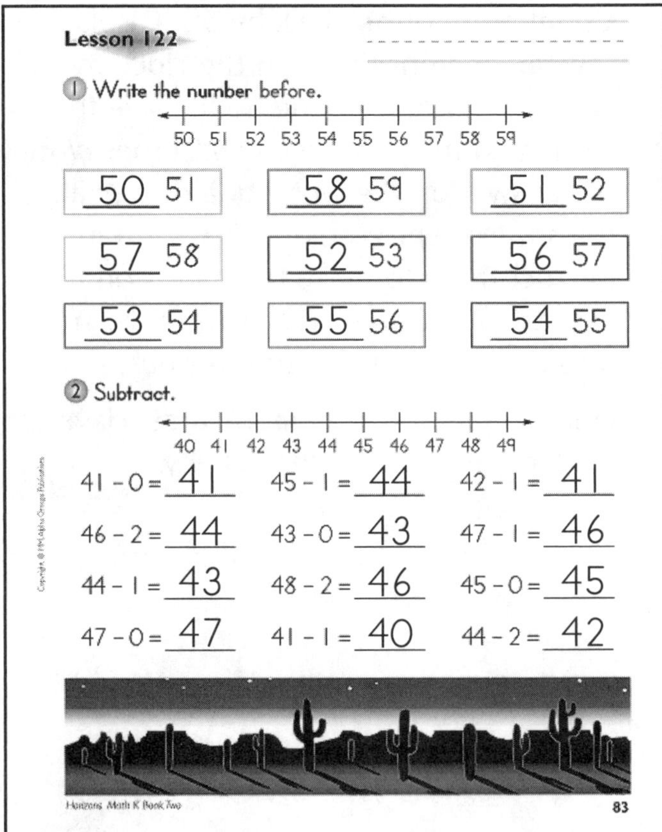

② Drill subtraction 1's with flash cards. Review subtraction on the number line. Instruct the student(s) to complete the activity.

③ Review the pennies, nickels, dimes, quarters, half dollars and dollar coins. Review counting quarters by 25¢ to $1. Review counting by 5's and 10's. Count by 5's and 10's from the 25 numbers. Instruct the student(s) to circle the correct number of coins in each box. Assist them if necessary.

④ Demonstrate how to write 15 minutes after the hour. Say an hour time and ask the student(s) to say the 15 minutes after time for that hour.

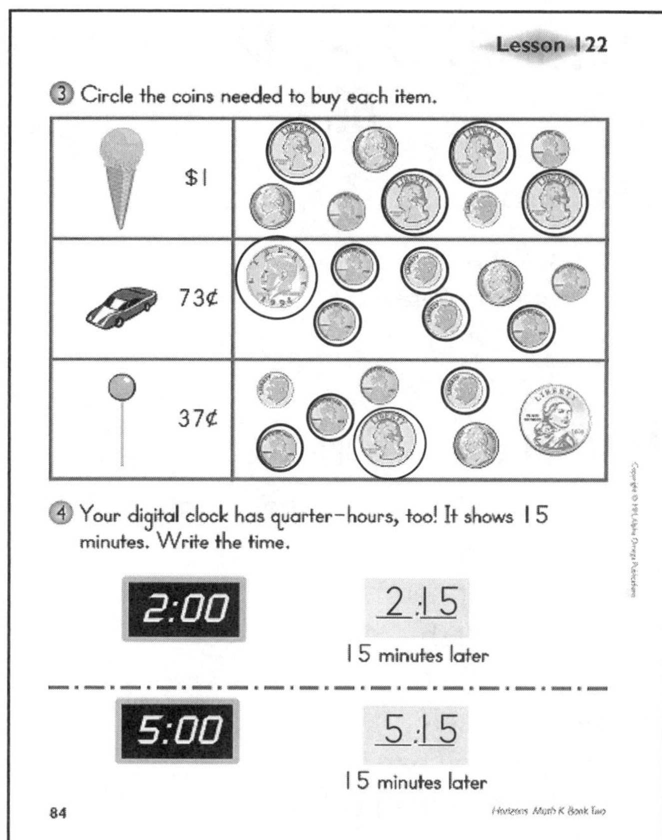

Lesson 123 - Place Value 60's

Overview:

- Place value 60's
- Number before 50's
- Subtract 40's
- 1/4 hour

Materials and Supplies:

- Teacher's Guide & Student Workbook
- White board
- Objects for counters
- Number flash cards
- Number chart
- Clock models
- Place value chart
- Subtraction flash cards 1's
- Addition flash cards 1's
- Number line strips

Teaching Tips:

Teach place value 60's.
Review subtraction 50's.
Review time – quarter-hour.
Drill subtraction 1's family.
Drill addition 1's family.
Review oral counting to 100.

Activities:

① Review place value with a place value chart or blocks. Practice a few numbers in the 60's family. Instruct the student(s) to complete the activity. Alert them to the two different types of problems in the activity.

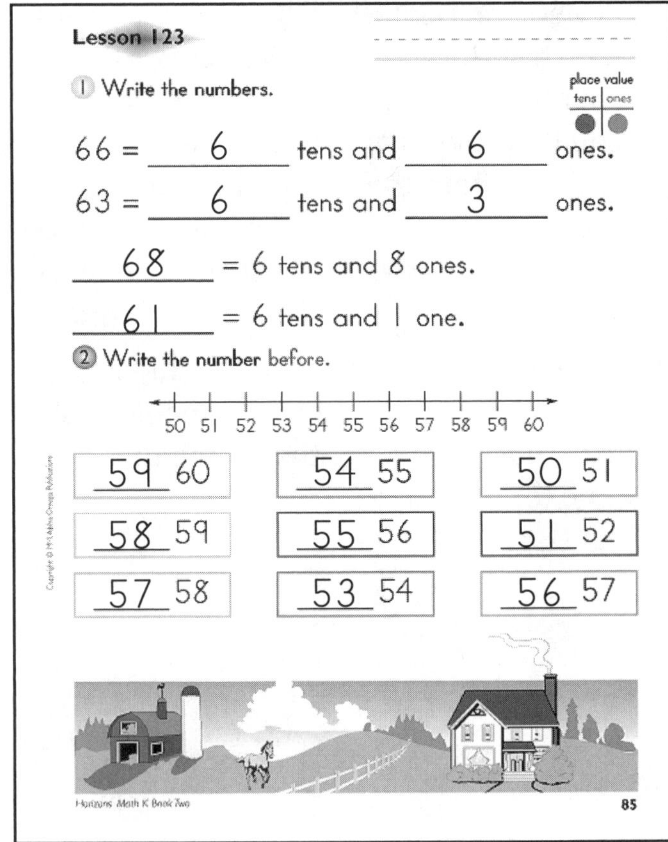
Lesson 123

① Write the numbers.

place value
tens | ones

66 = 6 tens and 6 ones.

63 = 6 tens and 3 ones.

68 = 6 tens and 8 ones.

61 = 6 tens and 1 one.

② Write the number before.

50 51 52 53 54 55 56 57 58 59 60

59 60	54 55	50 51
58 59	55 56	51 52
57 58	53 54	56 57

Horizons Math K Book Two 85

② Review number sequence by pointing to a number chart and asking the student(s) to say the number before 50's. Read the instruction and have the student(s) complete the activity.

③ The student(s) may use the number line at the top of the page to answer these subtraction problems for the 40's.

④ Demonstrate how to write 15 minutes after the hour. Say an hour time and ask the student(s) to say the 15 minutes after time for that hour.

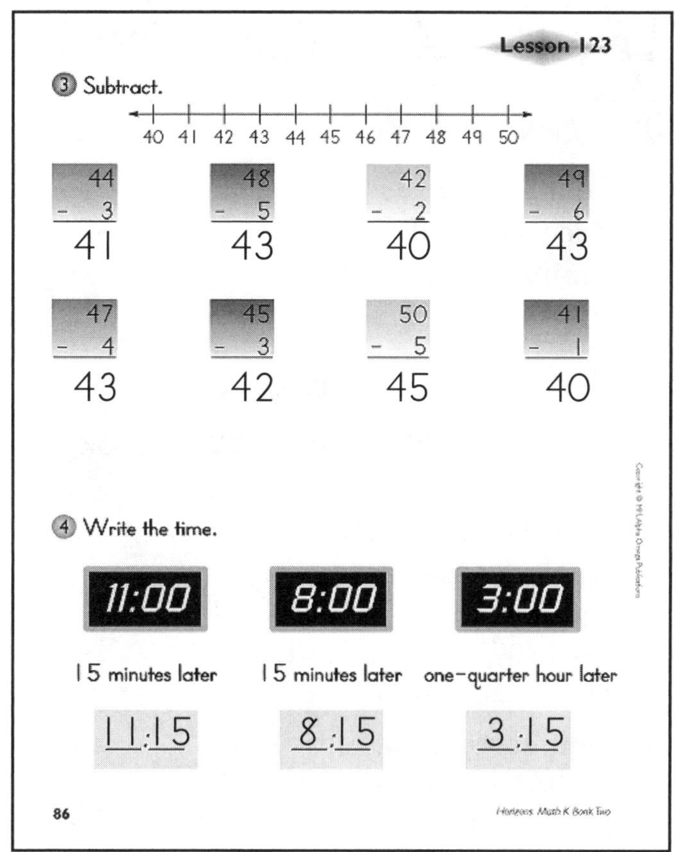

Lesson 124 - Count by 4's

Overview:

- Count by 4's
- Place value 60's
- Number before 50's
- Subtract 40's

Materials and Supplies:

- Teacher's Guide & Student Workbook
- White board
- Objects for counters
- Number flash cards
- Number chart
- Count by 4's flash cards
- Place value chart
- Subtraction flash cards 1's
- Addition flash cards 1's
- Number line strips
- Worksheet 35

Teaching Tips:

Teach counting by 4's to 100.
Review place value 60's.
Review number before 40's & 50's.
Review subtraction 40's.
Drill subtraction 1's family.
Drill addition 1's family.
Review oral counting to 100.

Activities:

① Count out loud by fours to 100 using the number chart. Discuss with the student(s) that counting by fours means to count over four on the number chart or to add four to each number. Read the instruction for Activity ①. After they have counted by 4's looking at the chart have them trace the 4's.

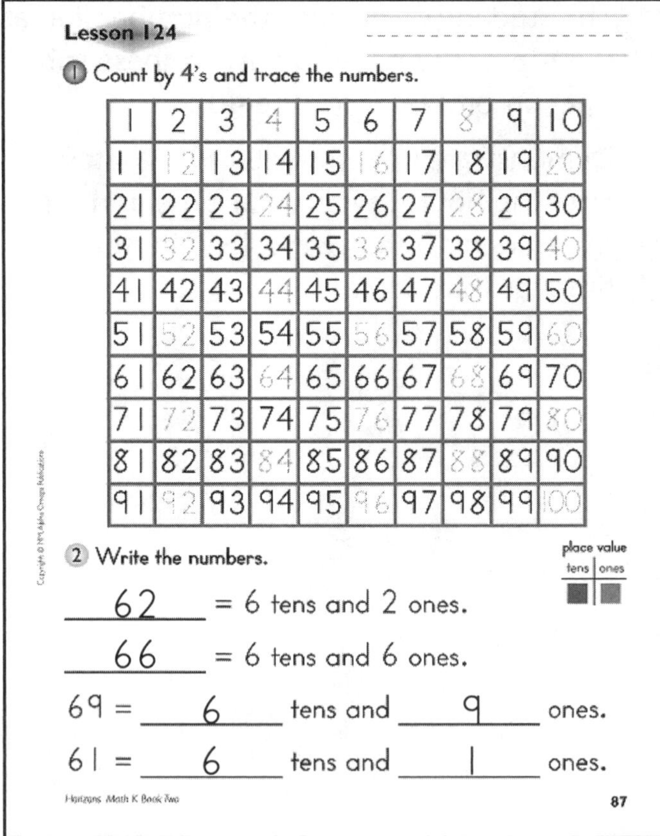

Lesson 124

① Count by 4's and trace the numbers.

1	2	3	4	5	6	7	8	9	10
11	12	13	14	15	16	17	18	19	20
21	22	23	24	25	26	27	28	29	30
31	32	33	34	35	36	37	38	39	40
41	42	43	44	45	46	47	48	49	50
51	52	53	54	55	56	57	58	59	60
61	62	63	64	65	66	67	68	69	70
71	72	73	74	75	76	77	78	79	80
81	82	83	84	85	86	87	88	89	90
91	92	93	94	95	96	97	98	99	100

② Write the numbers.

place value
tens | ones

62 = 6 tens and 2 ones.
66 = 6 tens and 6 ones.
69 = 6 tens and 9 ones.
61 = 6 tens and 1 ones.

Horizons Math K Book Two 87

② Review place value by counting the 60's. "60 is 6 tens and 0 ones, 61 is 6 tens and 1 one, 62 is 6 tens and 2 ones, etc."

③ Review number before 40's and 50's. This is a review activity. The student(s) should need very little help.

④ Drill subtraction 1's with flash cards. Review subtraction on the number line. Instruct the student(s) to complete the activity by using the number line at the top of the page.

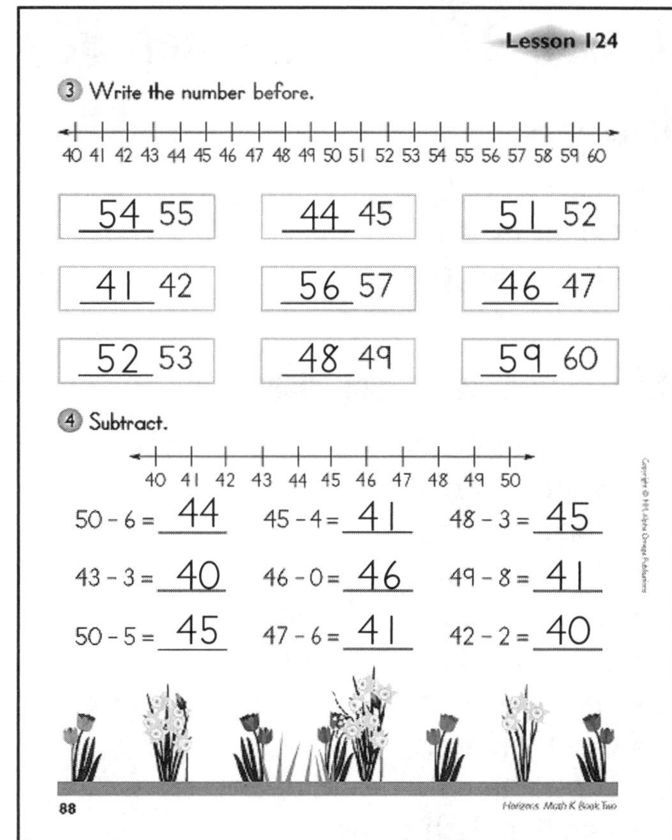

Lesson 125 - Subtract 50's

Overview:

- Subtract 50's
- Count by 4's
- Place value 60's
- 1/4 hour

Materials and Supplies:

- Teacher's Guide & Student Workbook
- White board
- Objects for counters
- Number flash cards
- Number chart
- Count by 4's flash cards
- Place value chart
- Clock models
- Subtraction flash cards 1's
- Addition flash cards 1's
- Number line strips

Teaching Tips:

Teach subtraction 50's.
Review count by 4's to 100.
Review place value 30's–60's.
Review time – quarter-hour.
Drill subtraction 1's family.
Drill addition 1's family.
Review oral counting to 100.

Activities:

① This is the first time the student(s) have subtracted from the 50's family. Review with them using the number line to find the answer to a subtraction problem. Only 0, 1 and 2 are being taken away from the 50's family.

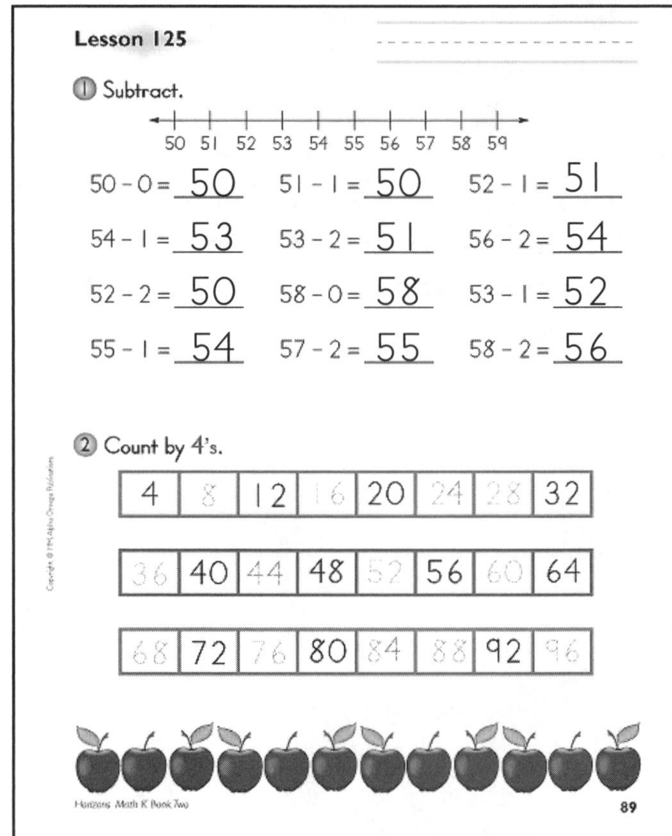

② Count out loud by fours to 100 using the number chart. Discuss with the student(s) that counting by fours means to count over four on the number chart or to add four to each number. Read the instruction for Activity ②. After they have counted by 4's looking at the chart, have them trace the 4's.

③ Review place value by drawing random number cards from the 30's–60's. Say the number (47) 47 equals 4 tens and 7 ones. Have a student pick from a set of 1's number cards the 4 and the 7 and have them place the cards on a place value chart.

④ Review how to write 15 minutes after the hour. Review several hours and 15 minutes with a digital clock model. Set a digital clock model to a 15-minute time. Have a student set the hands on a clock model to match the time.

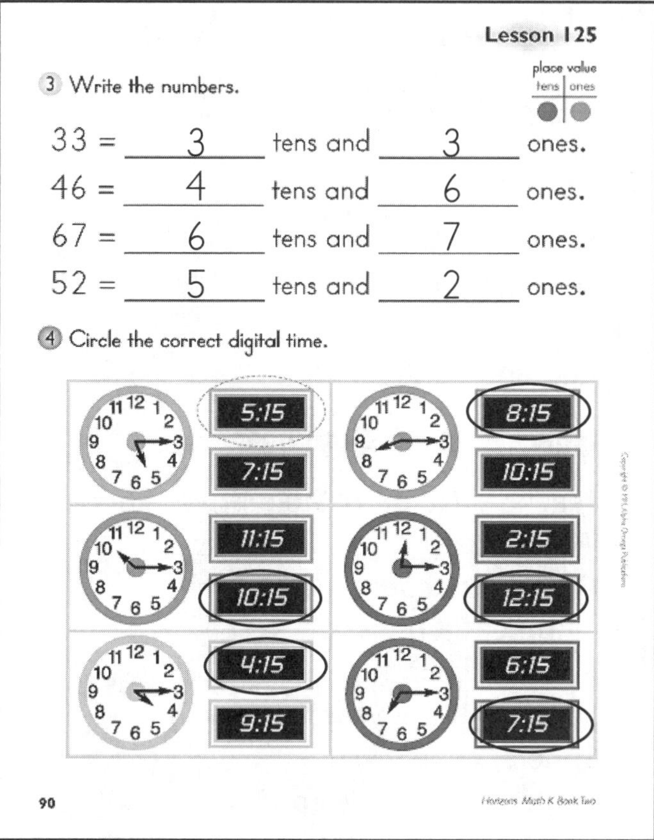

Lesson 126 - Number Before 60's

Overview:

- Number before 60's
- Subtract 50's
- Count by 4's
- Add and Subtract 1's

Materials and Supplies:

- Teacher's Guide & Student Workbook
- White board
- Objects for counters
- Number flash cards
- Number chart
- Seasons of the year flash cards
- Sphere, cone, cylinder
- Subtraction flash cards 1's
- Addition flash cards 1's
- Number line strips

Teaching Tips:

Teach number before 60's.
Review subtraction 50's.
Review count by 4's to 100.
Drill subtraction 1's family.
Drill addition 1's family.
Review oral counting to 100.

Activities:

① Review number sequence by pointing to a number chart and asking the student(s) to say the number before 60's. The numbers in this activity are from the 60's family. (60–69) Read the instruction and have the student(s) complete the activity.

Lesson 126

① Write the number before.

50 51 52 53 54 55 56 57 58 59 60 61 62 63 64 65 66 67 68 69

65 66	62 63	67 68
63 64	60 61	66 67
61 62	64 65	68 69

② Subtract.

56 − 2 = 54	58 − 2 = 56	54 − 2 = 52	59 − 2 = 57
57 − 3 = 54	59 − 3 = 56	55 − 3 = 52	60 − 3 = 57
58 − 4 = 54	60 − 4 = 56	56 − 4 = 52	57 − 4 = 53

Horizons Math K Book Two 91

② Drill subtraction 1's with flash cards. Review subtraction on the number line. Instruct the student(s) to complete the activity. Instruct the student(s) to use the number line in Activity ① for this activity.

③ Count out loud by fours to 100 using the number chart. Discuss with the student(s) that counting by fours means to count over four on the number chart or to add four to each number. Read the instruction for Activity ③. After they have circled the numbers by 4's count them out loud again.

④ Drill subtraction 1's with flash cards. Instruct the student(s) to complete the activity.

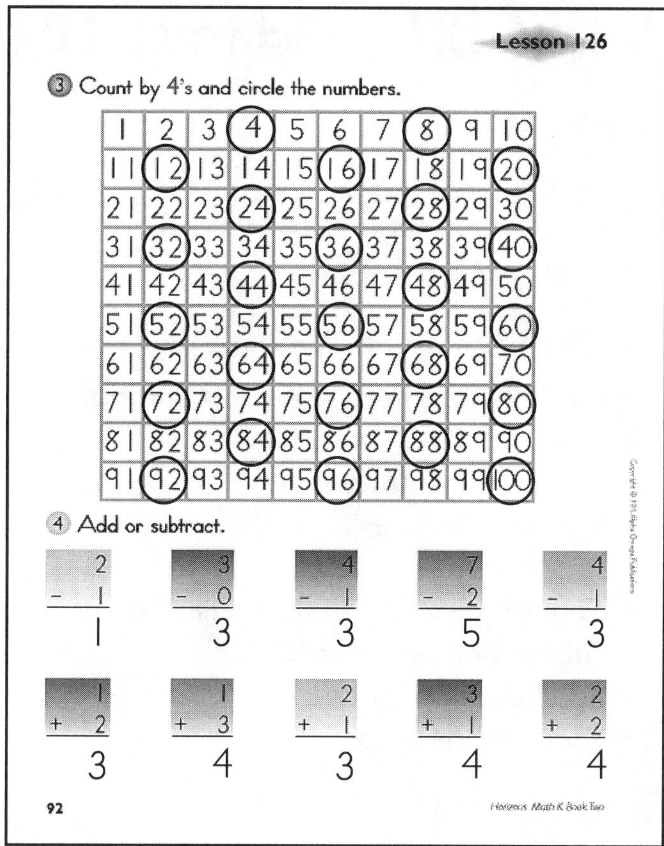

Lesson 127 - Subtract 60's

Overview:

- Subtract 60's
- Word problems
- Count by 1's, 2's, 3's, 4's, 5's

Materials and Supplies:

- Teacher's Guide & Student Workbook
- White board
- Objects for counters
- Number flash cards
- Number chart
- Count by 2's, 3's, 4's & 5's flash cards
- Subtraction flash cards 1's
- Addition flash cards 1's
- Number line strips

Teaching Tips:

Teach subtraction 60's.
Teach word problems subtraction.
Review count by evens to 20.
Review count by odds to 20.
Review count by 3's to 20.
Review count by 4's to 20.
Review count by 5's to 20.
Drill subtraction 1's family.
Drill addition 1's family.
Review oral counting to 100.

Activities:

① This is the first time the student(s) have subtracted from the 60's family. Review with them using the number line to find the answer to a subtraction problem. Only 0, 1, 2 and 3 are being taken away from the 60's family.

② Write a simple subtraction word problem on the white board. Have the student(s) use counting chips at their desks to demonstrate what the problem is telling them. Discuss what the key word is that tells them if they are to add or subtract (left). Write the subtraction fact on the white board as the student(s) tell it to you. Discuss what the label for the answer would be. Follow the same procedure for Activity ②, guiding the student(s) through each step.

③ Review counting by evens, odds, 3's , 4's and 5's. The arrows in the activity indicate what numbers need to be brought to the boxes. Instruct the student(s) to work left to right as they fill in the numbers. Read each row together after they have completed their work.

④ Instruct the student(s) to fill in the charts using the numbers from Activity ③.

Lesson 127

③ Fill in the numbers to complete each row.

1 2 3 4 5 6 7 8 9 10 11 12 13 14 15 16 17 18 19 20

evens	2	4	6	8	10	12	14	16	18	20
odds	1	3	5	7	9	11	13	15	17	19
3's	3	6	9	12	15	18				
4's	4	8	12	16	20					
5's	5	10	15	20						

④ Complete these rows from the chart above.

2	4	6	8	10	12	14	16	18	20
1	3	5	7	9	11	13	15	17	19
3	6	9	12	15	18				
4	8	12	16	20					
5	10	15	20						

94 Horizons Math K Book Two

Lesson 128 - Number Before 70's

Overview:

- Number before 70's
- Subtract 60's
- 1/2, 1/4 hour
- Months & seasons

Materials and Supplies:

- Teacher's Guide & Student Workbook
- White board
- Number flash cards
- Objects for counters
- Number chart
- Clock models
- Months of the year flash cards
- Seasons of the year flash cards
- Subtraction flash cards 1's
- Addition flash cards 1's
- Number line strips

Teaching Tips:

Teach number before 70's.
Review subtraction 60's.
Review half-hour and quarter-hour.
Review seasons.
Review months.
Drill subtraction 1's family.
Drill addition 1's family.
Review oral counting to 100.

Activities:

① Review number sequence by pointing to a number chart and asking the student(s) to say the number before 70's. The numbers in this activity are from the 70's family. (70–79) Read the instruction and have the student(s) complete the activity.

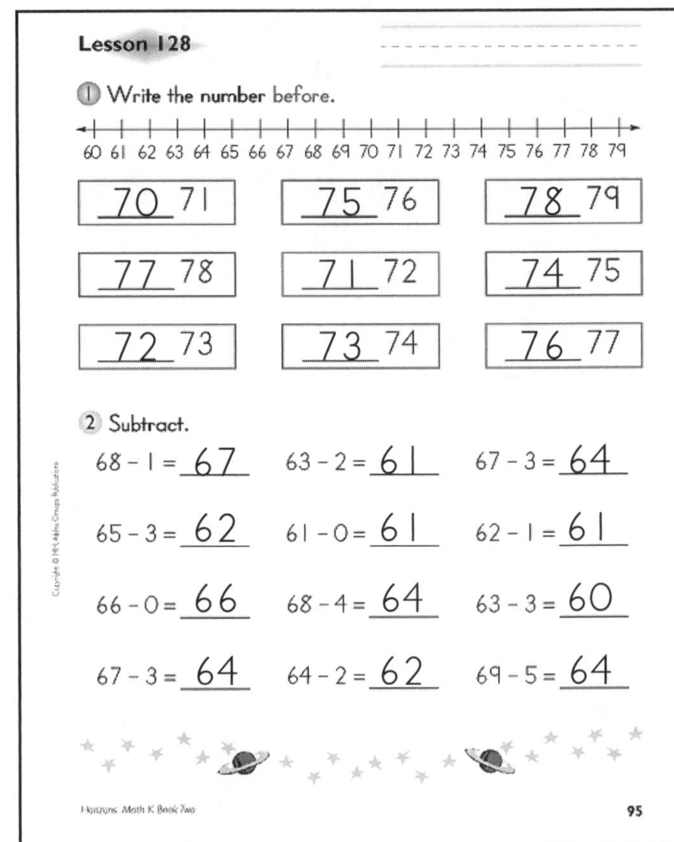

② Drill subtraction 1's with flash cards. Review subtraction on the number line. Instruct the student(s) to complete the activity.

③ Give the student(s) small clock models. Have them set their clocks to match the times you have written on the white board. They should check their clocks with your clock model. Encourage them to set the minute hand first and then the hour hand. After reading the instruction for Activity ③ instruct the student(s) to draw a line from each clock to the same time on a digital clock.

④ Review the months of the year and their names. Talk about the seasons and in what month they begin. Write each season on the white board. Under the name list the month that the season begins and the rest of the months of that season. For example under spring the last month to list is June. Under summer list June as the month it begins. Draw an arrow from the June under spring to the June under summer to show that June has days in both seasons. Read the instruction for Activity ④ and each phrase that the student(s) are to complete.

Lesson 129 - Subtract 70's

Overview:

- Subtract 70's
- Count by 10's & 4's
- Subtract 10's
- Identify whole, 1/2, 1/3, 1/4

Materials and Supplies:

- Teacher's Guide & Student Workbook
- White board
- Number flash cards
- Objects for counters
- Number chart
- Count by 3's, 4's, 5's & 10's flash cards
- Subtraction flash cards 1's
- Addition flash cards 1's
- Number line strips

Teaching Tips:

Teach subtraction 70's.
Review whole, 1/2, 1/3 & 1/4.
Review subtraction 10's.
Review counting by 3's, 4's, 5's & 10's.
Drill subtraction 1's family.
Drill addition 1's family.
Review oral counting to 100.

Activities:

① This is the first time the student(s) have subtracted from the 70's family. Review with them using the number line to find the answer to a subtraction problem. Only 0, 1, 2 and 3 are being taken away from the 70's family.

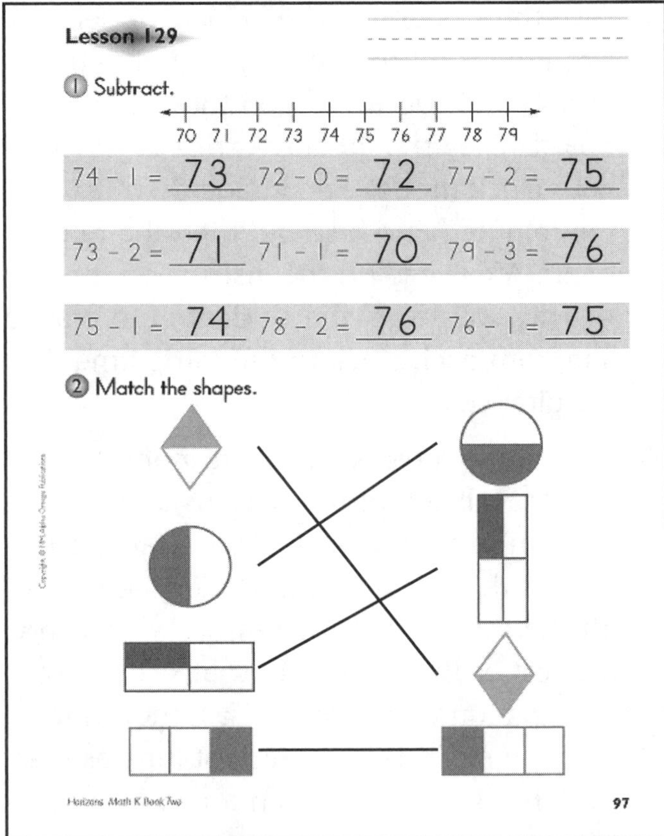

② Review shapes divided into 2, 3 or 4 equal parts. Review the names of the shapes. Instruct the student(s) to match the shapes in Activity ②.

③ Review the numbers in the 10's family from a number chart or line. These are review problems that the student(s) should be able to do independently.

④ Review counting by evens, odds, 3's , 4's 5's and 10's. There are one or two numbers missing in each set of flower petals. The center number is the starting number. It also tells what to count by. The numbers go around the petals in order. Instruct the student(s) to complete the activity.

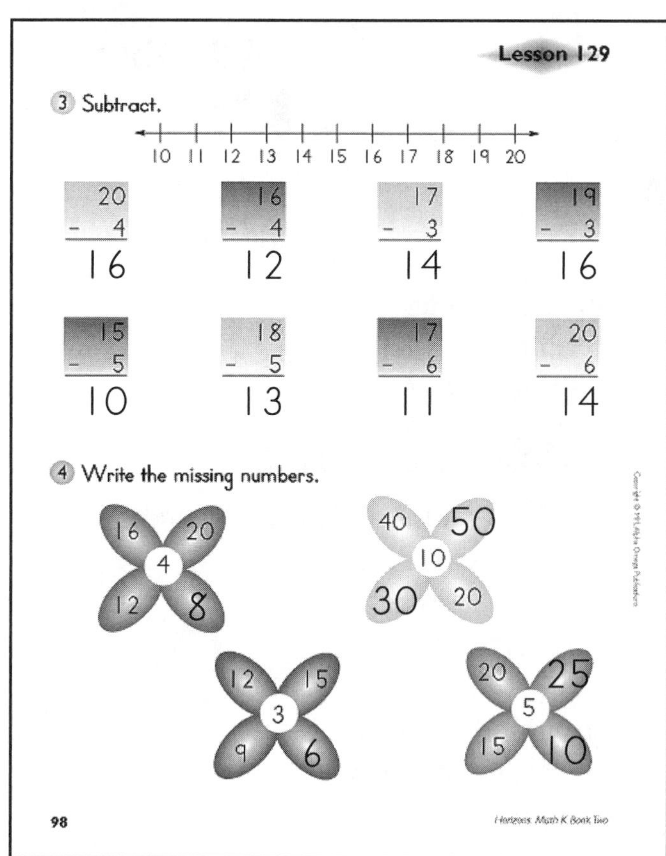

Lesson 130 - Number Before 80's

Overview:

- Number before 80's
- Subtract 70's
- Addition 60's & 70's
- Subtract 10's

Materials and Supplies:

- Teacher's Guide & Student Workbook
- White board
- Number flash cards
- Objects for counters
- Subtraction flash cards 1's
- Addition flash cards 1's
- Number line strips
- Number chart

Teaching Tips:

Teach number before 80's.
Review subtraction 70's.
Review addition 60's & 70's.
Review subtraction 10's.
Drill subtraction 1's family.
Drill addition 1's family.
Review oral counting to 100.

Activities:

① Review number sequence by pointing to a number chart and asking the student(s) to say the number before 80's. The numbers in this activity are from the 80's family. (80–89) Read the instruction and have the student(s) complete the activity.

Lesson 130

① Write the number before.

71 72 73 74 75 76 77 78 79 80 81 82 83 84 85 86 87 88 89 90

83 84	88 89	82 83
86 87	84 85	87 88
80 81	89 90	85 86

② Subtract.

78 − 3 = 75	74 − 2 = 72	78 − 4 = 74	73 − 3 = 70
79 − 5 = 74	75 − 3 = 72	76 − 0 = 76	71 − 1 = 70
77 − 4 = 73	74 − 3 = 71	80 − 4 = 76	72 − 1 = 71

Horizons Math K Book Two 99

② Drill subtraction 1's with flash cards. Review subtraction on the number line. Instruct the student(s) to complete the activity. Instruct the student(s) to use the number line in Activity ① for this activity.

③ Do some addition review using the 60's and 70's families. If the student(s) can quickly answer the problems using a number line, additional review is not necessary.

④ Review the numbers in the 10's family from a number chart or line. Count backwards from 20 by looking at a number chart. The student(s) should be able to complete the activity independently.

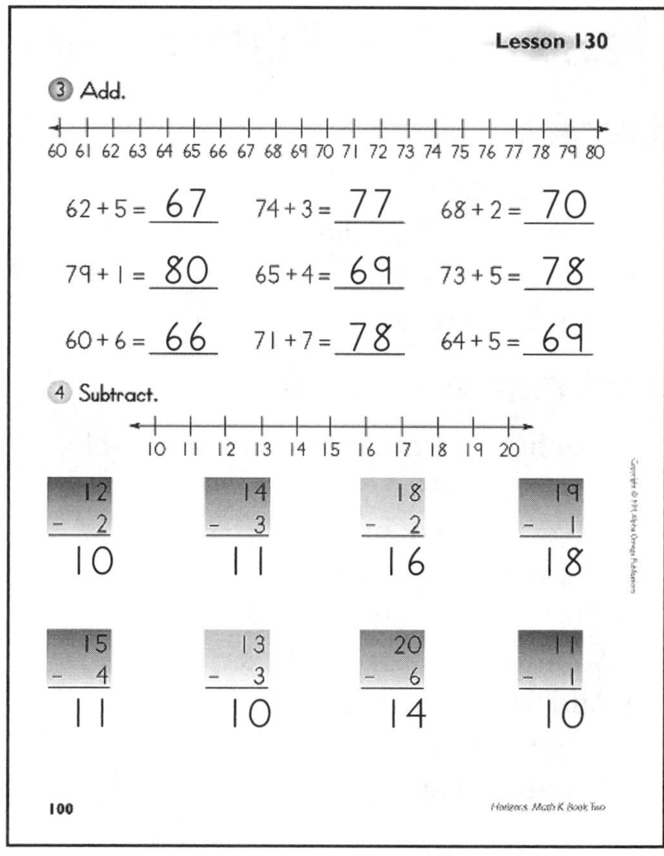

Lesson 131 - Subtract 80's

Overview:

- Subtract 80's
- Money, word problems
- Addition 60's & 70's
- Number after 90's

Materials and Supplies:

- Teacher's Guide & Student Workbook
- White board
- Objects for counters
- Number flash cards
- Objects for counters
- Subtraction flash cards 1's
- Addition flash cards 1's
- Number line strips
- Number chart

Teaching Tips:

Teach subtraction 80's.
Review word problems addition.
Review addition 60's & 70's.
Review number after 90's.
Drill subtraction 1's family.
Drill addition 1's family.
Review oral counting to 100.

Activities:

① This is the first time the student(s) have subtracted from the 80's family. Review with them using the number line to find the answer to a subtraction problem. Only 0, 1, 2 and 3 are being taken away from the 80's family.

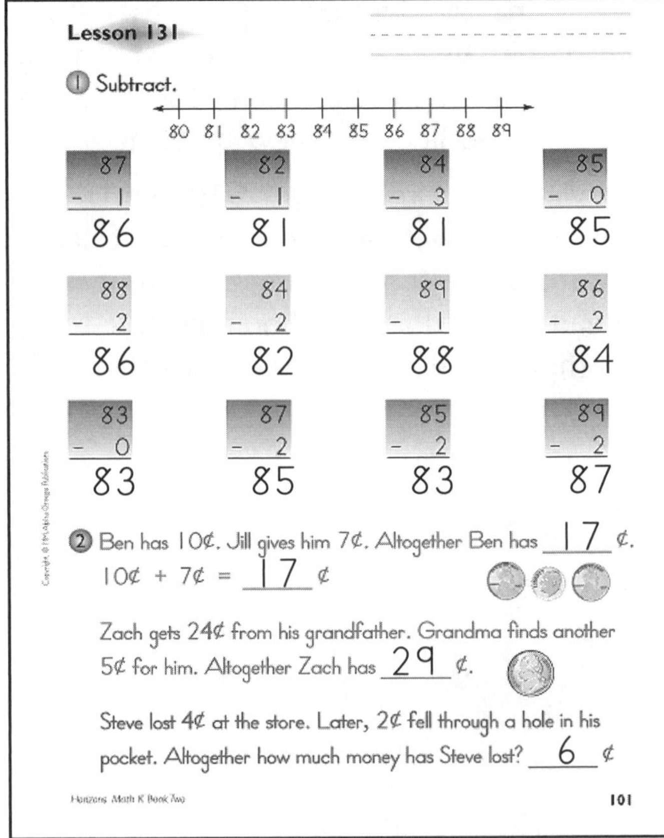

② Discuss what makes an addition word problem with the student(s). Ask what the key word is (altogether). Talk about the fact that something has to be added to. See if they can tell you a simple addition word problem that you could then write on the white board. If they can't, make one up for them. Visualize the problem using counting chips. Have the student(s) tell you the addition fact that supports the answer. Read the word problems in the activity. Allow the student(s) to write the addition fact, write the answer on their own, and then discuss the results with them.

③ This is a review activity of subtraction of the 60's & 70's families. Review with them using the number line to find the answer to a subtraction problem. 0–7 are being taken away from the 60's or 70's families.

④ This is a review activity of number after. The format has been changed to prepare the student(s) for future problems in the *Horizons Math* programs. Allow the use of a number line if it is needed.

Lesson 132 - Number Before 90's

Overview:

- Number before 90's
- Subtract 80's
- Identify geometric solids
- Seasons

Material and Supplies:

- Teacher's Guide & Student Workbook
- White board
- Objects for counters
- Number flash cards
- Seasons of the year flash cards
- Sphere, cone, cylinder
- Subtraction flash cards 1's
- Addition flash cards 1's
- Number line strips
- Number chart

Teaching Tips:

Teach number before 90's.
Review subtraction 80's.
Review sphere, cone & cylinder.
Review seasons.
Drill subtraction 1's family.
Drill addition 1's family.
Review oral counting to 100.

Activities:

① Review number sequence by pointing to a number chart and asking the student(s) to say the number before 90's. The numbers in this activity are from the 90's family. (90–99) Read the instruction and have the student(s) complete the activity. The student(s) have reached another milestone in their kindergarten math experience because another concept has reached 100.

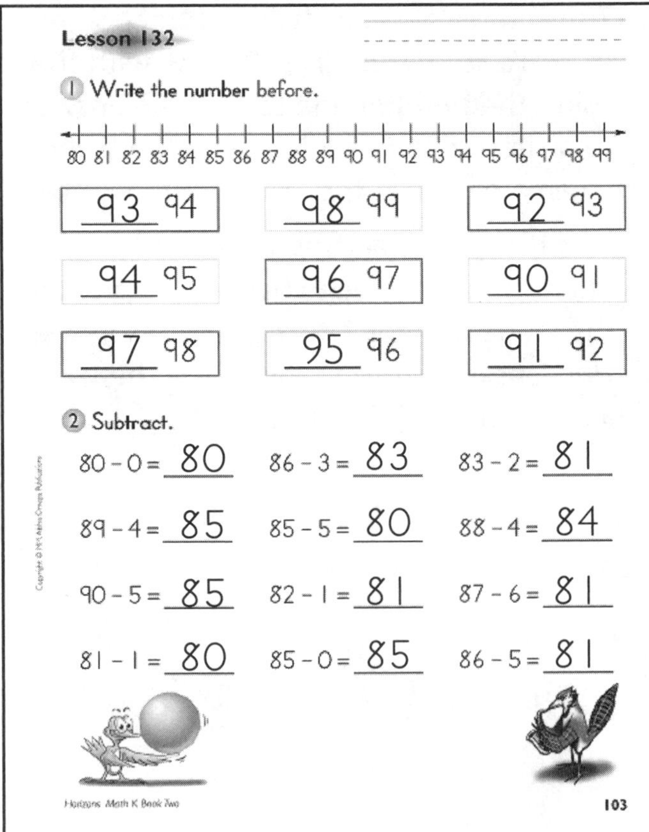

② This is the second time the student(s) have subtracted from the 80's family. Review with them using the number line to find the answer to a subtraction problem. 0–6 are being taken away from the 80's family. They can use the number line in Activity ① for these problems.

③ Review the solid shapes with models or flash cards. Review the characteristics of cones and cylinders. Instruct the student(s) to circle the cones and to put an X on the cylinders. Remind them that some shapes have more than one.

④ Review the season words with the student(s). Write each season on the white board and ask them for some examples of things that happen during a season.

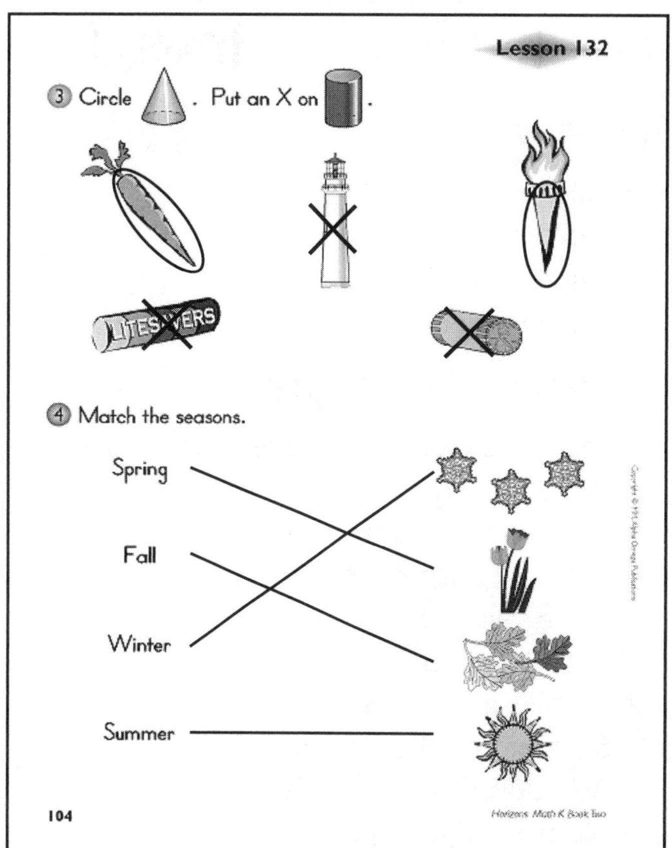

Lesson 133 - Subtract 90's

Overview:

- Subtract 90's
- Word problems, $1
- Place value 70's
- Money

Materials and Supplies:

- Teacher's Guide & Student Workbook
- White board
- Objects for counters
- Number flash cards
- Place value chart
- Base 10 blocks
- $1 bills and coins
- Subtraction flash cards 1's
- Addition flash cards 1's
- Number line strips
- Number chart

Teaching Tips:

Teach subtraction 90's.
Review word problems, addition.
Teach place value 70's.
Review $1 bill & $1 coin.
Drill subtraction 1's family.
Drill addition 1's family.
Review oral counting to 100.

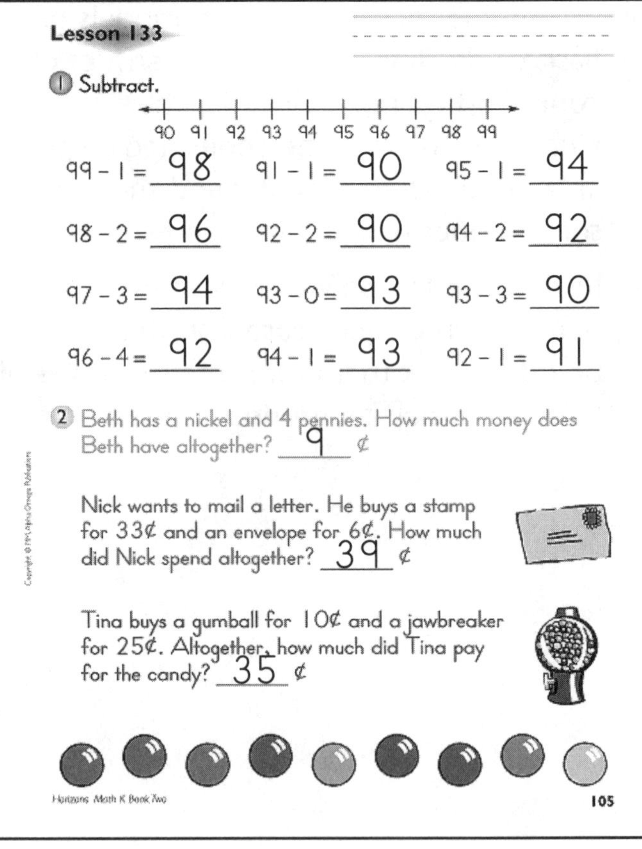
Lesson 133

① Subtract.

90 91 92 93 94 95 96 97 98 99

99 - 1 = 98	91 - 1 = 90	95 - 1 = 94
98 - 2 = 96	92 - 2 = 90	94 - 2 = 92
97 - 3 = 94	93 - 0 = 93	93 - 3 = 90
96 - 4 = 92	94 - 1 = 93	92 - 1 = 91

② Beth has a nickel and 4 pennies. How much money does Beth have altogether? 9 ¢

Nick wants to mail a letter. He buys a stamp for 33¢ and an envelope for 6¢. How much did Nick spend altogether? 39 ¢

Tina buys a gumball for 10¢ and a jawbreaker for 25¢. Altogether, how much did Tina pay for the candy? 35 ¢

Horizons Math K Book Two 105

Activities:

① This is the first time the student(s) have subtracted from the 90's family. Review with them using the number line to find the answer to a subtraction problem. Only 0, 1, 2 and 3 are being taken away from the 90's family. This is yet another milestone for the student(s). They have reached the 100's family in subtraction.

② Discuss what makes an addition word problem with the student(s). Ask what the key word is (altogether). Talk about the fact that something has to be added to. See if they can tell you a simple addition word problem that you could then write on the white board. If they can't, make one up for them. Visualize the problem using counting chips. Have the student(s) tell you the addition fact that supports the answer. Read the word problems in the activity. Allow the student(s) to write the addition fact and to write the answer on their own. Then discuss the results with them. Complete the activity.

③ Teach place value by counting the 70's. "70 is 7 tens and 0 ones, 71 is 7 tens and 1 one, 72 is 7 tens and 2 ones, etc." Instruct the student(s) to count the tens' blocks for the number in the tens' place and to count the ones for the number in the ones' place.

④ Review the $1 bill and the $1 coin. Instruct the student(s) to count the money.

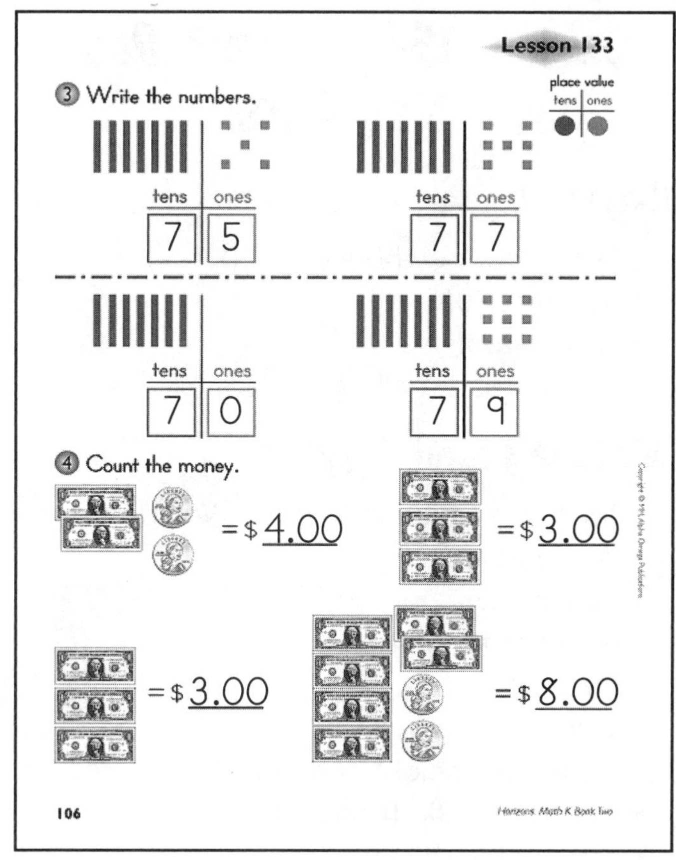

Lesson 134 - Next Door Neighbors

Overview:

- Next door neighbors
- Subtract 90's
- Word problems
- Count quart, gallon, cup & liter

Materials and Supplies:

- Teacher's Guide & Student Workbook
- White board
- Objects for counters
- Number flash cards
- Place value chart
- Volume containers
- Next door neighbor chart
- Subtraction flash cards 1's
- Addition flash cards 1's
- Number line strips
- Number chart

Teaching Tips:

Teach next door neighbors.
Review subtraction 90's.
Review word problems, addition.
Review volumes.
Drill subtraction 1's family.
Drill addition 1's family.
Review oral counting to 100.

Activities:

① Discuss with the student(s) different aspects of *after* and *before* other than numbers when doing this activity. What day comes after Monday? What month is before July? What year comes after 2001? Next door neighbors are the number before and the number after. Construct a neighbor house like the one pictured in the student activity. Choose a flash card at

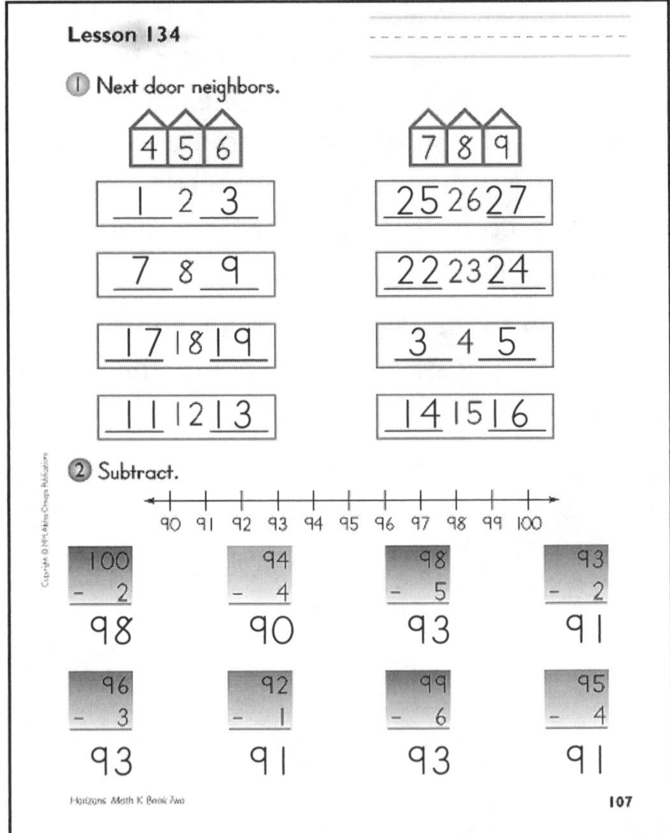

random and place it on the center house. Use a number line to practice the before and after number for the card that was selected.

② This is the second time the student(s) have subtracted from the 90's family. Review with them using the number line to find the answer to a subtraction problem. 1–6 are being taken away from the 90's family. Inform the student(s) that 100 appears in one of the problems.

③ Discuss what makes an addition word problem with the student(s). Read the first problem to the class. Ask what the key word is (altogether). Visualize the problem using counting chips. Have the student(s) tell you the addition fact that supports the answer. Allow the student(s) to write the answer. Allow the student(s) to write the addition fact and to write the answer on their own. Then discuss the results with them. Complete the activity.

④ Review the volume containers with the student(s) then have them complete the activity on their own.

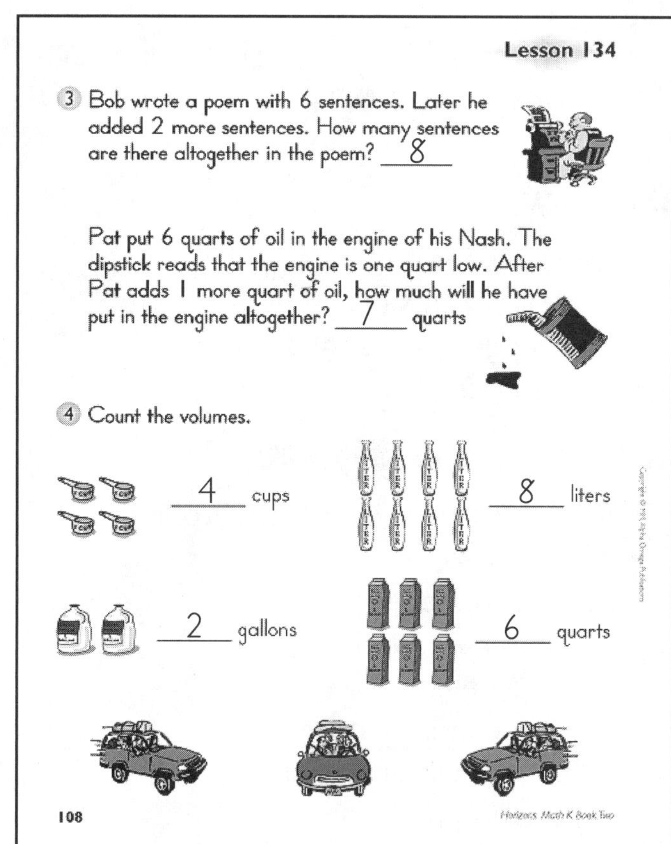
Lesson 134

③ Bob wrote a poem with 6 sentences. Later he added 2 more sentences. How many sentences are there altogether in the poem? 8

Pat put 6 quarts of oil in the engine of his Nash. The dipstick reads that the engine is one quart low. After Pat adds 1 more quart of oil, how much will he have put in the engine altogether? 7 quarts

④ Count the volumes.

4 cups

8 liters

2 gallons

6 quarts

108

Horizons Math K Book Two

Lesson 135 - Place Value 80's

Overview:

- Place value 80's
- Word problems (+)
- Identify geometric solids
- Count by 5's, $5 bill

Materials and Supplies:

- Teacher's Guide & Student Workbook
- White board
- Objects for counters
- Number flash cards
- Place value chart
- Sphere, cone, cylinder
- $5 bill, nickels and pennies
- Subtraction flash cards 1's
- Addition flash cards 1's
- Number line strips
- Number chart

Teaching Tips:

Teach place value 80's.
Review word problems, addition.
Review geometric solids.
Teach $5 bill.
Review counting by 5's.
Drill subtraction 1's family.
Drill addition 1's family.
Review oral counting to 100.

Activities:

① Review place value with a place value chart or blocks. Practice a few numbers in the 70's & 80's families. Instruct the student(s) to complete the activity. Alert them to the two different types of problems in the activity.

Lesson 135

① Write the numbers.

place value
tens | ones

84 = 8 tens and 4 ones.

88 = 8 tens and 8 ones.

86 = 8 tens and 6 ones.

80 = 8 tens and 0 ones.

② The instructions for warming a frozen sandwich are to microwave it for 4 minutes. Then remove the wrapper and microwave it for another 2 minutes. Altogether, how long will the sandwich be in the microwave? 6 minutes

Jan and Drew went hiking. The first trail was 5 miles long and the second trail was 3 miles. How far did they hike altogether on the 2 trails? 8 miles

Horizons Math K Book Two 109

② Review what makes an addition word problem. Read the first problem to the class. Ask what the key word is (altogether). Visualize the problem using counting chips. Have the student(s) tell you the addition fact that supports the answer. Allow the student(s) to write the addition fact and to write the answer on their own. Then discuss the results with them. Complete the activity.

③ Review geometric solids. Read the instructions to the student(s). They should be able to complete the activity without additional help.

④ Discuss the $5 bill and review counting by 5's. Review the nickel and review counting nickels by 5's. Count one row of pennies. Since each row has 5¢, the student(s) can count the pennies by 5's. Have the student(s) complete the activity.

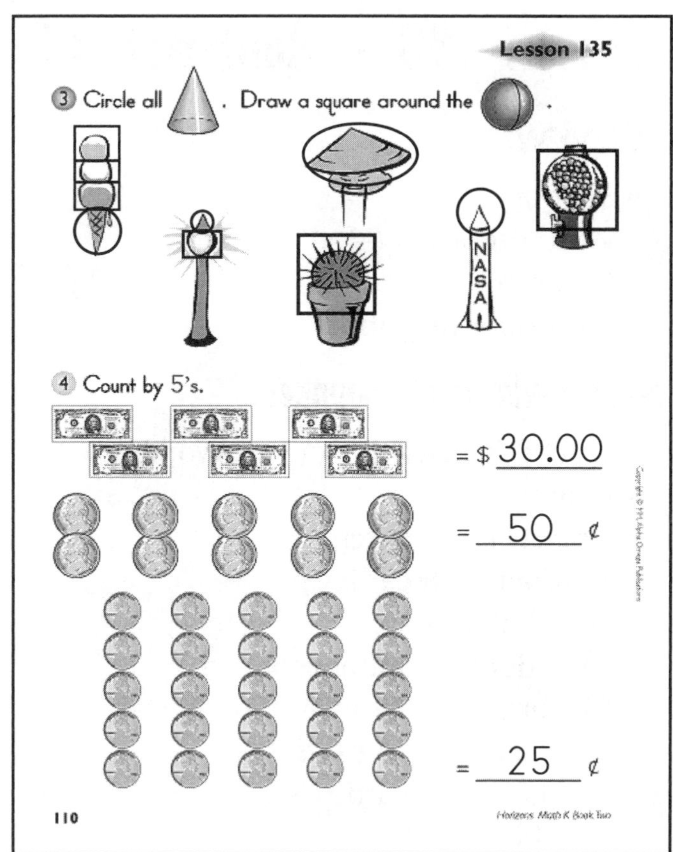

Lesson 136 - Subtract All

Overview:

- Subtract all
- Word problems (–)
- Count by 10's
- Next door neighbors

Materials and Supplies:

- Teacher's Guide & Student Workbook
- White board
- Objects for counters
- Number flash cards
- Place value chart
- Next door neighbor chart
- \$10 bill, \$1 bill, dimes and pennies
- Subtraction flash cards 1's
- Addition flash cards 1's
- Number line strips
- Number chart

Teaching Tips:

Review subtraction 1's & 10's.
Teach \$10 bill.
Review word problems, subtraction.
Review next door neighbors.
Drill subtraction 1's family.
Drill addition 1's family.
Review oral counting to 100.

Activities:

① This is the first of several subtraction review exercises. Only you as the teacher of the student(s) can decide how much drill or review is necessary at this time. Remind the student(s) to find the first number on the number line and to count back to subtract.

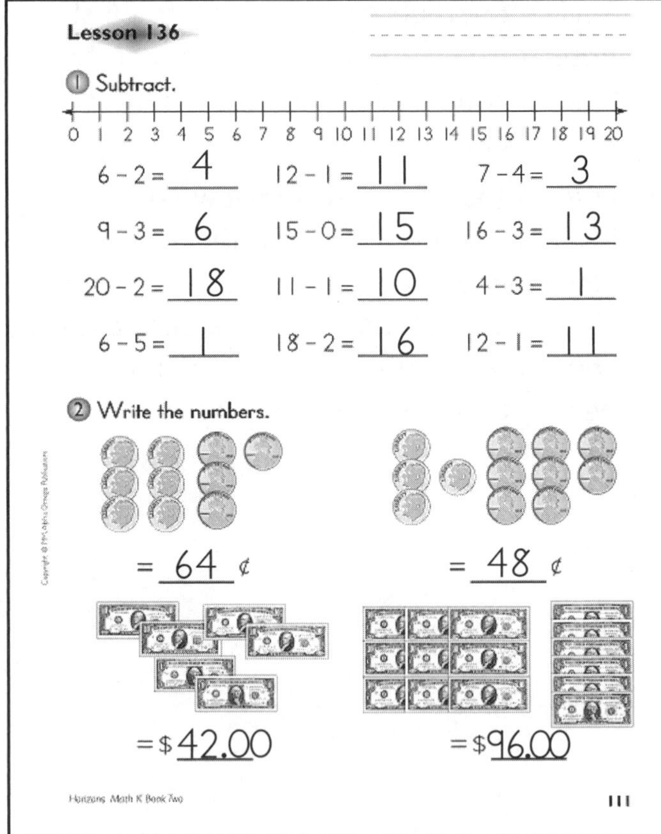

② Talk about a \$10 bill. Relate it to the base 10 blocks and to dimes. Both dimes and \$10 bills are the number of 10's. The \$10 bill is 10 dollars. A dime is 10¢. Instruct the students to count by 10's first and then to continue counting by 1's to find the totals. Do this together as a class activity if the student(s) need the help.

③ Read the first word problem to the class. Ask the student(s) to tell you the key word (left). Visualize the problem using counting chips if necessary. Have the student(s) tell you the subtraction fact that supports the answer. Allow the student(s) to write the subtraction fact and to write the answer on their own Then discuss the results with them. Complete the activity.

④ Review next door neighbors (before & after) with number flash cards and a next door neighbor chart. Allow the student(s) to use a number chart if necessary.

Lesson 137 - Add & Subtract 20's

Overview:

- Add & subtract 20's
- Bar graph
- Count by 2's
- Find the largest of 3 numbers

Materials and Supplies:

- Teacher's Guide & Student Workbook
- White board
- Objects for counters
- Number flash cards
- Count by 2's flash cards
- Subtraction flash cards 1's
- Addition flash cards 1's
- Number line strips
- Number chart

Teaching Tips:

Review addition & subtraction 20's.
Review bar graph.
Review counting by 2's.
Teach largest of 3 numbers.
Drill subtraction 1's family.
Drill addition 1's family.
Review oral counting to 100.

Activities:

① Review the addition and subtraction signs that occur in Activity ①. For the remainder of the lessons the student will be asked to do both addition and subtraction for review activities. Instruct the student(s) to begin the activity. After several have completed the addition problems and have started the subtraction, stop the class and ask if they are remembering to subtract on the second row of problems.

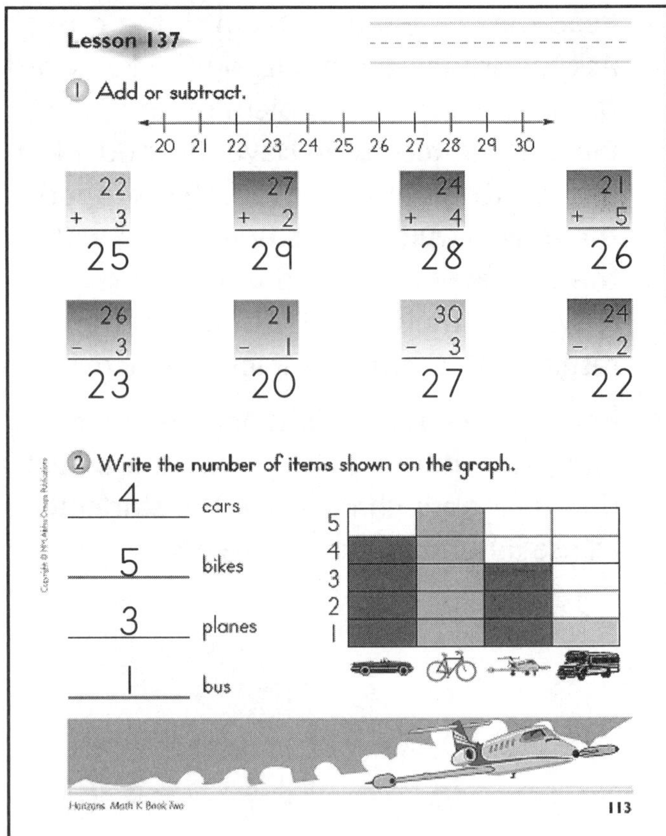

② Review bar graphs as is necessary. Go over the words for the pictures and have the student(s) complete the activity.

③ Count out loud with the student(s) by 2's to 100. Have them count by 2's in Activity ③ by writing the missing numbers. Display the 2's flash cards or a number chart for them to refer to if it is needed.

④ Give the student(s) about 20 counters. Have them make 3 different sets choosing numbers for which they have enough counters. (5, 9, 7) Ask them to tell you how many are in the largest group. Read the instruction and have the student(s) complete the activity.

Lesson 137

③ Write the missing numbers by 2's.

2 6 8

12 18

22 26

50

④ Circle the largest number in each group.

5 9 3	6 3 8
17 15 13	17 13 10

114 Horizons Math K Book Two

Lesson 138 - Place Value 90's

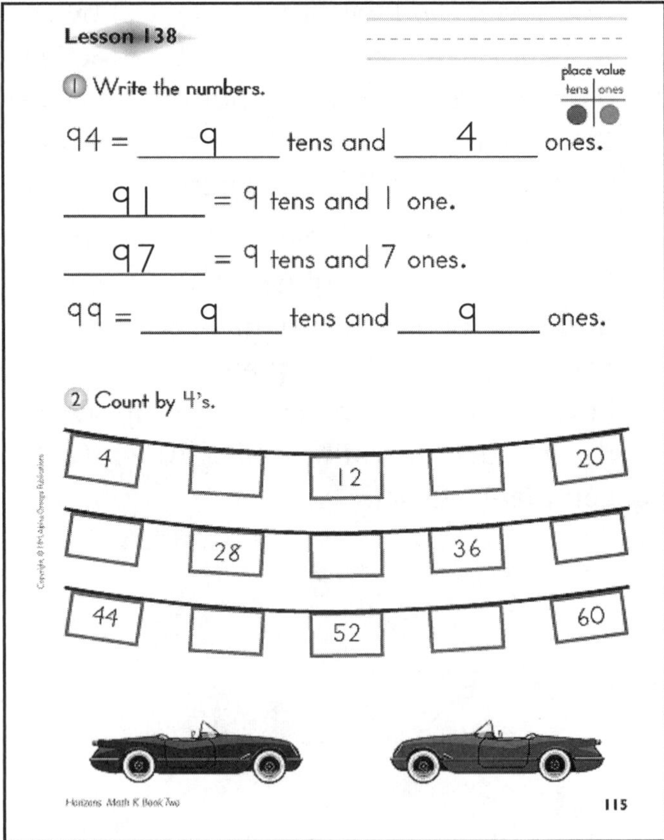

Lesson 138

① Write the numbers.

place value
tens | ones

94 = 9 tens and 4 ones.

91 = 9 tens and 1 one.

97 = 9 tens and 7 ones.

99 = 9 tens and 9 ones.

② Count by 4's.

4		12		20
	28		36	
44		52		60

Horizons Math K Book Two 115

Overview:

- Place value 90's
- Count by 4's
- Subtract 30's
- Word problems (+)

Materials and Supplies:

- Teacher's Guide & Student Workbook
- White board
- Objects for counters
- Number flash cards
- Count by 4's flash cards
- Place value chart
- Subtraction flash cards 1's
- Addition flash cards 1's
- Number line strips
- Number chart

Teaching Tips:

Teach place value 90's.
Review counting by 4's.
Review subtraction 30's.
Review word problems, addition.
Drill subtraction 1's family.
Drill addition 1's family.
Review oral counting to 100.

Activities:

① Review place value with a place value chart or blocks. Practice a few numbers in the 90's family. Instruct the student(s) to complete the activity. Alert them to the two different types of problems in the activity.

② Count out loud with the student(s) by 4's to 100. Have them count by 4's in Activity ② by writing the missing numbers. Display the 4's flash cards or a number chart for them to refer to if it is needed.

③ Review subtraction with a number line if it is needed. If no review is needed the student(s) may do this activity independently.

④ Review what makes a addition word problem. Read the first problem to the class. Ask what the key word is (altogether). Visualize the problem using counting chips. Have the student(s) tell you the addition fact that supports the answer. Allow the student(s) to write the addition fact and to write the answer on their own Then discuss the results with them. Have them complete the activity.

Lesson 138

③ Subtract.

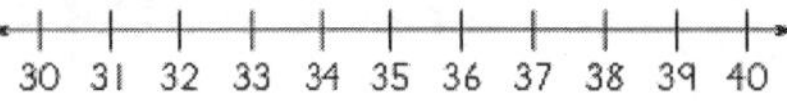

39 - 4 = 35	35 - 4 = 31	31 - 0 = 31
38 - 5 = 33	32 - 2 = 30	37 - 6 = 31
33 - 0 = 33	40 - 5 = 35	34 - 2 = 32

④ 3 boys are in a line. Then 6 more get in line. How many boys are there altogether in the line?

9 boys

Judy has 5 big books and 3 little books. How many books does Judy have altogether?

8 books

If it takes 10 minutes to do the first page of a lesson and 5 minutes to do the second page, altogether how long will you work on the lesson?

15 minutes

116 Horizons Math K Book Two

Lesson 139 - Measure with Centimeters

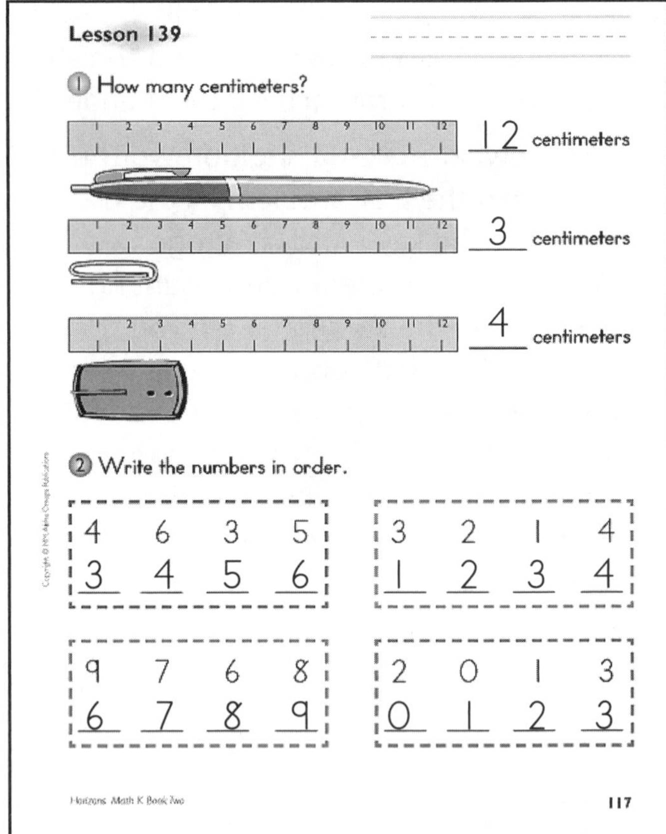

Overview:

- Measure with centimeters
- Put numbers in order 1's
- Count by 3's
- Smallest of 3 numbers

Materials and Supplies:

- Teacher's Guide & Student Workbook
- White board
- Objects for counters
- Number flash cards
- Count by 3's flash cards
- Ruler – centimeters
- Subtraction flash cards 1's
- Addition flash cards 1's
- Number line strips
- Number chart

Teaching Tips:

Teach ruler – centimeters.
Teach number order.
Review counting by 3's.
Teach finding the smallest of three numbers.
Drill subtraction 1's family.
Drill addition 1's family.
Review oral counting to 100.

Activities:

① Discuss with the student(s) that there are two different rulers that can be used to measure lengths – the inch ruler and the centimeter ruler. Tell them the centimeter ruler is a metric measure like the liter volume, while the inch ruler is an English measure. Have them take a look at the rulers in this activity that have centimeters on them. Tell them to compare this ruler to an inch ruler. Explain that you use a centimeter ruler in the same way that you use an inch ruler. Ask the student(s) to tell you the length of each object in the activity and then have them write it on the blank.

② Teach number order by giving a student four mixed-up consecutive number cards from the 1's and have put them in order from smallest to largest. They can use a number line or number chart to determine the number order, if necessary.

③ Count out loud with the student(s) by 3's to 100. Have them count by 3's in Activity ③ by writing the missing numbers. Display the 3's flash cards or a number chart for them to refer to if it is needed.

④ Give the student(s) about 20 counters. Have them make 3 different sets choosing numbers for which they have enough counters. (5, 9, 7) Ask them to tell you how many are in the smallest group. Read the instruction and have the student(s) complete the activity.

Lesson 139

③ Count by 3's.

3 6 12 15

21 24

33 39 42

48 54 57

④ Circle the smallest number in each box.

6 3 8	5 9 3
17 13 10	17 15 13
42 39 75	56 38 79

118 Horizons Math K Book Two

Lesson 140 - Subtract & Add 30's

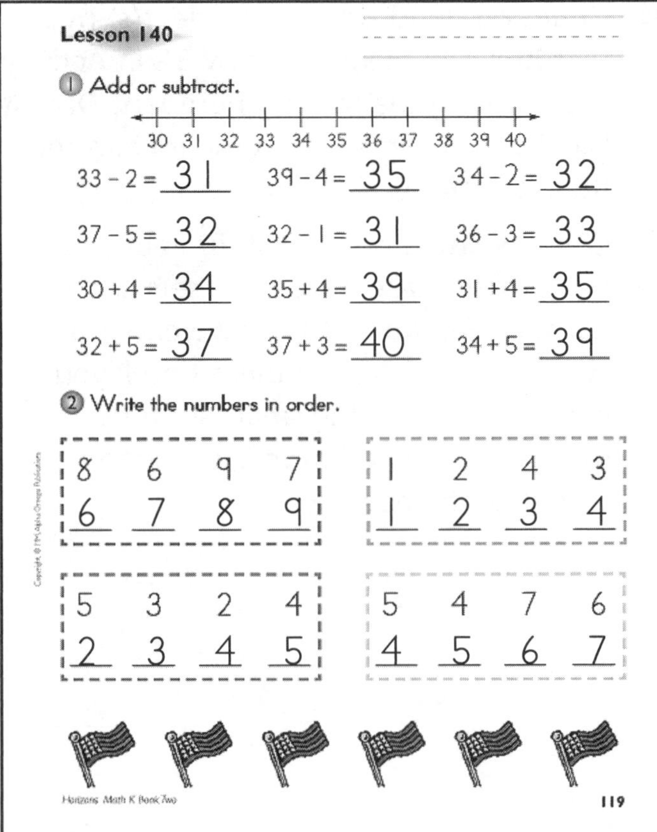

Overview:

- Subtract & add 30's
- Put numbers in order 1's
- Money, word problems
- Subtract 40's

Materials and Supplies:

- Teacher's Guide & Student Workbook
- White board
- Objects for counters
- Number flash cards
- Subtraction flash cards 1's
- Addition flash cards 1's
- Number line strips
- Number chart

Teaching Tips:

Review addition & subtraction 30's.
Review number order.
Review word problems, addition.
Review subtraction 40's.
Drill subtraction 1's family.
Drill addition 1's family.
Review oral counting to 100.

Activities:

① Review the addition and subtraction signs that occur in Activity ①. For the remainder of the lessons the student will be asked to do both addition and subtraction for review activities. Instruct the student(s) to begin the activity. After several have completed the subtraction problems and have started the addition stop the class and ask if they are remembering to add on the third row of problems.

② Review number order by giving a student four mixed-up consecutive number cards from the 1's and have put them in order from smallest to largest. They can use a number line or number chart to determine the number order, if necessary.

③ Review what makes an addition word problem. Read the first problem to the class. Ask what the key word is (and). Visualize the problem using counting chips. Have the student(s) tell you the addition fact that supports the answer. Allow the student(s) to write the answer on their own, then discuss the results with them. Read the remaining problem for the student(s) so they can complete the activity.

④ Review subtraction with a number line if it is needed. If no review is needed the student(s) may do this activity independently.

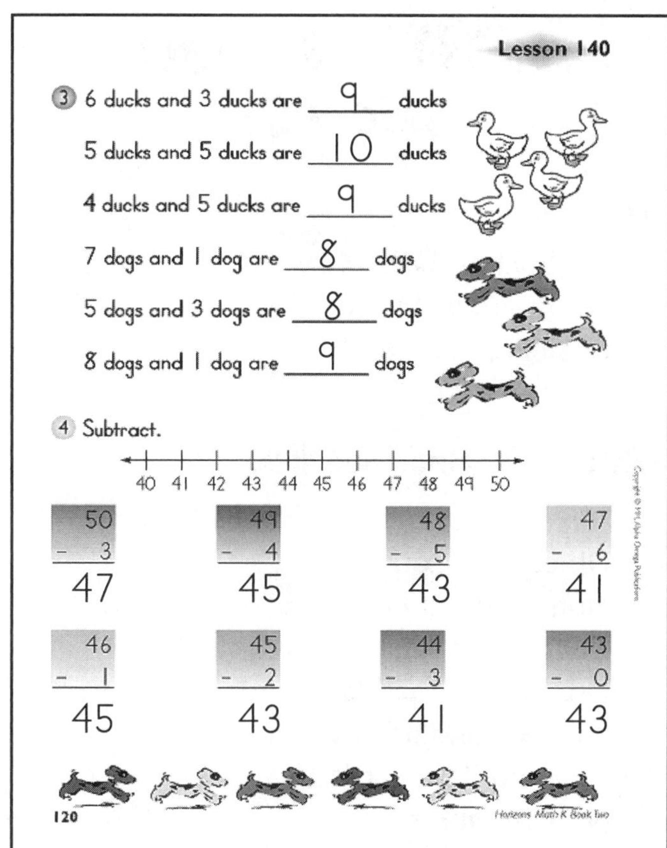

Lesson 141 - Subtract and Add 40's

Overview:

- Subtract and add 40's
- Put numbers in order 1's
- Ordinals, first–tenth
- Count by 3's

Materials and Supplies:

- Teacher's Guide & Student Workbook
- Objects for counters
- Number flash cards
- Count by 3's flash cards
- Ordinal number flash cards
- Subtraction flash cards 1's
- Addition flash cards 1's
- Number line strips
- Number chart

Teaching Tips:

Review addition & subtraction 40's.
Review number order.
Review ordinal numbers.
Review counting by 3's.
Drill subtraction 1's family.
Drill addition 1's family.
Review oral counting to 100.

Activities:

① Review the addition and subtraction signs that occur in Activity ①. For the remainder of the lessons the student will be asked to do both addition and subtraction for review activities. Instruct the student(s) to begin the activity. After several have completed the addition problems and have started the subtraction, stop the class and ask if they are remembering to subtract on the third row of problems.

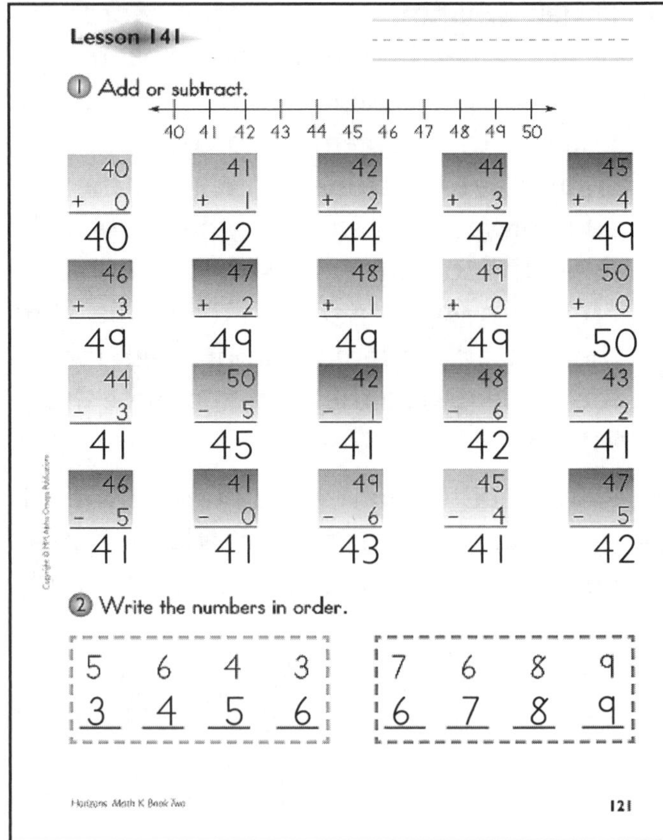

Lesson 141

① Add or subtract.

40 41 42 43 44 45 46 47 48 49 50

40 + 0 = 40	41 + 1 = 42	42 + 2 = 44	44 + 3 = 47	45 + 4 = 49
46 + 3 = 49	47 + 2 = 49	48 + 1 = 49	49 + 0 = 49	50 + 0 = 50
44 - 3 = 41	50 - 5 = 45	42 - 1 = 41	48 - 6 = 42	43 - 2 = 41
46 - 5 = 41	41 - 0 = 41	49 - 6 = 43	45 - 4 = 41	47 - 5 = 42

② Write the numbers in order.

5 6 4 3 → 3 4 5 6

7 6 8 9 → 6 7 8 9

Horizons Math K Book Two 121

② Review number order by giving a student four mixed-up consecutive number cards from the 1's and have put them in order from smallest to largest. They can use a number line or number chart to determine the number order, if necessary.

③ Review the ordinal numbers. The dogs are lined up in order. Instruct the student(s) to match the ordinal number to the dog's ribbon.

④ Count by 3's to 100. Each box in this activity has one number that is *not* a count by 3's number. Have the student(s) refer to a count by 3's chart if necessary.

Lesson 141

③ These are the winners at the dog show. Match their place in the row with the number for the ribbon.

2nd 5th 1st 3rd 6th 4th

④ Cross out the number that does not belong when you count by 3's.

3 9 6 ~~4~~	15 ~~7~~ 18 12	24 ~~32~~ 30 27
42 45 48 ~~52~~	60 63 57 ~~65~~	75 ~~83~~ 72 78

122 Horizons Math K Book Two

Lesson 142 - Time-Minutes

Overview:

- Time – minutes
- Count by 4's
- Subtract and add 40's
- Word problems

Materials and Supplies:

- Teacher's Guide & Student Workbook
- White board
- Objects for counters
- Number flash cards
- Count by 4's & 5's flash cards
- Clock models
- Subtraction flash cards 1's
- Addition flash cards 1's
- Number line strips
- Number chart

Teaching Tips:

Review counting by 5's.
Review counting by 4's.
Review addition & subtraction 30's & 40's.
Review word problems, addition.
Drill subtraction 1's family.
Drill addition 1's family.
Review oral counting to 100.

Activities:

① Count by 5's to 100. Using a clock model, have the student(s) count the minutes by 5's. Have the student(s) trace the first 5 in this activity and write the remaining 5's around the clock.

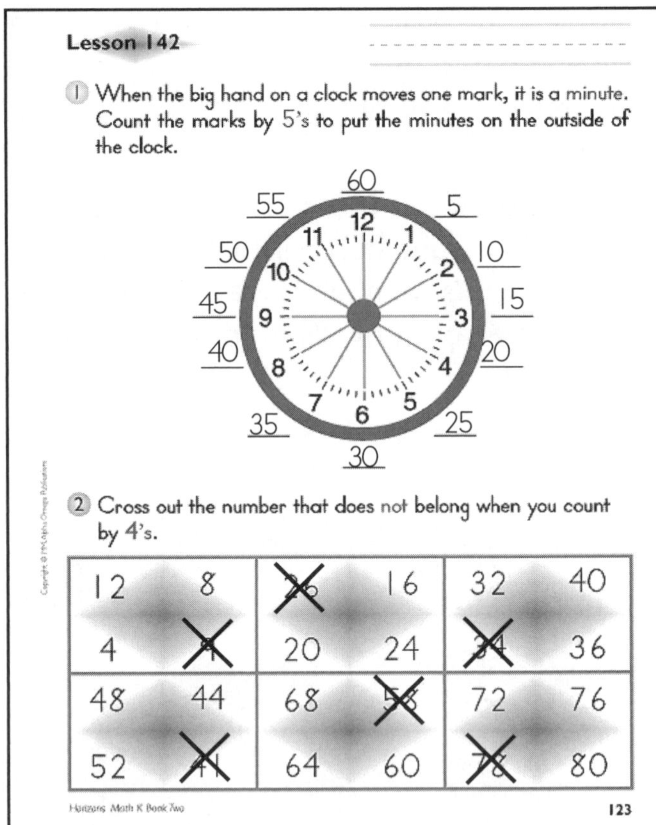

② Count by 4's to 100. Each box in this activity has one number that is not a count by 4's number. Have the student(s) refer to a count by 4's chart if necessary.

③ Review the addition and subtraction signs that occur in Activity ③. Instruct the student(s) to begin the activity. After several have completed the first row of problems and have started the second, stop the class and ask if they are remembering to look at the signs.

④ Review what makes an addition word problem. Read the first problem to the class. Ask what the key word is (and). Visualize the problem using counting chips. Have the student(s) tell you the addition fact that supports the answer. Allow the student(s) to write the answer on their own Then discuss the results with them. Read the remaining problems to the student(s) to complete the activity.

Lesson 142

③ Add or subtract.

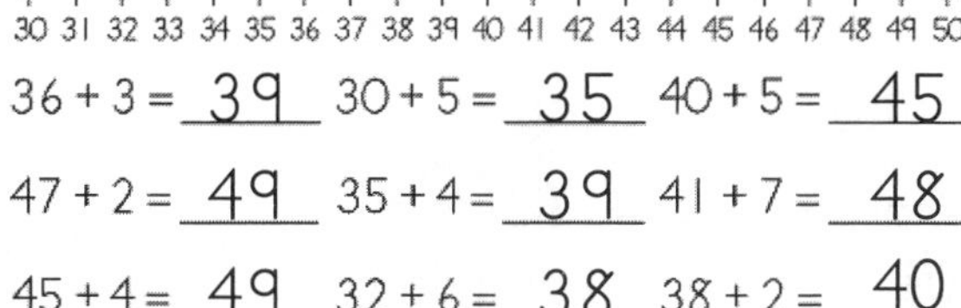

30 31 32 33 34 35 36 37 38 39 40 41 42 43 44 45 46 47 48 49 50

36 + 3 = 39	30 + 5 = 35	40 + 5 = 45
47 + 2 = 49	35 + 4 = 39	41 + 7 = 48
45 + 4 = 49	32 + 6 = 38	38 + 2 = 40
36 − 3 = 33	50 − 5 = 45	40 − 5 = 35
47 − 2 = 45	35 − 4 = 31	48 − 7 = 41
45 − 4 = 41	39 − 6 = 33	38 − 2 = 36

④ Write the numbers.

2 bottles and 4 bottles are 6 bottles.

3 inches and 5 inches are 8 inches.

4 centimeters and 11 centimeters are 15 centimeters.

8 books and 1 book are 9 books.

124 Horizons Math K Book Two

Lesson 143 - Subtract and Add 50's

Overview:

- Subtract and add 50's
- Measure with centimeters
- Addition 80's
- Perimeter, inches

Materials and Supplies:

- Teacher's Guide & Student Workbook
- White board
- Objects for counters
- Number flash cards
- Ruler – inches
- Ruler – centimeters
- Subtraction flash cards 1's
- Addition flash cards 1's
- Number line strips
- Number chart

Teaching Tips:

Review addition & subtraction 50's.
Review ruler – centimeters.
Review addition 80's.
Review perimeter – inches.
Drill subtraction 1's family.
Drill addition 1's family.
Review oral counting to 100.

Activities:

① Review the addition and subtraction signs that occur in Activity ①. Instruct the student(s) to begin the activity. After several have completed the first row of problems and have started the second, stop the class and ask if they are remembering to look at the signs.

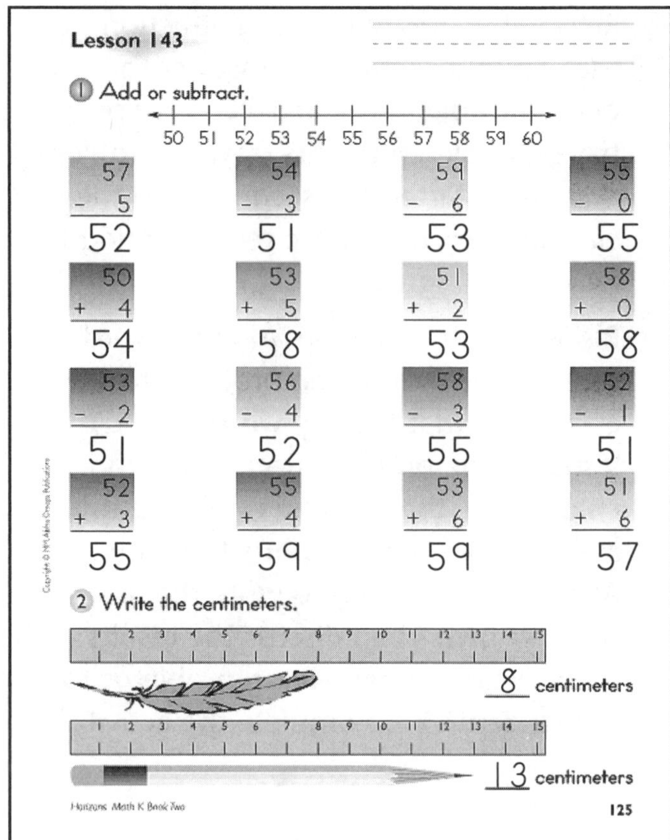

② Have the student(s) look at the centimeter rulers. To measure the length of the feather the end is set on zero. Then read the point at which the other end of the feather stops. This is the measurement in centimeters. They should be able to measure the pencil by themselves.

③ Review the 80's family. These are review problems. The student(s) should be able to do them independently.

④ Review perimeter as the distance around an object. Have them count the inches around the rectangle and write their answer on the blank.

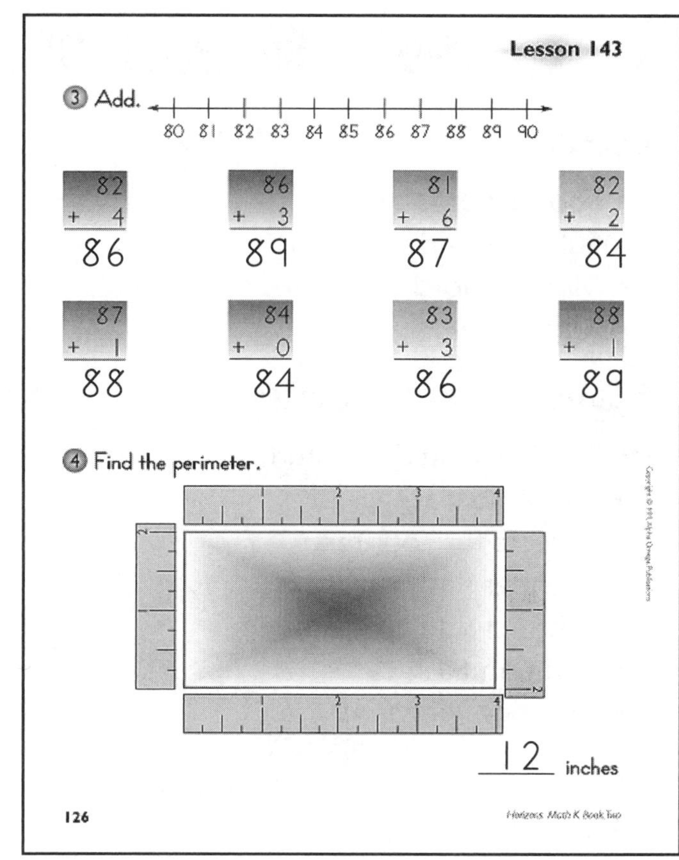

Lesson 144 - Subtract 90's

Overview:

- Subtract 90's
- Subtract and add 50's
- Money, word problems, subtract
- Addition 80's

Materials and Supplies:

- Teacher's Guide & Student Workbook
- White board
- Objects for counters
- Number flash cards
- Subtraction flash cards 1's
- Addition flash cards 1's
- Number line strips
- Number chart

Teaching Tips:

Review subtraction 90's.
Review addition & subtraction 50's.
Review word problems, subtraction.
Review addition 80's.
Drill subtraction 1's family.
Drill addition 1's family.
Review oral counting to 100.

Activities:

① Review the 90's family. These are review problems. The student(s) should be able to do them independently.

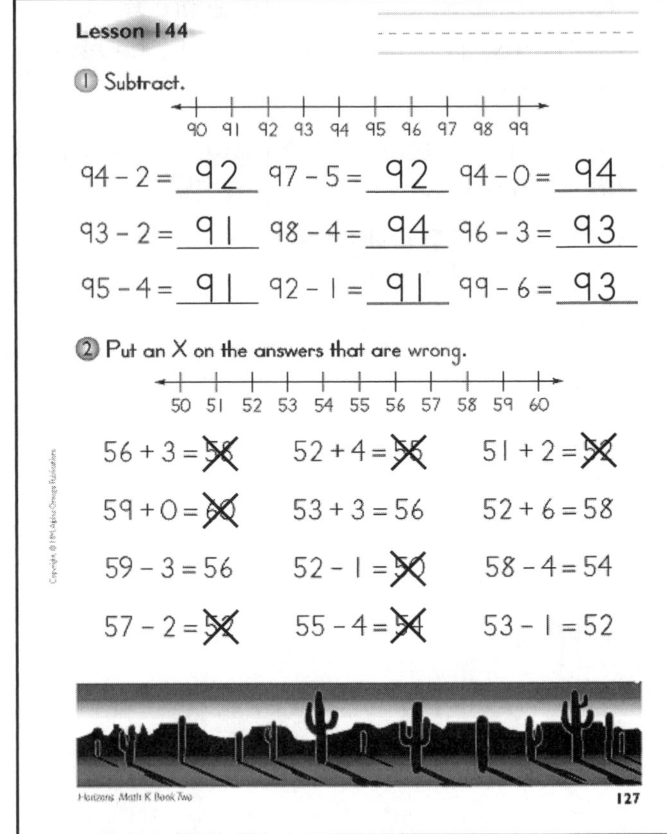

Lesson 144

① Subtract.

90 91 92 93 94 95 96 97 98 99

94 - 2 = 92 97 - 5 = 92 94 - 0 = 94
93 - 2 = 91 98 - 4 = 94 96 - 3 = 93
95 - 4 = 91 92 - 1 = 91 99 - 6 = 93

② Put an X on the answers that are wrong.

50 51 52 53 54 55 56 57 58 59 60

56 + 3 = 58 X 52 + 4 = 55 X 51 + 2 = 52 X
59 + 0 = 60 X 53 + 3 = 56 52 + 6 = 58
59 - 3 = 56 52 - 1 = 50 X 58 - 4 = 54
57 - 2 = 52 X 55 - 4 = 54 X 53 - 1 = 52

Horizons Math K Book Two 127

② This is a new activity. Put several sample problems on the white board, some with the correct answers and others without. Cover the answer to the first problem and ask a student for the answer. After they have given an answer, check to see if it matches the answer you wrote down. Instruct them to do all of the problems in this activity in similar fashion. Some of these problems are addition and some are subtraction.

③ Read the first word problem to the class. Ask the student(s) to tell you the key word (left). Visualize the problem counting coins if necessary. Have the student(s) tell you the subtraction fact. Allow the student(s) to write the subtraction fact and to write the answer on their own Then discuss the results with them. Complete the activity by reading the remaining questions to the student(s).

④ This is another new activity. Instruct the student(s) to do the problems just like they have been all year long, but this time instead of writing the answer, they need to match the answer to the problem.

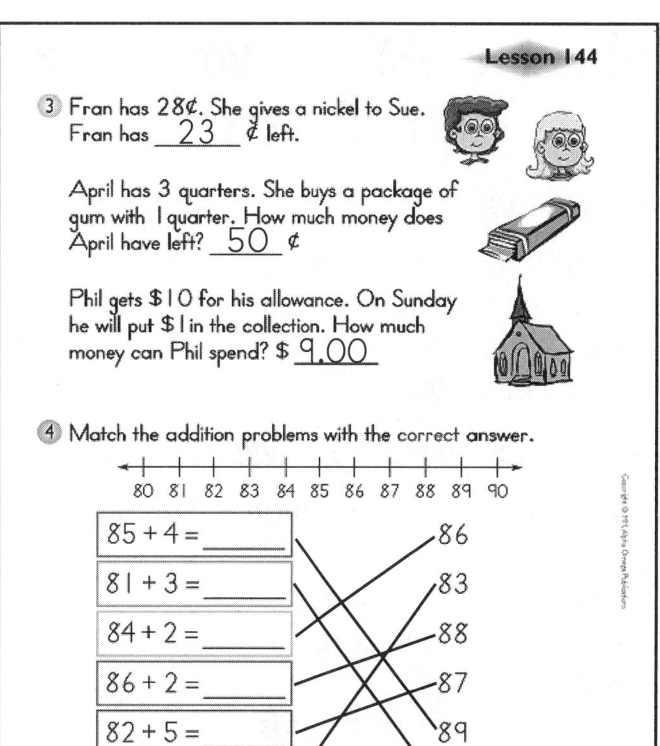
Lesson 144

③ Fran has 28¢. She gives a nickel to Sue. Fran has 23 ¢ left.

April has 3 quarters. She buys a package of gum with 1 quarter. How much money does April have left? 50 ¢

Phil gets $10 for his allowance. On Sunday he will put $1 in the collection. How much money can Phil spend? $ 9.00

④ Match the addition problems with the correct answer.

80 81 82 83 84 85 86 87 88 89 90

85 + 4 = ______	86
81 + 3 = ______	83
84 + 2 = ______	88
86 + 2 = ______	87
82 + 5 = ______	89
83 + 0 = ______	84

128 Horizons Math K Book Two

Lesson 145 - Subtract & Add 60's

Overview:

- Subtract & add 60's
- Time – minutes
- Subtract 90's
- Addition 90's

Materials and Supplies:

- Teacher's Guide & Student Workbook
- White board
- Objects for counters
- Number flash cards
- Clock models
- Count by 5's flash cards
- Subtraction flash cards 1's
- Addition flash cards 1's
- Number line strips
- Number chart

Teaching Tips:

Review addition & subtraction 60's.
Review counting by 5's.
Review time – hour & minutes.
Review subtraction 90's.
Review addition 90's.
Drill subtraction 1's family.
Drill addition 1's family.
Review oral counting to 100.

Activities:

① Review the addition and subtraction signs that occur in Activity ①. Instruct the student(s) to begin the activity. Stop the class after a few minutes and ask if they are remembering to look at the signs.

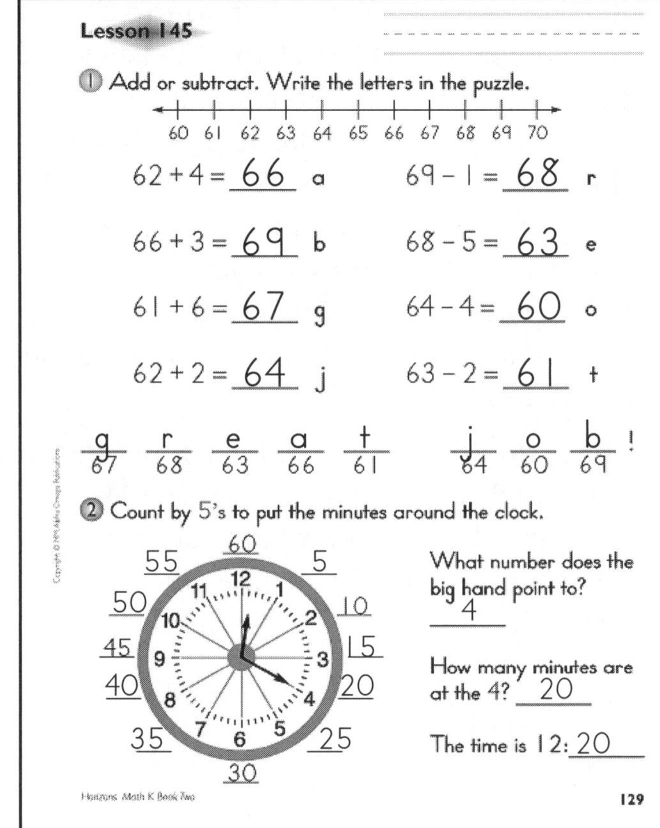

Lesson 145

① Add or subtract. Write the letters in the puzzle.

60 61 62 63 64 65 66 67 68 69 70

62 + 4 = 66 a
69 − 1 = 68 r
66 + 3 = 69 b
68 − 5 = 63 e
61 + 6 = 67 g
64 − 4 = 60 o
62 + 2 = 64 j
63 − 2 = 61 t

g	r	e	a	t		j	o	b	!
67	68	63	66	61		64	60	69	

② Count by 5's to put the minutes around the clock.

What number does the big hand point to? 4

How many minutes are at the 4? 20

The time is 12:20

Horizons Math K Book Two

129

② Count by 5's to 100. Using a clock model, have the student(s) count the minutes by 5's. Have the student(s) complete writing the remaining 5's around the clock. Read the questions to the student(s) and have them write their answers.

③ Review the 90's family. These are review problems. The student(s) should be able to do them independently.

④ Review the 90's family. These are review problems. The student(s) should be able to do them independently.

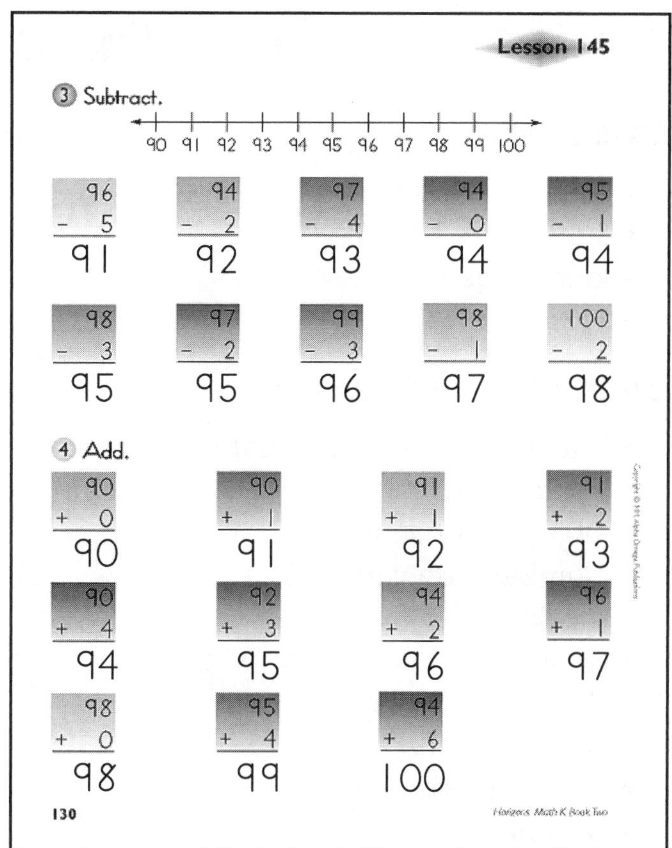

Lesson 146 - Time-Minutes

Overview:

- Time – minutes
- Subtract & add 60's
- Identify geometric solids
- 1/2, 1/3, 1/4

Materials and Supplies:

- Teacher's Guide & Student Workbook
- White board
- Objects for counters
- Number flash cards
- Clock models
- Count by 5's flash cards
- Cone, cylinder & sphere
- Subtraction flash cards 1's
- Addition flash cards 1's
- Number line strips
- Number chart

Teaching Tips:

Review time – hour & minutes.
Review addition & subtraction 60's.
Review geometric solids.
Review whole, 1/2, 1/3 & 1/4.
Drill subtraction 1's family.
Drill addition 1's family.
Review oral counting to 100.

Activities:

① Count by 5's to 100. Using a clock model have the student(s) count the minutes by 5's. Have them do the same thing on their own to write the minutes in this activity.

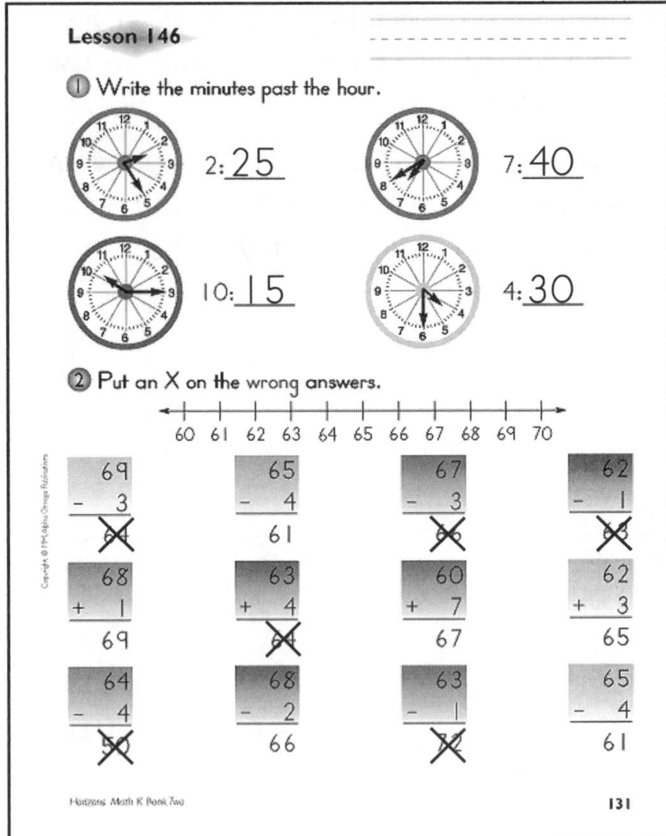

② Put several sample problems on the white board, some with the correct answers and others without. Cover the answer to the first problem and ask a student for the answer. After they have given an answer, check to see if it matches the answer you wrote down. Instruct them to do all of the problems in this activity in similar fashion. Some of these problems are addition and some are subtraction.

③ Review geometric solids. Instruct the students to match the shape on the left to the ones on the right. Some items contain more than one shape.

④ Review equal parts. Instruct them to write their answer for the figures in this activity.

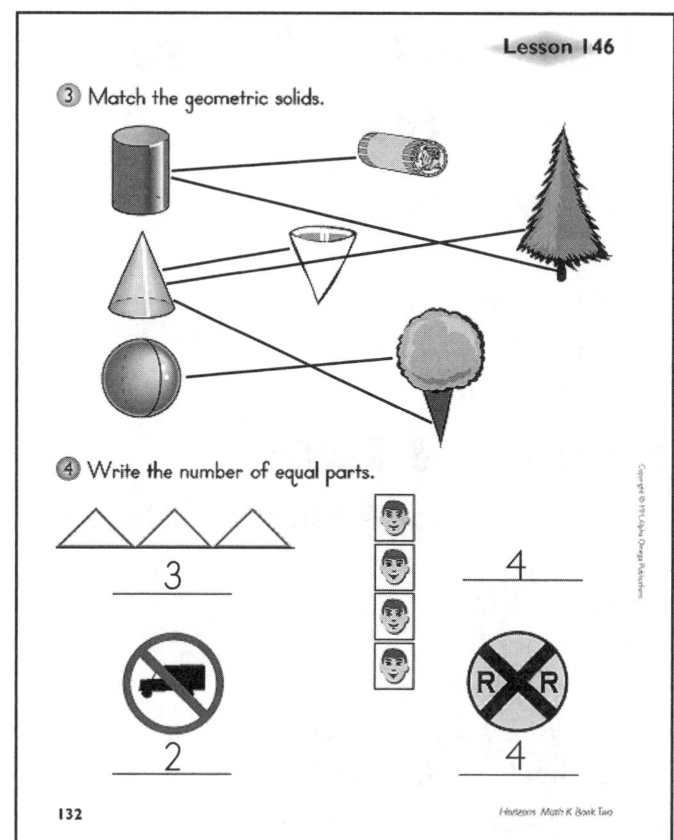

Lesson 147 - Subtract & Add 70's

Overview:

- Subtract & add 70's
- Time – minutes
- Days of the week
- Addition 90's

Materials and Supplies:

- Teacher's Guide & Student Workbook
- White board
- Objects for counters
- Number flash cards
- Clock models
- Count by 5's flash cards
- Ordinal number flash cards
- Days of the week flash cards
- Subtraction flash cards 1's
- Addition flash cards 1's
- Number line strips
- Number chart

Teaching Tips:

Review addition & subtraction 70's.
Review time – hour & minutes.
Review counting by 5's.
Review days of the week.
Review ordinal numbers.
Review addition 90's.
Drill subtraction 1's family.
Drill addition 1's family.
Review oral counting to 100.

Activities:

① Review the addition and subtraction signs that occur in Activity ①. Instruct the student(s) to begin the activity. Stop the class after a few minutes and ask if they are remembering to look at the signs.

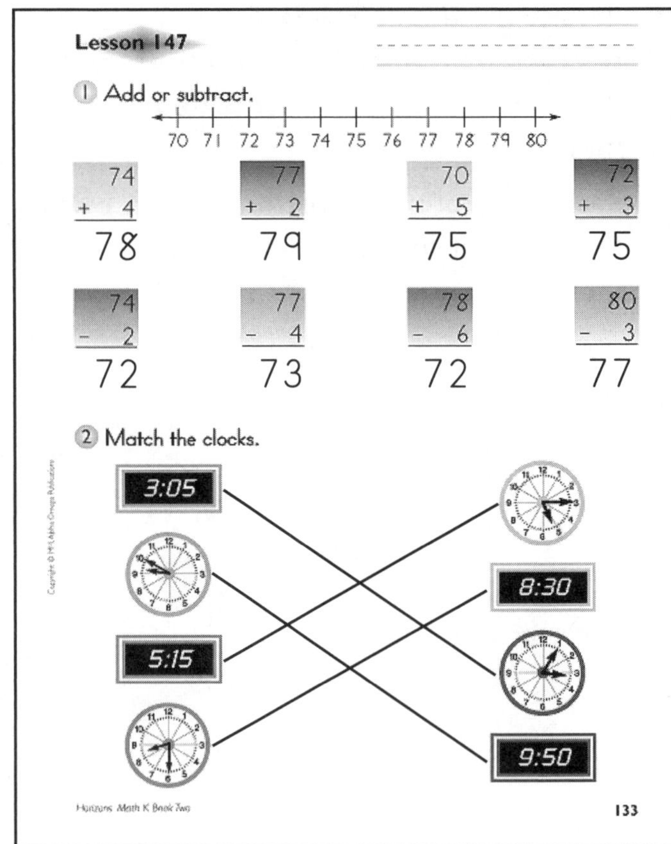

② Count by 5's to 100. Using a clock model have the student(s) count the minutes by 5's. Have them do the same thing on their own to match the clocks that have the same minutes in this activity.

③ Review ordinal numbers. Review the days of the week. Read the instruction and ask the student(s) to complete the activity.

④ This is a new activity. Instruct your student(s) to do all of the problems in this activity. Point out the letters by the answer blanks. If they have answered the problem correctly, the same number is on the bottom of the page. They are to write the letter over the number for the answer to the problem. Demonstrate this on the white board. If the letters are placed on the blanks correctly, they should spell a word.

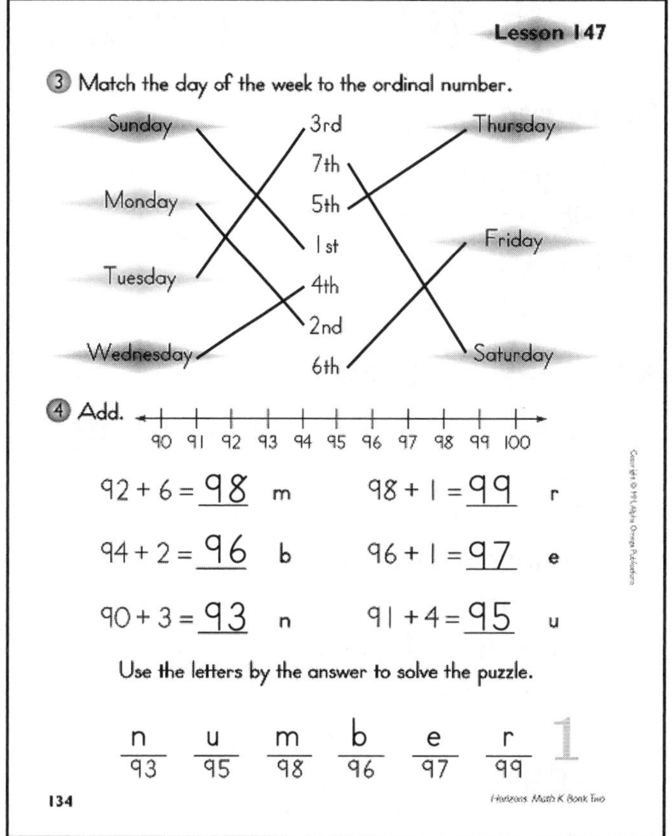

Lesson 148 – Bar Graphs

Overview:

- Bar graphs
- Subtract & add 70's
- 1/4 & 1/2 hour
- Count by 5's

Materials and Supplies:

- Teacher's Guide & Student Workbook
- White board
- Objects for counters
- Number flash cards
- Clock models
- Count by 5's flash cards
- Crayons
- Subtraction flash cards 1's
- Addition flash cards 1's
- Number line strips
- Number chart

Teaching Tips:

Review bar graphs.
Review addition & subtraction 60's & 70's.
Review time – half past.
Review counting by 5's.
Drill subtraction 1's family.
Drill addition 1's family.
Review oral counting to 100.

Activities:

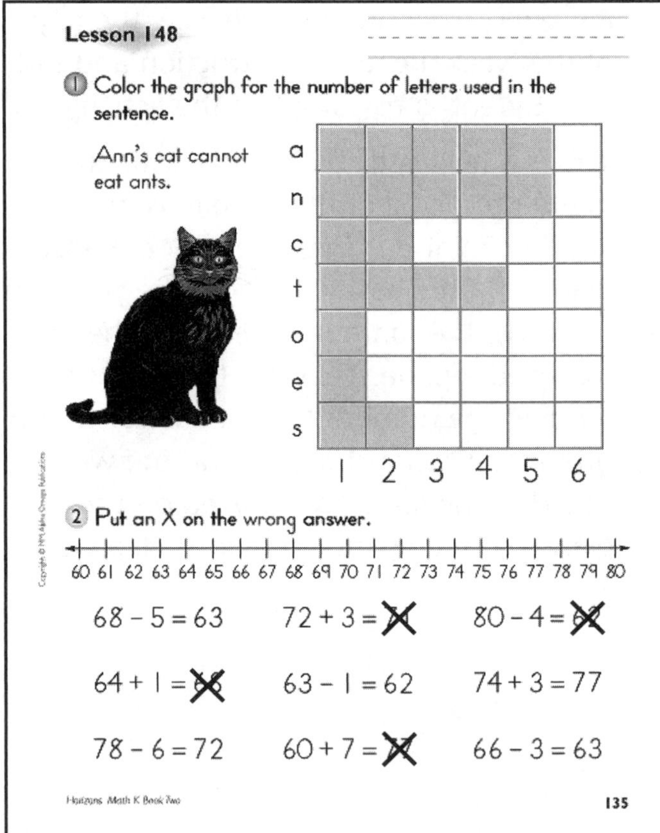

Lesson 148

① Color the graph for the number of letters used in the sentence.

Ann's cat cannot eat ants.

② Put an X on the wrong answer.

68 – 5 = 63 72 + 3 = X 80 – 4 = X

64 + 1 = X 63 – 1 = 62 74 + 3 = 77

78 – 6 = 72 60 + 7 = X 66 – 3 = 63

Horizons Math K Book Two 135

① Read the sentence in this activity together with the class. Ask a student to count the letter a's in the sentence. Direct the student(s) to the letter (a) at the top of the graph. Instruct them to color the number of squares for the number of letter a's in the sentence. They should color by rows as they complete this activity.

② Put several sample problems on the white board, some with the correct answers and others without. Cover the answer to the first problem and ask a student for the answer. After they have given an answer, check to see if it matches the answer you wrote down. Instruct them to do all of the problems in this activity in similar fashion. Some of these problems are addition and some are subtraction.

③ Review half past and 30 minutes. Read the instruction for the activity to the student(s). Have them complete the activity.

④ Count by 5's to 100. Each box in this activity has one number that is not a count by 5's number. Have the student(s) refer to a count by 5's chart is necessary.

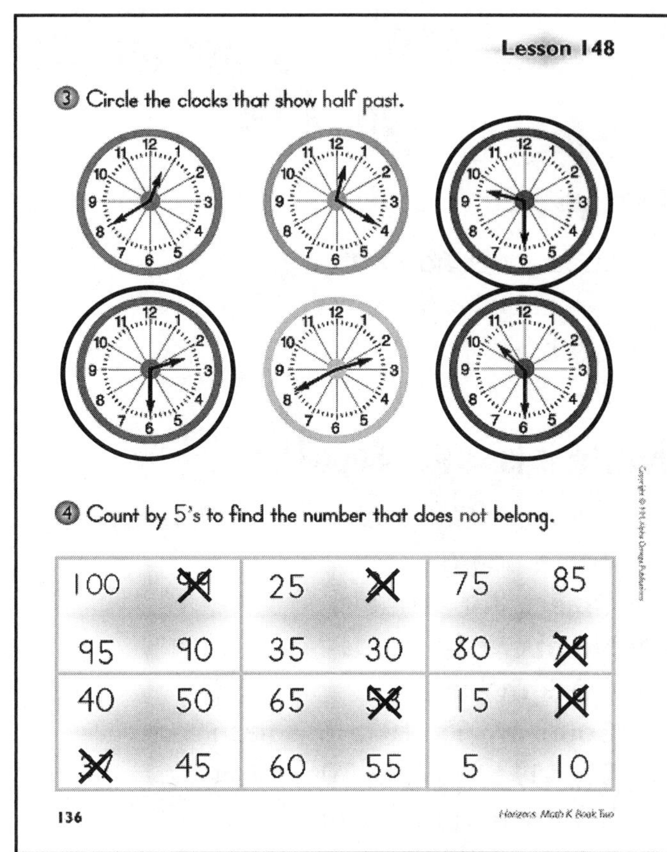

③ Circle the clocks that show half past.

④ Count by 5's to find the number that does not belong.

100	~~94~~	25	~~21~~	75	85
95	90	35	30	80	~~74~~
40	50	65	~~53~~	15	~~14~~
~~37~~	45	60	55	5	10

Lesson 149 - Subtract & Add 80's

Overview:

- Subtract & add 80's
- Largest of 3 numbers
- 1/4 hour
- $1, 25 cents

Materials and Supplies:

- Teacher's Guide & Student Workbook
- White board
- Objects for counters
- Number flash cards
- Clock models
- Count by 5's, 10's, 25's flash cards
- $5, $1, 50¢, 25¢, 10¢, 5¢ & 1¢
- Subtraction flash cards 1's
- Addition flash cards 1's
- Number line strips
- Number chart

Teaching Tips:

Review addition & subtraction 80's.
Review finding the largest of three numbers.
Review time – quarter past.
Review counting by 5's, 10's & 25's.
Drill subtraction 1's family.
Drill addition 1's family.
Review oral counting to 100.

Activities:

① Review the addition and subtraction signs that occur in Activity ①. Instruct the student(s) to begin the activity. Remind the class after a few minutes to look at the signs.

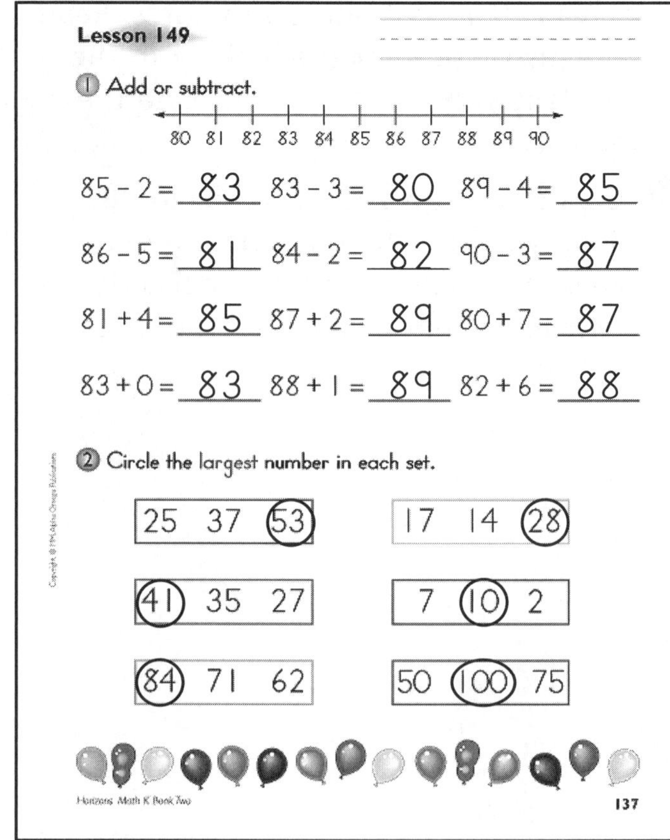

② Choose three number flash cards (0–100) at random. Ask your student(s) to choose the largest number of the three. Read the instruction and have the student(s) complete the activity.

③ Review quarter past and 15 minutes. Read the instruction for the activity to the student(s). Have them complete the activity.

④ Review counting by 5's &10's. Count the amount of coins and bills together with the students.

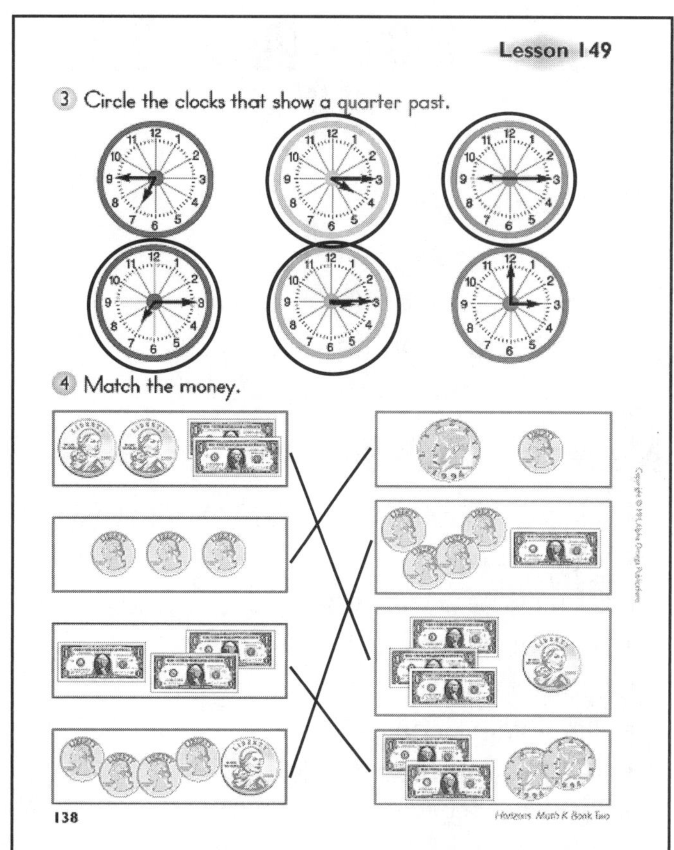

Lesson 150 - Place Value All

Overview:

- Place value all
- Subtract & add 80's
- Smallest of 3 numbers
- Time – minutes

Materials and Supplies:

- Teacher's Guide & Student Workbook
- White board
- Objects for counters
- Number flash cards
- Clock models
- Place value chart
- Subtraction flash cards 1's
- Addition flash cards 1's
- Number line strips
- Number chart

Teaching Tips:

Review place value 0–99.
Review addition & subtraction 80's.
Review finding the smallest of three numbers.
Review time – 5 minutes.
Review counting by 5's, 10's & 25's.
Drill subtraction 1's family.
Drill addition 1's family.
Review oral counting to 100.

Activities:

① Review place value by drawing random number cards 0–99. Say the place value sentence for the number. (37 is 3 tens and 7 ones) After three cards have been drawn, ask for the largest and the smallest of the three numbers as review for Activity ③. Also do several examples of the reverse where you say the last part of the sentence and the student(s) give you the number. (blank is 7 tens and 3 ones)

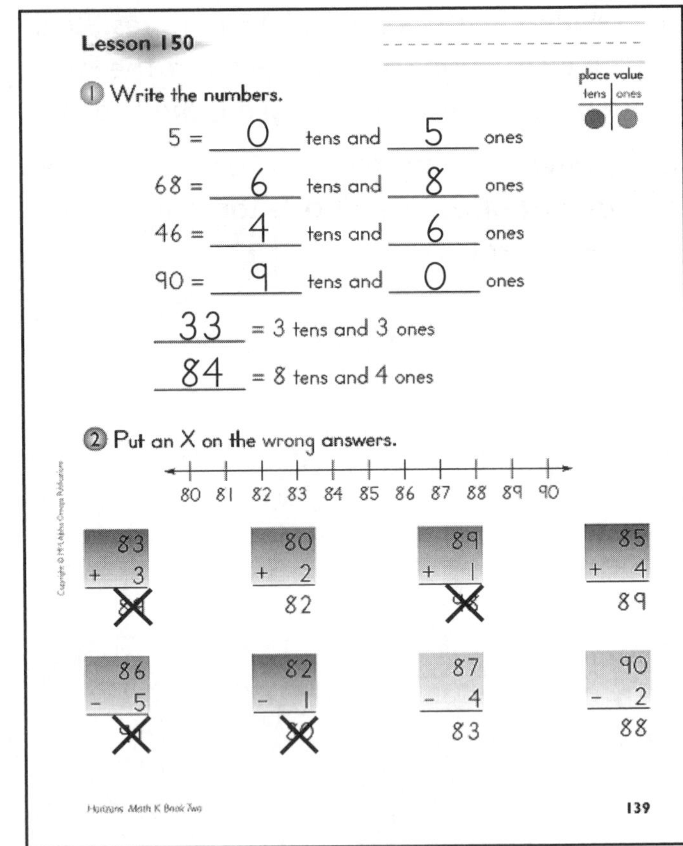

Lesson 150

① Write the numbers.

place value: tens | ones

5 = 0 tens and 5 ones
68 = 6 tens and 8 ones
46 = 4 tens and 6 ones
90 = 9 tens and 0 ones
33 = 3 tens and 3 ones
84 = 8 tens and 4 ones

② Put an X on the wrong answers.

80 81 82 83 84 85 86 87 88 89 90

83 + 3 = X
80 + 2 = 82
89 + 1 = X
85 + 4 = 89
86 − 5 = X
82 − 1 = X
87 − 4 = 83
90 − 2 = 88

Horizons Math K Book Two 139

② Put several sample problems, 80's, on the white board, some with the correct answers and others without. Cover the answer to the first problem and ask a student for the answer. After they have given an answer, check to see if it matches the answer you wrote down. Instruct them to do all the problems in this activity in similar fashion. Review the addition and subtraction signs that occur in Activity ②. Instruct the student(s) to begin the activity. Remind the class after a few minutes to look at the signs.

③ Choose three number flash cards (0–100) at random. Ask your student(s) to choose the smallest number of the three. Read the instruction and have the student(s) complete the activity.

④ Review counting around the clock by 5's. Set the clock to an hour time and say all the 5 minute times for that hour. 8:00, 8:05, 8:10, 8:15, 8:20, etc. Instruct them to match the clocks to the digital time.

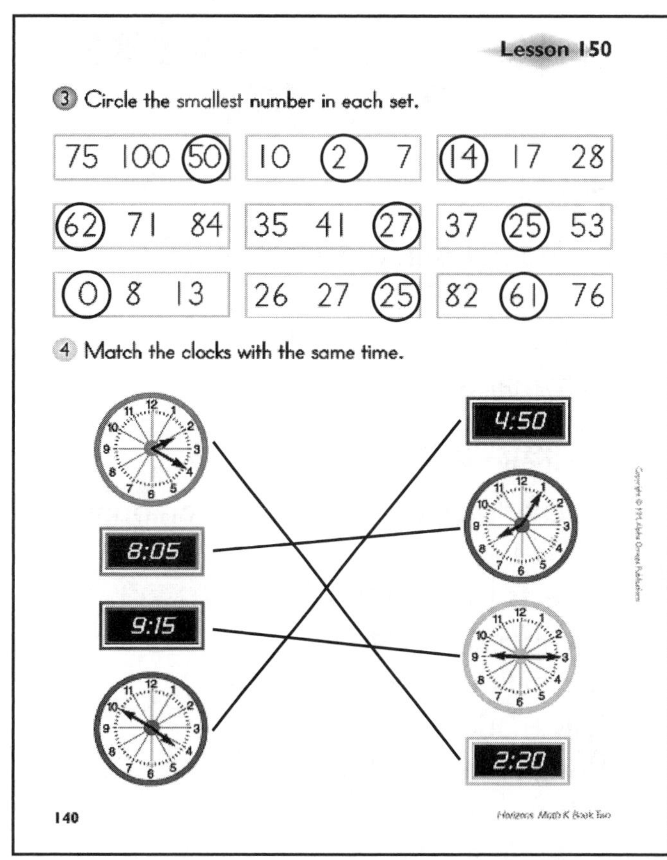

Lesson 151 - Numbers Order 10's

Overview:

- Put numbers in order 10's
- Ordinals, first–tenth
- Number before and after 1's
- Tally marks

Materials and Supplies:

- Teacher's Guide & Student Workbook
- White board
- Objects for counters
- Number flash cards
- Ordinal number flash cards
- Tally marks flash cards
- Next door neighbor chart
- Subtraction flash cards 1's
- Addition flash cards 1's
- Number line strips
- Number chart

Teaching Tips:

Teach number order 10's.
Review ordinal numbers.
Review number before and after 1's.
Review tally marks.
Drill subtraction 1's family.
Drill addition 1's family.
Review oral counting to 100.

Activities:

① Pick 4 consecutive number cards – 10's family. Mix the cards up and ask the student(s) to put them in number order. Do this several times with the student(s). Read the instruction for the activity and help them with the first problem. They should be able to complete the activity independently.

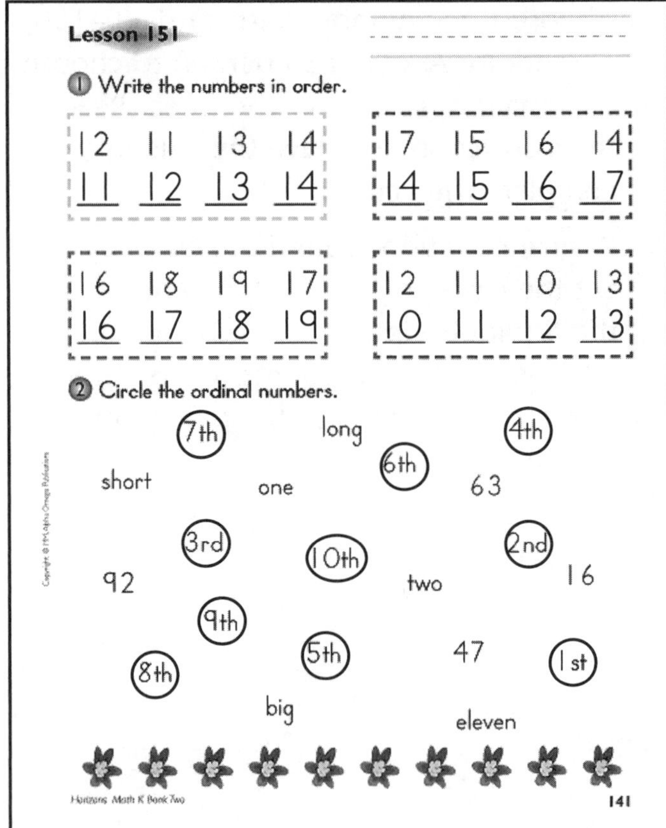
Lesson 151

① Write the numbers in order.

12 11 13 14
11 12 13 14

17 15 16 14
14 15 16 17

16 18 19 17
16 17 18 19

12 11 10 13
10 11 12 13

② Circle the ordinal numbers.

7th long 4th short one 6th 63 3rd 10th 2nd 92 two 16 9th 5th 47 1st 8th big eleven

Horizons Math K Book Two 141

② Review the ordinal numbers with flash cards. Read the instruction and have the student(s) do the activity. Encourage them to check over the ones they have circled after they have finished.

③ Choose a random number flash cards (0–10). Ask your student(s) to tell you the number before and the number after. This activity has also been called the *next door neighbors*. Read the instruction and have the student(s) complete the activity.

④ Do a short review of tally marks. Choose a random tally mark flash card and call on a student to give you the number.

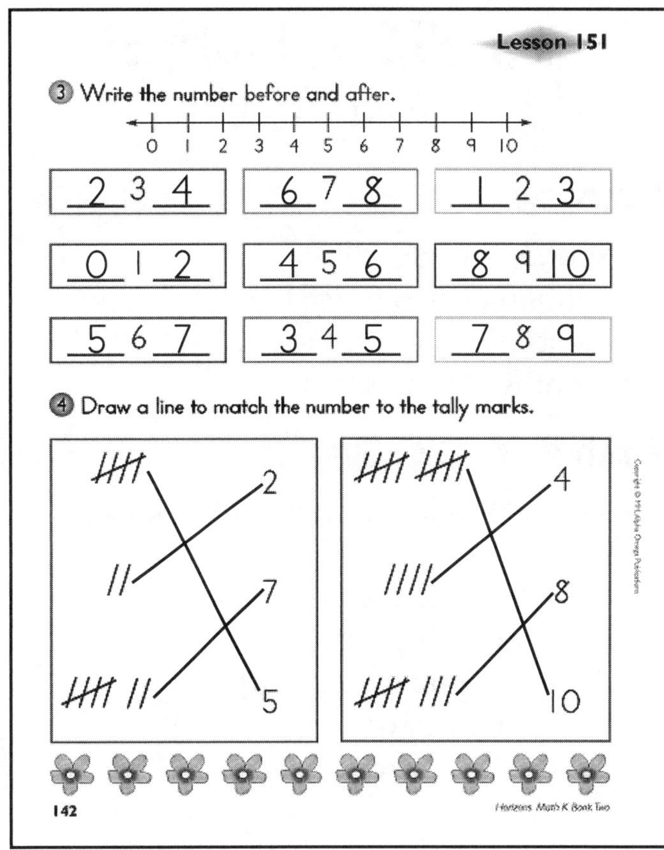

Lesson 152 - Subtract & Add 90's

Overview:

- Subtract & add 90's
- Put numbers in order 10's
- Identify whole, 1/2, 1/3 & 1/4
- Months of year, seasons

Materials and Supplies:

- Teacher's Guide & Student Workbook
- White board
- Objects for counters
- Number flash cards
- Ordinal number flash cards
- Shape flash cards
- Season flash cards
- Crayons
- Subtraction flash cards 1's
- Addition flash cards 1's
- Number line strips
- Number chart

Teaching Tips:

Review addition & subtraction 90's.
Review number order 10's.
Review equal parts.
Review seasons.
Drill subtraction 1's family.
Drill addition 1's family.
Review oral counting to 100.

Activities:

① Review the addition and subtraction signs that occur in Activity ①. Instruct the student(s) to begin the activity. Remind the class after a few minutes to check the signs.

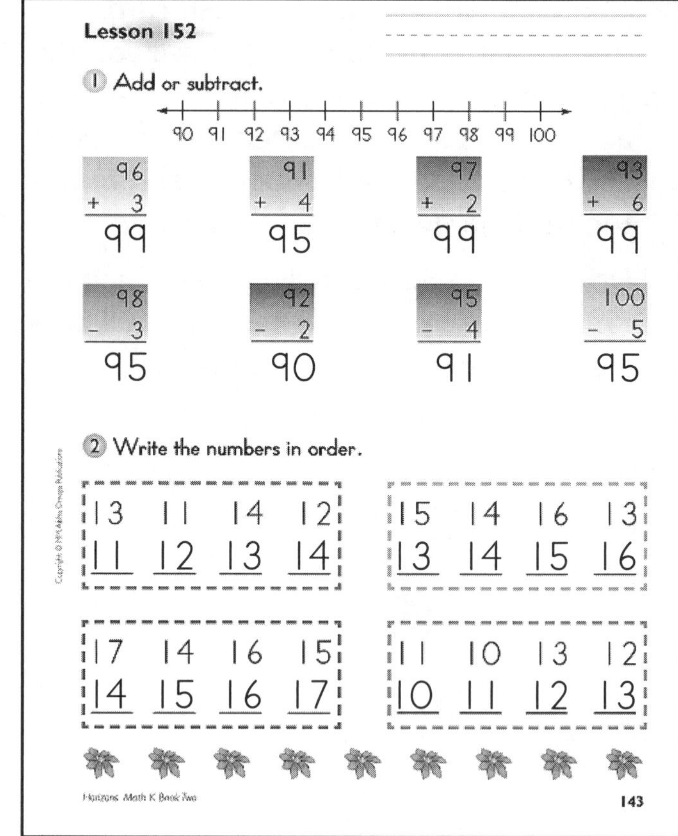

② Pick 4 consecutive number cards – 10's family. Mix the cards up and ask the student(s) to put them in number order. Do this several times with the student(s). Read the instruction for the activity. They should be able to complete the activity independently.

③ Review shapes: circle, square, star, rectangle, diamond, hexagon, triangle and octagon. Review dividing shapes into equal parts. Read the instruction for the activity. point out the "not" in the instruction.

④ Review the names of the seasons and some of the typical things that happen in them. Their pictures can be very simple like a sun, a brown leaf, a snowflake and a flower. Encourage them to do their best.

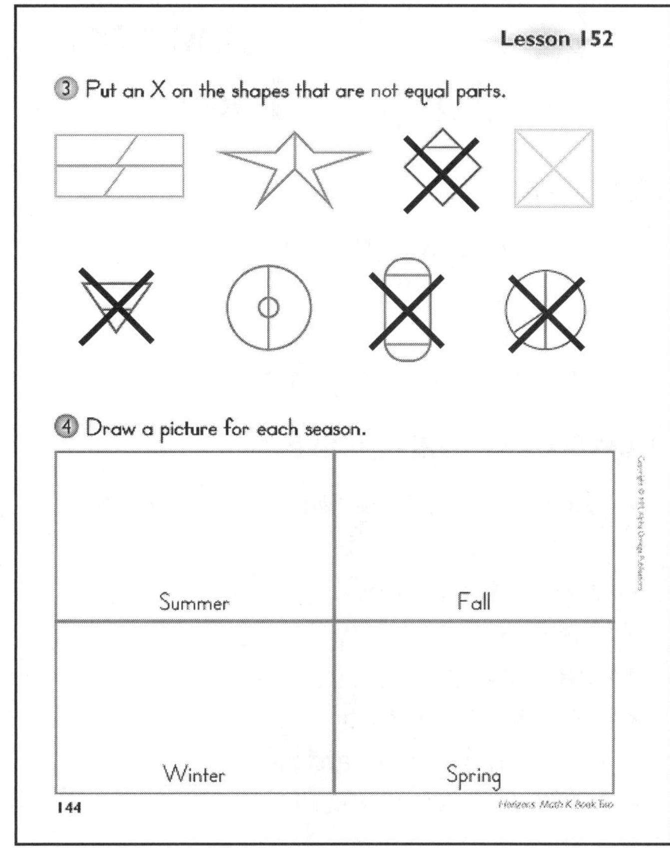

Lesson 153 - Number Between 1-100

Overview:

- Number between 1–100
- Subtract & add 90's
- 1/4, 1/2 hour
- Put numbers in order 10's

Materials and Supplies:

- Teacher's Guide & Student Workbook
- White board
- Objects for counters
- Number flash cards
- Clock models
- Next door neighbor chart
- Subtraction flash cards 1's
- Addition flash cards 1's
- Number line strips
- Number chart

Teaching Tips:

Review number between 0–100.
Review addition & subtraction 90's.
Review time – half-hour and quarter-hour.
Review number order 10's.
Drill subtraction 1's family.
Drill addition 1's family.
Review oral counting to 100.

Activities:

① Review the number between with the *next door neighbor chart*. Instead of leaving the outside houses blank, put numbers in the outside houses and ask the student(s) for the number between.

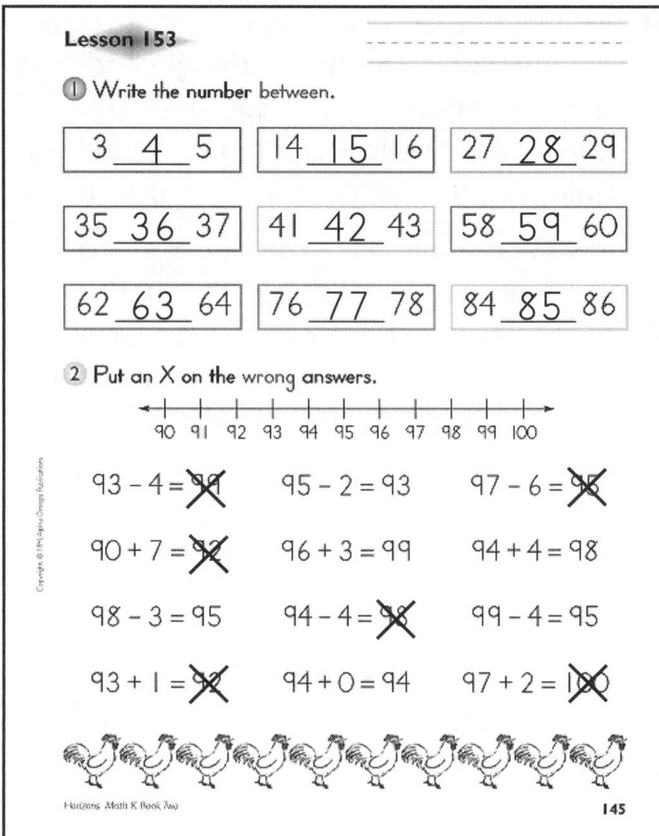
Lesson 153

① Write the number between.

3 4 5	14 15 16	27 28 29
35 36 37	41 42 43	58 59 60
62 63 64	76 77 78	84 85 86

② Put an X on the wrong answers.

93 – 4 = ~~99~~ X	95 – 2 = 93	97 – 6 = ~~95~~ X
90 + 7 = ~~92~~ X	96 + 3 = 99	94 + 4 = 98
98 – 3 = 95	94 – 4 = ~~98~~ X	99 – 4 = 95
93 + 1 = ~~92~~ X	94 + 0 = 94	97 + 2 = ~~100~~ X

Horizons Math K Book Two 145

② Put several sample problems, 90's, on the white board, some with the correct answers and others without. Cover the answer to the first problem and ask a student for the answer. After they have given an answer, check to see if it matches the answer you wrote down. Instruct them to do all of the problems in this activity in similar fashion. Review the addition and subtraction signs. Instruct the student(s) to begin the activity. Remind the class after a few minutes to check the signs.

③ Give each student a small clock model. Write several quarter-hour and half-hour times on the white board. Tell the student(s) to set the hands on their clock and check their work with your clock. Ask them which hand to place first (long or minute hand). Remind them that the minute hand tells them where to place the short (hour) hand. Let them do the activity independently.

④ Review only as is necessary for this activity.

Lesson 153

③ Draw hands to show half past.

Draw hands to show quarter past.

④ Write the numbers in order.

18 20 19 17
17 18 19 20

19 16 17 18
16 17 18 19

15 17 18 16
15 16 17 18

16 17 14 15
14 15 16 17

146 Horizons Math K Book Two

Lesson 154 - Review 1's & 10's, Addition & Subtraction

Overview:

- Review 1's & 10's, addition & subtraction
- Number between 1–100
- Bar graph
- Put numbers in order 1's & 10's

Materials and Supplies:

- Teacher's Guide & Student Workbook
- White board
- Objects for counters
- Number flash cards
- Clock models
- Next door neighbor chart
- Subtraction flash cards 1's
- Addition flash cards 1's
- Number line strips
- Number chart

Teaching Tips:

Review addition & subtraction 1's & 10's.
Review number between 0–100.
Review bar graphs.
Review number order 1's & 10's.
Drill subtraction 1's family.
Drill addition 1's family.
Review oral counting to 100.

Activities:

① The next several addition and subtraction review activities will include numbers from two number families. In this activity are 1's and 10's family problems. Review as is necessary and needed for the student(s). Most student(s) should be able to do this without additional practice.

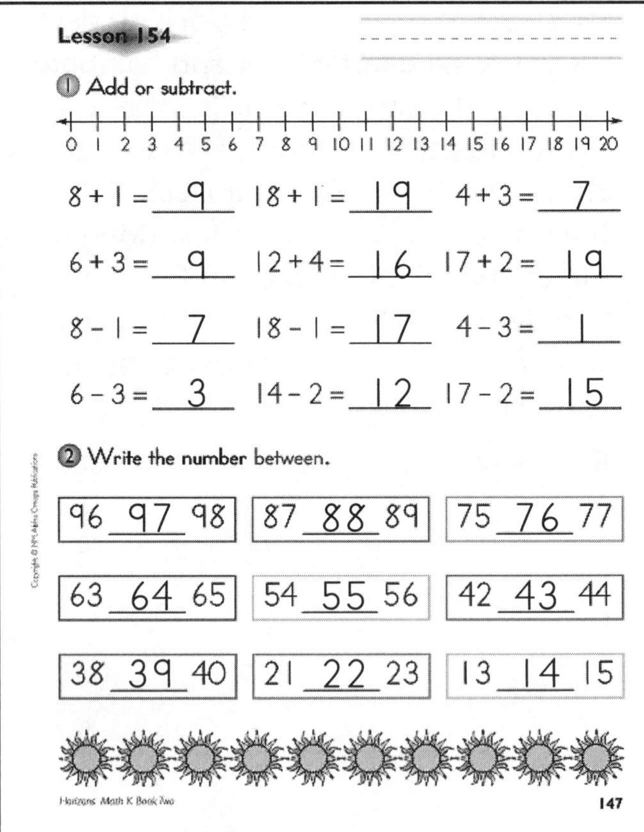
Lesson 154

① Add or subtract.

0 1 2 3 4 5 6 7 8 9 10 11 12 13 14 15 16 17 18 19 20

8 + 1 = 9	18 + 1 = 19	4 + 3 = 7
6 + 3 = 9	12 + 4 = 16	17 + 2 = 19
8 - 1 = 7	18 - 1 = 17	4 - 3 = 1
6 - 3 = 3	14 - 2 = 12	17 - 2 = 15

② Write the number between.

96 97 98	87 88 89	75 76 77
63 64 65	54 55 56	42 43 44
38 39 40	21 22 23	13 14 15

Horizons Math K Book Two 147

② Review the number between with the *next door neighbor chart*. Instead of leaving the outside houses blank, put numbers in the outside houses and ask the student(s) for the number between. Review numbers 0–100.

③ Review bar graphs. Have a student read each of the questions in the activity. Instruct the student(s) to complete the activity independently.

④ Review only as is necessary for this activity.

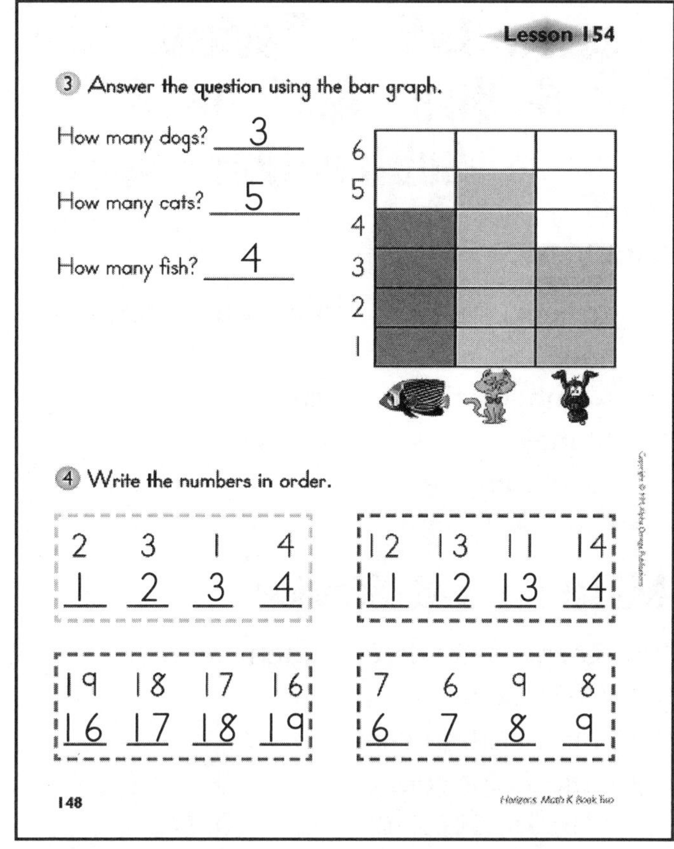

Lesson 154

③ Answer the question using the bar graph.

How many dogs? 3

How many cats? 5

How many fish? 4

④ Write the numbers in order.

2	3	1	4
1	2	3	4

12	13	11	14
11	12	13	14

19	18	17	16
16	17	18	19

7	6	9	8
6	7	8	9

148 Horizons Math K Book Two

Lesson 155 - Review 20's & 30's, Addition & Subtraction

Overview:

- Review 20's & 30's, addition & subtraction
- Number before and after 20's
- Money
- Lesser number
- Greater number

Materials and Supplies:

- Teacher's Guide & Student Workbook
- White board
- Number flash cards
- Objects for counters
- \$10, \$5, \$1, 25¢, 10¢, 5¢ & 1¢
- Next door neighbor chart
- Subtraction flash cards 1's
- Addition flash cards 1's
- Number line strips
- Number chart

Teaching Tips:

Review addition & subtraction 20's & 30's.
Review number before and after 20's.
Review \$10, \$5, \$1, 25¢, 10¢, 5¢ and 1¢.
Review greater and smaller number.
Drill subtraction 1's family.
Drill addition 1's family.
Review oral counting to 100.

Activities:

① This activity includes numbers from two number families. In this activity are there are 20's and 30's family problems. Review as is necessary and needed for the student(s). Most student(s) should be able to do this without additional practice.

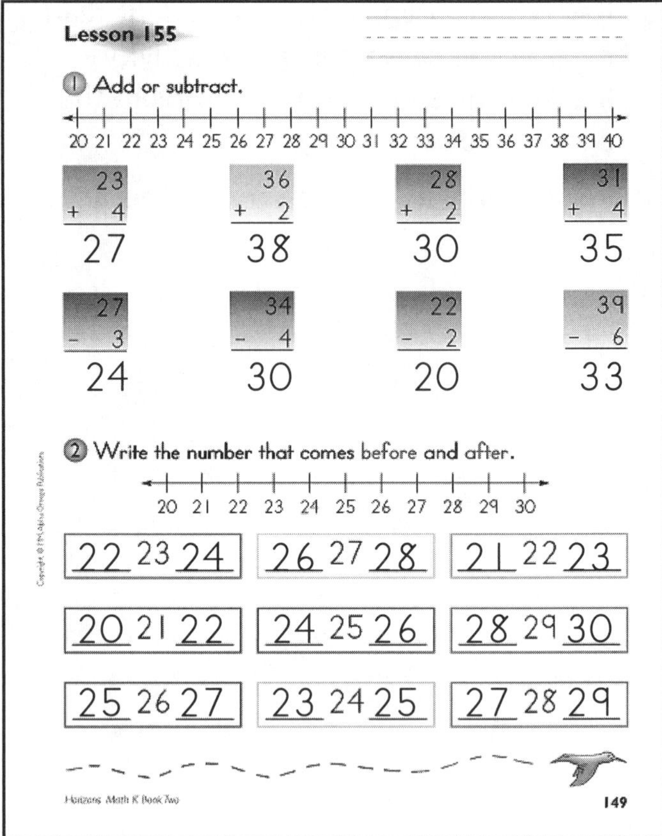

② Review the number before and after with the *next door neighbor chart*. Put a number in the center house and ask for the next door neighbors. Review numbers 0–100.

③ Review counting by 5's 10's & 25's. Read the instruction for the activity and have the student(s) complete it.

④ Choose two number flash cards from the 1's family. Ask the student(s) to tell you the number that is less (smaller). Do this several times. Review the instruction for the activity.

⑤ Choose two number flash cards from the 1's family. Ask the student(s) to tell you the number that is greater. Do this several times. Review the instruction for the activity.

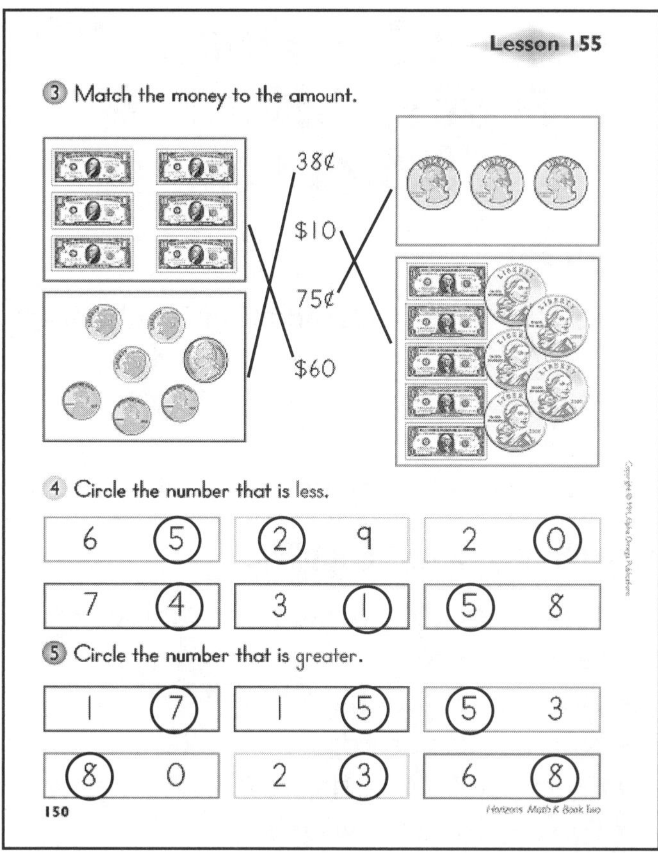

Lesson 156 - Review 40's & 50's, Addition & Subtraction

Overview:

- Review 40's & 50's, addition & subtraction
- Count by 10's
- Geometric solids
- Place value 10's & 1's

Materials and Supplies:

- Teacher's Guide & Student Workbook
- White board
- Objects for counters
- Number flash cards
- Count by 10's flash cards
- Sphere, cone & cylinder
- Place value chart
- Base 10 blocks
- Subtraction flash cards 1's
- Addition flash cards 1's
- Number line strips
- Number chart

Teaching Tips:

Review addition & subtraction 40's & 50's.
Review counting by 10's.
Review sphere, cone & cylinder.
Review place value.
Drill subtraction 1's family.
Drill addition 1's family.
Review oral counting to 100.

Activities:

① This activity includes numbers from two number families. In this activity there are 40's and 50's family problems. Review as is necessary and needed for the student(s). Most student(s) should be able to do this without additional practice.

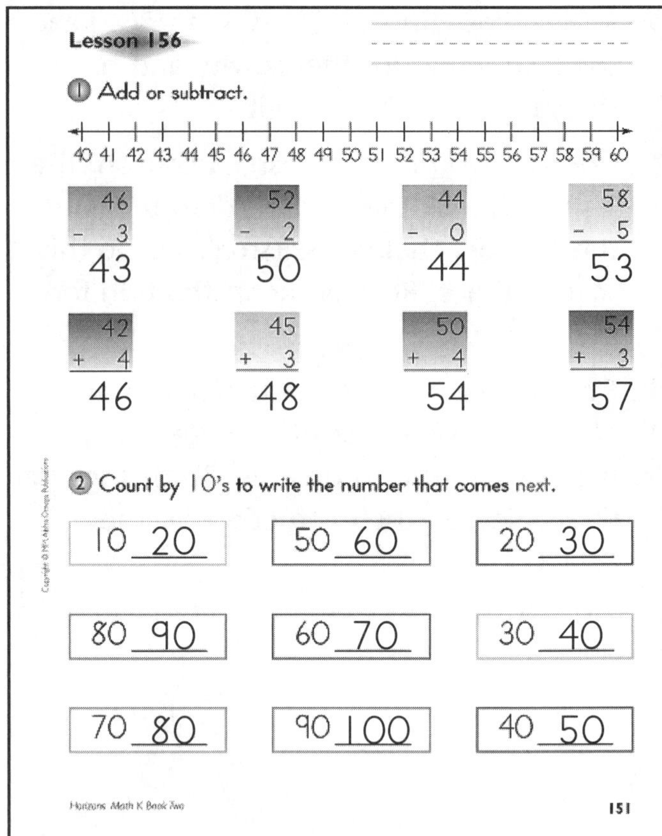

Lesson 156

① Add or subtract.

40 41 42 43 44 45 46 47 48 49 50 51 52 53 54 55 56 57 58 59 60

46 − 3 = 43	52 − 2 = 50	44 − 0 = 44	58 − 5 = 53
42 + 4 = 46	45 + 3 = 48	50 + 4 = 54	54 + 3 = 57

② Count by 10's to write the number that comes next.

10 20	50 60	20 30
80 90	60 70	30 40
70 80	90 100	40 50

Horizons Math K Book Two 151

② Review counting by 10's with flash cards. Randomly choose a 10's flash card and ask a student to give you the next 10. Do this several times before instructing the student(s) to complete the activity.

③ Review geometric solids. Instruct the students to match the shape on the left to the ones on the right.

④ Review place value with 10's and 1's blocks. Do several combinations before having the student(s) complete the activity.

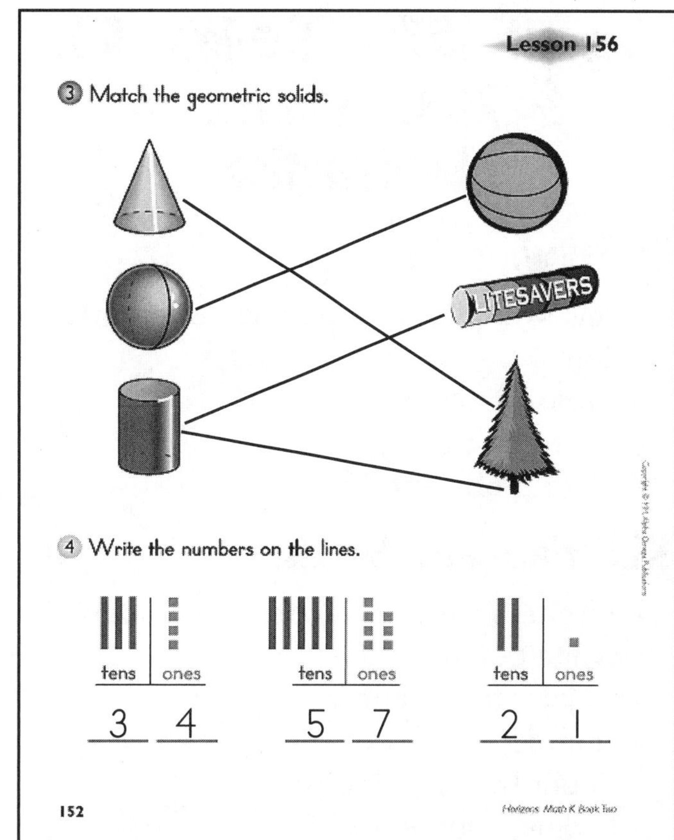

Lesson 157 - Review 60's & 70's, Addition & Subtraction

Overview:

- Review 60's & 70's, addition & subtraction
- Ordinal numbers
- Count by 5's
- Word problems

Materials and Supplies:

- Teacher's Guide & Student Workbook
- White board
- Objects for counters
- Number flash cards
- Count by 5's flash cards
- Ordinal number flash cards
- Subtraction flash cards 1's
- Addition flash cards 1's
- Number line strips
- Number chart

Teaching Tips:

Review addition & subtraction 60's & 70's.
Review ordinal numbers.
Review counting by 5's.
Review word problems – addition.
Drill subtraction 1's family.
Drill addition 1's family.
Review oral counting to 100.

Activities:

① This activity includes numbers from two number families. In this activity there are 60's and 70's family problems. Review as is necessary and needed for the student(s). Most student(s) should be able to do this without additional practice.

Lesson 157

① Add or subtract.

60 61 62 63 64 65 66 67 68 69 70 71 72 73 74 75 76 77 78 79 80

70 + 2 = 72	76 + 3 = 79	60 + 6 = 66
67 + 2 = 69	74 + 5 = 79	61 + 4 = 65
69 + 0 = 69	63 + 4 = 67	72 + 5 = 77
75 − 5 = 70	66 − 3 = 63	69 − 3 = 66
77 − 2 = 75	69 − 5 = 64	72 − 2 = 70
64 − 3 = 61	73 − 3 = 70	65 − 4 = 61

② Circle the third teddy bear. Put an X on the sixth teddy bear. Put a box around the ninth teddy bear.

Horizons Math K Book Two 153

② Review the ordinal numbers. Read the instructions for the activity and have the student(s) mark their answers.

③ Review counting by 5's with flash cards. Randomly choose a 5's flash card and ask a student to give you the next 5. Do this several times before instructing the student(s) to complete the activity.

④ Review what makes an addition word problem. Read the first problem to the class. Ask what the key word is (altogether). Visualize the problem using counting chips. Have the student(s) tell you the addition fact that supports the answer. Allow the student(s) to write the answer on their own. Then discuss the results with them. Read the remaining problem for the student(s) so they can complete the activity.

Lesson 157

③ Count by 5's to write the number after.

5 10	25 30	40 45
70 75	10 15	55 60
35 40	90 95	75 80
15 20	50 55	20 25

④ John has 5 balls. Sal gave him 4 more balls. How many balls does John have altogether? 9

Joe has 3 pears. Dick has 5 pears. How many pears do the boys have altogether? 8

154 Horizons Math K Book Two

Lesson 158 - Review 80's & 90's, Addition & Subtraction

Overview:

- Review 80's & 90's, addition & subtraction
- Tally marks
- Count quart, gallon, cup & liter
- Count by 2's

Material and Supplies:

- Teacher's Guide & Student Workbook
- White board
- Objects for counters
- Number flash cards
- Count by 2's flash cards
- Volume containers
- Tally marks flash cards
- Subtraction flash cards 1's
- Addition flash cards 1's
- Number line strips
- Number chart

Teaching Tips:

Review addition & subtraction 80's & 90's.
Review tally marks.
Review volume containers.
Review counting by 2's.
Drill subtraction 1's family.
Drill addition 1's family.
Review oral counting to 100.

Activities:

① This activity includes numbers from two number families. In this activity there are 80's and 90's family problems. Review as is necessary and needed for the student(s). Most student(s) should be able to do this without additional practice.

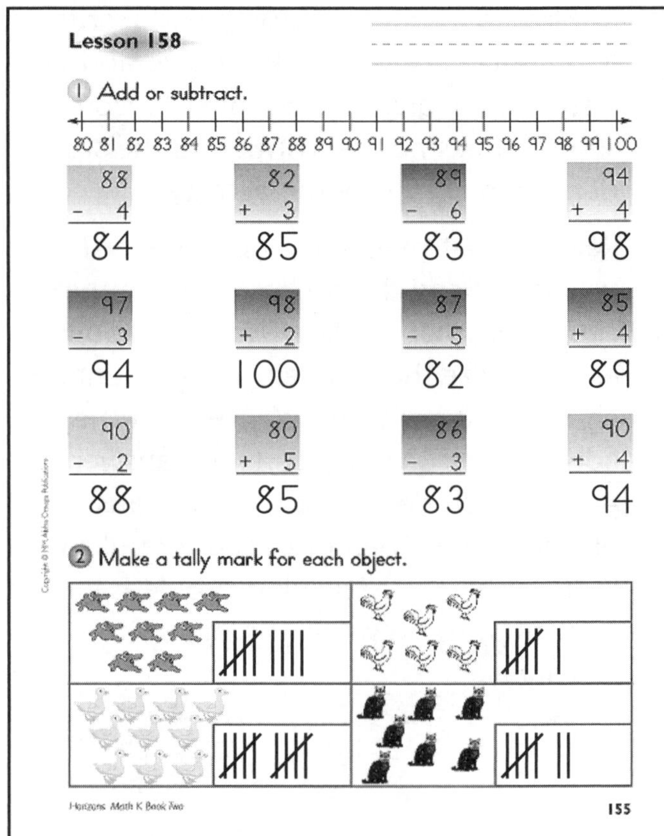

② Review tally marks and how to make them. Review how to do a 5 and a 10 with tally marks, also 6–9. Instruct the student(s) to put their tally marks for each group in the box by the set.

③ Review the names of the volume containers. Let the student(s) do this activity independently.

④ Review counting by 2's with flash cards. Randomly choose a 2's flash card and ask a student to give you the next 2. Do this several times before instructing the student(s) to complete the activity.

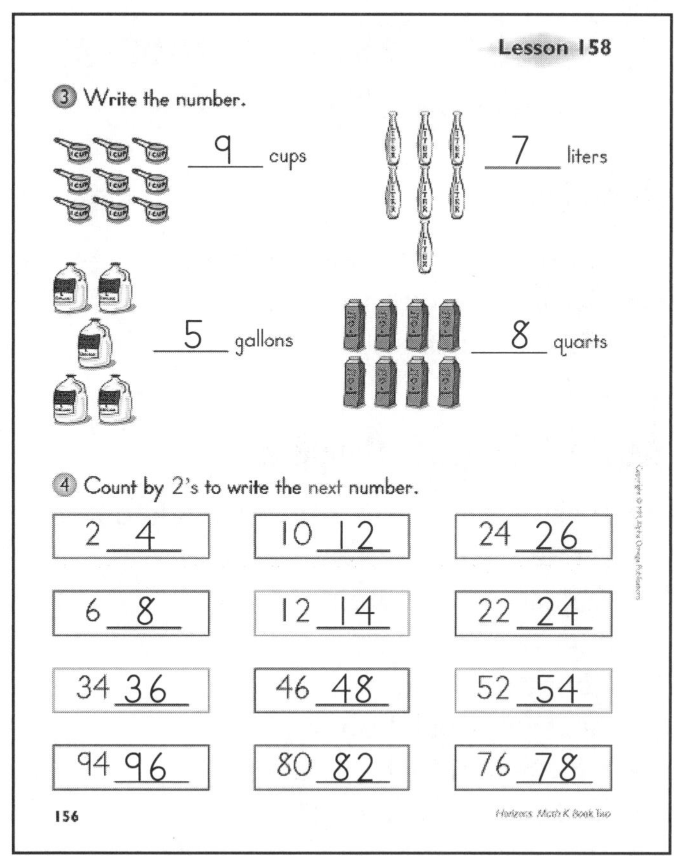

Lesson 159 - Numbers Order 1's & 10's

Overview:

- Put numbers in order 1's & 10's
- Number between 1–100
- Word problems
- Count by 3's

Materials and Supplies:

- Teacher's Guide & Student Workbook
- White board
- Objects for counters
- Number flash cards
- Count by 3's flash cards
- Next door neighbor chart
- Subtraction flash cards 1's
- Addition flash cards 1's
- Number line strips
- Number chart

Teaching Tips:

Review number order 1's & 10's.
Review number between 0–100.
Review word problems – subtraction.
Review counting by 3's.
Drill subtraction 1's family.
Drill addition 1's family.
Review oral counting to 100.

Activities:

① Pick four consecutive number cards – 1's & 10's families. Mix the cards up and ask the student(s) to put them in number order. Do this several times with the student(s). Read the instruction for the activity. They should be able to complete the activity independently.

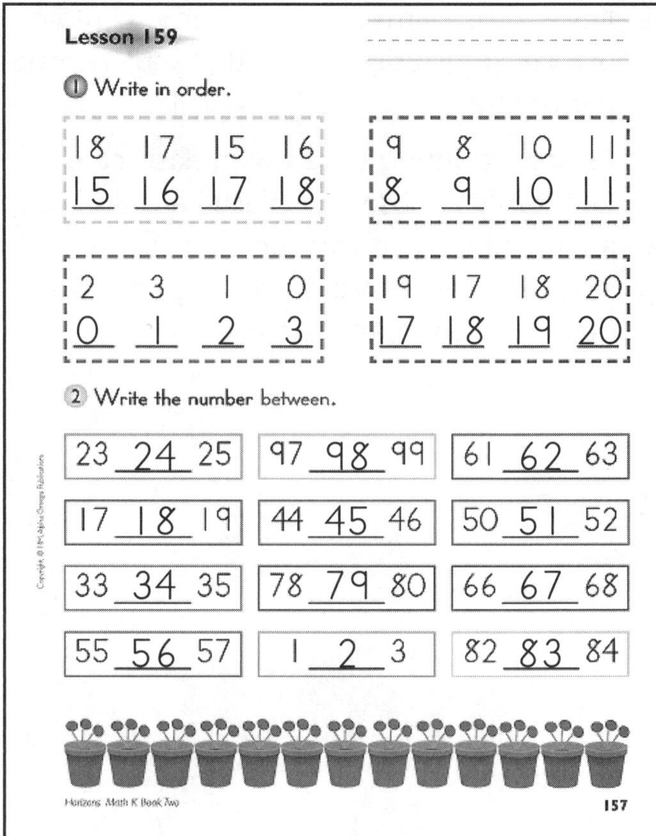
Lesson 159

① Write in order.

18 17 15 16
15 16 17 18

9 8 10 11
8 9 10 11

2 3 1 0
0 1 2 3

19 17 18 20
17 18 19 20

② Write the number between.

23 24 25	97 98 99	61 62 63
17 18 19	44 45 46	50 51 52
33 34 35	78 79 80	66 67 68
55 56 57	1 2 3	82 83 84

Horizons Math K Book Two 157

② Review the number between with the *next door neighbor chart*. Instead of leaving the outside houses blank put numbers in the outside houses and ask the student(s) for the number between. Review numbers 0–100.

③ Read the first word problem to the class. Ask the student(s) to tell you the key word (left). Visualize the problem using counters if necessary. Have the student(s) tell you the subtraction fact. Allow the student(s) to write the subtraction fact and to write the answer on their own, then discuss the results with them. Complete the activity by reading the remaining question to the student(s).

④ Review counting by 3's with flash cards. Randomly choose a 3's flash card and ask a student to give you the next 3. Do this several times before instructing the student(s) to complete the activity.

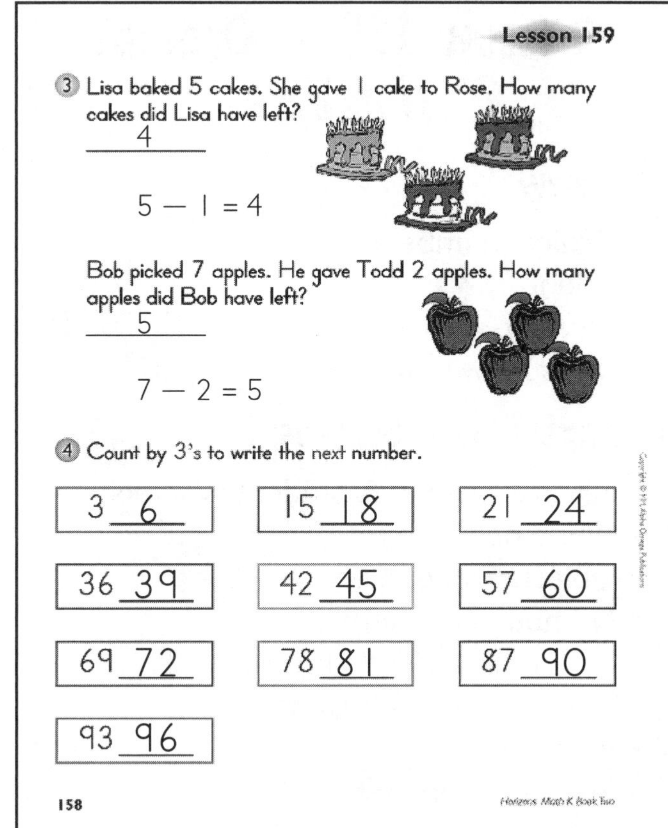

Lesson 159

③ Lisa baked 5 cakes. She gave 1 cake to Rose. How many cakes did Lisa have left?

4

5 − 1 = 4

Bob picked 7 apples. He gave Todd 2 apples. How many apples did Bob have left?

5

7 − 2 = 5

④ Count by 3's to write the next number.

3 6	15 18	21 24
36 39	42 45	57 60
69 72	78 81	87 90
93 96		

158 Horizons Math K Book Two

Lesson 160 - Ordinal Numbers

Overview:

- Ordinal numbers
- Count by 4's
- Measure with centimeter
- Measure with inches

Material and Supplies:

- Teacher's Guide & Student Workbook
- White board
- Objects for counters
- Number flash cards
- Ordinal number flash cards
- Count by 4's flash cards
- Ruler – inches
- Ruler – centimeters
- Subtraction flash cards 1's
- Addition flash cards 1's
- Number line strips
- Number chart

Teaching Tips:

Review ordinal numbers.
Review counting by 4's.
Review ruler – centimeters.
Review ruler – inches.
Drill subtraction 1's family.
Drill addition 1's family.
Review oral counting to 100.

Activities:

① Discuss the days of creation. Instruct the student(s) to write the number of the day under the picture. After all 7 days have been covered, instruct the student(s) to match the day to the ordinal number.

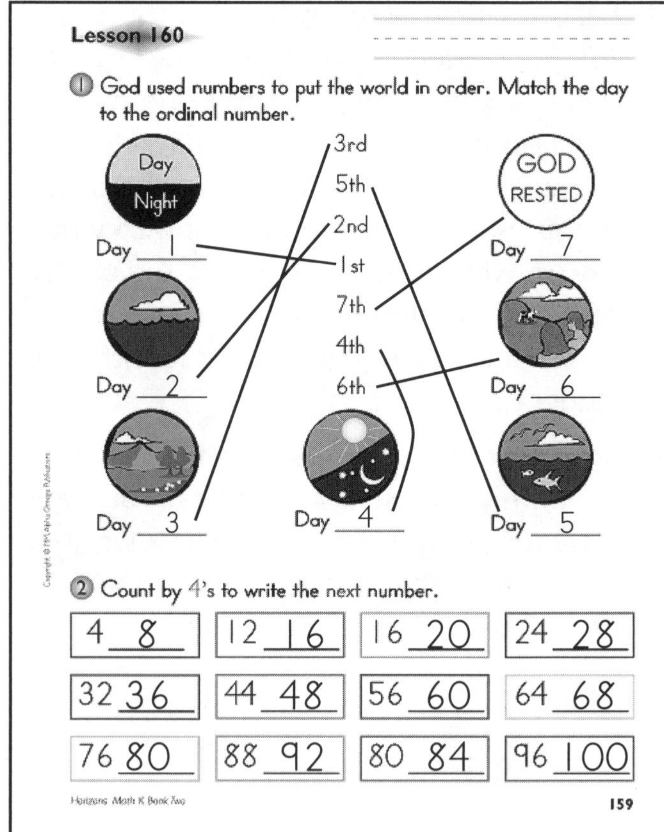

Lesson 160

① God used numbers to put the world in order. Match the day to the ordinal number.

Day / Night — Day 1
Day 2
Day 3
Day 4
Day 5
Day 6
GOD RESTED — Day 7

3rd
5th
2nd
1st
7th
4th
6th

② Count by 4's to write the next number.

4 8	12 16	16 20	24 28
32 36	44 48	56 60	64 68
76 80	88 92	80 84	96 100

Horizons Math K Book Two — 159

② Review counting by 4's with flash cards. Randomly choose a 4's flash card and ask a student to give you the next 4. Do this several times before instructing the student(s) to complete the activity.

③ Review the centimeter ruler. Point out some examples of where the student(s) might commonly see metric numbers: tools, packaging, tires, etc. Instruct them to place their finger at the end of each bar in this activity and trace up to the number on the ruler. These are measurements, so the number is labeled with the units, centimeters.

④ Review the inch ruler. Point out some examples of where the student(s) might commonly see English numbers. Lumber, road signs, speedometers, clothing, etc. Instruct them to place their finger at the end of each bar in this activity and trace up to the number on the ruler. These are measurements, so the number is labeled with the units, inches.

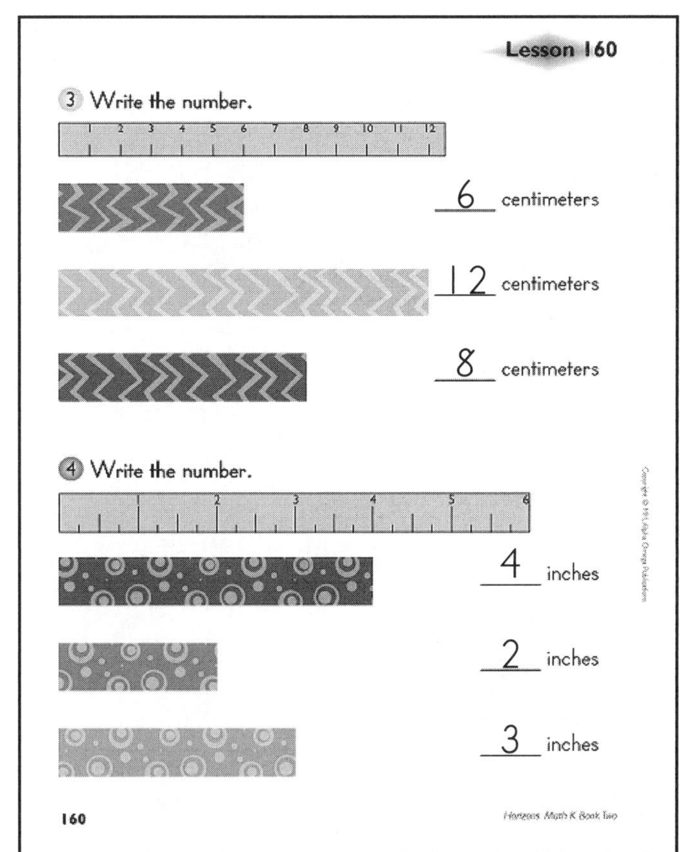

Worksheets

Worksheet 1

This number chart counts from 0 to 100.

0	1	2	3	4	5	6	7	8	9
10	11	12	13	14	15	16	17	18	19
20	21	22	23	24	25	26	27	28	29
30	31	32	33	34	35	36	37	38	39
40	41	42	43	44	45	46	47	48	49
50	51	52	53	54	55	56	57	58	59
60	61	62	63	64	65	66	67	68	69
70	71	72	73	74	75	76	77	78	79
80	81	82	83	84	85	86	87	88	89
90	91	92	93	94	95	96	97	98	99
100									

Worksheet 2

Practice writing the number 1.

Worksheet 3

Practice writing the number 2.

2 2 2 2 2 2 2 2

2 2 2 2 2 2 2

2 2 2 2 2 2

2 2 2 2 2

2 2 2 2

2 2 2

2 2

2

Worksheet 4

Practice writing the number 3.

Worksheet 5

Practice writing the number 4.

4 4 4 4 4 4 4 4

4 4 4 4 4 4 4

4 4 4 4 4 4

4 4 4 4 4

4 4 4 4

4 4 4

4 4

4

Worksheet 6

Practice writing the number 5.

5 5 5 5 5 5 5 5

5 5 5 5 5 5 5

5 5 5 5 5 5

5 5 5 5 5

5 5 5 5

5 5 5

5 5

5

Worksheet 7

Practice writing the number 6.

Worksheet 8

Practice writing the number 7.

Worksheet 9

Practice writing the number 8.

8 8 8 8 8 8 8 8

8 8 8 8 8 8 8

8 8 8 8 8 8

8 8 8 8 8

8 8 8 8

8 8 8

8 8

8

Worksheet 10

Practice writing the number 9.

Worksheet 11

Practice writing the number 0.

Worksheet 12

Write a row of each of these numbers.

0

1

2

3

4

5

6

7

8

9

Worksheet

Write a row of each of these numbers.

0

1

2

3

4

5

6

7

8

9

Worksheet

Write a row of each of these numbers.

20

21

22

23

24

25

26

27

28

29

Worksheet 15

Write a row of each of these numbers.

30

31

32

33

34

35

36

37

38

39

Worksheet 16

Write a row of each of these numbers.

40

41

42

43

44

45

46

47

48

49

Worksheet 17

Write a row of each of these numbers.

50

51

52

53

54

55

56

57

58

59

Worksheet 18

Write a row of each of these numbers.

60

61

62

63

64

65

66

67

68

69

Worksheet 19

Write a row of each of these numbers.

70

71

72

73

74

75

76

77

78

79

Worksheet 20

Write a row of each of these numbers.

80

81

82

83

84

85

86

87

88

89

Worksheet 21

Write a row of each of these numbers.

90

91

92

93

94

95

96

97

98

99

Worksheet 22

Circle the number your teacher reads.

1.

3.

2.

4.

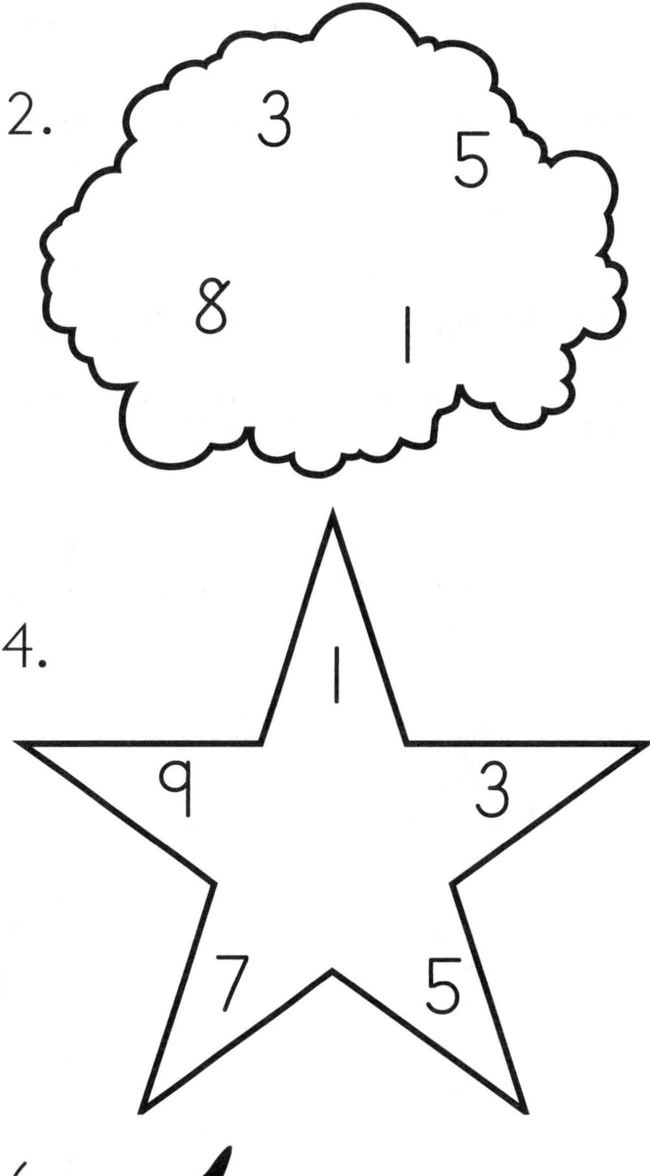

5.

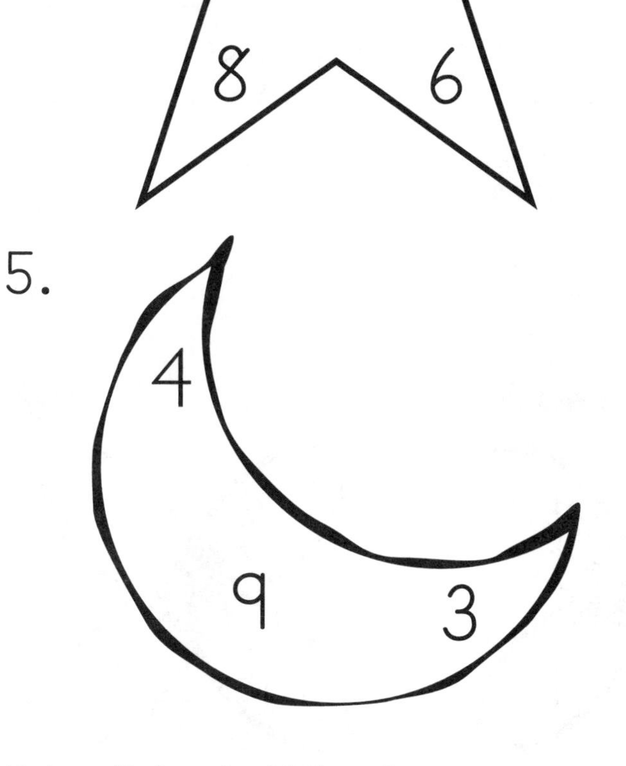

6.

Worksheet 23

① Circle the number your teacher reads.

② Write the number that comes after.

14 ____ 18 ____ 13 ____

16 ____ 12 ____ 11 ____

19 ____ 17 ____ 15 ____

10 ____

③ Circle the number your teacher reads.

Worksheet 24

Circle the number your teacher reads.

1.

2.

3.

4.

5.

6.

Worksheet 25

① Circle the number your teacher reads.

② Write the number that comes after.

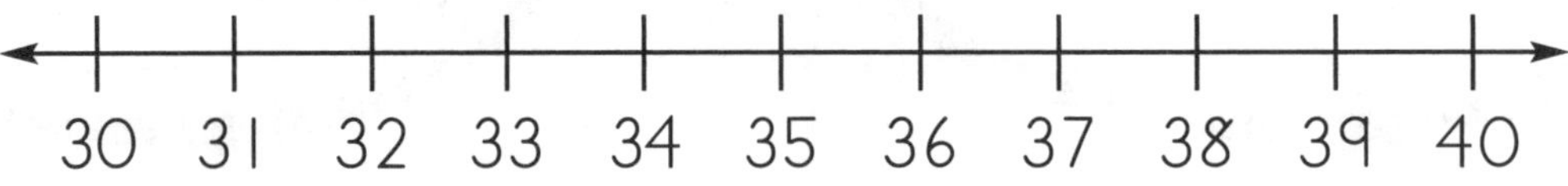

35 ____ 37 ____ 34 ____

33 ____ 30 ____ 32 ____

38 ____ 39 ____ 31 ____

36 ____

③ Circle the number your teacher reads.

Worksheet 26

① Write the number that comes after.

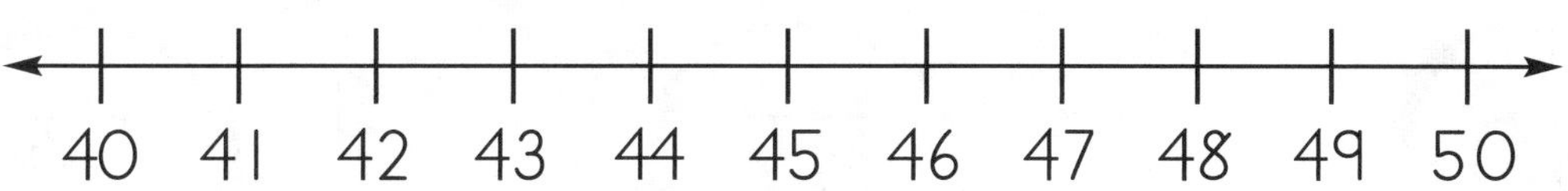

42 ____ 46 ____ 44 ____

45 ____ 43 ____ 48 ____

41 ____ 49 ____ 49 ____

47 ____

② Circle the number your teacher reads.

1.

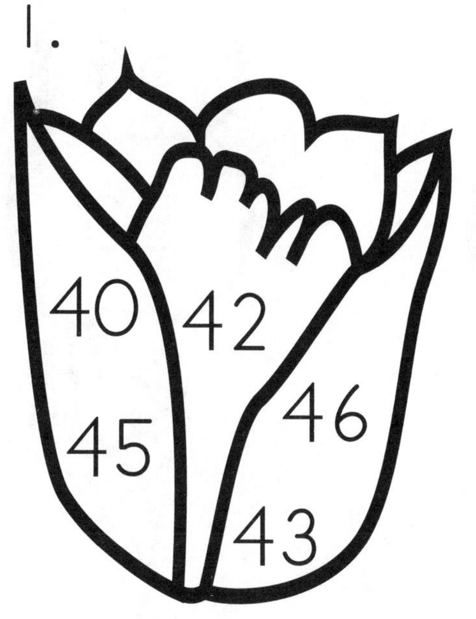

2.

41 44
49 42
48

3.

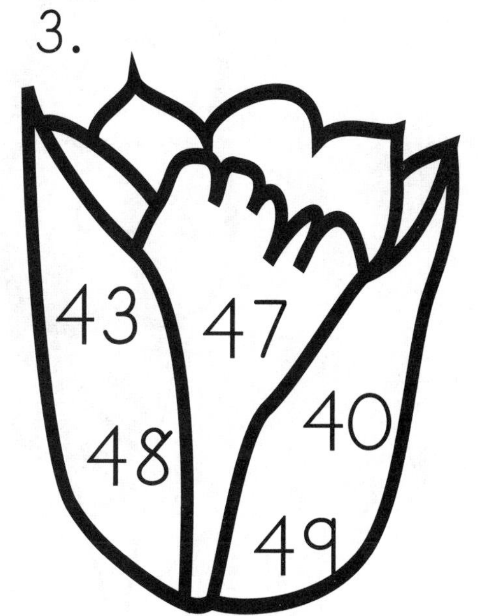

Worksheet 27

Circle the number your teacher reads.

1.

50
58
51

2.

57
59
52

3.

54
56
55

4.

50
53

59

5.

52
57
58

6.

57
54
50

Worksheet 28

Circle the number your teacher reads.

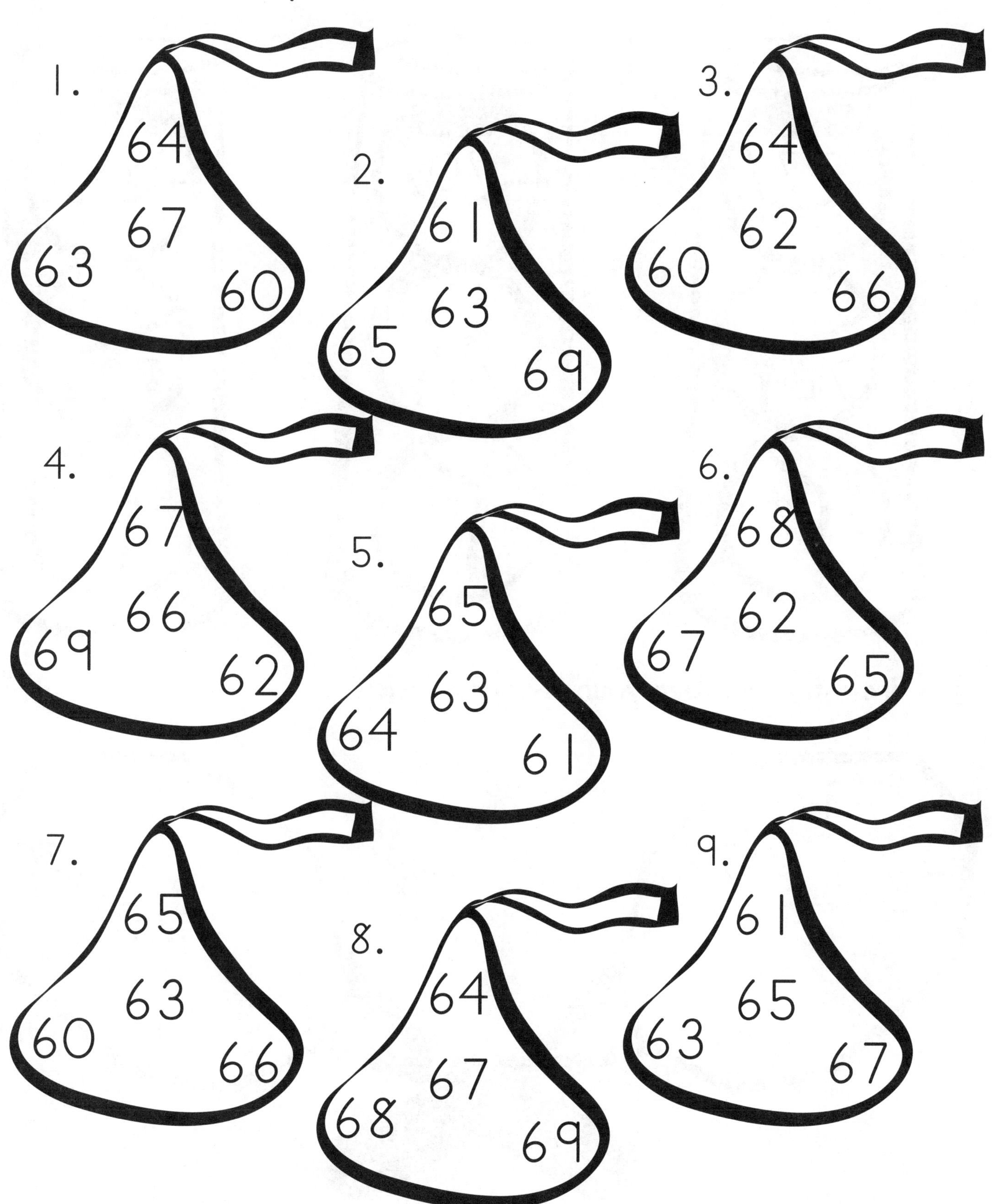

Worksheet 29

① Circle the number your teacher reads.

1.

2.

3.

② Circle the number your teacher reads.

1. 2.

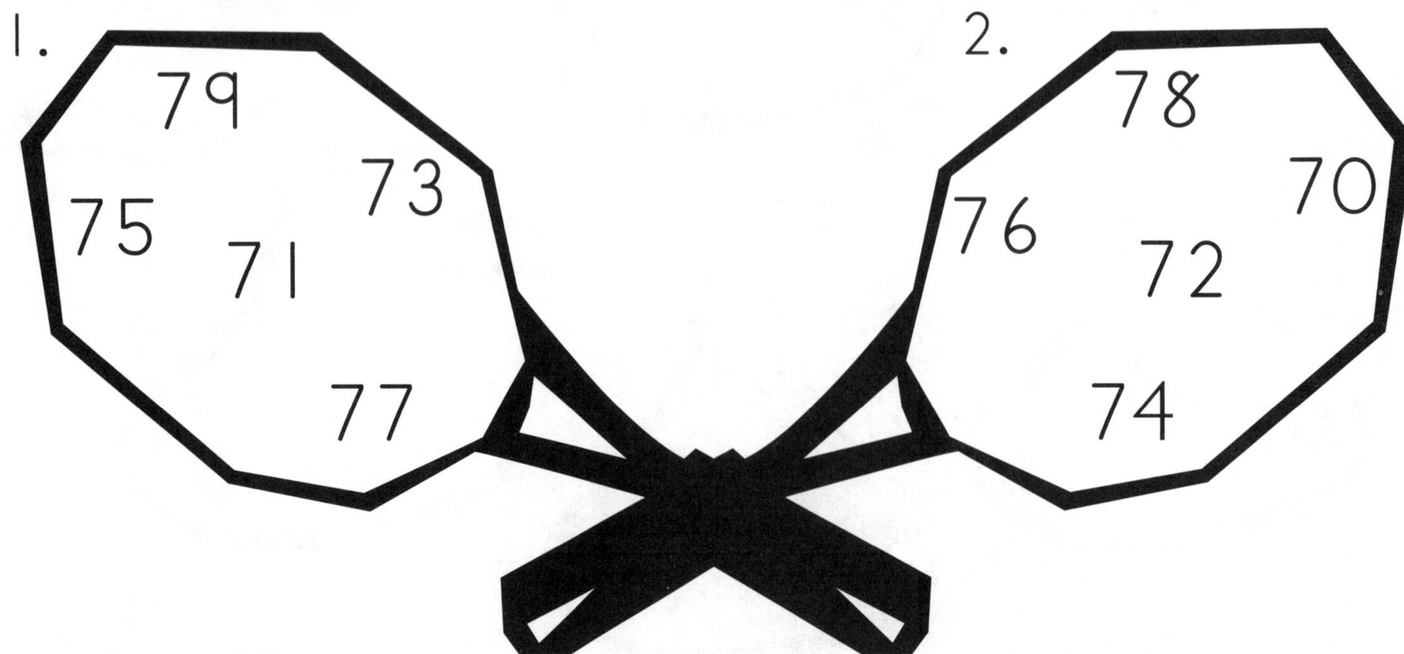

Worksheet 30

① Write the number that comes after.

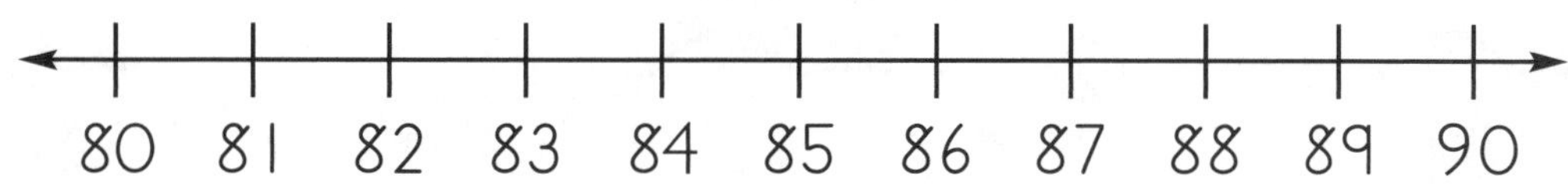

86 ____ 81 ____ 84 ____

80 ____ 85 ____ 87 ____

82 ____ 89 ____ 88 ____

83 ____

② Circle the number your teacher reads.

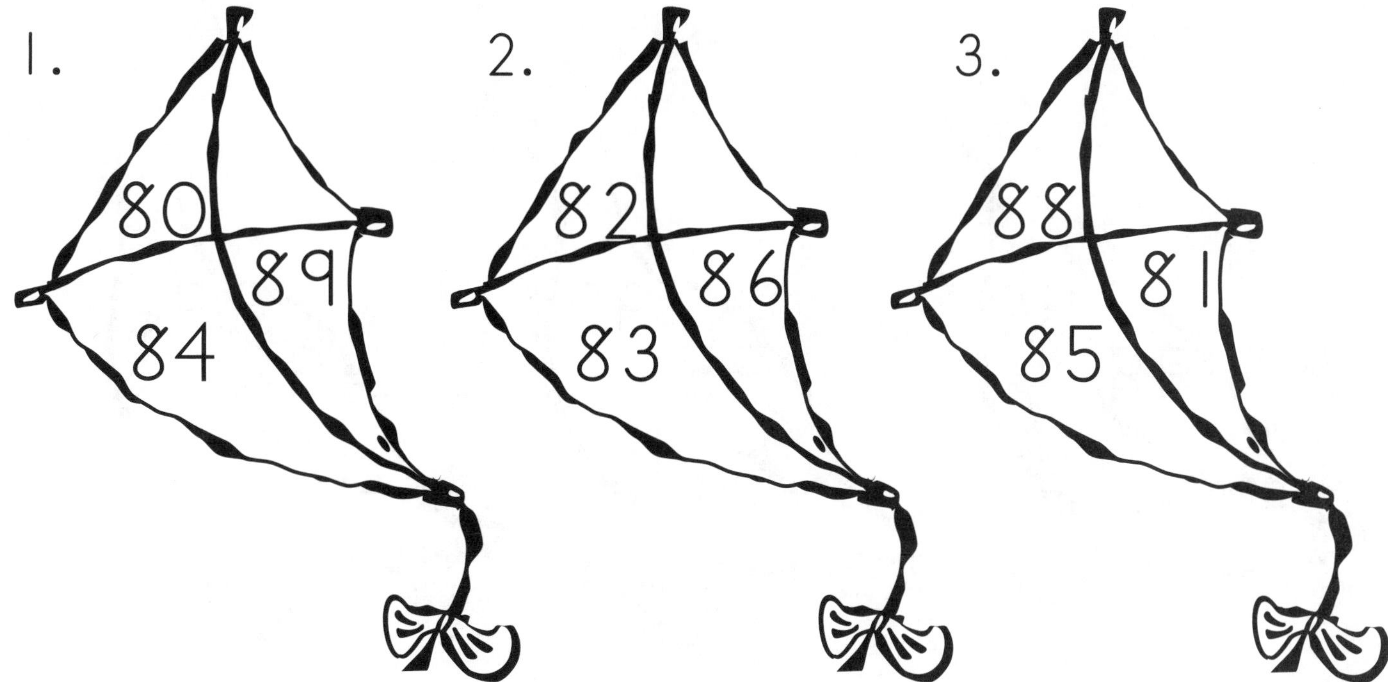

Worksheet 31

Circle the number your teacher reads.

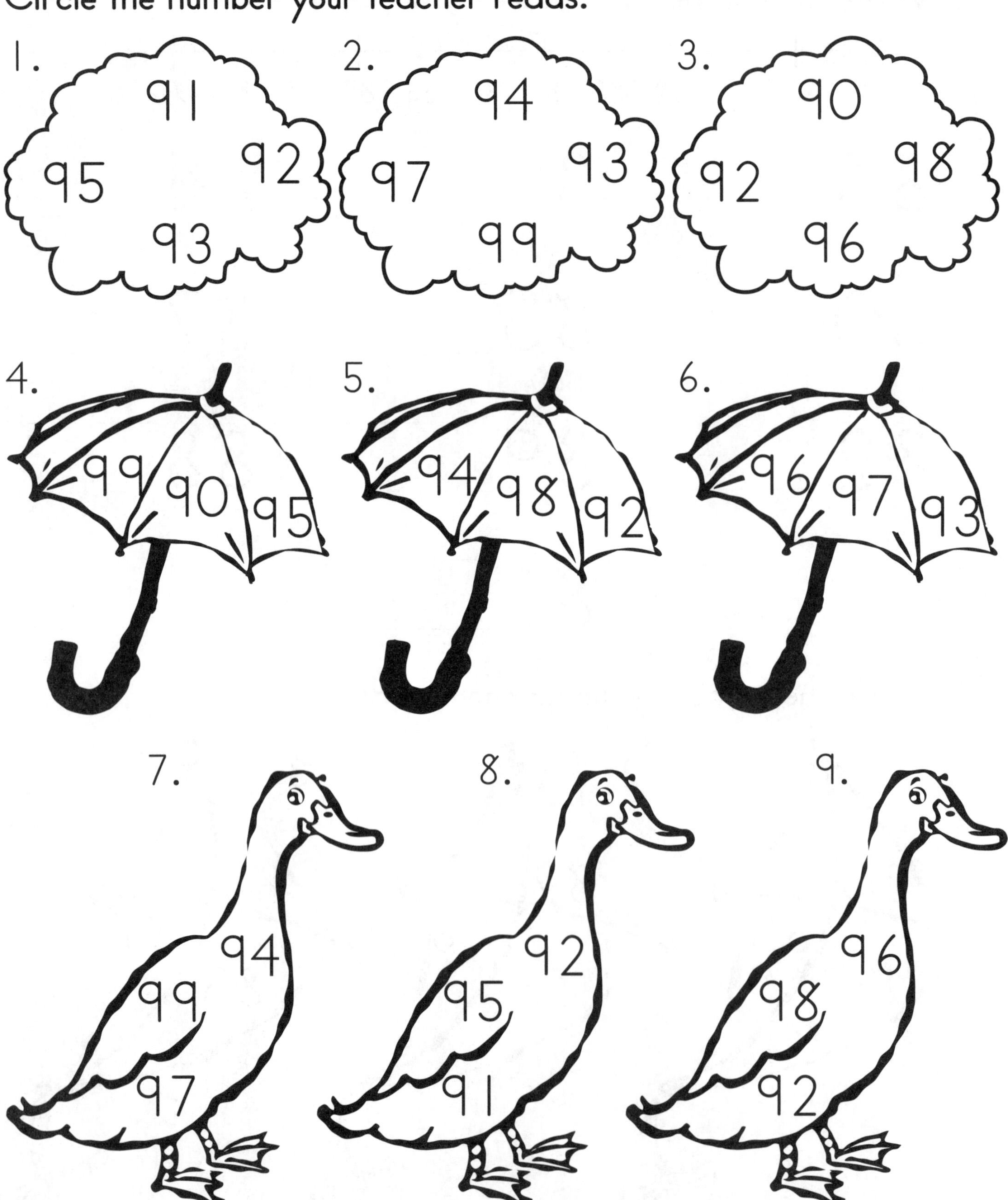

Worksheet 32

Count by 2's and write the even numbers.

1		3		5		7		9	
11		13		15		17		19	
21		23		25		27		29	
31		33		35		37		39	
41		43		45		47		49	
51		53		55		57		59	
61		63		65		67		69	
71		73		75		77		79	
81		83		85		87		89	
91		93		95		97		99	

Worksheet 33

Write the odd numbers.

	2		4		6		8		10
	12		14		16		18		20
	22		24		26		28		30
	32		34		36		38		40
	42		44		46		48		50
	52		54		56		58		60
	62		64		66		68		70
	72		74		76		78		80
	82		84		86		88		90
	92		94		96		98		100

Worksheet 34

Count by 3's.

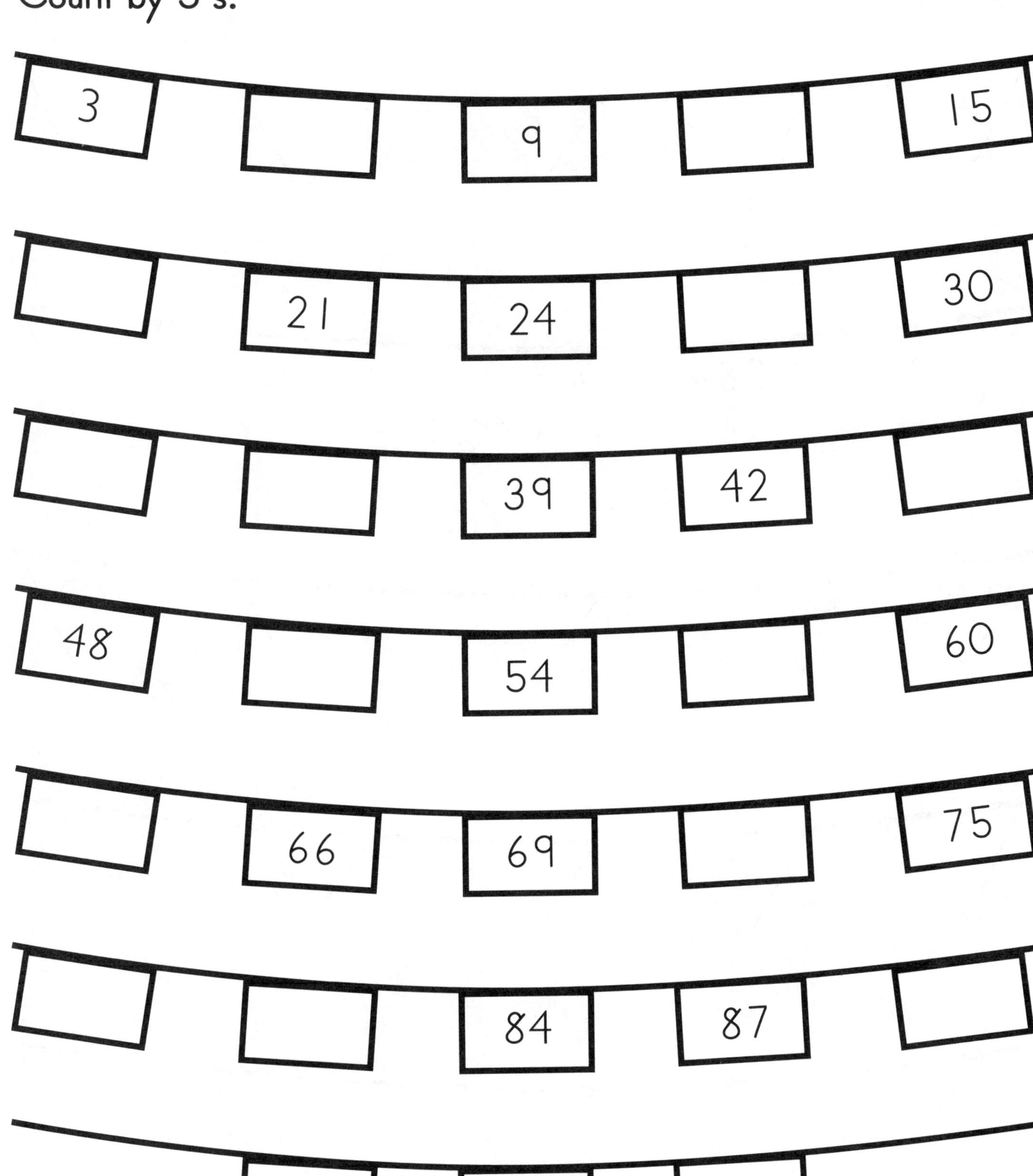

Worksheet 35

Count by 4's.

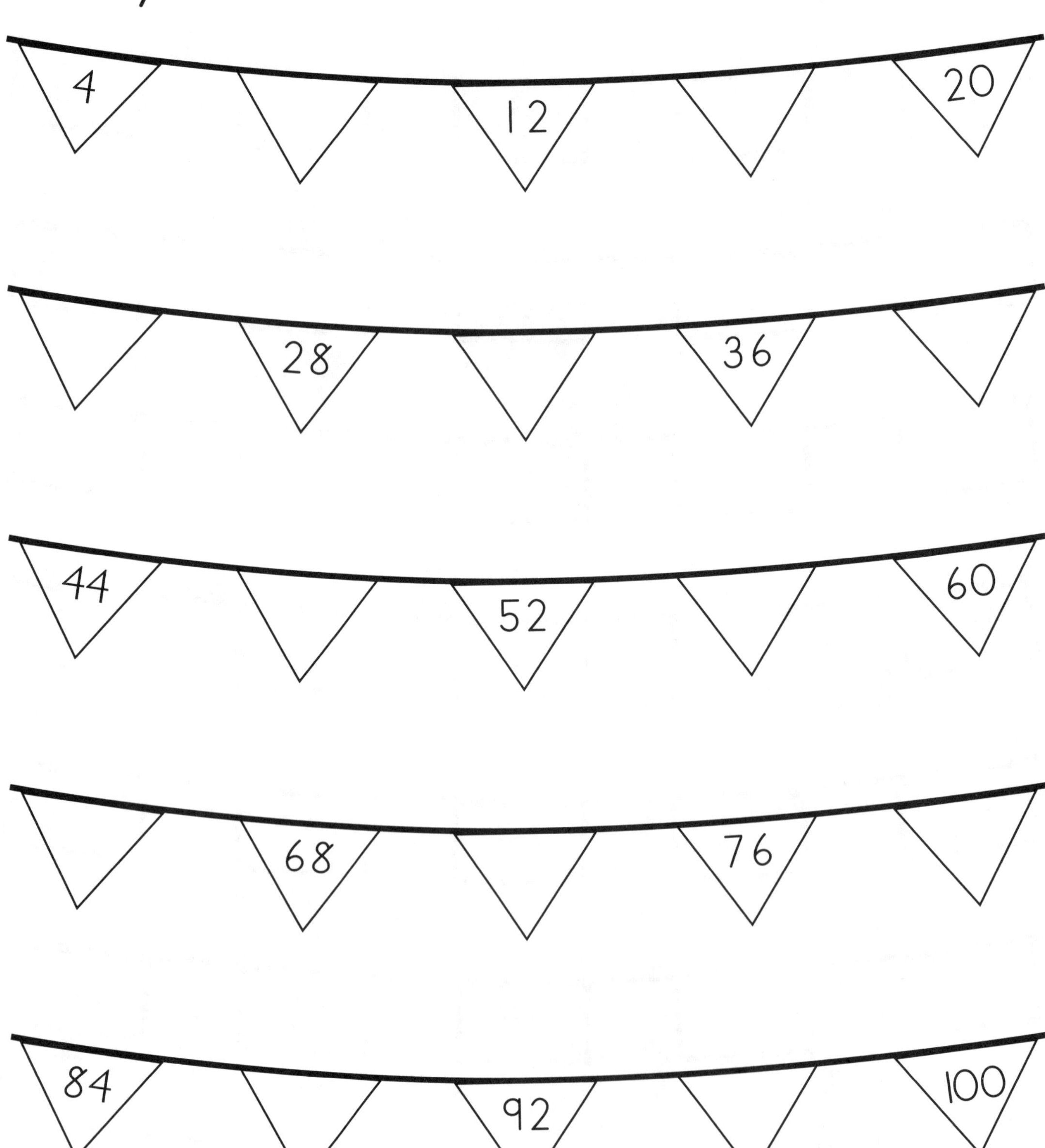

Worksheet 36

Count by 5's and write the missing number.

5 _____	60 _____	75 _____
10 _____	45 _____	80 _____
15 _____	50 _____	35 _____
90 _____	30 _____	20 _____
25 _____	85 _____	70 _____
55 _____	65 _____	40 _____
	95 _____	

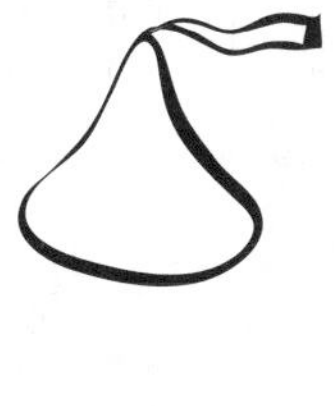

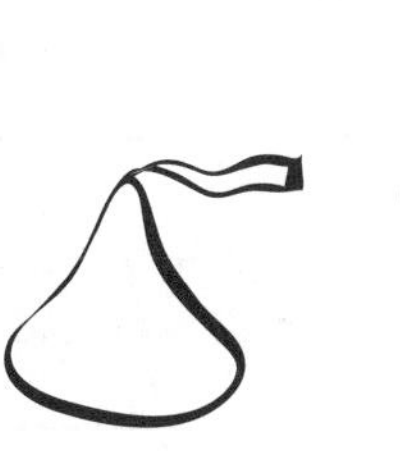

Worksheet 37

Count by 10's and fill in the missing numbers.

0	1	2	3	4	5	6	7	8	9
	11	12	13	14	15	16	17	18	19
	21	22	23	24	25	26	27	28	29
	31	32	33	34	35	36	37	38	39
	41	42	43	44	45	46	47	48	49
	51	52	53	54	55	56	57	58	59
	61	62	63	64	65	66	67	68	69
	71	72	73	74	75	76	77	78	79
	81	82	83	84	85	86	87	88	89
	91	92	93	94	95	96	97	98	99

Worksheet 38

Color:

5th –
green

8th –
blue

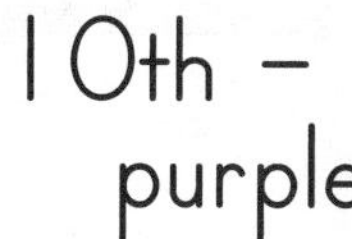

2nd –
black

6th –
orange

9th –
red

4th –
brown

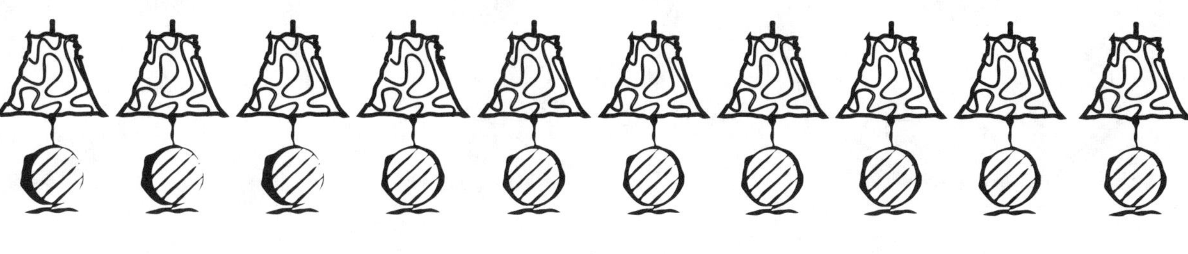

1st –
purple

7th –
yellow

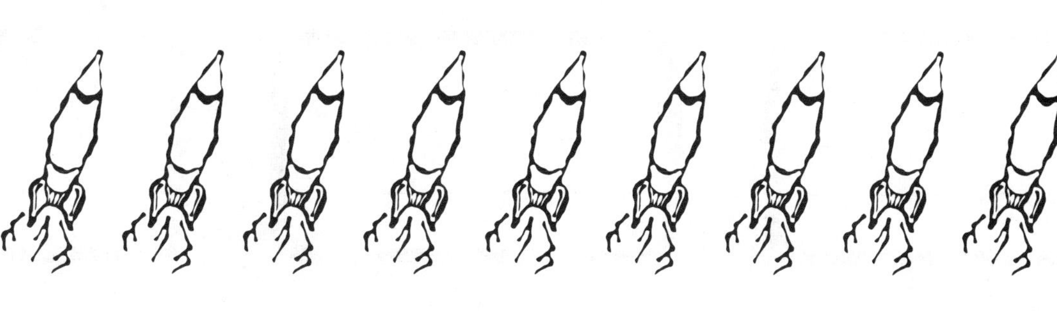

Worksheet 39

Write the time your teacher says.

1.

2.

3.

4.

___ : ___

5.

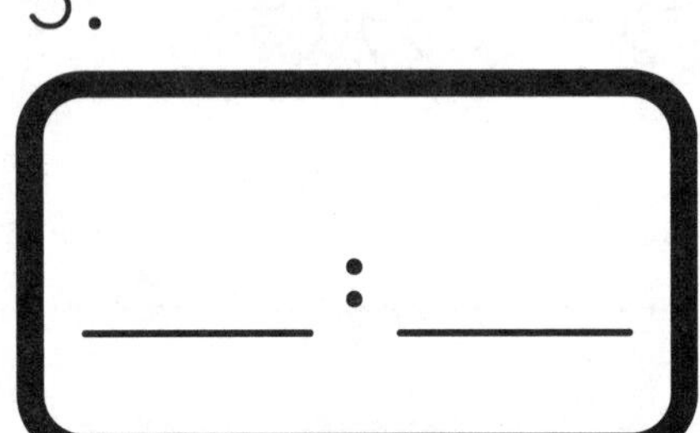

6.

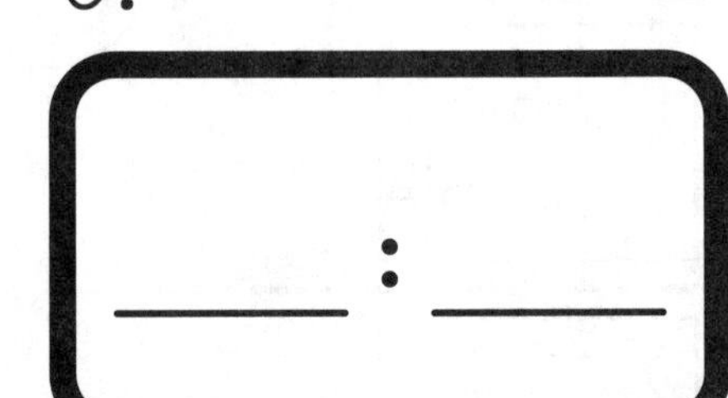

7.

8.

9.

10.

___ : ___

11.

___ : ___

12.

___ : ___

Worksheet 40

The number lines on this page and the next are for student use. Cut on the dotted lines and use the number lines to aid the students in adding number families.

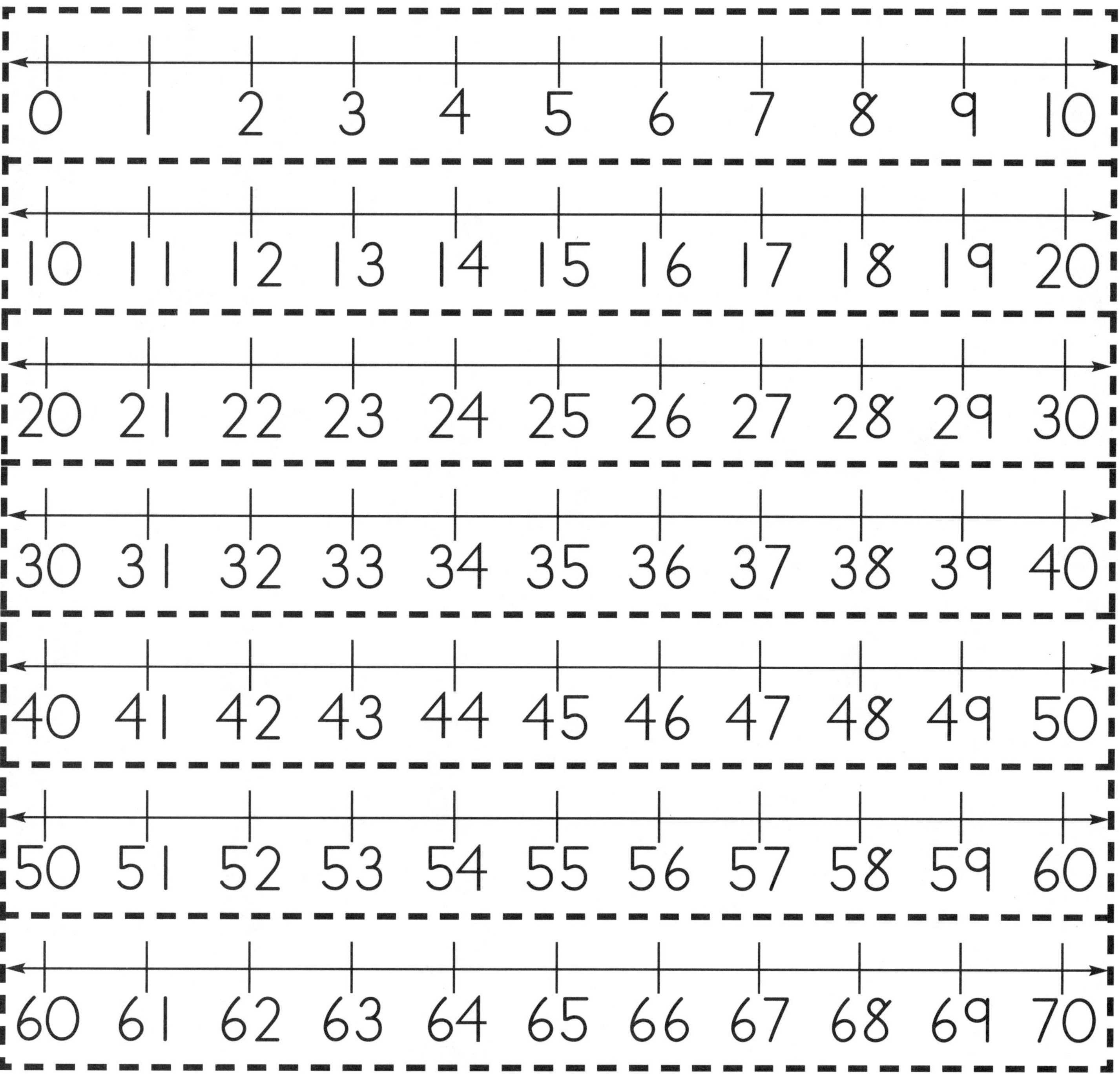

These number lines are for student use. Cut on the dotted lines and use the number lines to aid the students in adding number families.

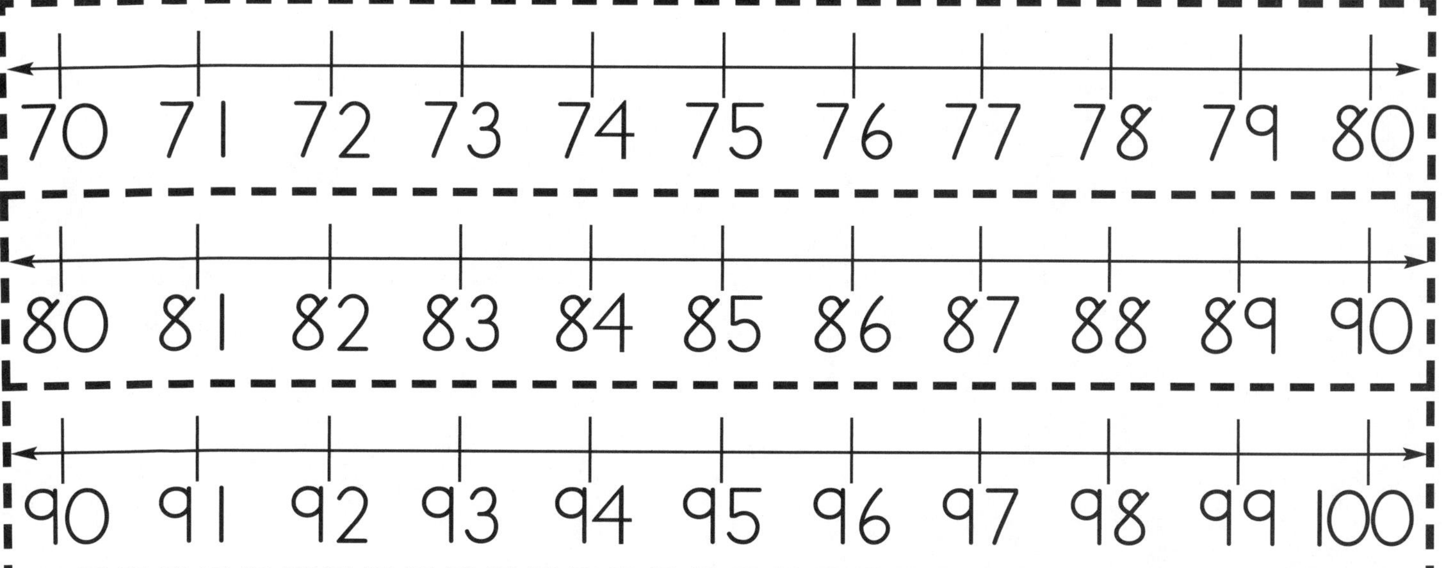